SURVEY
OF
SOCIAL
SCIENCE

SURVEY
OF
SOCIAL
SCIENCE

PSYCHOLOGY SERIES

Volume 6
2329-2698

Social Schemata—Z

Edited by

FRANK N. MAGILL

Consulting Editor

JACLYN RODRIGUEZ
OCCIDENTAL COLLEGE

SALEM PRESS

Pasadena, California   Englewood Cliffs, New Jersey

Library of Congress Cataloging-in-Publication Data
Survey of social science. Psychology series/edited by
Frank N. Magill; consulting editor, Jaclyn Rodriguez.
    p. cm.
    Includes bibliographical references and index.
    1. Psychology—Encyclopedias. I. Magill, Frank Nor-
then, 1907-   . II. Rodriguez, Jaclyn.
BF31.S79   1993   93-34708
150′.3—dc20   CIP
ISBN 0-89356-732-9 (set)
ISBN 0-89356-738-8 (volume 6)

Second Printing

PRINTED IN THE UNITED STATES OF AMERICA

CONTENTS

PSYCHOLOGY

SURVEY
OF
SOCIAL
SCIENCE

SOCIAL SCHEMATA

Type of psychology: Social psychology
Field of study: Social perception and cognition

Social schemata are certain clusters of information that people have stored in their memories; each cluster concerns a person, group of persons, or social event. Having such clusters of information already stored in memory can help people understand their social world yet can also lead people to have a biased perception of their social world.

Principal terms

COGNITION: a thought; also, the processing of information

COGNITIVE PROCESSES: the processes of thought, which include attending to an event, storing information in memory, recalling information, and making sense of information

SCHEMA (pl. SCHEMATA): a cluster of information, which may include facts, opinions, or personal experiences, stored in memory about a topic

SELF-FULFILLING PROPHECY: the phenomenon of one's own beliefs leading to events that then provide confirmation of those very beliefs

SELF-SCHEMATA: the schemata that one has about oneself

SOCIAL COGNITION: the area of social psychology concerned with how people make sense of social events, including the actions of others

STEREOTYPE: one's thoughts and beliefs about a group of people; one type of schema

Overview

Imagine how complicated life would be if people did not have the ability to store things in memory or to organize the information that did get stored; people would have to relearn information over and over. Because of memories of past experiences, people do not have to relearn what an apple is, for example, or what to do with it each time they come in contact with one.

A well-organized memory system also helps people make educated guesses. One is able to conclude that, because of an apple's texture, it will not make a satisfactory baseball. One is able to make educated guesses because the human brain has the ability to categorize objects and to generalize from past experiences to new experiences. Indeed, social psychologists believe that the brain not only has the ability to categorize, it also has the tendency to do so. For example, a very young city child who is taken to the zoo may point to a goat and say, "Doggy!"

The brain's memory system categorizes objects, people, and events by somehow connecting different pieces of related information together. Social psychologists call this collection of related information a schema. The young child knows that "doggies," for example, have fur, four legs, and wet noses. Somehow, the brain links these pieces of information together. In the child's mind, there is an idea of the typical characteristics an object must have in order for it to be a "doggy."

All people have many schemata, and the range of topics they cover includes all those topics about which a given person knows things. Some of these topics are social in nature, some are not. If the content of a schema concerns a person, group of people, or social event, the schema is called a social schema. One type of social schema is a "script." A script is a schema about a social event, such as a "good party" or "going to class." Another type of social schema is a stereotype, which is a schema about a group of people. If one were to list, for example, everything one could think of regarding "criminals," including one's opinions or personal experiences, one would have listed the contents of one's "criminal" stereotype.

A third type of social schema is a self-schema. Each of a person's many self-schemata combine to make up the person's overall self-concept. A person might, for example, have a self-schema regarding him- or herself as a student, another one as a male or female, and yet another regarding his or her athletic abilities. Each self-schema might have many, or few, pieces of information. One's self-schema as a student, for example, might include information about where one goes to school, which classes one is taking, whether one enjoys being a student, memories of oneself in one's first kindergarten class, or of books one read that made an impact. Notice that some of these pieces of information might also be included in other schemata; the information stored in the "student" self-schema might also be stored in a script about school, for example.

Schemata, whether they are self-schemata, scripts, stereotypes, or other types of schemata, help people organize and understand new events. Just as one's schema for an apple helps one recognize and know what to do with an apple, one's social schemata help one function in social situations. For example, most high school juniors know what to do in a new classroom without having to be told because their "classroom" schema, created during previous semesters, already holds information about how to behave in class. Schemata, then, help people simplify the world; they do not constantly have to relearn information about events, concepts, objects, or people.

To understand how social schemata help people simplify the world, social psychologists study the cognitive processes that schemata affect. Cognitive processes are thinking processes, such as paying attention, that enable the brain to perceive events. Research has shown that schemata affect what people pay attention to, what they store in permanent memory and then later recall, how they interpret events, and even how people behave (although "behaving" is not considered a cognitive process).

This area of study is called social cognition. Research in social cognition shows that having a schema makes it more likely that a person will pay attention to events that are relevant to the schema than to events that are irrelevant. Schemata also make it more likely that a person will store in permanent memory and later recall new information that confirms the beliefs that person already has in his or her schemata.

Schemata also affect how people interpret events. When people have a schema for an event or person, they are likely to interpret that event or the person's behavior in a way that is consistent with the beliefs already held in the schema. Finally, people tend to act in ways that are consistent with the schemata they hold in memory, and their actions can affect the actions of others in such a way as to confirm the original beliefs. All these cognitive memory biases result in confirmation of the beliefs that are already held; thus, these biases produce self-fulfilling prophecies.

Applications

Although social schemata can facilitate people's understanding of their social world, they also can bias people's perceptions. Often, people are not accurate recorders of the world around them; rather, their own beliefs and expectations, clustered and stored as schemata, distort their perceptions of social events. Such distortions help answer the social psychological question, Why are stereotypes so difficult to change?

Imagine that a person has a schema, a stereotype, about criminals. If he or she then meets a man who is introduced as a criminal, his or her perceptions of this person can be biased by the schema. Since schemata affect what people notice, this person will be more likely to notice things about this man that are consistent with his or her schema than things that are irrelevant. Perhaps the person believes that criminals use foul language but has no expectations regarding the type of listening skills a criminal might have. In this case, the person might be more likely to notice when the criminal swears than to notice his empathic listening skills. Then, because schemata affect what is stored in and recalled from memory, the person might be more likely to put into memory, and later remember, the criminal's swearing. Even if the person did notice his good listening skills, he or she would be less likely to store that in memory, or to recall it later, than to store information about his swearing.

On the other hand, if a person believes that criminals are not very empathic, he or she might be especially likely to notice this new acquaintance's empathic listening skills. It is unlikely, though, that a person would change his or her schema to fit this new information; what is more likely is that he or she would interpret this information in such a way as to make it fit the stereotype—for example, consider this one criminal to be the exception to the rule, or conclude he developed his listening skills as a con to get out of jail more quickly. Finally, a person very well might treat a criminal in a way that fits his or her beliefs about him. For example, a person who believes criminals lie might express doubt over things he says. The criminal might then respond to these doubts by acting defensively, which might then confirm the other person's belief that criminals act aggressively or that they have reasons to feel guilty. The criminal also might respond to doubting comments by actually lying. He might have the attitude, "If you expect me to lie, I might as well." What has happened, in this case, is this: A person's beliefs have affected his or her behavior, which in turn has affected the criminal's behavior, and the criminal's behavior now confirms the person's stereotype. This chain of events is one of the problems created by schemata. Very often, negative beliefs make it more likely that a person will find or produce confirmation for these beliefs.

These biases in information processing also can apply to how people perceive themselves, and thus explain why it can be difficult to change a negative self-concept. If a woman sees herself as incompetent, for example, she is likely to notice when her own behavior or thoughts are less than adequate; she is likely to store those examples in memory; and she is likely later to recall such examples from memory. Furthermore, if she engages in an activity and her performance is up for interpretation, she will be more likely to evaluate that performance as incompetent than as competent. Finally, if she believes she is incompetent, this can lead her actually to act that way. For example, her belief may lead her to feel nervous when it is time to perform, and her nervousness might then lead her to perform less competently than she otherwise might have. This provides her with more proof of her own incompetence, another self-fulfilling prophecy.

In the 1970's and 1980's, Aaron T. Beck demonstrated that individuals who are depressed have a self-schema for depression and also a hopeless schema about the world in general. Beck's work has been extremely influential in the understanding of depression. Because of his work, one of the major approaches to treating depression is to help the depressed individual change his or her thoughts and cognitive processes.

Understanding that schemata can bias people's thinking can help people resist such biases. Resisting the biases can help people change parts of their self-concepts, their stereotypes of others, or even their schemata about their loved ones. If one sees one's roommate as messy, for example, one might be especially likely to notice and remember his messy behaviors, and it is possible that one might respond to his messiness by cleaning up after him, nagging, or becoming more messy oneself. The roommate might then rebel against all these responses by becoming even more messy himself, resulting in a downward spiral. If one's roommate also is one's spouse, this can lead to marital problems. Not all self-fulfilling prophecies have these types of unpleasant consequences, but to stop the cycle of those that do, people need to search actively for evidence that disconfirms their schemata.

Context

Research in social cognition, the area of social psychology that focuses on social schemata, evolved as a hybrid from two areas of psychology: social psychology and cognitive psychology. In 1924, Floyd Allport published a book entitled *Social Psychology*; this early text was the first to assert that an individual's behavior is affected by the presence and actions of other individuals. In the 1950's, though, Kurt Lewin asserted, as social psychologists still assert, that an individual is more influenced by his or her perceptions of other individuals than by what the other individuals actually are doing. For many years after, a popular subfield in social psychology was person perception. Researchers studying person perception discovered many factors that influence people's judgments and impressions of others. For example, researchers showed that individuals are more influenced by unpleasant than by pleasant information when forming an impression of a stranger. Person perception research focused on how individuals perceive others, rather than on how individuals are influenced by others, and such research provided one of the main foundations for the field of social cognition.

The second main foundation was research on cognitive processes. In the 1980's, researchers studying person perception realized they could better understand why people perceive others as they do by learning more about cognitive psychology. Cognitive psychology was first developed to explain how individuals learn—for example, to explain the relationship between a child's ability to pay attention, put information into memory, and recall information and the child's ability to learn information from a textbook. As cognitive psychologists created techniques for studying these cognitive processes, researchers studying person perception realized that the same processes that affect a schoolchild's ability to learn textbook material also might affect how individuals learn about other individuals. As these new cognitive research techniques began answering many questions in the field of person perception, that field branched into a second field, the field called social cognition.

One of the first main contributions from this new field was a better understanding of interracial problems. Prior to their understanding of social schemata, social psychologists had been interested in discovering the factors that lead to unpleasant feelings toward other racial groups and the conditions that would eliminate such feelings. Research on social schemata helped explain unpleasant intergroup relations by showing that thoughts, that is, schemata, can be resistant to change for reasons that have nothing to do with unpleasant feelings toward a group; the biases in attention, storing information in memory, recalling information, and interpreting events can occur even when unpleasant feelings are not present. Just as a young child's brain perceives a goat to be a "doggy," an adult's brain also tends to perceive new events in ways that fit information already held in memory.

Social psychologists now understand that cognitive processes also affect many other psychological phenomena that formerly were explained by emotional processes alone. For example, social schemata contribute to psychologists' understanding of why crime victims do not always receive help, why bullies initiate fights, and why some teenagers are so angry with their parents.

Social schemata, studied by social psychologists, have such far-reaching effects that researchers in areas of psychology other than social psychology also study them. For example, personality psychologists study how social schemata affect self-concept, and clinical psychologists study how social schemata can inhibit or facilitate therapy sessions. Social schemata themselves may simplify people's understanding of social events, but the study of schemata has greatly enriched the understanding of the social perceiver.

Bibliography

Beck, Aaron T. *Love Is Never Enough*. New York: Harper & Row, 1988. A famous therapist and researcher explains how negative thoughts can interfere in a marriage and teaches the reader how to change unrealistic scripts regarding relationships. Not a typical self-help book; the tone and writing style are serious, although not difficult.

Brehm, Sharon S., and Saul M. Kassin. "Social Perception: Thinking About Ourselves and Others." In *Social Psychology*. Boston: Houghton Mifflin, 1989. This section of Brehm and Kassin's social psychology textbook includes three chapters on person perception and social cognition, including a section on sexism. A clear discussion of self-perception, self-esteem, and self-presentation also is included. The writing is accessible and thought provoking.

Burns, David D. *Intimate Connections*. New York: Signet, 1985. This popular self-help book by a colleague of Aaron Beck shows how beliefs and expectations can influence people's feelings toward themselves and others. Includes a helpful chapter on how to change such thoughts, and another on how to overcome feelings of inferiority. Also addresses unrealistic relationship scripts.

Fiske, Susan T., and Shelley E. Taylor. *Social Cognition*. New York: McGraw-Hill, 1991. Explains how memory, attitudes, emotions, and motivation combine to affect people's perceptions of others and themselves. Although the writing includes the terminology used by social psychologists, the authors provide many definitions and examples. One of the most comprehensive books available on social cognition.

Plotnik, Rodney J. "Social Cognition." In *Introduction to Psychology*. 2d ed. New York: Random House, 1989. Interesting and easy to read. The discussion of social schemata includes good examples, as well as descriptions of original and famous research studies on social schemata. Also included is a discussion of other topics in social cognition, among them attitude formation and change.

Julie A. Felender

Cross-References

Abnormality: Sociocultural Models, 82; Attributional Biases, 338; Causal Attribution, 487; Cognitive Psychology: An Overview, 572; Theories of Intergroup Relations, 1356; Effects of Prejudice, 1848; Reduction of Prejudice, 1855; Racism, 2037; Social Perception: Others, 2311.

SOUND LOCALIZATION

Type of psychology: Sensation and perception
Field of study: Auditory, chemical, cutaneous, and body senses

The behavioral skill of localizing the source of a perceived sound in three-dimensional space is referred to as sound localization. The primary cues used for this task, mainly as a result of the separation of the ears, are differences in the intensity or in the time of arrival of the signals at the two ears.

> *Principal terms*
> ACOUSTIC: relating to the physical nature of sounds and the sense of hearing
> AUDITORY: of or relating to hearing
> DICHOTIC: referring to the simultaneous stimulation of the two ears by stimuli differing in some parameter
> DIOTIC: referring to the simultaneous stimulation of the two ears by identical stimuli
> MONOTIC: referring to the stimulation of only one ear
> PHASE: the fractional part of a cycle through which a periodic oscillation, as of pure tones, has progressed, measured from an arbitrary starting point

Overview

In order to solve the problem of localizing a sound in the three-dimensional space surrounding a listener, the nervous system works with several different parameters. One of these is the time of arrival of the sound waves at the eardrum (tympanic membrane) of each ear, referred to as the interaural time delay (ITD). Another is the intensity of the sound waves as they impinge on each tympanic membrane, referred to as the interaural intensity difference (IID). These are also known as the dichotic cues which are available to the listener.

In 1916, the German philosopher and psychologist Carl Stumpf introduced the terms "dichotic" (referring to the simultaneous stimulation of the two ears by different stimuli), "diotic" (simultaneously stimulating the two ears by the same stimuli), and "monotic" (referring to the stimulation of only one ear). A stimulus can be simultaneously diotic and dichotic, as when the frequency of a binaural (two-ear) signal is diotic but the intensity of the signal is dichotic (as explained below).

These dichotic cues exist because of a simple anatomical fact: The two tympanic membranes are physically separated by the head. When a sound source is equally distant from each tympanic membrane, its emitted sound waves will arrive simultaneously at the membranes (that is, the ITD will be zero); otherwise, the ITD will be different from zero as the membrane nearer to the sound source receives the sound stimulus first.

Another consequence of the presence of the head's being between the two tympanic membranes is that the head can actually serve as a sound barrier for the ear that is more distant from the sound source. In other words, the head casts an "acoustic shadow" that results in an interaural intensity difference (IID).

A listener's ability to localize a sound source can be studied by positioning a sound source along two spatial dimensions. One of these describes the source's distance along the horizontal plane, usually referred to as the azimuth. The other dimension refers to the distance above the horizontal plane that the source is located, usually referred to as the elevation. A sound source placed directly in front of the subject therefore is located at 0 degrees of azimuth and 0 degrees of elevation (called the origin); when directly above the subject, it is at 0 degrees of azimuth and 90 degrees of elevation; when directly before the subject's right ear canal, the source is at 90 degrees of azimuth and 0 degrees of elevation, and so forth.

Experimental results indicate that the type of sound used as a stimulus can have a large effect upon a subject's ability to localize the sound. The duration of the stimulus and the range of sound frequencies present in it both have a significant influence on the listener's success at localization. This has made it somewhat difficult to compare directly the experimental results obtained in different laboratories. Nevertheless, a clear picture has emerged.

The subjects invariably perform best when the sound source is positioned directly to the front, in which case the errors in localization are smallest (errors of about 2 to 3 degrees of azimuth and elevation) and the results are most consistent—that is, they show the least variability. As the source is positioned farther away from the origin, the errors become progressively larger, approaching 20 degrees for positions behind the subject's head.

Although a subject is much better able to localize sound using two ears, it is somewhat possible to localize sounds using only one ear. For example, when subjects are localizing noise signals using monotic stimulation, the error in elevation is only slightly larger than when using binaural (two-ear) stimulation—12 degrees for monaural versus 9 degrees for binaural stimulation. Localization of the sound in the azimuth, however, produces much greater errors—30 to 40 degrees for monaural versus 5 to 10 degrees for binaural stimulation.

Human abilities to localize the distance of a sound source are not particularly good. When the intensity of the sound source is already known—for example, in the case of a voice at normal conversational intensity—then the distance judgments can be fairly accurate and depend almost entirely on the intensity of the sound signal at the tympanic membrane. Sound localization can also refer to the identification of the motion of a sound source, such as a change in the elevation or in the azimuth or in both, or a change in the distance of a sound.

For changes in the distance of a sound, there are cues available from the changing intensity of the sound as well as from Doppler shifts in the stimulus frequency. Doppler shifts result in the listener hearing a higher-frequency tone when the sound source is approaching the listener and a lower-frequency tone when the source is moving away from the listener. In order to use Doppler shifts as cues, it is necessary either for the listener to know the frequency of the sound when its source is stationary or for the sound source to change its direction of motion (for example, from approaching the listener to moving away from the listener).

When the distance is not a factor that is changing, researchers often measure the minimum audible movement angle (MAMA). The MAMA is the least change in position of a moving sound source that can be detected by a listener under a given set of conditions. At 0 degrees azimuth, the MAMA is smallest, and it increases with increasing azimuth. In general, MAMAs increase (that is, performance becomes worse) as the velocity of the sound source increases.

Applications

In the nineteenth century, sound localization research was centered on the problem of providing spatiality for tones. Compared to objects, which are seen or touched and obviously have positions in three-dimensional space, sounds were denied any extension. Nineteenth century psychologists were interested in explaining possible ways that the senses of touch and kinesthesis (the sense of body position and movement in space) might be used to give tones spatiality. This problem of how nonspatial tones become localized in three-dimensional space by a listener is referred to as a genetic problem. The geneticists tried to devise explanations that would somehow permit the other senses to build a listener's subjective auditory space.

In the 1880's, various experiments were performed that were claimed to demonstrate the theory that the semicircular canals of the inner ear (which are responsible for a person's sense of dynamic equilibrium) contribute to the construction of this auditory space. One idea was that the movements of the head and its semicircular canals impart information that was used to build up auditory space and to place the nonspatial sounds within this subjective space.

Evidence against this idea is simply the fact that two different sounds (for example, a ticking watch and a whistle) can be localized simultaneously, although the head cannot move in two directions at once, as the theory would have required. In addition, it was deemed impossible for a sound to pass through the external ear canal, through the middle ear bones, and into the internal ear, where it would then stimulate the three semicircular canals to different degrees to indicate its original position in three-dimensional space.

By the twentieth century, researchers lost interest in the genesis of a subjective auditory space and turned their attention to more quantifiable questions, such as the precision with which listeners can localize a sound and the nature of the physiological mechanisms by which this can be done. Investigators began to seek knowledge of the important functional relations that enable sound localization. They looked for the answers to their questions in terms of the physics and physiology of the experimental situation.

An excellent example of this is the finding reported in 1906 by the physicist John William Strutt, the third Baron Rayleigh, that high-frequency tones are better localized than lower-frequency tones. Lord Rayleigh, applying his great skills as a physicist to the problem, recognized the importance of the separation of the listener's two ears by the head and the acoustic shadow that the head produced. This acoustic-shadow effect results in the ear most distant from a sound source receiving a less intense stimulation than the ear nearer to the source (that is, the IID is different from zero).

Rayleigh computed the wavelengths of different frequencies of sounds and found that for tones below 1,000 hertz (1,000 cycles per second), the wavelength of the tones is actually several times larger than the diameter of the human head. His calculations also indicated that for such tones, the IID would not be large enough to be used for sound localization. Nevertheless, listeners are able to localize sounds whose frequencies are less than 1,000 hertz.

Given that IID's could not be used to explain a listener's ability to localize a low-frequency tone, the only alternative explanation available was that the interaural time delay (ITD) was able to be used as a cue. Because of the periodic-wave nature of tonal stimuli, saying that an ITD is different from zero also implies that the phase of the waves arriving at the two ears from a single sound source is not necessarily the same. This explanation, however, ran contrary to the widespread belief at that time that humans are incapable of perceiving phase differences.

Knowing that listeners can localize low-frequency sounds without resorting to IID cues, Rayleigh pursued this question, performing experiments which extended those of Silvanus Thompson, who had instigated the scientific reexamination of phase perception with his ingenious experiments in 1877 and 1878. In an initial experiment, Thompson utilized two tuning forks, one tuned to 128 hertz and the other tuned slightly differently. He then used two rubber tubes, one of which transmitted the tones from one of the forks to the left ear while the other tube transmitted the tones from the other fork to the right ear. The listener reported hearing beats even though the resulting sound heard was reported as continuous. In another experiment, Thompson used two forks, one at 256 hertz and the other at 512 hertz, and transmitted their sounds through a single tube which divided and went to both ears. By rotating one of the forks around its axis, it is possible to change the phase relationship of its tone with respect to the other fork's tone. Extending this type of experiment and making use of the new technological device of his time, the telephone, Thompson transmitted the tone from each fork by means of its own telephone. Thus, one fork's signal went to the subject's left ear, and the other fork's signal went to the right ear. Then, by reversing the electrical connections on one of the telephones, it was possible to alter the phase of the tone signal being transmitted over that telephone with respect to the tone signal being sent over the other telephone.

It was as a result of experiments such as these that evidence began to accumulate in favor of interaural phase differences (IPDs) acting as cues for sound localization, especially for lower-frequency tones. The development of modern research equipment now permits investigators to construct virtually any sort of auditory stimulus desired, systematically and precisely to change any parameter of the stimulus in order to determine its importance for sound localization, and to measure a listener's ability to distinguish small changes in the stimulus parameters.

Context

The history of sound localization research illustrates the conceptual difficulties that early investigators faced. To begin with, it is obvious that things which one sees and touches exist in three-dimensional space, where they have definite positions, sizes, and shapes. The situation is not so clear with respect to sounds. In the nineteenth century, most psychologists even held that there was no such phenomenon as auditory space perception.

The nineteenth century German physician and natural scientist Hermann von Helmholtz conducted studies of the phase of sound waves and concluded that phase was not important in the perception of vowels or other complex patterns. As a result, most researchers thought that organisms could not perceive phase; therefore, they did not consider phase to be an important cue for sound localization. Many, such as the Scottish philosopher and psychologist Alexander Bain, explained human sound localization skills as resulting simply from experience. He proposed, for example, that when a subject hears a sound whose intensity is known, its distance can be deduced by noting its loudness and by the recall of previous learned experiences involving distances and loudness differences.

In 1838, the German physiologist and anatomist Johannes Peter Müller proposed that the directional specification of sound sources must result from the spatial separation of the two ears. This would, he reasoned, permit interaural intensity differences (IIDs) to be used as cues for sound localization. It was not until 1876, however, that Lord Rayleigh performed the first detailed experimental investigations into the phenomenon of sound localization. Rayleigh stood in the middle of a circle of his assistants outdoors on a lawn with his eyes closed. Then one of the assistants would speak, and Rayleigh would try to localize the voice by pointing. He showed that this could be done accurately to within several degrees. His further experiments using tuning forks demonstrated the fact that the IID was dependent upon the frequency of the sound.

Lord Rayleigh's contributions to sound localization research were very significant and include demonstrating that the IID is often important for localization; that high-frequency tones are better localized than lower-frequency tones; that pure-tone sounds are better localized than noises or voices; that the location of a sound at the front midline is often mistakenly localized at a symmetrical position at the rear midline (and vice versa); and that location confusion does not occur with respect to left and right.

In 1878, Silvanus Thompson began studies that culminated in Rayleigh's phase theory in 1907, which held that interaural phase differences (IPDs) could be cues for sound localization. A variety of clever experiments by numerous investigators provided convincing evidence for the validity of Lord Rayleigh's theory. Thus, the erroneous conclusion by von Helmholtz that humans could not utilize phase information to localize sounds was finally corrected.

The time theory of sound localization, proposed in 1920 by the Austrians Erich von Hornbostel and Max Wertheimer, stated that interaural time delays (ITDs) can be used as cues in localizing sounds. During the 1920's, it became evident that the three theories—intensity theory, phase theory, and time theory—actually represent different physiological mechanisms for the localization of sounds.

Bibliography

Middlebrooks, John C., and David M. Green. "Sound Localization by Human Listeners." In *Annual Review of Psychology* 42. Stanford, Calif.: Annual Reviews, 1991. As the title implies, this easy-to-read review concerns studies of human listeners. The subject is divided into sections dealing with two-dimensional sound localization, horizontal localization, vertical localization, monaural localization, distance perception, motion detection, dynamic cues for localization, and simulating external sources over headphones.

Perkins, William H., and Raymond D. Kent. *Functional Anatomy of Speech, Language, and Hearing.* San Diego, Calif.: College-Hill Press, 1986. An excellent text for the serious high school or college student. Good appendices are included for anatomical terminology, fetal development, and selected readings. There are also excellent self-study sections at the end of each chapter and an appendix containing their answers. Another appendix lists a variety of relevant audiovisual materials.

Phillips, Dennis P., and John F. Brugge. "Progress in Neurophysiology of Sound Localization." In *Annual Review of Psychology* 36. Stanford, Calif.: Annual Reviews, 1985. This comprehensive review of the scientific literature is surprisingly easy to read for the college student, considering the technical nature of the subject. There is no glossary of terms, which requires the reader to look elsewhere for help with the anatomy. The biological mechanisms used in sound localization are covered quite well.

Stebbins, William C. *The Acoustic Sense of Animals.* Cambridge, Mass.: Harvard University Press, 1983. Excellent for the general high school or higher-level reader. Discusses insects, fish, birds, reptiles, amphibians, and all sorts of mammals. Introductory background information is combined with explanations of important experimental methods and discussions of the results. Sound localization is nicely discussed throughout the text.

_____, ed. *Animal Psychophysics: The Design and Conduct of Sensory Experiments.* New York: Appleton-Century-Crofts, 1970. A very useful book for those interested in conducting experiments of their own. High school and college readers will learn much about the correct design and execution of animal experiments, although the text is not strictly for learning about sound localization.

John V. Urbas

Cross-References

SPEECH DISORDERS

Type of psychology: Language
Fields of study: Behavioral therapies; infancy and childhood; organic disorders

Speech disorders may have an organic or learned origin, and they often affect a person's ability to communicate efficiently. As a result of a speech disorder, a person may exhibit a number of behavioral effects, such as the avoidance of talking with others and low self-esteem.

Principal terms
> COMMUNICATION: the exchange of information and ideas between
> participants, often in the form of speech
> SELF-ESTEEM: the evaluative part of the self-concept; self-worth
> SOCIAL INTERACTION: a communication act from one individual directed
> toward another
> SPEECH: the process of producing sounds in the form of words
> THERAPY: the systematic habilitation of a disorder
> VOCAL FOLDS: folds of skin found in the larynx and attached to cartilage
> that vibrate to make speech; often called vocal cords

Overview

The ability to communicate is one of the most basic human characteristics. Communication is essential to learning, working, and, perhaps most important, social interaction. Normal communication involves hearing sounds, interpreting and organizing sounds, and making meaningful sounds. The ear first takes in sounds, changes them into electrical impulses, and relays these impulses to the brain. The brain interprets the impulses, assigns meaning, and prepares a response. This response is then coded into the precisely coordinated changes in muscles, breath, vocal folds, tongue, jaw, lips, and so on that produce understandable speech.

Between 5 and 10 percent of Americans experience speech and/or language difficulties, often referred to as speech disorders. For these individuals, a breakdown occurs in one of the processes of normal communication described above. People with speech disorders may exhibit one or more of the following problems: They may be difficult to understand, use and produce words incorrectly, consistently use incorrect grammar, be unable to hear appropriately or to understand others, consistently speak too loudly, demonstrate a hesitating speech pattern, or simply be unable to speak. Speech disorders can be categorized as one of three disorder types: disorders of articulation, of fluency, or of voice. Articulation disorders are difficulties in the formation and stringing together of sounds to produce words. Fluency disorders, commonly referred to as stuttering, are interruptions in the flow or rhythm of speech. Finally, voice disorders are characterized by deviations in a person's voice quality, pitch, or loudness.

Articulation disorders are the most common types of speech errors in children. Articulation errors may take the form of substitutions, omissions, or distortions of sounds. An example of a substitution would be if the *w* sound were substituted for the *r* sound, as in "wabbit" for "rabbit." Substitutions are the most common form of articulation errors. An example of an omission would be if the *d* sound was left out of the word "bed," as in "be____." Finally, sounds can also be distorted, as in "shleep" for "sleep."

Stuttering is defined as an interruption in the flow or rhythm of speech. Stuttering can be characterized by hesitations, interjections, repetitions, or prolongations of a sound, syllable, word, or phrase. "I wa-wa-want that" is an example of a part-word repetition, while "I, I, I want that" is an example of a whole-word repetition. When a word or group of words such as "uh," "you know," "well," or "oh" is inserted into an utterance, it is termed an interjection. "I want uh, uh, you know, uh, that" is an example of a sentence containing interjections. There may also be secondary behaviors associated with stuttering. In order for an individual to extricate himself or herself from a stuttering incident, secondary behaviors may be used. A stutterer may blink the eyes, turn the head, tap his or her leg, look away, or perform some other interruptive behavior to stop the stuttering. In therapy, secondary behaviors are very difficult to extinguish.

While articulation disorders and stuttering are often seen in children, voice disorders are common among adults. Voice disorders are categorized into disorders of pitch, intensity, nasality, and quality. A person with a voice disorder of pitch may have a vocal pitch which is too high. A person may speak too softly and thus exhibit a voice disorder of intensity. Still others may sound as though they talk through their nose (hypernasality) or always have a cold (hyponasality). The most common voice disorder is a disorder of quality. Examples of disorders of vocal quality include a voice that sounds hoarse, breathy, harsh, or rough. This type of voice disorder may be caused by vocal abuse, or an overusage of the voice, and might be found among singers, actors, or other individuals who abuse or overuse their voices. If the vocal abuse continues, vocal nodules (like calluses) may appear on the vocal folds. Vocal nodules may be surgically removed, and a person may be put on an extended period of vocal rest.

Speech disorders may be caused by a variety of factors. They may result from physical problems, health problems, or other problems. Physical problems such as cleft lip and palate, misaligned teeth, difficulty in controlling movements of the tongue, injury to the head, neck, or spinal cord, poor hearing, mental retardation, and cerebral palsy can contribute to poor articulation. The exact causes of stuttering are not known; however, a variety of factors are thought to be involved, including learning problems, emotional difficulties, biological defects, and neurological problems. Problems with voice quality can be caused by too much strain on the vocal folds (for example, yelling too much or clearing the throat too often), hearing loss, inflammation or growths on the vocal folds (vocal nodules), or emotional problems.

Applications

Speaking, hearing, and understanding are essential to human communication. A disorder in one or more of these abilities can interfere with a person's capacity to communicate. Impaired communication can influence all aspects of a person's life, creating many problems for an individual. Behavioral effects resulting from the speech disorder can be found in both children and adults. Children with speech disorders can experience difficulties in learning and find it hard to establish relationships with others. Speech disorders in adults can adversely affect social interactions and often create emotional problems, which may interfere with a person's ability to earn a living. Disorders such as those described above can interfere with a person's relationships, independence, well-being, and ability to learn. People who have trouble communicating thoughts and ideas may have trouble relating to others, possibly resulting in depression and isolation. Furthermore, job opportunities are often limited for people who cannot communicate effectively. Thus, they may have trouble leading independent, satisfying lives. Emotional problems may develop in people who exhibit speech disorders as a result of embarrassment, rejection, or poor self-image. Finally, learning is difficult and frustrating for people with speech disorders. As a consequence, their performance and progress at school and on the job can suffer.

When trying to communicate with others, individuals with speech disorders may experience other negative behavioral effects as a result of the disorder. These effects include frustration, anxiety, guilt, and hostility. The emotional experience of speech-disordered persons is often a result of their experiences in trying to communicate with others. Both the listener and the speech-disordered person react to the disordered person's attempts to communicate. In addition, the listener's reactions may influence the disordered individual. These reactions may include embarrassment, guilt, frustration, and anger and may cause the disordered individual to experience a sense of helplessness that can subsequently lower the person's sense of self-worth. Many speech-disordered people respond to their problem by being overly aggressive, by denying its existence, by projecting reactions in listeners, and/or by feeling anxious or timid.

Treatment of speech disorders attempts to eliminate or minimize the disorder and related problems. Many professionals may be involved in providing therapy, special equipment, or surgery. In therapy, specialists teach clients more effective ways of communicating. They may also help families learn to communicate with the disordered individual. Therapy may also include dealing with the negative behavioral effects of having a speech disorder, such as frustration, anxiety, and a feeling of low self-worth. In some cases, surgery can correct structural problems that may be causing speech disorders, such as cleft palate or misaligned teeth. For children with articulation disorders, therapy begins with awareness training of the misarticulations and the correct sound productions. After awareness is established, the new sound's productions are taught. For individuals who exhibit voice disorders, therapy is designed to find the cause of the disorder, eliminate or correct the cause, and retrain the individuals to use their voices correctly. Therapy for stutterers, however, is an entirely different matter. There are many methods for treating stuttering. Some are self-proclaimed "cures," while others help individuals live with their stuttering. Still other types of stuttering therapy help the stutterer overcome his or her fear of communicating, or help him or her develop a more normal breathing pattern.

Though there are many ways to treat speech disorders, disorder prevention is even more important. Certain things can be done to help prevent many speech disorders. All the methods focus on preventing speech disorders in childhood. Children should be encouraged to talk, but they should not be pushed into speaking. Pushing a child may cause that child to associate anxiety or frustration with communicating. Infants do not simply start talking; they need to experiment with their voice, lips, and tongue. This experimentation is often called babbling, and it should not be discouraged. Later on, one can slowly introduce words and help with correct pronunciation. When talking with young children, one should talk slowly and naturally, avoiding "baby talk" and gibberish. Children will have difficulty distinguishing between the baby-talk word (for example, "baba") and the real word ("bottle"). Having children point to and name things in picture books and in real-world surroundings allows the child to put labels (words) on the objects in his or her environment. Increases in the number of labels the child has learned can subsequently increase the number of topics about which the child can communicate. It is most important to listen to what the child is trying to say rather than to how the child is saying it. Such prevention strategies will encourage positive behavioral effects regarding the act of communicating. These positive effects include feelings of self-efficiency, independence, and a positive self-image.

Context

Early identification of a speech disorder improves the chances for successful treatment, and early treatment can help prevent a speech disorder from developing into a lifelong handicap. Professionals who identify, evaluate, and treat communication disorders in individuals have preparations in the field of speech-language pathology. A speech-language pathologist is a professional who has been educated in the study of human communication, its development, and its disorders. By evaluating the speech and language skills of children and adults, the speech-language pathologist determines if communication problems exist and decides on the most appropriate way of treating these problems.

Speech-language pathology services are provided in many public and private schools, community clinics, hospitals, rehabilitation centers, private practices, health departments, colleges and universities, and state and federal governmental agencies. There are more than fourteen hundred clinical facilities and hundreds of full-time private practitioners providing speech services to people throughout the United States. Service facilities exist in many cities in every state. A speech-language pathologist will have a master's or doctoral degree and should hold a Certificate of Clinical Competence (CCC) from the American Speech-Language-Hearing Association and/or a license from his or her state.

Responsibilities of a speech-language pathologist include evaluation and diagnosis, therapy, and referral to other specialists involved with speech disorders. By gathering background information and by direct observation and testing, the speech-language pathologist can determine the extent of the disorder as well as a probable cause. The speech-language pathologist chooses an appropriate treatment to correct or lessen the communication problem and attempts to help the patient and family understand the problem. When other treatment is needed to correct the problem, the patient is referred to another specialist. Audiologists, special educators, psychologists, social workers, neurologists, pediatricians, otolaryngologists (also known as ear, nose, and throat specialists), and other medical and dental specialists may be involved in the diagnosis and treatment of a speech disorder. For example, psychologists may be best suited to treat the emotional or behavioral aspects of having a speech disorder (that is, anxiety, frustration, anger, denial, and so on). Otolaryngologists are often involved in the diagnosis of voice disorders. Audiologists determine whether an individual's hearing is affecting or causing a speech disorder.

Speech disorders can affect anyone at any time. The chances are good that everyone at one time has either had, or known someone with, a speech disorder. Since communication is so overwhelmingly a part of life, disordered speech is not something to take lightly. With good prevention, early identification, and early treatment, lifelong difficulties with communication can be prevented.

Bibliography

Curlee, Richard F. "Counseling in Speech, Language, and Hearing." *Seminars in Speech and Language* 9, no. 3 (1988). In his introductory article to this issue, Curlee presents a clear and interesting overview of counseling strategies for the speech-language pathologist. Counseling of parents and spouses of persons with speech disorders is detailed.

Riekehof, Lottie L. *The Joy of Signing.* Springfield, Mo.: Gospel Publishing House, 1987. A comprehensive book of sign language. Includes origins of the signs, usage of the signs, and sign variations.

Shames, George H., and Elizabeth H. Wiig, eds. *Human Communication Disorders.* Columbus, Ohio: Charles E. Merrill, 1986. This general text covers a wide range of communication disorders. Includes a section on speech-language pathology as a profession. Also includes sections on cleft palate, aphasia, and cerebral palsy.

The Speech Foundation of America. *Counseling Stutterers.* Memphis, Tenn.: Author, 1989. The Speech Foundation of America is a nonprofit, charitable organization dedicated to the prevention and treatment of stuttering. It provides a variety of low-cost publications about stuttering and stuttering therapy. This publication is written to give clinicians a better understanding of the counseling aspect of therapy and to suggest ways in which it can be used most effectively.

_____. *Therapy for Stutterers.* Memphis, Tenn.: Author, 1989. A general guide to help those who work or plan to work in therapy with adult and older-adolescent stutterers.

Jennifer A. Sanders Wann
Daniel L. Wann

Cross-References

Aphasias, 279; Grammar and Speech, 1100; Infant Perceptual Systems, 1290; Language Acquisition Theories, 1394; Language and Cognition, 1401; Stuttering, 2483.

SPEECH PERCEPTION

Type of psychology: Sensation and perception
Field of study: Auditory, chemical, cutaneous, and body senses

Speech perception involves a set of enigmatic phenomena, and no completely acceptable theory explaining all of its aspects has been developed. During speech perception, people rapidly extract meanings from a complex spoken signal in the face of many apparently insurmountable obstacles.

Principal terms
    ACOUSTIC: relating to the physical nature of sounds and the sense of
      hearing
    ARTICULATION: the act or manner of pronouncing speech sounds
    FORMANT: a narrow range of sound frequencies that becomes enhanced
      during vowel sound production
    MOTOR NEURONS: the cells of the central nervous system responsible for
      causing muscular activity
    PHONEME: a basic unit of a language considered to be the smallest unit
      of speech
    PHONETIC: relating to spoken language or speech sounds

Overview

The perception of human speech signals involve a variety of phenomena which initially appear trivial; upon closer inspection, however, the phenomena are found to be exceedingly complex. The basic phenomena are the ability to perceive the same speech message correctly when it is presented by various speakers, or by the same speaker performing under different conditions (the phenomenon of perceptual constancy); differences in the perceptual processing of speech and nonspeech sounds; the ability to discriminate well among sounds from different speech sound categories, but only poorly among sounds from within the same speech sound category (categorical perception of speech); and the problems presented by the signal's immediate speech sound (or phonetic) context for the correct identification of the signal (the phenomenon of context-sensitive cues).

Each of these phenomena is so complex primarily because of the nature of the speech signal. A spoken language is perceived by a native listener as a sequence of discrete units, commonly called words. The physical nature of the typical speech signal, however, is more accurately described as a continuous, complex acoustic wave. In this signal, not only do the sounds associated with consecutive syllables often overlap considerably, but also the sounds of consecutive words often overlap.

The ultimate goal of speech perception research is the development of a theory which explains the various phenomena associated with the perception of the human speech signal. To achieve this goal, two basic types of information are needed: a detailed description of the speech signal, to test whether any acoustic cues exist that could be used by listeners; and accurate measurements of the acts of speech perception, to test hypotheses related to the different theories of speech perception.

When describing the speech signal for a given language, researchers have noted that the signal is composed of a set of basic units called phonemes, which are considered to be the smallest units of speech. The phonemes can be thought of (though this analogy is imprecise) as corresponding somewhat to the letters in a written word. For example, American English is said to comprise twenty-five consonant phonemes and seventeen vowel phonemes. The distinction between consonant and vowel speech sounds is based on the degree to which the vocal tract is closed. Consonants are generated with partial or complete closure of the vocal tract during some point of their production. Vowels are created with the vocal tract in a more open state.

Since consonants are produced by closing or nearly closing the vocal tract, they contain relatively little acoustic energy. Because of the dynamic changes occurring in the shape of the resonant cavities of the vocal tract during consonant production, the consonants are difficult to specify exactly in terms of acoustic patterns. Consonants commonly contain bursts of noise, rapid changes of frequencies, or even brief periods of silence, which all may take place within twenty-thousandths of a second.

Vowels have less complex acoustical characteristics, primarily because they are produced with the vocal tract open and not changing its shape so dramatically. They are of relatively long duration and tend to have more constant acoustical features than consonants. The most important features of vowel sounds are their formants, which are narrow ranges of sound frequencies that become enhanced during vowel production. The formants result from basic physical characteristics of the vocal tract, chief among these being its shape for a particular vowel, which cause most of the vocal frequencies to become suppressed, while only a few narrow bands of frequencies (the formants) are reinforced. Formants are numbered in increasing order from the lowest- to the highest-frequency band. The relative-frequency relationships among the formants of a vowel sound characterize that vowel.

Experiments show that the vowel sounds in English speech can be distinguished from one another by reference to the frequency values of formants one and two. For any given vowel sound, however, there is a range of frequencies that typically occurs for the formants, depending on the person speaking and the conditions under which he or she speaks. There is even some overlap between the ranges for some vowels.

Vowels and consonants can be further subdivided according to the articulatory features that characterize production of the sound. Articulatory features include the location of the greatest constriction in the vocal tract, the degree of rounding of the lips, the place of articulation (that is, where in the vocal tract the sound tends to be primarily produced, such as at the lips or in the nasal cavity), and the manner of articulation (for example, "voiced" means the vocal folds are vibrating, and "voiceless" means the vocal folds do not vibrate). These factors are important because of their possible use by a listener during the process of speech perception.

The nervous system can be viewed as consisting of two main subdivisions: transmission systems and integrative systems. For speech perception, the transmission systems both transmit and process the nervous signals that are produced by acoustic stimulation of the sensory structures for hearing. The integrative systems further process the incoming signals from the transmission systems by combining and comparing them with previously stored information. Both systems are actively involved in the processes of speech perception. Much research has been done concerning the exact mechanisms of signal processing in the nervous system and how they enable listeners to analyze complex acoustic speech signals to extract their meaning.

Theories of speech perception can be described in several ways. One way of categorizing the theories labels them as being either "top down" or "bottom up." Top-down theories state that a listener perceives a speech signal based upon a series of ongoing hypotheses. The hypotheses evolve at a rather high level of complexity (the "top") and are formed as a result of such things as the listener's knowledge of the situation, or the predictability of the further occurrence of certain words in a partially completed sequence. Bottom-up theories take the position that perception is guided simply by reference to the incoming acoustic signal and its acoustic cues. The listener then combines phonemes to derive the words, and the words to produce sentences, thereby proceeding from the simplest elements (the "bottom") up toward progressively more complex levels.

Another contrasting description is that of "active" versus "passive" theories. Active theories state that the listener actively generates hypotheses about the meaning of the incoming speech signal based upon various types of information available both in the signal and in its overall context (for example, what has already been said). The listener is said to be using more than simply acoustic cues to give meaning to what has been heard. Passive theories state that the listener automatically (passively) interprets the speech signal based upon the acoustic cues that are discerned.

Applications

Often, major differences in acoustic waves are produced by different speakers (or the same speaker performing under different conditions) even when speaking the same speech message. Nevertheless, native listeners typically have little trouble understanding the message. This phenomenon, known as perceptual constancy, is probably the most complex problem in the field of speech perception.

Variations in the rate of speaking, the pitch of the voice, the accent of the speaker, the loudness of signal, the absence of particular frequency components (for example, when the signal is heard over a telephone), and other factors are handled with amazing speed and ability by the typical listener. Many variations result in drastic changes or even total elimination of many acoustic cues normally present in the signal.

There is experimental evidence to support the hypothesis that when speech occurs at a higher-than-normal rate, the listener uses both syllable and vowel durations as triggers to adjust the usual stored acoustic cues toward shorter and faster values. This automatic adjustment permits accurate speech perception even when the speaking rate approaches four hundred words per minute.

Another difficult task is to explain the ease with which a listener can understand speech produced by different persons. The largest variations in vocal tract size (especially length) and shape occur between children and adults. Even among adults, significant differences are found, the average woman's vocal tract being nearly 15 percent shorter than that of the average male. These differences introduce quite drastic shifts in formant frequencies and other frequency-dependent acoustic cues. Nevertheless, experiments show that even very young children generally have no difficulty understanding the speech of complete strangers, which indicates that the nervous system is able to compensate automatically even before much speech perception experience has been garnered.

Studies of human perceptual processing using speech and nonspeech sounds as stimuli provide evidence for differences in the way people deal with these two categories of sounds. The implication is that specialized speech-processing mechanisms exist in the human nervous system. A major difference is a person's ability to process speech signals at a higher rate than nonspeech signals. Experiments show that phonetic segment information can be perceived as speech at rates as high as thirty segments per second (normal conversation rates transmit about ten segments per second). The rate of perception for comparable nonspeech signals, however, is only about four sounds per second.

The phenomenon of categorical perception of speech refers to the fact that people discriminate quite well among sounds from different speech sound categories (for example, a /b/ as opposed to a /p/ sound, as might occur in the two words "big" and "pig"); however, people's discrimination of different acoustic examples of sounds from within the same speech sound category (for example, variations of the /b/ sound) is not as good. One theory to explain categorical perception proposes that the auditory system is composed of nerve cells or groups of nerve cells which function as "feature detectors" that respond whenever a particular acoustic feature is present in a signal. In the example of the sounds /b/ and /p/ from the spoken words "big" and "pig," according to this theory, there are feature detectors which respond specifically to one or the other of these two consonants, but not to both of them, because of the different acoustic features that they each possess. One problem for proponents of the theory is to describe the particular features to which the detectors respond. Another problem is the number of different feature detectors a person might have or need. For example, is one detector for the consonant /b/ sufficient, or are there multiple /b/ detectors which permit a person to perceive /b/ correctly regardless of the speaker or the context in which the /b/ is spoken (and the consequent variations in the acoustic patterns for the /b/ that are produced)?

Although variations in the immediate speech sound (or phonetic) context often result in major changes in the acoustic signature of a phoneme (the phenomenon of context-sensitive cues), a person's ability to identify the phoneme is remarkable. People can recognize phonemes even though the variations found in the acoustic signatures of a given phoneme when spoken by even a single speaker but in different contexts (for example, for /d/ in the syllables "di," "de," "da," "do," and "du") make it difficult to specify any characteristic acoustic features of the phoneme.

Research shows that many acoustic cues (such as short periods of silence, formant changes, or noise bursts) interact with one another in determining a person's perception of phonemes. Thus, there is no unique cue indicating the occurrence of a particular phoneme in a signal since the cues depend on the context of the phoneme. Even the same acoustic cue can indicate different phonemes, according to the context. A complete theory of speech perception would have to account for all these phenomena, as well as others not mentioned.

Context

Speech sounds represent meanings in a language, and a listener extracts the meanings from a speech signal. What has remained unclear is how the nervous system performs this decoding. One hypothesis is that there are sensory mechanisms which are specialized to decode speech signals. This idea is suggested by the experimental results which indicate differences in the processing of speech and nonspeech signals. An alternative hypothesis is that special speech-processing mechanisms exist at a "higher" level, operating on the outputs of generalized auditory sensory mechanisms.

In the 1960's, the study of speech perception developed rapidly; three major theories were presented. These motivated a wealth of research projects, assisted by advances in electronic instrumentation, and have formed a basis for the development of newer theories. All three theories specify an interaction between the sensory representation of the incoming speech signal and the neuromotor commands (that is, the pattern of signals that the nervous system would have to generate to activate the muscles for speaking) which would be involved in the production of that same signal. Two of the theories are briefly described below.

The first and probably most influential of the theories is Alvin M. Liberman's motor theory of speech perception. Briefly stated, the motor theory maintains that a listener decodes the incoming speech signal by reference to the neuromotor commands that would be required to produce it. The process of speech perception therefore involves a sort of reverse process to that of speech production, in which a speaker has a message to send and generates appropriate neuromotor commands to enable the articulatory muscles to produce the speech signal. According to the motor theory of speech perception, the listener has an internal neural pattern, generated by the incoming speech signal's effects on the sensory apparatus. This pattern can be "followed back" to the neuromotor commands that would be necessary to produce an acoustic signal like the one which had just produced the internal (sensory) neural pattern. At this point, the listener recognizes the speech signal, and perception occurs by the listener's associating the neuromotor commands with the meanings they would encode if the listener were to produce such commands when speaking.

Among the problems facing the motor theory, a major one has been to explain how infants are able to perceive surprisingly small differences in speech signals before they are able to produce these same signals, since it would seem that they do not possess the necessary neuromotor commands. Another problem has been the inability for the supporters of the theory to explain how the "following back" from the incoming signal's generated neural activity patterns to the appropriate neuromotor commands occurs.

At the other end of the theoretical spectrum from the motor theory, Gunnar Fant's auditory model of speech perception places greater emphasis on an auditory analysis of the speech signal. This theory proposes that the speech signal is first analyzed by the nervous system so that distinctive acoustic features get extracted or represented in the activity patterns of the nervous system. Then these features are combined into the phonemes and syllables which the listener can recognize. Much as in the motor theory, this recognition depends on the listener possessing basic knowledge about the articulatory processes involved in speech production—in particular, the distinctive phonetic features possible in the language being heard.

In contrast to the motor theory, Fant's model supposes an ability of the listener's auditory system to pick out distinctive acoustic features from the phonetic segments being heard. The auditory model, therefore, separates the auditory and articulatory functions more distinctly than the motor theory does.

One of the problems of the auditory model is that distinctive acoustic features of phonetic segments are difficult to specify unambiguously. Supporters of the model argue that the important features are more complex than the relatively simple ones normally proposed and represent characteristic relationships between various parts of the signal.

Bibliography

Eimas, Peter D. "The Perception of Speech in Early Infancy." *Scientific American* 252 (January, 1985): 46-52. Discusses the human infant's ability to detect phonemic categories long before the age at which speech production has begun. This clearly presented article explains some of the speech perception research techniques that can be used with infants. The results suggest that at least some speech perception mechanisms are innate.

Fodor, Jerry A. *The Modularity of Mind.* Cambridge, Mass.: MIT Press, 1983. Although this is a philosophical presentation of Fodor's theory of mind, much of the text is concerned with speech and language. The discussions may be difficult for high school students, but they are valuable lessons in an alternate approach to what may seem to be a topic restricted to scientists.

Liberman, Alvin M. "On Finding That Speech Is Special." *American Psychologist* 37, no. 2 (1982): 148-167. The author is the chief developer of the motor theory of speech perception. This explanation of the theory and critical experimental results that support it includes many good figures, but most references are to articles in specialist journals. Good for advanced high school and college-level readers.

Matthei, Edward, and Thomas Roeper. *Understanding and Producing Speech.* New York: Universe Books, 1985. Recommended for high school and college readers, this text about psycholinguistics contains clearly written chapters about both human speech production and perception. Includes a good index and suggestions for further reading.

Perkins, William H., and Raymond D. Kent. *Functional Anatomy of Speech, Language, and Hearing.* San Diego, Calif.: College-Hill Press, 1986. An excellent text for the serious high school or college student. One chapter is dedicated to speech acoustics, while three chapters treat the neurology of speech (input processing, central processing, and output processing). Good appendixes are included for anatomical terminology and selected readings.

John V. Urbas

Cross-References

Aphasias, 279; Bilingualism: Acquisition, Storage, and Processing, 408; The Cerebral Cortex, 500; Language: The Developmental Sequence, 1387; Language Acquisition Theories, 1394; Language and Cognition, 1401; Linguistic Structure: Phonemes and Morphemes, 1457; Psycholinguistics, 1918; Split-Brain Studies, 2355.

SPLIT-BRAIN STUDIES

Type of psychology: Biological bases of behavior
Fields of study: Cognitive processes; nervous system

Split-brain studies provide insight into cognitive asymmetries in hemispheric functioning following surgery to sever the major interconnecting fiber tracts that allow communication between the cerebral hemispheres. Knowledge of hemispheric asymmetries is useful for understanding the organization and information-processing abilities of the human brain.

Principal terms

CEREBRAL COMMISSURES: fiber tracts, such as the corpus callosum and anterior commissure, that connect and allow neural communication between the cerebral hemispheres

CEREBRAL HEMISPHERES: two anatomically similar hemispheres that make up the outer surface of the brain (the cerebral cortex); separated by the cerebral longitudinal fissure

COMMISSUROTOMY: surgery performed to sever the major cerebral commissures that serve as interconnecting fiber tracts between the cerebral hemispheres

DICHOTIC LISTENING: the simultaneous presentation of competing auditory information to both ears through headphones

DYSLEXIA: difficulties in reading, often occurring after damage to the left cerebral hemisphere

EXPRESSIVE APHASIA: difficulties in expressing language, usually after damage to Broca's area in the left frontal lobe of the cerebral cortex

HEMISPHERIC ASYMMETRIES: asymmetric specialization of psychological functions in the cerebral hemispheres

LATERALITIES: asymmetric specialization of the brain and body; hemispheric asymmetries are an example of one type of laterality

RECEPTIVE APHASIA: difficulties in comprehending language, usually after damage to Wernicke's area in the left temporal lobe of the cerebral cortex

TACHISTOSCOPE: an experimental apparatus for presenting visual information very briefly to the right or left visual field; sometimes called a T-scope

Overview

The study of laterality, or the specialized asymmetric functions throughout the body, is not a new and novel field, as might be suggested by the popularization of "left brain-right brain" dichotomies. Lateralization of functions in the brain, sometimes referred to as hemispheric asymmetries, was demonstrated in 1861 by Paul Broca, a well-known physician at the time. He found that patients suffering from damage to certain regions of the left cerebral hemisphere exhibited more frequent speech and language disorders than did those with right cerebral hemisphere damage. Based on these findings, Broca correctly reasoned that the left hemisphere is specialized for speech and language in the vast majority of people. Unfortunately, these results were quickly transformed into an overly simplistic dichotomization of cerebral functioning in which the left hemisphere was conceptualized as the dominant hemisphere and the right hemisphere as a rather minor, perhaps even unimportant, hemisphere. From split-brain studies performed since 1940, it has become obvious that the right hemisphere is essential for normal visuospatial functioning.

Split-brain surgery, sometimes referred to as commissurotomy, was first performed on a human patient by the neurosurgeon William Van Wagenen in 1940 to reduce the severity of life-threatening epileptic seizures. Other early commissurotomies were performed by two neurosurgeons, Phillip Vogel and Joseph Bogen. The rationale for commissurotomies is rather simple: By severing the cerebral commissures, the major interconnecting fiber bundles that allow communication between the cerebral hemispheres, epileptic seizures will be prevented from spreading beyond their focal hemisphere. Commissurotomies are performed only as a last resort, after traditional drug therapy fails to control seizure activity.

Surprising as it may seem, commissurotomy patients show few long-term alterations in behavior. All subjects suffer from "acute disconnection syndrome," in which they are mute and partially paralyzed on the left side of the body for an interval ranging from a few days to a few weeks. Otherwise, commissurotomy patients exhibit relatively normal behavior. Moreover, the severity and frequency of seizure activity declines, sometimes quite dramatically, in response to this surgical procedure. Upon closer tachistoscopic examination of split-brain patients, however, hemispheric asymmetries in information processing are evident. These asymmetries are investigated in T-scope or divided visual field studies. The split-brain patient is required to fixate on a central point, while visual stimulation is presented to the right or left visual field. Assuming that the patient is fixated on the central point, stimulation in the right visual field is projected to the left hemisphere, and left visual field stimulation to the right hemisphere. Once the information is available to the left or right hemisphere of a split-brain patient, it is not able to cross the cerebral commissures, principally the corpus callosum, since those fibers have been partially or completely severed.

The pioneering studies of the divided visual field in split-brain patients are described in *The Bisected Brain* (1970) by Michael Gazzaniga, who was a co-principal investigator with Roger Sperry in those studies. In one of their investigations, pictures of common objects were presented to either the right visual field or the left visual field of split-brain patients. All patients were able to identify the information verbally when it was presented in the right visual field (left hemisphere), but not in the left visual field (right hemisphere). These results suggested specialization for verbal tasks in the left cerebral hemisphere but did not address functioning in the right cerebral hemisphere.

To assess the psychological functions of the right cerebral hemisphere, the procedure described in the previous experiment was repeated, except that subjects were asked to reach under a curtain with their left or right hand to select the object from among several alternatives (rather than verbally identifying the picture of the object). Subjects were able to perform this task competently with their left hand, which is controlled primarily by the right cerebral hemisphere. Therefore, stimulation presented to the left visual field is projected to the right cerebral hemisphere, which controls the left hand. The opposite is true for stimulation presented to the right visual field. Correct identification of objects with the left hand indicated right cerebral hemisphere involvement in recognition of nonverbal stimuli.

Support for the superiority of the right hemisphere on visuospatial tasks came from a study in which split-brain patients were required to assemble patterned blocks into particular designs. Even though all patients were right-handed, they were much better at this task with the left hand, presumably because the right cerebral hemisphere controls that hand. Yet another test of the abilities of the left cerebral hemisphere was performed by requesting subjects to copy pictures of line drawings. Again, despite being right-handed, all subjects performed better with the left hand. Their left-handed efforts were rather clumsy, but the spatial dimensions of the line drawings were proportionally correct. Overall, split-brain studies seem to indicate left-hemisphere superiority on verbal tasks and right-hemisphere superiority on nonverbal, visuospatial tasks.

Further proposals for differences between the right and left hemispheres have been suggested from split-brain research. For example, it now appears that the left hemisphere is specialized for verbal tasks, but only as a consequence of its analytical, logical, information-processing style—of which language is one manifestation. Similarly, the right hemisphere is specialized for visuospatial tasks because of its synthetic, holistic manner of processing information. Support for these hemispheric asymmetries was derived from a 1974 study conducted by Jere Levy in which split-brain patients were given ambiguous instructions; they were simply to match similar pictorial stimuli. These pictures could be matched either by their functions, such as a cake on a plate matched with either a spoon or a fork, or by their appearance, such as a cake on a plate matched with a hat with a brim. When the pictures were presented to the right visual field (left hemisphere), matching was accomplished by function, while pictures projected in the left visual field (right hemisphere) were matched according to appearance. Matching by function was construed to involve logical, analytical information processing; matching by appearance was interpreted as involving holistic, synthetic information processing.

Most of the basic findings on hemispheric asymmetries in split-brain patients have been extended to normal subjects whose cerebral commissures are intact, with the exception that right-hemisphere superiority for visuospatial tasks seems to be slightly weaker in normal subjects. Investigations with normal subjects require measurement of reaction time, because information projected to one visual field can quickly and easily transfer to the opposite hemisphere.

Applications

When generalizing basic laboratory research findings to real-world situations, it is important to note that information transfer across the cerebral commissures is nearly instantaneous in normal subjects. In addition, the real-world environment provides prolonged visual stimulation, which is typically scanned with continuous eye movements. In these situations, environmental stimulation is available to both cerebral hemispheres. Therefore, one must be cautious not to overstate the case for a relationship between hemispheric asymmetries and real-world phenomena. The two cerebral hemispheres do work in combination as a unified brain in normal subjects. Even in split-brain patients, the prolonged availability of environmental stimulation and continuous eye scanning movements result, for the most part, in unified overt behavior. Behavioral, perceptual, and motor differences in split-brain patients are only evident with highly specialized and artificial laboratory testing with such instruments as the tachistoscope. Generalizations, then, from divided visual field studies of asymmetry to everyday situations require actual research evidence rather than the speculation that is popular among some segments of both the scientific and lay community.

Stuttering is one real-world phenomenon for which laterality research has practical implications. There is some evidence that stutterers are bilaterally represented for speech and language to a greater extent than are nonstutterers. In one investigation, R. K. Jones, a neurosurgeon, was presented with four stutterers who had blood clots or tumors located near the normal speech center in the left hemisphere. Because of concern that removal of the blood clots or tumors would produce muteness in his patients by damaging the speech center, Jones performed the Wada test to determine where the speech center was located in each patient. This test involves the injection of an anesthetic agent, sodium amobarbital, into the right or left carotid artery. The carotid arteries provide the frontal regions of the brain, where the speech center is located, with oxygenated blood. The sodium amobarbital anesthetizes the particular hemisphere into whose carotid artery the drug is injected. If speech is disrupted by this procedure, either the speech center is located in the opposite hemisphere or the patient is bilaterally represented for speech. Additional testing of the opposite hemisphere will reveal whether the patient is bilaterally represented.

Using this procedure, Jones found that all four stutterers possessed bilateral speech representation. After the surgery, all four patients stopped stuttering and began to speak normally. These findings raise the question as to why stuttering is related to bilateralization of speech functions. One explanation is that stuttering occurs in these patients because, unlike normal people, the speech center in one hemisphere is competitive with the speech center in the opposite hemisphere. Neural impulses from the two speech centers arrive out of synchrony at the muscles that control speech, which produces stuttering. What are the practical implications of these findings? It is quite obvious that producing irreparable damage to the brain for the sole purpose of eliminating a speech disorder, such as stuttering, would be highly unethical at current levels of medical technology and knowledge about the brain. Additional research on the hemispheric basis of stuttering will need to be conducted, and technological advances will be required before stuttering can be eliminated in bilaterally represented patients through the use of neurosurgery; however, findings such as these may be increasingly useful in future applications of laterality research.

Yet another phenomenon linked with laterality research is dyslexia, a disorder of reading that is not associated with sensory impairment, retardation, or emotional disturbances. A physician by the name of Samuel T. Orton (1937) was the first to propose a link between hemispheric asymmetries and dyslexia. He observed mirror-image reversals of letters and words in reading and writing among children with reading problems. Orton also noted that many of these children exhibited unstable hand preferences, often accomplishing tasks normally reserved for a preferred hand with either hand on a given occasion. To account for these observations, Orton proposed that these children were insufficiently lateralized for speech and language functions. In other words, neither hemisphere was specialized for speech and language.

Evidence to support the hypothesis that dyslexia is attributable to incomplete lateralization has been generated by E. B. Zurif and G. Carson (1970), who compared the performance of fourteen normal readers in the fourth grade with fourteen dyslexic fourth graders on a dichotic listening task. Dichotic listening involves presenting simultaneous, competing verbal stimuli of differing content to each ear through headphones. The subjects' task is to identify the words, letters, or digits presented to each ear. Since the right ear primarily transmits auditory input to the left hemisphere, and the left ear to the right hemisphere, detectable differences in the processing of verbal stimulation can be used to suggest hemispheric asymmetries. In the foregoing study, presentation of a dichotic digits task showed a significant right-ear (left-hemisphere) advantage for the normal children and a weak, insignificant left-ear (right-hemisphere) advantage for the dyslexic children. Failure to find a significant hemispheric advantage in processing dichotically presented verbal stimulation suggests that dyslexic children may, indeed, be incompletely lateralized for speech and language. Before practical applications of this finding are realized, further explorations on the development of hemispheric asymmetries will be necessary to determine whether lateralization of functions can be influenced by environmental manipulation. Only if such modifications are possible can the development of incomplete lateralization be altered in dyslexics.

Context

Modern research on hemispheric asymmetries has its origins in a short paper read at an 1836 medical conference in Montpellier, France. Marc Dax, an obscure country physician, reported that aphasia, a disorder of speech and language, is related to left-hemisphere brain damage and concluded that each hemisphere is specialized for different functions. Unfortunately, the paper received little attention and Dax died the following year, never knowing that he had anticipated one of the most exciting and productive research fields to emerge in the twentieth century. Because Dax's paper was not widely known, credit for the discovery of hemispheric asymmetries was incorrectly given to Paul Broca, who presented a similar paper in 1861 to a meeting of the Society of Anthropology in Paris. Broca does deserve some of the credit for the discovery of hemispheric asymmetries in that he suggested an exact area of the left frontal lobe that produces an expressive aphasia when damaged. Furthermore, Broca presented a much more impressive case for left-hemisphere lateralization of speech and language; his paper was received with enthusiasm and controversy.

In 1868, a British neurologist, John Hughlings Jackson, proposed the idea of a "leading" hemisphere, which preceded the modern concept of "cerebral dominance," the idea that one hemisphere is dominant for psychological functions over the other hemisphere. By 1870, Karl Wernicke, a German neurologist, had presented evidence that a specific region of the temporal lobe in the left cerebral hemisphere is essential for comprehending language and, when damaged, produces a receptive aphasia. In combination, these findings led to a widely held position that one hemisphere, usually the left, is dominant for verbal tasks and other higher functions, while the opposite hemisphere, usually the right, possesses no special function or only minor, limited functions. Even though the term "cerebral dominance" is still used today, it is generally recognized that there are no "major" or "minor" hemispheres; they are simply specialized for different tasks and information-processing styles.

The strongest early evidence for a specific function mediated primarily by the right hemisphere came from widespread assessment of brain-damaged patients on spatial relationship tests. After testing more than two hundred brain-damaged patients, T. Weisenberg and K. E. McBride (1935) concluded that the right hemisphere is specialized for spatial relationships. These results refuted the notion of a single dominant hemisphere for all psychological functions.

Modern contributions made by Roger Sperry, Michael Gazzaniga, and their colleagues have been, perhaps, most instrumental in establishing the functions of the cerebral hemispheres. Their results, as well as those of neuropsychologists, have been incorporated into such areas as biological psychology, cognition, and perception. Biological psychologists are concerned with establishing the functions of various brain structures in normal subjects, including the cerebral hemispheres. Neuropsychologists contribute to laterality research by specifying the cognitive, motor, and behavioral deficits that arise following brain damage to a specific region in the cerebral cortex. Laterality research also provides information about hemispheric specialization for cognitive and perceptual processes.

Future explorations on laterality will continue to examine performance for specific tasks and information-processing strategies in each hemisphere, but with greater emphasis on localizing functions to specific brain structures. In addition, more effort will be expended on developing practical applications of laterality research in clinical and educational settings.

Bibliography

Bradshaw, John L., and Norman C. Nettleton. *Human Cerebral Asymmetry.* Englewood Cliffs, N.J.: Prentice-Hall, 1983. Bradshaw and Nettleton examine hemispheric asymmetries in split-brain and normal subjects, focusing particular attention on differences in cognitive processes and information-processing capacities between the two hemispheres. This book is moderately difficult to read and is recommended for college students and advanced high school students.

Bryden, M. P. *Laterality: Functional Asymmetry in the Intact Brain.* New York: Academic Press, 1982. A comprehensive book on laterality research and methods for each sensory modality. In addition, such specialized topics as the genetics and development of laterality, sex differences in laterality, and individual differences in laterality are reviewed. Although very comprehensive, the book is highly technical and would be appropriate only for advanced students.

Corballis, Michael C. *Human Laterality.* New York: Academic Press, 1983. Corballis draws on evidence for laterality from split-brain and normal subjects, examining laterality from comparative, developmental, evolutionary, and genetic perspectives. Examines the relationship between hemispheric asymmetries and such language disorders as dyslexia and stuttering. Well-written and moderately easy to read; highly recommended for college students and high school students.

Corballis, Michael C., and Ivan L. Beale. *The Ambivalent Mind: The Neuropsychology of Left and Right.* Chicago: Nelson-Hall, 1983. Corballis and Beale examine the concepts of left and right and the nature of handedness as it relates to behavior. In addition, they address practical applications of hemispheric asymmetry research for dyslexia, stuttering, and the development of academic skills. This book is moderately difficult and is recommended for college students and advanced high school students.

Segalowitz, Sidney J. *Two Sides of the Brain: Brain Lateralization Explored.* Englewood Cliffs, N.J.: Prentice-Hall, 1983. A basic book on hemispheric asymmetries found in split-brain and normal subjects. In addition, Segalowitz addresses developmental issues, individual differences, and implications of brain lateralization for human behavior. Highly accessible to the student and lay reader.

Springer, Sally P., and Georg Deutsch. *Left Brain, Right Brain.* 3d ed. New York: W. H. Freeman, 1989. Springer and Deutsch have written a comprehensive introductory book on laterality. They address research with split-brain and normal subjects in considerable detail, and provide thorough coverage of potential practical applications of laterality research. The book is very readable and is highly recommended for high school students, college students, and adult readers.

Richard P. Atkinson

Cross-References

Altered States of Consciousness, 220; Aphasias, 279; Brain Injuries: Concussions, Contusions, and Strokes, 448; Brain Specialization, 455; The Cerebral Cortex, 500; Neural Anatomy and Cognition, 1640; Neural Damage and Plasticity, 1655; Speech Disorders, 2342; Speech Perception, 2348; Stuttering, 2483.

SPORT PSYCHOLOGY

Type of psychology: Motivation
Fields of study: Motivation theory; social motives

Involvement in sports as a participant or a spectator serves similar psychological functions for individuals: Both help people create and maintain a positive self-concept, allow them to feel a part of important social groups, and provide a pleasant source of stimulation.

Principal terms

ATTRIBUTION: assigning event outcomes to particular causal factors
EUSTRESS: positive arousal or stress
EXTRINSIC MOTIVATION: behavior motivation caused by rewards that are external to the task performance itself
IMAGERY: the use of visualization to imagine the physical movements involved in executing a skill
INTRINSIC MOTIVATION: motivation based on the desire to achieve or perform a task for its own sake, without external rewards
SELF-CONCEPT: beliefs about one's personal qualities or traits
SELF-ESTEEM: the evaluative part of the self-concept; one's feeling of self-worth
SOCIAL IDENTITY THEORY: a theory maintaining that people are motivated to create and maintain a positive identity in terms of personal qualities and, especially, group memberships

Overview

An individual's motivational level is a critical determinant of his or her involvement in sports, either as a participant or as a spectator. Involvement in sports by both participants and spectators is a result of similar motivational factors: the desire to maintain a positive self-concept, the need to affiliate with or belong to meaningful social groups, and the need for positive levels of stress.

As illustrated by the work of social psychologists such as Henri Tajfel, John Turner, and Jennifer Crocker, who have all tested aspects of social identity theory, people attempt to maintain a positive view of themselves. Evaluations that people make of the groups to which they belong have consequences for their social identity. For many persons, the goal of feeling positive about themselves can be accomplished, at least in part, through involvement with athletics—either actively as participants or passively as spectators. For the athlete, self-esteem begins to play an important motivational role in early childhood. Children tend to choose activities in which they are successful, allowing them to feel proud of their accomplishments. Those children who find success in athletic games played at the gym or at recess begin to prefer them to other recreational or intellectual activities; however, physical ability also plays a role in children's decisions to participate in sports. Those with the most skill (presumably a genetic predisposition derived from athletic parents) tend to show the most enthusiasm for sports participation. Success and its subsequent self-esteem benefits fuel their desire to continue or increase their participation in athletics.

When studying the motivation of children, it is important to distinguish between intrinsic motivation and extrinsic motivation. When an individual is intrinsically motivated to complete a task, that person is moved by internal factors such as feelings of competence or an interest in the task itself. Persons who are extrinsically motivated are driven by external rewards, such as money, trophies, or praise from coaches and parents. Ideally, children should become involved in sports for intrinsic reasons, and most do become involved as a result of such motives. When intrinsically motivated children are given external rewards for their performance, however, the result can be a reduced overall motivation to participate in sports. That is, when children believe that they are no longer participating simply because of an inherent enjoyment of sports, they tend to become less interested.

The desire to maintain positive levels of self-esteem continues to be a primary motivational force for both adolescent and adult athletes. For these persons, participation in athletics allows them the opportunity to feel good about themselves by helping to fulfill their need for achievement and status. Successful athletic performance provides them with a feeling of accomplishment and mastery.

In addition to motivating the participants, a desire to feel good about oneself also serves as a motivational force for sports spectators. Although spectators do not personally accomplish performance goals as do the athletes, feelings of satisfaction and accomplishment can be experienced by the fans. Sports fans report elation following their team's victory and sorrow after their team's defeat with levels of intensity similar to those of the players. When one's favorite team is successful, feelings of pride and increased self-esteem are the result. Thus, spectators can improve their self-concept without requiring any special athletic skills.

Nyla Branscombe and Daniel Wann performed a series of studies showing that spectators may experience increases in self-esteem even if their favorite team is not of championship caliber. Fans of the local team, regardless of the success of that team, tend to have higher self-esteem, experience fewer negative emotions, and report greater life satisfaction than do persons who are not fans of the team. Such high self-esteem seems to be caused by the feelings of belonging and the social support gained through interactions with other fans. Supporting the local team allows one the opportunity to affiliate with others similar to oneself and to belong to something greater than oneself.

The desire to affiliate with, and belong to, certain groups also motivates sports participants. Humans are social animals and usually enjoy being members of various groups and organizations. As adolescents begin to detach themselves from their families, social groups involving their peers become increasingly important. A primary source of peer-group memberships is sports teams. Membership in such teams permits adolescents to be accepted by their peers, extends their social network, gives them a sense of belonging, and helps establish their social identity. Adults also may satisfy their need for affiliation and belonging by playing in recreational sports leagues.

A third factor shown to motivate both the athlete and the spectator is a desire for positive levels of stress. Unlike the negative stress that often accompanies academic or work endeavors, positive stress, called eustress, is reflective of people's desire to find stimulation in life. For both participants and spectators, an athletic event involving their chosen team can be very stimulating. Hearts begin to race, people may feel nervous, and, in general, the event can be quite arousing—much like a roller-coaster ride. This stimulation is actively sought by many people, and involvement in sports is an easy way to obtain it.

Applications

The motivational forces described above help to explain a wide variety of the behaviors exhibited by athletic participants and spectators. For example, the importance of maintaining a positive self-concept has been used to explain the self-serving attributions of both players and fans. Attributions are the explanations that people give when explaining why certain events occur. Attributions can be either external (the "A" grade was attributable to luck or easy questions) or internal (the "A" on a test was attributable to intelligence or intensive studying). Because of the desire for a positive self-concept, people tend to use external attributions to explain their failures (thereby protecting their self-concept) while forming internal attributions concerning their successes (thereby enhancing their self-concept). This self-serving attributional bias can be found in many areas, including athletics. Research has demonstrated that when a participant or a spectator's team has failed a competition, people tend to form external attributions as a means of explaining the defeat. For example, when asked to explain why they lost, athletes often blame the officials, bad luck, or the opponents' dirty play. They do not perceive the failure to be internal (attributable to a lack of skill or ability on their part); hence, their self-concept is protected. Conversely, when victorious, athletes tend to assign internal, not external, causes for their success. That is, when the match was won, they state that it was attributable to their skill rather than to luck.

This pattern of self-serving attributions is also found among sports spectators. When their favorite team is successful, sports fans tend to give internal attributions similar to those of the players. When their team loses, spectators choose external attributions to explain the defeat. This bias, used most frequently by the highly allegiant or identified fans, is driven by a desire to maintain the belief that the groups with which they are associated are good. Spectators can increase their self-esteem through a related process, called "basking in reflected glory" by Robert Cialdini and his colleagues. Cialdini has found that spectators enhance their self-esteem by increasing their association with successful teams and protect their self-esteem by decreasing their association with failing teams. In one study, students at a large university were telephoned and asked to describe the most recent game of the university's football team. When the team had won, people tended to give statements such as

"We won" or "We were victorious." When the team had lost, however, the typical reply was "They lost" or "They were defeated." In a second study, the day after their college team played, more students wore clothing that identified their university affiliation following a victory compared to when the team had been defeated. The most allegiant fans, however, tend to continue showing support for their team even when it loses over long periods of time. This is consistent with observation of some sports fans (such as members of the Chicago Cubs Die-hard Fan Club) who continue supporting teams even though they have a long history of losing.

The findings on the intrinsic-extrinsic motivational dichotomy have been used to help individuals who are trying to establish youth sports leagues. In the early stages of a league, intrinsic motives should be emphasized. Increases in extrinsic motivation via rewards and trophies will probably result in a reduction of intrinsic motivation and interest in the activity. In fact, simply having children come to expect their parents' praise can reduce intrinsic motivation. Unexpected praise and rewards are less likely to reduce intrinsic motivation. In general, it is probably best to take a "hands off" approach to children's athletic games. Less structure and parental influence will most likely result in greater enjoyment of the activity by children.

Coaches often try to increase the motivation of athletes as a means of increasing their performance. For example, by increasing a player's motivation to achieve a specific goal, a coach will probably increase that player's performance; however, increasing the player's motivation is only one method of enhancing performance. Another popular technique, called imagery, involves having the athlete mentally rehearse the athletic situations occurring in a competition. For example, prior to shooting the ball, a basketball player might form a mental image of himself or herself taking the correct stances, completing the correct follow-through, and so on. The results of research investigating the impact of imagery on performance have been quite positive. For example, L. Verdelle Clark had varsity and junior-varsity high school basketball players practice their free-throw shooting through either mental imagery or physical practice. The results indicated that the mental practice technique was almost as effective as the physical practice method.

The final factor motivating sports participants and spectators is eustress, or an individual's need for positive stimulation. The notion that people attend or participate in athletics to become aroused has important implications for their aggressive behavior. Considerable literature has noted that higher levels of arousal often result in increases in aggression. Thus, as either the players or the fans become excited (and many become involved with that purpose in mind), they are more likely to act aggressively toward either the players or the spectators of the opposing team. Consequently, at many sporting events, the stage is set for violence.

Context

Sport psychology is a relatively young specialty area within psychology. In fact, most of the national and international professional organizations designed to examine issues in sport psychology were founded fewer than twenty years ago, and it was not until 1986 that the American Psychological Association recognized sport psychology as a separate academic division. The topic of motivation, however, is one of the major areas of emphasis within the discipline of sport psychology, and it has attracted considerable research and theoretical attention.

Increased interest in the factors underlying the motivation of sports participants and spectators has been driven by the fact that sports have become one of the most popular leisure-time activities. The vast majority of individuals living in the United States are involved in sports in some form or another, many on a daily basis. In fact, families who share an interest in sports are almost twice as likely to express satisfaction with their leisure time as are persons who are not actively involved with sports. Furthermore, satisfaction with leisure-time activities greatly influences other areas of an individual's life, such as school or work.

Questions such as why some individuals are motivated to become involved in athletics, why some discontinue their involvement, and what the effects of sport involvement are should receive additional research attention in the future. Many of the initial questions examined in this area focused on ways of assisting athletic coaches in improving athletes' motor performance. Research into casual sports participation, and spectatorship in particular, is only beginning.

Understanding the motivations of sport spectators and participants is important for several reasons. First, most individuals begin their involvement with sports at a young age, usually by early adolescence. As a consequence of the large impact of peer relations on the development of young persons' personalities, insight into these relationships is important; it can be gained by studying athletic team formation and cohesion. Second, because self-esteem plays such a critical role in determining whether individuals will become involved in sports, the positive emotional impact of athletics may be used for therapeutic purposes. For example, a clinical psychologist might suggest to clients that they become involved in sports as one means of improving their self-concepts. Third, professional sports is a very big business with many millions of dollars at stake. If an individual's performance could be increased by increasing motivation, the result could be quite profitable. In fact, many professional sports organizations, as well as the United States Olympic Committee, now have their own sport psychologists on staff to help players with motivational issues, adjustment difficulties, and stress. As sport psychology continues to flourish, so too will research on the determinants of athletic participation and spectatorship.

Bibliography

Branscombe, Nyla R., and Daniel L. Wann. "The Positive Social and Self-Concept Consequences of Sports Team Identification." *Journal of Sport and Social Issues* 15, no. 2 (1991): 115-127. This paper reports on the consequences of sports-team identification for spectators. Specifically, the importance of self-esteem, feelings of belonging, and the team's record as motivating factors are reviewed. Other emotional consequences for sports spectators such as depression and alienation are considered.

Cialdini, Robert, et al. "Basking in Reflected Glory: Three (Football) Field Studies." *Journal of Personality and Social Psychology* 34 (September, 1976): 366-375. This interesting article investigates the self-esteem protecting and enhancing technique of basking in reflected glory. The authors discuss their own research on college students and point out the implications of that work for self-esteem maintenance via affiliation.

Clark, L. V. "Effect of Mental Practice on the Development of a Certain Motor Skill." *Research Quarterly* 31 (1960): 560-569. This easy-to-read journal article provides an excellent example of the effects of mental imagery on athletic performance, in addition to reviewing the methodology employed in this type of research. Much of the early work on imagery is cited and discussed.

Cox, Richard H. *Sport Psychology: Concepts and Applications.* Dubuque, Iowa: Wm. C. Brown, 1985. This book examines sport psychology primarily from a social psychological perspective. While many interesting topics within sport psychology are reviewed, the informative discussion of attributional biases adds substantially to this volume.

Cratty, Bryant J. *Psychology in Contemporary Sport.* 3d ed. Englewood Cliffs, N.J.: Prentice-Hall, 1989. This well-written text is a "must read" for persons interested in sport psychology, especially issues related to motivation. The author provides a comprehensive discussion of the literature by reviewing the impact of motivational variables at various life stages. Topics include genetic influences, social influences, and the need for stress.

Deci, E. L. "Intrinsic Motivation: Theory and Application." In *Psychology of Motor Behavior and Sport*, edited by Daniel M. Landers and Robert W. Christina. Champaign, Ill. Human Kinetics, 1977. Deci conducted many of the early experiments examining the detrimental effects of extrinsic rewards on intrinsic motivation. This chapter applies the research to the sports world in addition to reviewing past research in the area of intrinsic motivation.

Sloan, L. R. "The Function and Impact of Sports for Fans: A Review of Theory and Contemporary Research." In *Sports, Games, and Play: Social and Psychological Viewpoints*, edited by Jeffrey H. Goldstein. Hillsdale, N.J.: Lawrence Erlbaum, 1979. Explores the rewards that sports provide for spectators. Many motivational issues are discussed, including basking in reflected glory, stimulus seeking (eustress), and sports aggression. The author provides numerous real-life examples to illustrate the concepts.

Nyla R. Branscombe
Daniel L. Wann

Cross-References

S-R THEORY: MILLER AND DOLLARD

Type of psychology: Personality
Fields of study: Behavioral and cognitive models; models of abnormality;
 personality theory

Miller and Dollard developed a personality theory that was based on Clark Hull's stimulus-reponse learning theory. They used this theory and a number of psychoanalytic concepts to explain how neurosis developed. They also showed how psychotherapy could be conceptualized as a learning process by using an S-R model of higher mental processes.

Principal terms

CONFLICT: the result of incompatible motives or responses, as, for example, when a person simultaneously tries to approach and avoid the same goal

CUE: a distinctive stimulus that determines when and where a person will respond and what response will occur

CUE-PRODUCING RESPONSE: a response which serves as a cue for other responses; words (speech) can cue behaviors, and thoughts can cue other thoughts

DRIVE: an intense stimulus that forces action, such as a biological state (primary drive) such as hunger, thirst, or pain

HABIT: an association or connection between a cue and a response, such as stopping (response) at a red light (cue)

IMITATION: copying or matching the behavior of another person

REINFORCEMENT: the process of strengthening a habit; occurs when a response results in reduction of a drive

RESPONSE: an action; responses are elicited by cues and are energized by drives

RESPONSE HIERARCHY: an arrangement of alternative responses to a cue, in a hierarchy from that most likely to occur to that least likely to occur

SECONDARY DRIVE: a primary drive that is elicited by a neutral cue

Overview

Much, if not most, human behavior is learned. How human beings learn is one of the central, and most controversial, topics in psychology. Neal E. Miller and John Dollard used principles of learning developed by Clark Hull, who studied how animals learn, and applied them to explain complex human behavior.

According to Miller and Dollard, human behavior occurs in response to cues. A red traffic light, for example, is a cue to stop, whereas green is a cue to go. A cue is simply any stimulus that is recognized as different from other stimuli. A cue may bring about a variety of responses, but some responses are more likely to occur than others. The response most likely to occur to a cue is called the dominant response. Responses to a cue are arranged in a response hierarchy, from the dominant response to the response least likely to occur. A person's response hierarchy can change. The hierarchy that a person has originally is called the initial hierarchy. If the initial hierarchy is inborn, it is known as the innate hierarchy. When a hierarchy changes, the result is known as the resultant hierarchy.

Change in a response hierarchy occurs as a result of learning. There are four fundamental considerations in the explanation of how learning occurs: drive, cue, response, and reinforcement.

A drive is an intense stimulus, such as hunger, that motivates a response. The cue is the stimulus that elicits the response. If the dominant response in the hierarchy results in a reduction in the drive, then reinforcement will occur. Reinforcement means that the association, or connection, between the cue (stimulus) and response is strengthened; the next time the cue occurs, therefore, that response will be even more likely to occur. Reinforcement occurs when a person realizes that the response has led to a reward, although such awareness is not always necessary; reinforcement can also occur automatically. In other words, Miller and Dollard's theory states that for persons to learn, they must want something (drive), must do something (response) in the presence of a distinct stimulus (cue), and must get some reward for their actions (reinforcement).

If the dominant response does not result in a reward, the chance that the dominant reponse will occur again is gradually lessened. This process is called extinction. Eventually, the next response in the hierarchy will occur (in other words, the person will try something else). If that response results in reward, it will be reinforced and may become the dominant response in the hierarchy. In this way, according to Miller and Dollard, humans learn and change their behavior. According to this theory, connections between stimulus and response are learned; these are called habits. Theories that view learning in this way are called stimulus-response, or S-R, theories. The total collection of a person's habits make up his or her personality.

Drives, as previously noted, motivate and reinforce responses. Some drives, such as hunger, thirst, sex, and pain, are inborn and are known as primary drives. These drives are naturally aroused by certain physiological conditions; through learning, however, they may also be aroused by cues to which they are not innately connected. For example, one may feel hungry when one sees a favorite restaurant even though one has recently eaten. Drives aroused in this way (that is, by previously neutral cues) are called secondary, or learned, drives.

The natural reaction to an aversive stimulus is pain. Pain is a primary drive; it motivates a person to act, and any response which reduces pain will be reinforced. Neutral cues associated with pain may also produce a response related to pain called fear (or anxiety). Fear motivates a person to act; a response which reduces fear will be reinforced. Fear is therefore a drive; it is a drive which is especially important for understanding neurotic behavior, according to Miller and Dollard. For example, a fear of a harmless cue such as an elevator (an elevator phobia) will motivate a person to avoid elevators, and such avoidance will be reinforced by reduction of fear.

A response learned to one cue may also occur to cues which are physically similar to that cue; in other words, what one learns to do in one situation will occur in other, similar situations. This phenomenon is called stimulus generalization.

Many responses are instrumental responses, that is, they act on and change some aspect of the environment. Other responses are known as cue-producing responses; the cues from these reponses serve to bring about other responses. Words are especially important cue-producing responses; someone says a word and another person responds, or one thinks a word and this is a cue for another word. Thinking can be considered as chains of cue-producing responses—that is, as a sequence of associated words; in this way Miller and Dollard sought to describe the higher mental processes such as thinking, reasoning, and planning.

Applications

In their book *Social Learning and Imitation* (1941), Miller and Dollard pointed out that to understand human behavior one must know not only the process of learning (as described above) but also the social conditions under which learning occurs. Human learning is social—that is, it occurs in a social context, which can range from the societal level to the interpersonal level. The process of imitation is one example of how what an individual learns to do depends on the social context.

Imitation involves matching, or copying, the behavior of another person. If the matching behavior is rewarded, it will be reinforced, and the individual will therefore continue to imitate. The cue that elicits the imitating response is the person being imitated (the model), so that the imitative behavior, in Miller and Dollard's analysis, is dependent on the presence of the model. In this way, Miller and Dollard used S-R theory to explain how individuals learn what to do from others and thereby learn how to conform to society. In their best-known work, *Personality and Psychotherapy: An Analysis in Terms of Learning, Thinking, and Culture* (1950), Dollard and Miller applied S-R theory to explain how neurosis is learned and how it can be treated using learning principles. They pointed out three central characteristics of neurosis that require explanation: misery, stupidity, and symptoms.

The misery that neurotics experience is a result of conflict. Conflict exists when incompatible responses are elicited in an individual. An approach-approach conflict exists when a person has to choose between two desirable goals; once a choice is made, the conflict is easily resolved. An avoidance-avoidance conflict exists when an individual must choose between two undesirable goals. An approach-avoidance conflict exists when an individual is motivated both to approach and to avoid the same goal. The last two types of conflicts may be difficult to resolve and under certain conditions may result in a neurosis.

Dollard and Miller tried to explain some aspects of psychoanalytic theory in S-R terms; like Sigmund Freud, the founder of psychoanalysis, they emphasized the role of four critical childhood training situations in producing conflicts that can result in neurosis. These are the feeding situation, cleanliness training, sex training, and anger-anxiety conflicts. Unfortunate training experiences during these stages of childhood may result in emotional problems. Childhood conflicts arising from such problems may be repressed and may thereore operate unconsciously.

The "stupidity" of the neurotic is related to the fact that conflicts which produce misery are repressed and unconscious. Dollard and Miller explained the psychoanalytic concept of repression in terms of S-R theory in the following manner. Thinking about an experience involves the use of cue-producing responses (that is, the use of words) in thinking. If no words are available to label an experience, then a person is unable to think about it—that is, the experience is unconscious. Some experiences are unconscious because they were never labeled; early childhood experiences before the development of speech and experiences for which the culture and language do not provide adequate labels are examples of experiences which are unconscious because they are unlabeled. Labeled painful experiences may also become unconscious if a person stops thinking about them. Consciously deciding to stop thinking about an unpleasant topic is called suppression. Repression is similar to suppression except that it is automatic—that is, it occurs without one consciously planning to stop thinking. For Dollard and Miller, therefore, repression is the automatic response of stopping thinking about very painful thoughts; it is reinforced by drive reduction and eventually becomes a very strong habit.

The third characteristic of neuroses requiring explanation are symptoms. Phobias, compulsions, hysteria, and alcoholism are examples of symptoms. Symptoms arise when an individual is in a state of conflict-produced misery. This misery is a result of the intense fear, and other intense drives (for example, sexual drives), involved in conflict. Because the conflict is unconscious, the individual cannot learn that the fear is unrealistic. Some symptoms of neurosis are physiological; these are direct effects of the fear and other drives which produce the conflict. Other symptoms, such as avoidance in a phobia, are learned behaviors that reduce the fear and/or drives of the conflict. These symptoms are reinforced, therefore, by drive reduction.

Dollard and Miller's explanation of psychotherapy is largely a presentation of key features of psychoanalysis described in S-R terms. Therapy is viewed as a situation in which new learning can occur. Because neurotic conflict is unconscious, new learning is required to remove repression so that conflict can be resolved. One technique for doing this, taken directly from psychoanalysis, is free association; here, neurotic patients are instructed to say whatever comes to their consciousness. Because this can be a painful experience, patients may resist doing this, but, because the therapist rewards patients for free associating, they eventually continue. While free associating, patients become aware of emotions related to their unconscious conflicts and so develop a better understanding of themselves.

Another technique borrowed from psychoanalysis involves a phenomenon known as transference. Patients experience and express feelings about the therapist. Such feelings really represent, in S-R terms, emotional reactions to parents, teachers, and other important persons in the patient's past, which, through stimulus generalization, have been transferred to the therapist. The therapist helps the patient to recognize and label these feelings and to see that they are generalized from significant persons in the patient's past. The patient in this way learns how she or he really feels. The patient learns much about herself or himself that was previously unconscious and learns how to think more adaptively about everyday life. The patient's symptoms are thereby alleviated.

Context

The S-R theory used by Miller and Dollard had its intellectual roots in the thinking of the seventeenth century, when human beings were thought of as being complicated machines which were set in motion by external stimuli. At the beginning of the twentieth century, the stimulus-response model was adopted by John B. Watson, the founder of behaviorism. Watson used the S-R model to explain observable behavior, but he avoided applying it to mental processes because he believed that mental processes could not be studied scientifically.

Miller and Dollard extended the behaviorism of Watson to the explanation of mental events through their concept of the cue-producing reponse and its role in the higher mental processes. This was an S-R explanation: Mental processes were seen as arising from associations between words that represent external objects; the words are cues producing responses. Miller and Dollard's approach, therefore, represented a significant departure from the behaviorism of Watson. Miller and Dollard tried to explain mental events in their book *Personality and Psychotherapy*, in which they attempted to explain many psychoanalytic concepts in S-R terms. Since psychoanalysis is largely a theory of the mind, it would have been impossible for them not to have attempted to describe mental processes.

The approach to explaining mental processes used by Miller and Dollard, though it represented a theoretical advance in the 1950's, was gradually replaced by other explanations beginning in the 1960's. The drive-reduction theory of learning that they advocated came under criticism, and the S-R view that humans passively react to external stimuli was criticized by many psychologists. As a result, new theories of learning emphasizing cognitive (mental) concepts were developed.

New ways of thinking about mental processes were also suggested by fields outside psychology; one of these was computer science. The computer and its program were seen as analogous to human mental processes, which, like computer programs, involve the input, storage, and retrieval of information. The computer and its program, therefore, suggested new ways of thinking about the human mind. Miller and Dollard's S-R theory has largely been replaced by concepts of contemporary cognitive science.

Miller and Dollard's theory still exercises an important influence on contemporary thinking in psychology. Their analysis of psychoanalysis in terms of learning theory made the important point that neuroses could be unlearned using the principles of learning. Behaviorally oriented treatments of emotional disorders owe a debt to the intellectual legacy of Miller and Dollard.

Bibliography

Dollard, John, et al. *Frustration and Aggression.* New Haven, Conn.: Yale University Press, 1939. An early application of S-R theory to complex human behavior. The presentation of the hypothesis that aggression is inevitably caused by frustration is seen here.

Dollard, John, and Neal E. Miller. *Personality and Psychotherapy: An Analysis in Terms of Learning, Thinking, and Culture.* New York: McGraw-Hill, 1950. The best known of the works of Miller and Dollard. Presents a theory of personality and an S-R presentation of psychoanalytic theory and psychoanalytic therapy.

Hall, Calvin Springer, and Gardner Lindzey. *Theories of Personality.* 3d ed. New York: John Wiley & Sons, 1978. This book has a chapter on S-R theory and presents a detailed overview of the theory of Miller and Dollard.

Miller, Neal E. "Studies of Fear as an Acquirable Drive: I. Fear as a Motivator and Fear-Reduction as Reinforcement in the Learning of New Responses." *Journal of Experimental Psychology* 38 (1948): 89-101. A classic paper that served as the experimental basis for postulating that fear is a secondary drive.

Miller, Neal E., and John Dollard. *Social Learning and Imitation.* New Haven, Conn.: Yale University Press, 1941. Presents an application of S-R theory to social motivation with a special emphasis on imitation.

Spence, Kenneth Wartenbee. *Behavior Theory and Conditioning.* New Haven, Conn.: Yale University Press, 1956. A succinct and lucid presentation of the Hullian type S-R learning theory which served as the basis for many concepts in Miller and Dollard's S-R theory of personality.

Sanford Golin

Cross-References

STATISTICAL SIGNIFICANCE TESTS

Type of psychology: Psychological methodologies
Field of study: Methodological issues

Statistical significance tests are techniques that help assess the importance of research findings; they are crucial in helping to determine what inferences can be drawn from the data gathered from a psychological study.

Principal terms

MEAN: the average value of a group of scores

NORMAL DISTRIBUTION: a bell-shaped curve that often provides an accurate description of the distribution of scores obtained in research; it forms the basis of many statistical tests

NULL HYPOTHESIS: the hypothesis that whatever variable is being studied has produced no effect

PROBABILITY: the odds of a particular event occurring

SIGNIFICANCE LEVEL: the degree of likelihood that research results are attributable to chance

STANDARD DEVIATION: a measure of how spread out a group of scores are from the mean

T-TEST: a statistical test of the significance of the difference between the means of two groups

Overview

Psychological researchers make extensive use of statistical methods in the analysis of data gathered in their research. Statistical methods serve two primary functions: descriptive, to provide a summary of large sets of data so that the important features are readily apparent, and inferential, to evaluate the extent to which the data support the hypothesis being studied as well as the extent to which the findings can be generalized to the population as a whole. It is this second function that makes use of statistical significance tests.

Researchers may employ these tests either to ascertain whether there is a significant difference in the performance of different groups being studied or to determine whether different variables (characteristics) of subjects have a strong relationship to one another. For example, in conducting an experiment to test the effect of a particular treatment on behavior, the experimenter would be interested in testing the differences in performance between the treatment group and a control group. Another researcher might be interested in looking at the strength of the relationship between two variables—such as scores on the Scholastic Aptitude Test (SAT) and college grade-point average. In both cases, statistical significance tests would be employed to find out whether the difference between groups or the strength of the relationship between variables was statistically significant.

The term "statistically significant" has a specific meaning based on the outcome of certain statistical procedures. Statistical significance tests have their basis in the laws of probability, specifically in the law of large numbers and conditional probability. Primarily, the law of large numbers states that as the number of events with a certain probabilistic outcome increases, the frequencies of occurrence that are observed should come closer and closer to matching the frequencies that would be expected based on the probabilities associated with those events. For example, with a coin flip, the probability associated with "heads" is .50 (50 percent), as is the probability associated with "tails." If a person flipped a coin ten times, it would not be too startling if he or she got eight heads; if the coin were flipped ten thousand times, however, the observed frequencies of heads and tails would be about 50 percent each. Thus, with large numbers of probabilistic events, the expected outcomes can be predicted with great precision.

Conditional probability refers to the probability of a second event, given that a certain first event has occurred. For example, if someone has already pulled one ace from a deck of cards, what is the probability of pulling a second ace on that person's next attempt (without replacing the first card)? The probability of pulling the first ace was four (the number of aces in the deck) out of fifty-two (the number of cards in the deck). The second draw has a conditional probability created by what happened on the first pick. Since an ace was drawn first, there are now three left in the deck, and since the card was not replaced, there are now fifty-one cards left in the deck. Therefore, the probability of pulling the second ace would be three out of fifty-one.

Armed with these two concepts, it is now possible to understand how statistical significance tests work. Researchers are always investigating hypothetical relationships between variables through experiments or other methodologies. These hypotheses can be about how strongly related two variables are or about differences between the average performance between groups—for example, an experimental and a control group. One possible hypothesis is that the variables have no relationship, or that the groups are not different in their performance. This is referred to as the null hypothesis (from the Latin *nullus*, meaning "none"), and it plays an important role in establishing statistical significance. A second possible hypothesis is that there is a relationship between variables, or that there is a difference between the mean performances of groups. This is referred to as the alternative hypothesis, and it is the hypothesis truly of interest to the researcher. It is not possible, however, to test this hypothesis directly; it is possible to test the null hypothesis. Since these two hypotheses are both mutually exclusive and exhaustive (only one can be true, but one *must* be true), if it can be shown from the data gathered that the null hypothesis is highly unlikely, then researchers are willing to accept the alternative hypothesis.

This works through a conditional probability strategy. First, one assumes that the null hypothesis is true. Then one looks at the data gathered during the research and asks the question, "How likely is it that we would have gotten this particular sample data if the null hypothesis were true?" In other words, researchers evaluate the probability of the data given the null hypothesis. If they find, after evaluation, that the data would be very unlikely if the null hypothesis were true, then they are able to reject the null hypothesis and accept the alternative hypothesis. In such a case, it can be said that the results were statistically significant.

Arbitrarily, the standard for statistical significance is usually a conditional probability of less than .05 (5 percent). This probability value required to reject the null hypothesis is referred to as the significance level. This criterion is set at a stringent level because science tends to be conservative; it does not want to reject old ideas and accept new ones too easily. The significance level actually represents the probability of making a certain type of error—of rejecting the null hypothesis when it is in fact true. The lower the significance level, the higher the confidence that the data obtained would be very unlikely if the null hypothesis were true and the observed effects are reliable.

Statistical significance tests are the procedures that allow one to evaluate the conditional probability of the data, given the null hypothesis. The data from one's study are used to compute a test statistic. This is a number whose size reflects the degree to which the data differ from what would be expected if the null hypothesis were true. Some commonly encountered test statistics are the t-ratio, the F-ratio, and the critical (Z) ratio. The probability associated with the test statistic can be established by consulting published tables, which give the probability of obtaining a particular value of the test statistic if the null hypothesis is true. The null hypothesis is rejected if the probability associated with the test statistic is less than a predetermined "critical" value (usually .05). If the probability turns out to be greater than the critical value, then one would fail to reject the null hypothesis; however, that does not mean that the null hypothesis is true. It could simply be that the research design was not powerful enough (for example, the sample size may have been too small, like flipping the coin only ten times) to detect real effects that were there, like a microscope that lacks sufficient power to observe a small object that is nevertheless present.

There is sometimes a difference between statistical significance and practical significance. The size of most test statistics can be increased simply by increasing the number of subjects in the sample that is studied. If samples are large enough, any effect at all will be statistically significant no matter how small that effect may be. Statistical significance tests tell researchers how reliable an effect is, but not whether that effect has any practical significance. For example, suppose a researcher were investigating the effectiveness of two diet plans and used groups of one thousand subjects for each diet. Upon analyzing the data, the researcher found that subjects following diet A had a significantly greater weight loss than subjects following diet B. Suppose, however, that the average difference between the two groups was only one-tenth of a pound. While this difference was statistically significant, it would have no practical significance whatsoever.

Applications

Statistical significance tests provide a measure of how likely it is that the results of a particular research study came about by chance. They accomplish this by putting a precise value on the confidence or probability that rerunning the same study would produce similar or stronger results. A specific test, the t-test, can provide an example of how this works in practice. The t-test is used to test the significance of the difference between the mean performance of two groups on some measure of behavior. It is one of the most widely used tests of significance in psychological research.

Suppose a professor of psychology is interested in whether the more "serious" students tend to choose the early-morning sections of classes. To test this hypothesis, the professor compares the performance on the final examination of two sections of an introductory psychology course, one that met at 8:00 A.M., and one that met at 2:00 P.M. In this example, the null hypothesis would state that there is no difference in the average examination scores for the two groups. The alternative hypothesis would state that the average score for the morning group will be higher. In calculating the mean scores for each of the two groups, the professor finds that the early-morning class had an average score of 82, while the afternoon class had an average score of 77. Before reaching any conclusion, however, the professor would have to find out how likely it is that this difference could be attributable to chance, so a t-test would be employed.

There are three factors that influence a test of significance such as the t-test. One is the size of the difference between the means. In general, the larger the measured difference, the more likely that the difference reflects an actual difference in performance and not chance factors. A second factor is the size of the sample, or the number of measurements being tested. In general, differences based on large numbers of observations are more likely to be significant than the same differences based on fewer observations (remember the coin-flipping example). This is true because with larger samples, random factors within a group (such as the presence of a "hotshot" student, or some students who were particularly sleepy on exam day) tend to be canceled out across groups. The third factor that influences a measure of statistical significance is the variability of the data, or how spread out the scores are from one another. If there is considerable variability in the scores, then the difference (variability) in the group means is more likely to be attributable to chance. The variability in the scores is usually measured by a statistic called the standard deviation, which could loosely be thought of as the average distance of a typical score from the mean of the group. As the standard deviation of the groups gets smaller, the size of the measure of statistical significance, such as the t, will get larger.

Knowing these three things—the size of the difference of the two groups, the number of scores for each group, and the standard deviations of the test scores of the two groups—the professor can calculate a t-statistic and then draw conclusions. The actual calculation of the t is beyond the scope of this article, but with a difference of mean test scores of five points, fifty students in each class, and standard deviations of 3.5 in the first class and 2.2 in the second, the value of t would be 1.71. To determine whether this t is significant, the professor would go to a published statistical table that contains the minimum values for significance of the t statistic based on the number of subjects in the calculation (more technically, the degrees of freedom, which is the total number of subjects minus the number of groups—in this case, 100 minus 2, or 98). If the computed value of t is larger than the critical value published in the table, the professor can reject the null hypothesis and conclude that the performance of the early morning class was significantly better than that of the afternoon class.

Many research studies in psychology involve more complex designs than simple comparisons between two groups. They may contain three or more groups and evaluate the effects of more than one treatment or condition. This more complex evaluation of statistical significance is usually carried out through a procedure known as the analysis of variance (or F-test). The details of this procedure are also beyond the scope of this article; but, like the t-test, the F-test is calculated based on the size of the group differences, the sizes of the groups, and the standard deviation of the groups.

Other tests of statistical significance are available, and the choice of the appropriate technique is determined by such factors as the kind of scale on which the data are measured, the number of groups, whether one is interested in assessing a difference in performance or the relationship between subject characteristics, and so on. One should bear in mind, however, that statistical significance tests are only tools and that numbers can be deceptive. It is important to remember that even the best statistical analysis means nothing if a research study is designed poorly.

Context

Tests of statistical significance have been important in psychological research since the early 1900's. Pioneers such as Sir Francis Galton, Karl Pearson, and Sir Ronald A. Fisher were instrumental in both developing and popularizing these methods. Galton was one of the first to recognize the importance of the normal distribution (the bell-shaped curve) for organizing psychological data. The properties of the normal distribution are the basis for many of the probabilistic judgments underlying inferential statistics. Pearson, strongly influenced by Galton's work, was able to develop the chi-squared "goodness of fit" test around 1900. This was the first test that enabled the determination of the probability of discrepancies between the observed number of occurrences of categories of phenomena and what would be expected by chance.

It was the publication of Fisher's book *Statistical Methods for Research Workers* in 1925, however, that popularized the method of hypothesis testing and the use of statistical significance tests. Even though he was not the first to suggest it, Fisher, in this book, established the .05 level of significance as the standard for scientific research. Fisher's second book, *The Design of Experiments* (1935), brought his theory of hypothesis testing to a wider audience, and he believed that he had developed the "perfectly rigorous" method of inductive inference. Among Fisher's accomplishments was the development of the method of analysis of variance for use with complex experimental designs (the F-test was named for Fisher). Prior to Fisher's work, the evaluation of whether the results of research were "significant" was based either on a simple "eyeballing" of the data or on an informal comparison of mean differences with standard deviations. Through the efforts of Fisher and some of his followers, hypothesis testing using statistical significance tests soon became an indispensable part of most scientific research. In particular, between 1940 and 1955, statistical methods became institutionalized in psychology during a period that has been called the "inference revolution." Many researchers believed that these techniques provided scientific legitimacy to the study of otherwise abstract psychological constructs.

There have been some problems, however, with the statistical revolution in psychological research. Many researchers routinely misinterpret, for example, the meaning of rejecting the null hypothesis. Employing statistical significance tests can only tell the probability of the data, given the null hypothesis. It cannot tell the probability of a hypothesis (either the null or the alternative), given the data. These are two different conditional probabilities. Yet many reseachers, and even some textbooks in psychology, claim that the level of significance specifies the probability that the null hypothesis is correct or the probability that the alternative hypothesis is wrong. Often the quality of research is measured by the level of significance, and researchers are often reluctant to submit, and journal editors reluctant to publish, research reports in which there was a failure to reject the null hypothesis. This tendency has led over the years to the publication of many statistically significant research results that have no practical significance and to the withholding by researchers of reports of worthwhile studies (that might have had practical significance) because of a failure to reject the null hypothesis.

Statistical significance tests are valuable techniques for the analysis of research results, but they must be applied correctly and analyzed properly in order to serve their intended function.

Bibliography

Cowles, M., and C. Davis. "On the Origins of the .05 Level of Statistical Significance." *American Psychologist* 37, no. 5 (1982): 553-558. Traces the historical development of the .05 criterion for statistical significance. It discusses many of the earlier standards that were applied informally by statisticians and researchers and discusses Fisher's role in formalizing and popularizing the .05 level.

Gigerenzer, Gerd, and David J. Murray. *Cognition as Intuitive Statistics.* Hillsdale, N.J.: Lawrence Erlbaum, 1987. A somewhat technical but readable account of the emergence of statistical inference in psychological research. The first chapter not only chronicles the important events in this revolution but also gives a very clear discussion of the misinterpretation and misuse of statistical significance tests.

Howell, David C. *Fundamental Statistics for the Behavioral Sciences.* Boston: PWS-Kent, 1989. An excellent text designed for an introductory statistics course in the behavioral sciences. It does not require a mathematics background beyond high school algebra, and it emphasizes the logic of statistical procedures rather than their mathematical derivation.

Phillips, John L. *How to Think About Statistics.* 3d ed. New York: W. H. Freeman, 1988. Takes a common-sense approach to the logic behind statistical analysis and problem solving. Not a textbook, it focuses more on the thinking behind the numbers than on computations. It also emphasizes the application of statistics, with numerous examples from psychology, education, politics, and sociology.

Pyrczak, Fred. *Statistics with a Sense of Humor.* Los Angeles: F. Pyrczak, 1989. This is a workbook that provides an excellent supplement to any statistics text. The author has a real gift for presenting statistical concepts in a clear manner, and his humorous examples and riddle format tend to make the principles easier to understand.

Rowntree, Derek. *Statistics Without Tears.* New York: Charles Scribner's Sons, 1981. Another excellent introduction to the main concepts and terminology of statistics. Concepts are presented through words and diagrams rather than by means of formulas and equations, which tends to reduce the impact of "math phobia."

Oliver W. Hill, Jr.

Cross-References

Data Description: Descriptive Statistics, 751; Data Description: Inferential Statistics, 757; Hypothesis Development and Testing, 1248; Sampling, 2122; The Scientific Method in Psychology, 2148; Survey Research: Questionnaires and Interviews, 2507.

STRATEGIC FAMILY THERAPY

Type of psychology: Psychotherapy
Field of study: Group and family therapies

Strategic theory and interventions have been highly influential in the founding of modern family therapy. Strategic family therapy focuses on influencing family members by carefully planned interventions and the issuance of directives for resolving problems. At times, these directives may appear to be in direct opposition to the goals of treatment (an approach referred to as paradox). Strategic therapy is one of the most widely studied, taught, and emulated approaches to treating family (and individual) dysfunction.

Principal terms

AGORAPHOBIA: an intense fear of being in places or situations in which help may not be available or escape could be difficult

DOUBLE BIND: receiving contradictory messages; a form of communication which often occurs when a family member sends two messages, requests, or commands that are logically inconsistent, contradictory, or impossible

PARADOXICAL INTERVENTION: a therapy technique in which a therapist gives a patient or family a task that appears to contradict the goals of treatment

REFRAMING: redefining an event or situation in order to alter its meaning

RESTRAINING STRATEGIES: a form of paradoxical intervention wherein the therapist discourages, restrains, or denies the possibility of change

SYMPTOM PRESCRIPTION: a form of paradoxical intervention wherein the therapist encourages or instructs patients to engage in behaviors that are to be eliminated or altered

Overview

Families engage in complex interactional sequences that involve both verbal and nonverbal (for example, gestures, posture, intonation, volume) patterns of communication. Family members continually send and receive complicated messages. Strategic family approaches are designed to alter psychological difficulties which emerge from problematic interactions between individuals. Specifically, strategic therapists view individual problems (for example, depression, anxiety) as manifestations of disturbances in the family. Psychological symptoms are seen as the consequences of misguided attempts at changing an existing disturbance. For example, concerned family members may attempt to "protect" an agoraphobic patient from anxiety by rearranging activities and outings so that the patient is never left alone; unfortunately, these efforts only serve to foster greater dependency, teach avoidant behaviors, and maintain agoraphobic symptoms. From a strategic viewpoint, symptoms are regarded as communicative in nature. That is, symptoms have distinct meanings within families and usually appear when a family member feels trapped and cannot break out of the situation via nonsymptomatic ways.

The strategic model views all behavior as an attempt to communicate. In fact, it is impossible not to communicate, just as it is impossible not to act. For example, an adolescent who runs away from home sends a message to his or her parents; similarly, the parents communicate different messages in terms of how they react. Frequently, the intended message behind these nonverbal forms of communication is difficult for family members to discern. Moreover, when contradictions appear between verbal and nonverbal messages, communication can become incongruent and clouded by mixed messages.

Gregory Bateson, who was trained as an anthropologist and developed much of the early theory behind strategic approaches, worked with other theorists to develop the double-bind theory of schizophrenia. A double-bind message is a particularly problematic form of mixed communication that occurs when a family member sends two messages, requests, or commands that are logically inconsistent, contradictory, or impossible. For example, problems arise when messages at the content level ("I love you" or "Stay close to me") conflict with nonverbal messages at another level ("I despise you" or "Keep your distance"). Eventually, it is argued, a child who is continually exposed to this mixed style of communication, that is, a "no-win" dilemma, may feel angered, helpless, and fearful, and responds by withdrawing.

Since Bateson's early work in communication theory and therapy, the strategic approach has undergone considerable revision. At least three divisions of strategic family therapy are frequently cited: the original Mental Research Institute (MRI) interactional view, the strategic approach advocated by therapists Jay Haley and Cloe Madanes, and the Milan systemic family therapy model. There is considerable overlap among these approaches, and the therapy tactics are generally similar.

The MRI interactional family therapy approach shares a common theoretical foundation with the other strategic approaches. In addition to Bateson, some of the prominent therapists who have been associated with the institute at one time or another are Don Jackson, Jay Haley, Virginia Satir, and Paul Watzlawick. As modified by Watzlawick's writings, including *The Invented Reality* (1984), the MRI model emphasizes that patients' attempts to solve problems often maintain or exacerbate difficulties. Problems may arise when the family either overreacts or underreacts to events. For example, ordinary life difficulties or transitions (for example, a child beginning school, an adult dealing with new work assignments) may be associated with family overreactions. Similarly, significant problems may be treated as no particular problem. The failure to handle such events in a constructive manner within the family system eventually leads to the problem taking on proportions and characteristics which may seem to have little similarity to the original difficulty. During family therapy, the MRI approach employs a step-by-step progression of suggested strategies toward the elimination of a symptom. Paradoxical procedures, which are described later, represent a mainstay of the MRI approach.

Haley and Madanes' approach to strategic family therapy argues that change occurs through the process of the family carrying out assignments (to be completed outside therapy) issued by the therapist. As described in Madanes' *Strategic Family Therapy* (1981), strategic therapists attempt to design a therapeutic strategy for each specific problem. Instead of "suggesting" strategies, as in the MRI approach, therapists issue directives which are designed deliberately to shift the organization of the family in order to resolve the presenting problem. Problems are viewed as serving a function in the family and always involve at least two or three individuals. As detailed in Haley's *Leaving Home: The Therapy of Disturbed Young People* (1980) and *Ordeal Therapy: Unusual Ways to Change Behavior* (1984), treatment includes intense involvement, carefully planned interventions designed to reach clear goals, frequent use of therapist-generated directives or assignments, and paradoxical procedures.

The Milan systemic family therapy model is easily distinguished from other strategic approaches because of its unique spacing of therapeutic sessions and innovative team approach to treatment. The original work of therapists Mara Selvini-Palazzoli, Luigi Boscolo, Gianfranco Cecchin, and Guiliana Prata has been described as "long brief" family therapy and was used to treat a wide variety of severe problems such as anorexia and schizophrenia. The first detailed description of the Milan group's approach was written by the four founding therapists and called *Paradox and Counterparadox: A New Model in the Therapy of the Family in Schizophrenic Transition* (1978). The original Milan approach incorporated monthly sessions for approximately one year. The unusual spacing of sessions was originally scheduled because many of the families seen in treatment traveled hundreds of miles by train to receive therapy. Later, however, the Milan group decided that many of their interventions, including paradox, required considerable time to work. Thus, they continued the long brief model. Another distinguishing factor of the Milan group was its use of therapist-observer teams who watched treatment sessions from behind a two-way mirror. From time to time, the therapist observers would request that the family therapist interrupt the session to confer about the treatment process. Following this discussion, the family therapist would rejoin the session and initiate interventions, including paradox, as discussed by the team of therapist observers who remained behind the mirror. In 1980, the four originators of the Milan group divided into two smaller groups (Boscolo and Cecchin; Selvini-Palazzoli and Prata). Shortly thereafter, Selvini-Palazzoli and Prata continued pursuing family research separately. The more recent work of Boscolo and Cecchin is described in *Milan Systemic Family Therapy* (1987), while Selvini-Palazzoli's new work is presented in *Family Games* (1989), which she wrote with several new colleagues.

Applications

Jay Haley argued that conventional mental health approaches were not providing effective treatment. Based on his work with schizophrenics, he observed that patients typically would improve during their hospitalizations, return home, and then quickly suffer relapses. He also suggested that if the patient did improve while away from the hospital, then a family crisis would often ensue, resulting in the patient's eventual rehospitalization. Thus, effective treatment from a strategic framework often required family members to weather crises and alter family patterns of communication so that constructive change could occur.

Related to Haley's work with hospitalized patients was his treatment of "disturbed" young adults who exhibited bizarre behavior and/or continually took illegal drugs. In *Leaving Home: The Therapy of Disturbed Young People*, Haley suggests that it is best to assume that the problem is not an individual problem, but a problem of the family and young person separating from each other. That is, young adults typically leave home as they succeed in work, school, or career and form other intimate relationships. Some families, however, become unstable, dysfunctional, or distressed as the son or daughter attempts to leave. In order to regain family stability, the young adult may fail in attempts to leave home (often via abnormal behavior). Furthermore, if the family organization does not shift, then the young adult may be destined to fail over and over again.

Haley's approach to treating such cases includes several stages of strategic therapy. First, the entire family attends the initial interview, and the parents are put in charge of solving their child's problems. During treatment, the parents are told that they are the best therapists for their child's problems. Because the family is assumed to be in conflict (as shown by the patient's problems), requiring the family to take charge and become active in the treatment of the identified patient allows for greater opportunities to intervene around the conflict. In particular, it is assumed that the hierarchy of the family is in confusion and that the parents must take an active role in shifting the family's organization. Also, all family members are encouraged to adopt a position in which they expect the identified patient's problems to become normal.

As the identified patient improves, the family will often experience a crisis and become unstable again. A relapse of the identified patient would follow the usual sequence for the family and return stability (and familiarity) to the system. Unfortunately, a relapse would only serve to perpetuate the dysfunction. Therefore, the therapist may further assist the family by dealing with concerns such as parental conflicts and fears, or attempt to assist the young adult by providing opportunities away from therapy sessions which foster continued growth. Eventually, termination is planned, based on the belief that treatment does not require the resolution of all family problems, but instead those centered on the young adult.

Strategic therapists share a common belief in the utility of paradoxical procedures. In fact, the history of modern paradoxical psychotherapy is frequently credited as beginning with the MRI group, although paradoxical techniques have been discussed by various theorists from other orientations. Paradox refers to a contradiction or an apparent inconsistency that defies logical deduction. That is, strategic paradox is employed as a means of altering behavior through the use of strategies in apparent opposition to treatment goals. The need for paradoxical procedures is based on the assumption that families are very resistant to change and frequently attempt to disrupt the therapist's effort to help them. Thus, if the therapist suggests common therapeutic tactics (for example, communication homework, parenting suggestions), then the family may resist (for example, may "forget" to do the homework, sabotaging the exercise) and fail to improve. On the other hand, if the therapist tells the family to do what they are already doing, then the family may resist by getting better.

A variety of explanations have been offered to explain the manner in which paradox works. In *Change: Principles of Problem Formation and Problem Resolution* (1974), written by Watzlawick and his colleagues, paradox is described as producing a special type of change among family members. That is, there are two levels of change: first-order and second-order change. First-order change is change within a family system (for example, a parent increasing punishment as the child's behavior becomes more disruptive). First-order change is typically conducted in a step-by-step fashion and involves the use of problem-solving strategies. On the other hand, second-order change refers to changing the family system itself, and it typically occurs in a sudden and radical manner. The therapist attempts to change the system by unexpected, illogical, or abrupt methods. Paradoxical procedures are designed to effect second-order change. A paradoxical approach might be to encourage the child to act out every time he or she believes that the parents are about to have a fight. In such a case, the family system may be transformed by family members receiving important feedback about the manner in which they operate, by increased understanding of one another's impact on the system, and by efforts to discard "old family rules" by initiating new procedures for effective family living.

Several different classes of paradoxical interventions are highlighted in Gerald Weeks and Luciano L'Abate's book *Paradoxical Psychotherapy: Theory and Practice with Individuals, Couples, and Families* (1982). These include reframing, prescribing the symptom, and restraining.

Reframing refers to providing an alternative meaning or viewpoint to explain an event. A common example of reframing is Tom Sawyer, who described the boredom of whitewashing a fence as pleasurable and collected cash from his peers for the opportunity to assist him. Reframing provides a new framework from which to evaluate interactions (for example, "Mom is smothering" versus "Mom is caring and concerned").

Prescribing the symptom refers to encouraging or instructing patients to engage in the behavior that is to be eliminated or altered. Symptom prescription is the most common form of paradox in the family therapy literature. Following the presentation of an appropriate rationale to the family (for example, to gain more assessment information), the therapist offers a paradoxical instruction to the family, typically as part of the week's homework. For example, a child who frequently throws temper tantrums may be specifically instructed to engage in tantrums, but only in certain locations at scheduled times. Another common use of paradox involves symptom prescription for insomniacs. A patient with onset insomnia (difficulty falling asleep) may be encouraged to remain awake in order to become more aware of his or her thoughts and feelings before falling asleep. As might be guessed, anxiety is often associated with onset insomnia, and such an intervention serves to decrease anxiety about failing to fall asleep by introducing the idea that the patient is supposed to stay awake. Frequently, patients describe difficulty completing the homework because they "keep falling asleep too quickly."

Restraining strategies include attempts to discourage, restrain, or even deny the possibility of change; the therapist might say, "Go slow," or, "The situation appears hopeless," or, "Don't change." The basis for restraining strategies is the belief that many patients may not wish to change. Why would patients seek treatment and spend money toward that end if they do not wish to improve? All change involves risk, and with risk comes danger and/or uncertainty. Moreover, the future may be less predictable following change. In fact, it is possible to conceive of most recurring patterns of family dysfunction or individual difficulties as a heavy overcoat. At times, the heavy overcoat serves a useful purpose by protecting one from harsh weather. As time passes, however, the overcoat becomes uncomfortable as the weather becomes warmer. Still, many people dread taking off the overcoat because they are used to it, it has become familiar, and the future seems uncertain without it. From the patient's viewpoint, discomfort may be more acceptable than change (and the uncertainty it brings).

Perhaps the most common restraining strategy is predicting a relapse. In predicting a relapse, the patient is told that a previous problem or symptom will reappear. By so doing, the therapist is in a no-lose situation. If the problem reappears, then it was predicted successfully by the therapist, is understood by the therapist, and can be dealt with by the therapist and patient. If the problem does not reappear, then the problem is being effectively controlled by the patient.

Context

Strategic approaches, based on communication theories, developed from research conducted at the Mental Research Institute (MRI) in Palo Alto, California, in the 1950's. In contrast to psychodynamic approaches, which emphasize the importance of past history, trauma, and inner conflicts, strategic therapies highlight the importance of the "here and now," and view psychological difficulties as emerging from problematic interactions between individuals (family members or married partners). Moreover, strategic therapists tend to follow a brief model of treatment, in contrast to many individual and family therapy approaches.

The effectiveness of family therapy approaches, including strategic approaches, is difficult to measure. Although there has been a clear increase in research evaluating the efficacy of family interventions since about 1980, the results are less than clear because of difficulties with research methodologies and diverse research populations. For example, psychodynamic therapists prefer to use case studies rather than experimental designs to determine effectiveness. Strategic therapists have conducted only a handful of research studies, but these results are encouraging. A structural-strategic approach developed by psychologist M. Duncan Stanton has demonstrated effectiveness in the treatment of drug abuse. Also, the Milan approach has been found to be effective for a variety of problems identified by families who partici-pated in a three-year research program. Further research is warranted, however, be-fore definitive conclusions about the empirical effectiveness of strategic approaches can be reached.

In conclusion, strategic family therapy has shaped the field of family therapy. Inno-vative approaches such as paradox have been associated with strategic therapy for years, and advances continue to be seen from the respective groups of strategic thera-pists. Although strategic approaches such as paradoxical directives are frequently re-garded as controversial and perhaps risky, the importance of some strategic contribu-tions to the field of family therapy—in particular, the recognition of multiple levels of communication, and of subtle nuances of power struggles in relationships—is widely accepted.

Bibliography

Goldenberg, Irene, and Herbert Goldenberg. *Family Therapy: An Overview.* 3d ed. Pacific Grove, Calif.: Brooks/Cole, 1991. An updated review of the major fam-ily therapy approaches, including strategic family therapy. Also provides a back-ground on family development, and highlights issues in family therapy research and training.

Haley, Jay. *Leaving Home: The Therapy of Disturbed Young People.* New York: McGraw-Hill, 1980. Presents a treatment program for disturbed young people and their families. Describes the use of intense involvement and rapid disengagement with such families. Haley is one of the foremost theorists and therapists in strate-gic approaches.

Madanes, Cloe. *Strategic Family Therapy.* San Francisco: Jossey-Bass, 1981. Pro-vides an overview of strategic family therapy from one of the primary therapists in the field. Describes the philosophy and common approaches employed by stra-tegic therapists in the treatment of a variety of presenting problems.

Stanton, M. Duncan. "Strategic Approaches to Family Therapy." In *Handbook of Family Therapy,* edited by Alan S. Gurman and David P. Kniskern. New York: Brunner/Mazel, 1981. Summarizes the strategic family therapy approach and high-lights the central components of the MRI group, Milan school, and other notable strategic therapists. Also highlights the dimensions of healthy and dysfunctional families from a strategic model. Finally, briefly outlines some research on the effectiveness of the model in treating a variety of disorders.

Weeks, Gerald R., and Luciano L'Abate. *Paradoxical Psychotherapy: Theory and Practice with Individuals, Couples, and Families.* New York: Brunner/Mazel, 1982. Provides an overview of paradoxical approaches and details a variety of consid-erations in using paradox in treatment. Presents a compilation of paradoxical meth-ods and describes some of the theories underlying these methods.

Gregory L. Wilson

Cross-References

ADAPTATION TO STRESS

Type of psychology: Stress
Field of study: Coping

Stress is an agitated physiological state in which the electrical transmission of information along neurons is heightened to the point that the nervous system may collapse and/or bodily functions may perform poorly. Most individuals pursue displacement activities to relieve stress; unfortunately, these efforts are halfway measures which often make the stressful situation worse. More effective, scientific methods are available for alleviating stress.

Principal terms

BIOFEEDBACK: a psychophysiological technique by which an individual monitors a specific, supposedly involuntary bodily function and consciously attempts to control this function

CANCER: an age- and stress-related disease in which normal body cells lose their differentiation capacity and mutate into a rapidly multiplying, uncontrollable mass of cells

CHAOS: a disruption of a normal, orderly physiological rhythm, often brought about by the slightest disturbance or stress to a system

DISPLACEMENT ACTIVITY: a behavior exhibited without explanation or purpose by an animal that is subject to a stressful situation or environment

ENDOCRINE SYSTEM: a system of ductless glands in the bodies of vertebrate animals that secretes hormones which travel through the bloodstream to target tissues, whose functioning is altered by the hormones

HOMEOSTASIS: the maintenance of constant, internal bodily conditions and physiological rhythms, the achievement of which is seriously compromised by stressful situations

LATERAL THINKING: an alternative means of looking at events and situations that runs counter to traditional, stressful approaches

NERVOUS SYSTEM: an array of billions of neurons (conducting nerve cells) that transmits electrical information throughout the body and thereby controls practically all bodily processes

STRESS: a heightened electrical activity within the neurons of the central and peripheral nervous systems such that various bodily systems begin to function improperly or fail altogether

Overview

Stress becomes an abnormally dangerous physiological condition when it is maintained for long periods of time without relaxation. It is caused by the increased electrical flow of information along neurons, the nerve cells which conduct information throughout the central and peripheral nervous systems of animals. It is also caused by the increased release of hormones from the endocrine system. Combined, the heightened nervous system activity and production of hormones affects organs and tissues within the body. The cells of these bodily structures will respond to such increased activity by deviating from their normal, stable physiological rhythms, descending into chaotic behavior and functioning improperly as a result.

Ultimately, the causes of stress come from an individual's external environment. The individual may be exposed to physical danger from other individuals of the same or a different species. The individual may be stressed from starvation, loneliness, or rejection. The individual's status within her or his social environment may be threatened. Regardless of the cause, all these events serve as environmental stimuli that trigger the stress response within the body of the individual. The individual becomes agitated from heightened nerve and hormonal activity—the "fight-or-flight" response.

Such a stressful response is critical for the survival of an individual in a harsh environment where the possibility of death via a predator or enemy lurks behind every corner. For most animals, such stressful conditions last for only a few minutes and quickly are followed by long periods of relaxation once the danger has passed. The stressful response, however, has been taken to extraordinary lengths by humans in a fast-paced technological society in which individuals are pushed to their physical limits to produce results or perish from the competition. In technological human societies, the fight-or-flight stress response is continuous, with little room for relaxation.

The results of this stressful society have been disastrous. Deaths of individuals from stroke, heart attack, cancer, and other stress-related diseases have skyrocketed. These diseases are caused primarily by the breakdown of normal bodily rhythms and tissue functions under the false information delivered to them by the hyperactivity of neurons and hormones triggered by the stressful conditions in which the individual lives. Blood vessels constrict under stress so that sufficient blood cannot reach certain tissues, leading to a stroke if that tissue is brain tissue, and a heart attack if that tissue is the heart muscle. Cells become abnormal, tumorous, and cancerous under stress. These cancer cells proliferate and spread, since stress also weakens the body's immune system, which otherwise would fight and destroy the abnormal cells.

Besides damage to body tissues, weakening of the immune system, and the occurrence of disease, stress causes the body to age prematurely. Stress causes overacceleration of all bodily functions. It wrecks homeostasis, the maintenance of orderly internal conditions for the body, in the process reducing bodily rhythms to chaotic randomness. Such chaotic disruptions of homeostatic body rhythms can lead to serious chemical imbalances within the body that may contribute to abnormal behavior, irritability, or violence.

When exposed to stressful situations and their inevitable disruptions to bodily rhythms, most animals adapt to the stressful environment by altering their behavior.

Often, they will exhibit displacement activities, behaviors which seem out of place and which are virtually unexplainable. For example, a stressed animal may start moving around in circles or attacking fellow group members without provocation. In mice, the stressful conditions of overcrowding lead to behaviors such as homosexuality and even cannibalism.

In many ways, human responses to stressful situations are similar to those of other animals; however, the strong social and cultural aspects of human society make human stress adaptations more varied. These adaptations may include constructive and antistress behaviors such as group association, athletics, self-imposed antistress strategies, and so on. Nevertheless, certain adaptations may create other problems: Overeating, smoking, precocious sexual behavior, and alcohol and drug abuse are stress adaptations that may contribute to further stress.

Participation in athletic events is a strong positive adaptation to stress. Physical exertion relaxes nervous tension and dilates blood vessels, thereby allowing increased blood flow and negating stress-related arteriosclerosis (hardening of the arteries) and other deleterious physiological conditions. Lack of exercise in prolonged high-stress situations can have very serious physiological ramifications.

Self-induced antistress strategies include methods such as meditation and biofeedback. Meditation involves disciplining one's mind and logically dealing with stress and stressful situations. It involves lateral thinking, an approach by which one establishes priorities and values in one's life that deemphasize the trivial preconceptions and preoccupations that produce most of the stress in human lives. The philosophy known as Zen Buddhism is a good example. In some ways, organized religions meet this aspect of stress adaptation, although most religions do so within the context of a social dominance hierarchy, which can cause stress of its own.

Biofeedback is an often-criticized technique which gained popularity in the 1970's and received scientific support in the 1990's. This technique involves the monitoring of some physiological condition (such as blood pressure) within one's own body with an appropriate instrument and mental concentration to control the condition. Such functions for the most part are involuntary; they are unconsciously controlled by the central nervous system of the individual. Biofeedback research has demonstrated that many such involuntary processes can be consciously regulated to a significant extent for the well-being of the individual. Such techniques have shown positive results for the rehabilitation of paralysis patients.

These positive adaptations to stress involve mental and physical discipline. In highly stressful, technological Western society, however, most individuals resort to "quick-fix" displacement adaptations which often propagate the stressful situation in a vicious circle. Such negative stress adaptations, which are practiced by millions of Americans, include overeating, smoking, excessive consumption of alcoholic beverages, drug abuse, and addictions to loud music and television. Most of these short-term stress alleviations involve immediate self-gratification. Such negative stress adaptations probably have contributed significantly to many social and medical problems in industrialized nations, including rising cases of mental illness, alcoholism, drug abuse, heart disease, cancer, infant mortality, child abuse, acts of violence, accidents, and the rapid spread of disease.

Applications

The biological effects of stress upon humans result in hundreds of thousands of deaths per year and billions of dollars in medical expenses. These effects are a needless tragedy and a drain upon the national and world economies. Stress must be reduced in American society, and individuals must participate in positive stress adaptations to protect themselves from the physiological disorders which are brought about by stress.

The most immediate applications of stress adaptation lie within the field of psychology. Probably the majority of behavioral problems studied by psychologists are stress-related to some degree. Psychologists and other social scientists attempt to devise stress adaptation strategies for use by individuals who are suffering from stressful situations. Among these strategies are various psychoanalytic techniques aimed at building individual self-esteem and self-worth. Psychologists and psychiatrists aim to tackle stress within individuals at the mental level.

Medical research employs both psychological and physiological techniques to minimize stress within the human brain and body. Such researches aim to understand the human nervous and endocrine systems and their effects upon the rest of the body. The human nervous system consists of a centralized brain and spinal cord containing several hundred billion neurons and a dispersed peripheral nervous system containing hundreds of billions of neurons that deliver and receive information from absolutely every region of the body. Sensory information comes from the body or outside the body along sensory peripheral nerves that relay the information to the spinal cord and brain. Complex networks of millions of neurons within the brain analyze the sensory information, a response decision is made, and a command is sent along many arrays of motor peripheral neurons to muscles and other target organs so that the body can respond to the initial stimulus.

In stressful situations, the body is barraged with external stimuli, which are carried along such sensory neurons to the brain and spinal cord. If the brain interprets the stimulus to be a danger or nuisance to the organism, then motor neurons will issue fight-or-flight commands to appropriate body regions. Such responses may occur over even the most trivial events which society deems important. The fight-or-flight response will employ not only the hyperactivity of sensory and motor neurons but also the increased activity of the endocrine system.

The endocrine system consists of ductless glands that release protein or steroid hormones to target the cells of specific body tissues. The bloodstream delivers these hormones to their targets, where they trigger a cascade of enzymatically controlled chemical reactions that activate or inactivate certain genes within the target cells. The result is reprogramming of the target cell's protein production, since cellular proteins are encoded by the cell's genes.

These nervous and endocrine effects occur much like a long chain of dominoes falling upon one another. Once a stressful stimulus is received by the body, a complex sequence of nervous and endocrine system-directed physiological changes is set into motion, a sequence which is very difficult to reverse. In the central nervous system, neural networks grow into specific patterns based upon the individual's personal experiences, thus producing memory. Long-term stress will fix a stress pattern into an individual's psychological and physical makeup so that the person's body will continuously be in the fight-or-flight response to some extent. Hormones and neurotransmitters will be set at specific, high production levels to maintain the stress state. Organ systems and bodily processes will begin to degrade if the neural and endocrine stress fixation is not reversed. Abnormally high hormone levels under stress can trigger abnormalities in cellular growth, in many cases leading to tumors and cancers. Growing evidence implicates stress in the occurrence of cancer and in the degradation of the immune system, which normally destroys abnormal cells.

A variety of medications, relaxants, and depressants are available to curtail the effects of stress in patients; however, these medications often have serious side effects and often are addictive, the latter being a stress situation in and of itself. Many of the displacement activities and negative stress adaptations give the individual temporary psychological relief from the stressful condition but do not remove the physical effects of the stress.

The only effective means of alleviating the psychological and physiological effects of stress are mental and physical discipline. Mental discipline (such as meditation, relaxation, and biofeedback) involves the concentrated easing of nervous tension and the realization that situations which cause stress usually are not worth the worry. Physical exertion via sports and exercise provides psychological relief and enables the body to reset itself to a calmer level. Without these positive stress adaptations, individuals usually slip into the easier negative stress adaptations and their physiological hazards. Perhaps the only true alleviation of stress is for people to live slower, more meaningful, and more understanding lives.

Context

Stress adaptation is a central focus in psychology because stress affects all people. Different individuals cope with stress in different ways. Some people handle stress very well. Other people are devastated by the slightest difficulties. Much of the difference between these two extremes can be traced to the genetics, physiologies, and life experiences of the people involved. The ability of any one person to handle stress is determined by the individual's psyche, which in turn is determined by the individual's inherited genes and life experience.

Stress and stressful situations can arise from personal discomfort with one's interactions with others, undesirable events (such as accidents or the death of a friend), and actual physical danger. The technological society that exists in North America and Europe is fast-paced, overpopulated, and oriented toward the rapid achievement of goals, money, and deadlines. Failure to achieve these artificial objectives is frowned upon, thereby leading to the generation of an incredible amount of stress in most people's lives. People are caught in an ever-accelerating situation of avoiding stress by avoiding failure, and in so doing they are generating more stress in a never-ending vicious cycle. The most amazing aspect of this technological stress is that, in reality, it poses no real threat to one's safety or survival: People perceive such a threat when none exists.

The net results of such stress are millions of cases of heart disease, cancer, stroke, obesity, eating disorders such as anorexia nervosa, behavioral disorders, alcoholism, drug use and abuse, sexual promiscuity, sexually transmitted diseases, smoking, depression, and crime. Stress is a major killer and disruptor of human lives. Billions of wasted dollars are spent by individuals to alleviate stress-related diseases; alleviating stressful environments and treating the physiological effects of stress have become a major priority in medicine.

Stress overburdens the human nervous and endocrine systems, in particular the central control regions of thought and biological processes within the brain. The human brain consists of approximately 100 billion neurons that are arranged in an incomprehensibly complex arrangement of neural networks that coordinate virtually all bodily processes via the billions of neurons in the spinal cord and peripheral nerves. Furthermore, the brain contains the hypothalamus and hypophysis (pituitary gland), which control virtually all hormonal secretions within the body and the genetic regulation of most cells within the body.

The disruption of homeostasis (the maintenance of orderly, rhythmic cycles within the body) produces the stress-related diseases described above. It affects some individuals more severely than others. Most individuals choose halfway measures to deal with stress on a temporary basis; however, studies clearly have demonstrated that mental and physical self-control are the best adaptations to stress. A slower but more physically active life-style is recommended. A correct diet with perhaps a small quantity of alcohol (such as a glass of wine) may also be helpful, according to some studies. Proper antistress adaptations should include mental and physical conditioning as well as physical exercise every day to counteract stressful situations. Sociologists and psychologists must emphasize the need for government, businesses, and industry to reorient their priorities and recognize stress as a major cause of disease. The reduction of stress in the human environment is a critical medical challenge.

Bibliography

Andrewartha, Herbert George. *Introduction to the Study of Animal Populations.* Chicago: University of Chicago Press, 1961. In this classic book by one of the pioneers in animal behavior research, Andrewartha discusses the principal behaviors of many different species, including dominance hierarchies, environmental stress, and displacement activities. The second half of the book is a useful guide to performing animal behavior experiments in the laboratory and the field.

Curtis, Helena. *Biology.* 3d ed. New York: Worth, 1979. Curtis presents an excellent introduction to biology for the beginning student in this thorough but clear book.

In chapter 34, "Integration and Control," she describes the functioning of the mammalian nervous and endocrine systems. Chapters 40, "Brain and Behavior," and 48, "Social Behavior," focus upon neurophysiological responses to the environment and to other organisms.

Lorenz, Konrad. *On Aggression.* Translated by Marjorie Kerr Wilson. New York: Harcourt, Brace and World, 1966. Lorenz, a Nobel laureate in physiology or medicine for his pioneering animal behavior research, describes animal behavior, especially aggressive behavior, in this exciting, simple book. He addresses one of the key causes of stress in human society and discusses human technological and social evolution within this context.

Manning, Aubrey. *An Introduction to Animal Behavior.* 3d ed. Reading, Mass.: Addison-Wesley, 1979. Manning's short but thorough book is an excellent introduction to animal behavior research. He describes numerous behavioral models for learning, displacement activities, and stress responses, and cites numerous experimental studies to support these models. Stress and displacement activities are addressed in chapter 5, "Conflict Behaviour."

Marler, Peter, and William J. Hamilton III. *Mechanisms of Animal Behavior.* New York: John Wiley & Sons, 1966. In this comprehensive survey and introduction to animal behavior research, Marler and Hamilton discuss major ethological theories and models, and numerous classical experiments which describe the behaviors of many different species. They describe defense mechanisms, threat displays, stress responses, aggression, and displacement activities in several mammalian and avian species.

Pirsig, Robert M. *Zen and the Art of Motorcycle Maintenance.* New York: Bantam, 1975. In this brilliant semi-autobiographical bestseller, philosopher Pirsig introduces the reader to value systems in human society. He attacks the stressful, meaningless aspects of daily life and challenges the reader to live life to its fullest. Stresses major concepts such as quality and "selfless climbing" instead of "ego-climbing" in the conduct of one's life.

Raven, Peter H., and George B. Johnson. *Biology.* 2d ed. St. Louis: Times Mirror/Mosby, 1989. Raven and Johnson's *Biology* is a beautifully illustrated and diagrammed introduction to biology. Major biological topics are presented with great simplicity in this lengthy text, including mammalian anatomy and physiology. Several chapters are devoted to the human nervous and endocrine systems as well as to the mechanisms of animal behavior.

David Wason Hollar, Jr.

Cross-References

STRESS: BEHAVIORAL AND PSYCHOLOGICAL RESPONSES

Type of psychology: Stress
Fields of study: Coping; critical issues in stress; stress and illness

Stress is an adaptive reaction to circumstances that are perceived as threatening. It motivates people and can enhance performance. Learning to cope with adversity is an important aspect of normal psychological development, but exposure to chronic stress can have severe negative consequences if effective coping mechanisms are not learned.

Principal terms
 COPING STRATEGIES: techniques used to lower one's stress level
 DAILY HASSLES: seemingly minor everyday events that are a constant source of stress
 PHOBIAS: stresses induced by unrealistic fear of specific situations
 STATE ANXIETY: often used interchangeably with *fear* and *stress*; denotes a momentary, transitory reaction to a situation that is perceived as threatening or dangerous
 TRAIT ANXIETY: relatively stable individual differences in proneness to experience state anxiety; people high in trait anxiety are especially threatened by situations involving fear of failure or social/ interpersonal threats

Overview

The term "stress" is used to designate how human beings respond when they confront circumstances that they appraise as dangerous or threatening and that tax their coping capability. Stressful events (stressors) elicit a wide range of responses in humans. They not only bring about immediate physiological changes but also affect one's emotional state, the use of one's intellectual abilities and one's efficiency at solving problems, and one's social behavior. When experiencing stress, people take steps to do something about the stressors eliciting the stress and to manage the emotional upset they are producing. These maneuvers are called coping responses. Coping is a key concept in the study of the stress process. Stress-management intervention techniques are designed to teach people the appropriate ways to cope with the stressors that they encounter in their everyday lives.

The emotional state most directly affected by stress is anxiety. In fact, the term "state anxiety" is often used interchangeably with the terms "fear" and "stress" to denote a transitory emotional reaction to a dangerous situation. Stress, fear, and state anxiety are distinguished from trait anxiety, which is conceptualized as a relatively stable personality disposition or trait. According to psychologist Charles Spielberger, people high in trait or "chronic" anxiety interpret more situations as dangerous or threatening than do people who are low in trait anxiety, and they respond to them with more intense stress (state anxiety) reactions. Instruments that measure trait anxiety ask people to characterize how they usually feel, and thus they measure how people characteristically respond to situations. Measures of trait anxiety (such as the trait anxiety scale of the State-Trait Anxiety Inventory) are especially useful in predicting whether people will experience high levels of stress in situations involving threats to self-esteem or threat of failure at evaluative tasks.

Common phobias or fears of specific situations, however, especially when the perceived threat has a strong physical component, are not related to individual differences in general trait anxiety level. Measures of general trait anxiety are therefore not good predictors of people's stress levels when they are confronted by snakes, an impending surgical operation, or the threat of electric shock. Such fears can be reliably predicted only by scales designed to evaluate proneness to experience fear in these particular situations.

Seemingly minor events that are a constant source of irritation can be very stressful, as can more focalized events that require major and sometimes sudden readjustments. Psychologists Richard Lazarus and Susan Folkman have dubbed these minor events "daily hassles." The media focus attention on disasters such as plane crashes, earthquakes, and epidemics that suddenly disrupt the lives of many people, or on particularly gruesome crimes or other occurrences that are likely to attract attention. For most people, however, much of the stress of daily life results from having to deal with ongoing problems pertaining to jobs, personal relationships, and everyday living circumstances. According to Lazarus and Folkman, exposure to such daily hassles is actually more predictive of negative health outcomes than is frequency of exposure to major life events.

People often have no actual experience of harm or unpleasantness regarding things that they come to fear. For example, most people are at least somewhat uneasy about flying on airplanes or about the prospect of having a nuclear power plant located near them, though few people have personally experienced harm caused by these things. Although people tend to pride themselves on how logical they are, they are often not very rational in appraising how dangerous or risky different events actually are. For example, there is great public concern about the safety of nuclear reactors, though they in fact have caused very few deaths. The same general public that smokes billions of cigarettes (a proved carcinogen) per year also supported banning an artificial sweetener because of a minuscule chance that it might cause cancer.

People tend to think of stress as being uniformly negative—something to be avoided or at least minimized as much as possible. Psychologists Carolyn Aldwin and Daniel Stokols point out, however, that studies using both animals and humans have indicated that exposure to stress also has beneficial effects. Rats handled as infants are less fearful, are more exploratory, are faster learners, and have more robust immune systems later in life. In humans, physical stature as adults is greater in cultures that expose children to stress (for example, circumcision, scarification, sleeping apart from parents) than in those that are careful to prevent stress exposure—

even when nutrition, climate, and other relevant variables are taken into account. Although failure experiences in dealing with stressful circumstances can inhibit future ability to function under stress, success experiences enable learning of important coping and problem-solving skills that are then used to deal effectively with future stressful encounters. Such success experiences also promote a positive self-concept and induce a generalized sense of self-efficacy that in turn enhances persistence in coping with future stressors.

Psychologists Stephen Auerbach and Sandra Gramling note that stress is a normal, adaptive reaction to threat. It signals danger and prepares people to take defensive action. Over time, individuals learn which coping strategies are successful for them in particular situations. This is part of the normal process of personal growth and maturation. Stress can, however, cause psychological problems if the demands posed by stressors overwhelm a person's coping capabilities. If a sense of being overwhelmed and unable to control events persists over a period of time, one's stress signaling system ceases to work in an adaptive way. One misreads and overinterprets the actual degree of threat posed by situations, makes poor decisions as to what coping strategies to use, and realizes that one is coping inefficiently; a cycle of increasing distress and ineffective coping may result. Some people who have experienced high-level stress for extended periods or who are attempting to deal with the aftereffects of traumatic stressors may become extremely socially withdrawn and show other signs of severe emotional dysfunction.

Applications

The fact that stress has both positive and negative effects can be exemplified in many ways. Interpersonally, stress brings out the "worst" and the "best" in people. A greater incidence of negative social behaviors, including less altruism and cooperation and more aggression, has generally been observed in stressful circumstances. Psychologist Kent Bailey points out that, in addition to any learning influences, this may result from the fact that stress signals real or imagined threats to survival and is therefore a potent elicitor of regressive, self-serving survival behaviors. The highly publicized murder of Kitty Genovese in Queens, New York, a number of years ago, which was witnessed by thirty-eight people (from the safety of their apartments) who ignored her pleas for help, exemplifies this tendency, as does the behavior during World War II of many Europeans who either did not stand up for the Jews and other minorities who were oppressed by the Nazis or conveniently turned their heads. Everyone has heard, however, of selfless acts of individual heroism being performed by seemingly ordinary people who in emergency situations rose to the occasion and risked their own lives to save others. Even in a Europe dominated by Adolf Hitler, there were people who risked great harm to themselves and their families to save others. In addition, in stressful circumstances in which cooperation and altruism have survival value for all concerned, as in the wake of a natural disaster, helping-oriented activities and resource sharing are among the most common short-term reactions.

Stress may enhance as well as hinder performance. For example, the classic view of the relationship between stress and performance is represented in the Yerkes-Dodson inverted-U model, which posits that both low and high levels of arousal decrease performance, whereas intermediate levels enhance performance. Although this model has not been unequivocally validated, it seems to be at least partially correct, and its correctness may depend upon the circumstances. On the one hand, psychologists Gary Evans and Sheldon Cohen concluded that, in learning and performance tasks, high levels of stress result in reduced levels of working-memory capacity and clearly interfere with performance of tasks that require rapid detection, sustained attention, or attention to multiple sources of input. On the other hand, psychologist Charles Spielberger found that in less complex tasks, as learning progresses, high stress levels may facilitate performance.

Psychologist Irving Janis examined the relationship between preoperative stress in surgical patients and how well they coped with the rigors of the postoperative convalescent period. He found that patients with moderate preoperative fear levels adjusted better after surgery than those with low or high preoperative fear. He reasoned that patients with moderate fear levels realistically appraised the situation, determined how they would deal with the stressful aspects of the recovery period, and thus were better able to tolerate those stressors. Patients low in preoperative fear engaged in unrealistic denial and thus were unprepared for the demands of the postoperative period, whereas those high in preoperative fear became overanxious and carried their inappropriately high stress levels over into the recovery period, in which that stress continued to inhibit them from realistically dealing with the demands of the situation. The negative effect of unrealistically low fear levels is also exemplified in the description by psychologists Walter Fenz and Seymour Epstein of two first-time sky divers who surprised everyone with their apparent total lack of concern during training and on the morning of their first jump. Their reactions changed dramatically, however, once they entered the aircraft. "One began vomiting, and the other developed a coarse tremor. Both pleaded for the aircraft to be turned back. Upon leaving, they stated that they were giving up jumping."

Janis' investigation was particularly influential because it drew attention to the question of how psychologists can work with people to help them cope with impending stressful events, especially those (such as surgery) that they are committed to confronting and over which they have little control. Findings by psychologists Thomas Strentz and Stephen Auerbach indicate that in such situations it may be more useful to teach people emotion-focused coping strategies (those designed to minimize stress and physiological arousal directly) than problem-focused strategies (those designed to change the stressful situation itself). In a study with volunteers who were abducted and held hostage for four days in a stressful simulation, they found that hostages who were taught to use emotion-focused coping techniques (such as deep breathing, muscular relaxation, and directed fantasy) adjusted better and experienced lower stress levels than those who were taught problem-focused techniques (such as nonverbal communication, how to interact with captors, and how to gather intelligence).

Context

Stress has many important adaptive functions. The experience of stress and learning how to cope with adversity is an essential aspect of normal growth and development. Coping strategies learned in particular situations must be generalized appropriately to new situations. Exposure to chronic stress that cannot be coped with effectively can have severe negative consequences. Work by pioneering stress researchers such as Hans Selye brought attention to the physiological changes produced by exposure to chronic stress, which contribute to diseases such as peptic ulcers, high blood pressure, and cardiovascular disorders. Subsequent research by psychiatrists Thomas Holmes and Richard Rahe and their colleagues indicated that exposure to a relatively large number of stressful life events is associated with the onset of other diseases such as cancer and psychiatric disorders, which are less directly a function of arousal in specific physiological systems.

Studies by these researchers have led psychologists to try to understand how best to teach people to manage and cope with stress. Learning to cope with stress is a complex matter because, as Richard Lazarus has emphasized, the stressfulness of given events is determined by how they are cognitively appraised, and this can vary considerably among individuals. Further, the source of stress may be in the past, the present, or the future. The prospect of an impending threatening encounter (such as a school exam) may evoke high-level stress, but people also experience stress when reflecting on past unpleasant or humiliating experiences or when dealing with an immediate, ongoing danger. Sometimes, people deal with past, present, and future stressors simultaneously.

It is important to distinguish among present, past, and future stressors, because psychological and behavioral responses to them differ, and different kinds of coping strategies are effective in dealing with them. For example, for stressors that may never occur but are so aversive that people want to avoid them if at all possible (for example, cancer or injury in an automobile accident), people engage in preventive coping behavior (they stop smoking, or they wear seat belts) even though they are not currently experiencing a high level of anxiety. In this kind of situation, an individual's anxiety level sometimes needs to be heightened in order to motivate coping behavior.

When known stressors are about to affect one (for example, a surgical operation the next morning), it is important for one to moderate one's anxiety level so that one can function effectively when actually confronting the stressor. The situation is much different when one is trying to deal with a significant stressor (such as sexual assault, death of a loved one, or a war experience) that has already occurred but continues to cause emotional distress. Some persons who cannot adjust adequately are diagnosed as having "post-traumatic stress disorder." Important aspects of coping with such stressors include conceptualizing one's response to the situation as normal and rational rather than "crazy" or inadequate, and reinstatement of the belief that one is in control of one's life and environment rather than subject to the whims of circumstance.

Bibliography

Auerbach, Stephen M. "Assumptions of Crisis Theory and Temporal Model of Crisis Intervention." In *Crisis Intervention with Children and Families*, edited by Stephen M. Auerbach and Arnold L. Stolberg. Washington, D.C.: Hemisphere, 1986. This chapter examines some basic issues pertaining to psychological responses to extremely stressful events, including the role of the passage of time, individual differences, and previous success in dealing with stressful events. Crisis intervention and other stress-management programs are also reviewed.

_____. "Temporal Factors in Stress and Coping: Intervention Implications." In *Personal Coping: Theory, Research, and Application*, edited by B. N. Carpenter. Westport, Conn.: Praeger, 1991. Focuses on how behavioral and psychological stress responses differ depending on whether the stressor is anticipated, currently ongoing, or has already occurred. The types of coping strategies that are likely to be most effective for each kind of stressor are described, and many examples are given.

Greenberg, Jerrold S. *Comprehensive Stress Management*. Dubuque, Iowa: Wm. C. Brown, 1990. An easy-to-read text giving an overview of psychological and physiological stress responses and stress-management techniques. Separate sections on applications to occupational stress, the college student, the family, and the elderly.

Janis, Irving Lester. *Psychological Stress*. New York: John Wiley & Sons, 1958. Describes some of Janis' early investigations evaluating relationships between stress and behavior. The focus is on his pioneering study evaluating the relationship between preoperative stress levels in surgical patients and their ability to adapt to the rigors of the postoperative convalescent period.

Monat, Alan, and Richard S. Lazarus, eds. *Stress and Coping*. 2d ed. New York: Columbia University Press, 1985. This anthology consists of twenty-six brief readings under the headings of effects of stress, stress and the environment, coping with the stresses of living, coping with death and dying, and stress management. The selections are readable as well as informative, and the editors give a useful overview prior to each section in which they summarize the relevance and importance of each reading.

Silver, R. L., and C. Wortman. "Coping with Undesirable Life Events." In *Human Helplessness*, edited by Judy Garber and Martin E. P. Seligman. New York: Academic Press, 1980. Silver and Wortman examine the behavioral consequences of encountering and adjusting to cataclysmic stressful events such as a disabling accident, a serious illness, or the death of a loved one. They review different theoretical formulations of reactions to stressful events and examine whether people's actual emotional and behavioral reactions are consistent with theories. They emphasize social support, the ability to find meaning in the outcome of the event, and experience with other stressors as important factors that determine how well people adjust.

Stephen M. Auerbach

Cross-References

STRESS: COGNITIVE APPRAISALS

Type of psychology: Stress
Fields of study: Cognitive processes; coping; critical issues in stress

Inducement of stress usually depends not only on the actual nature of a stressful event but also on an appraisal of the situation by the experiencing individual that it is indeed stressful. Cognitive appraisals also influence how a person copes with stress.

Principal terms

COGNITION: in this context, perceptions, thoughts, beliefs, attitudes, imaging, and judgments; some cognitive appraisals may be made without awareness

CONTROL: in this context, beliefs as to the degree of personal control over one's life, including beliefs about an ability to manage stress situations

EMOTION-FOCUSED COPING: coping strategies designed to lessen emotional distress, to increase distress, or to reappraise a situation cognitively so as to alter its significance

PRIMARY APPRAISAL: an evaluation of an event as irrelevant to one's life, benign in its implications, or stressful

PROBLEM-FOCUSED COPING: coping strategies directed toward the environment or back toward the self (reappraisals, for example) in an effort to alter problems produced by the stressor

PSYCHOLOGICAL STRESS: stress characterized by emphasis on psychological rather than biological considerations

SECONDARY APPRAISAL: an evaluation of a stress encounter in terms of what might or can be done in the way of coping

STRESS APPRAISAL: an evaluation as to whether harm or loss has already occurred, or the threat of harm or loss exists, or the situation presents a positive challenge

STRESS INOCULATION TRAINING: a technique, analogous to medical inoculation, meant to teach coping skills as a way to handle immediate and future problems

STRESSOR: a stimulus event capable of causing stress

Overview

Although there may be stressors that affect the individual in a direct, physiological way, most are susceptible to modification by psychological factors. The response to high environmental temperature is one example of a response that seems at first to be strictly physiological but has a psychological component. There are also situations in which psychological factors clearly play an integral role; perhaps the majority of stress situations fall into this category.

The research and theoretical writings of Richard S. Lazarus have been particularly influential in advancing the salience of cognition, specifically cognitive appraisal. His thinking may be taken as representative of theories emphasizing the role of personal assessment in stress situations. Lazarus distinguishes between primary and secondary appraisal. Primary appraisal has to do with a person's interpretation of an event. A stimulus can be judged to be irrelevant, that is, of no importance one way or the other for the person's well-being. A benign/positive appraisal might be made if the event appears to be of a helpful nature. The emotions involved are positive ones, such as joy, happiness, and love. A stress appraisal is made if some loss or damage has occurred (harm/loss appraisal) or there is the threat of loss or damage. Stress appraisals also include challenges, situations with the potential for producing growth and gains. The emotions associated with threat are negative, while those associated with challenge are positive. The situation can be quite complex, more than one kind of appraisal being present at the same or almost the same time.

Secondary appraisals have to do with coping with a threat or challenge. The designation is admittedly misleading, as neither order of appearance nor degree of importance is meant. Rather, secondary and primary appraisals interact to determine the degree of stress and the quality and intensity of emotional response. Complex and crucial processes are involved, relating to decisions as to what coping strategies are possible and applicable, the probability of success in accomplishing one's aims, and the effects of a strategy, given all the contingencies operating at a particular time.

Lazarus also discusses the possibility of reappraisal. On the basis of new information, the individual may modify the original appraisal. Thus, a decision might be made that an initial perception of threat was incorrect. A somewhat different form of reappraisal is called defensive reappraisal. Essentially a coping strategy, defensive reappraisal is an attempt to reinterpret events in such a way as to lessen implications of harm and threat. Although not all psychologists agree with the particulars of Lazarus' theory, what is significant is the generally accepted view that psychological stress involves appraisal processes concerned with judgments of stimuli as stressors, and with decisions as to how to cope with stressful events.

A central concern has long been the importance of "control." While the concept has proved to be far from clear and unitary, it essentially refers to the ability to control a situation. Whether control is real or illusory, beliefs about it can influence responses to stressors. For example, the way a potentially stressful event is interpreted can lessen its impact, and beliefs about causation may help to relieve stress by altering cognitive structure. The social psychologist Albert Bandura has written on self-efficacy: People will form expectations as to their ability to execute successful coping behaviors. Those with a strong sense of self-efficacy presumably show lesser psychological and physiological reactions to stress than those with a weaker sense. While an attempt can be made to distinguish between appraisal and expectancy, Bandura does seem to be discussing evaluations that will influence the person's judgment of the degree of environmental threat.

The sources of appraisals are many and varied; there is no doubt that the specifics of the situation are important. Thus, it is likely that a significant biological threat will be recognized as such. One could also argue that certain life changes, such as the death of a beloved spouse, will invariably lead to a high degree of psychological stress. In other words, it is unlikely that one would view certain events as other than threatening and harmful. As already discussed, however, some situations appraised as stressful may actually be viewed positively. For example, starting a new job may lead to a stress appraisal, but one that involves a challenge. There may be an intertwining of threat and challenge in such cases.

Aside from the specific, there may be general contingencies which cut across situations that lead to stress appraisals. For example, research on animals suggests that predictable noxious events are less stressful than those whose occurrence cannot be predicted. Similarly, there is reason to believe that high levels of stress occur in humans when uncertainty accompanies an event.

Personal characteristics of the appraising person are also of great importance. Bandura's self-efficacy, reflecting a held set of beliefs, has already been mentioned. Suzanne C. Kobasa and her collaborators have suggested a personality attribute that incorporates dimensions similar to many offered by other writers. In attempting to study the reasons a highly stressed individual need not be prone to illness, she identified a personality trait she called hardiness. Hardy individuals have a sense of personal control over events in their lives; are committed to what they are doing; have a strong sense of purpose; and view many potential stressors, such as changes in life, as challenges promoting growth and development rather than as threats. All these characteristics can influence how a person might perceive a potential stressor and how adaptively an individual reacts to a threat.

A number of factors, then, can influence the appraisal of what could be viewed as stressful situations. Not only particular factors, but also interactions among them are of importance. Thus, Kobasa writes that the committed person will minimize perceived threat. Following Lazarus and Susan Folkman, however, it can be suggested that a strong commitment to some outcome coupled with a sense of loss of control in threatening situations can produce great feelings of stress. On the other hand, a more sanguine attitude may be possible if, even in the face of little control of the situation, a person feels no such investment in what is happening.

Applications

Cognitive factors are important in the production of psychological stress. Psychological stress must be associated with emotions; it is likely, therefore, that the study of cognitive appraisal will enhance understanding of both stress and emotion. Basing their work on Lazarus' theories and on a view of stress as a "disturbed person-environment relationship," Susan Folkman and Richard S. Lazarus studied how appraisals, emotions, and coping might change as the stress situation changes.

Folkman and Lazarus studied students enrolled in a college course on stress and coping shortly before they were to take a midterm examination (time 1), after the test but before reception of grades (time 2), and some days after they had received their grades (time 3). Time 1 was viewed as "anticipatory," a time of great ambiguity because of lack of knowledge of the examination or the results of taking the test. Time 2 was thought of as a "waiting stage," and time 3 as the "outcome stage," because the student now knew his or her grade. Folkman and Lazarus viewed the procedure as providing a natural experiment to test hypotheses relating to stress and coping. In general, their findings supported the hypotheses tested.

The investigators believed that their results supported four general principles. First, stress encounters should be viewed as dynamic, developing events. The environment, in effect, changed with the time periods, and associated with the changes were appropriate alterations in appraisals, emotions, and ways of coping. Emotions associated with threat and challenge were very apparent in times 1 and 2 but were relatively rare in the third stage. In contrast, emotions associated with appraisals of harm and benefit ("mastery/gain") were least intense in time 1 and most prevalent in times 2 and 3.

Folkman and Lazarus have recognized two classes of coping. Problem-focused coping refers to attempts to alter or manage the situation. Emotion-focused coping, of which six types were studied, reflects attempts to regulate emotional response. Problem-focused coping was essentially seen in time 1 but then diminished sharply. An emotion-focused procedure, "emphasizing the positive," showed a similar pattern, as did "seeking social support," a mixed method of coping. These would not be unexpected changes, for the student would have early engaged in the reasonable activity of studying for the exam, a problem-focused approach, and seeking information from others (social support); such efforts in later periods would have been inappropriate. The patterns of changes found with some emotion-focused techniques (in addition to the positive emphasis) also appeared reasonable given the changing circumstances.

The second principle is that at any phase of the stress process, people may give evidence of experiencing apparently contradictory states of mind and emotions. For example, there was evidence that students felt emotions associated with both threat and challenge at all stages of the investigation. Ambiguity probably played a role, for these mixed emotions were highest in periods of greater ambiguity, while as the test results became apparent, there was a tendency to experience emotions associated with either harm appraisals or those connected to appraisals of benefit.

Third, coping is a very complex process. Students used on the average six or seven different types of coping. While degree of use of specific techniques varied over time periods, students used both problem-focused and emotion-focused coping at all stages of the study. The same was true for the use of social support, though the specific nature of the support varied somewhat; problem-focused techniques were more likely to predominate earlier, while emotional support gained more importance later. The results indicated that problem-focused coping is helped by emphasizing positive aspects of the stress encounter, but, the authors suggest, it may be hindered by other emotion-focused styles.

Finally, in addition to the general tendencies discussed, there are significant individual differences in felt emotions, differences resulting in large measure from differences in cognitive appraisals and coping. The students differed on a number of characteristics, the relative importance of specific variations being dependent on kind of appraisal and coping. Thus, while having a significant stake in the outcome was important to both threat and challenge emotions, it was especially important in the former case. Variation in anticipated exam difficulty influenced threat appraisals, while differences in feelings of control were significant for challenge and benefit emotions. Ways of coping contributed to individual variation as well. Factors other than grade obtained and, especially, grade point average, therefore, played a role in individual variation in emotion. A relatively straightforward and common situation, then, can be seen to offer information on the complex interactions among appraisals, emotion, and coping.

It should not be surprising that techniques attempting to alter cognitive appraisals have been introduced into therapeutic procedures. An example of such approaches is the stress inoculation training of Donald Meichenbaum and others. First applied to anxiety problems, the training, designed to "inoculate" the individual against stress, has been extended to other problems. Thus, it may even serve as a preventive. It can be said to consist of three stages. The first phase may be called the conceptualization stage. This is largely an educational experience. The individual learns about stress and a person's responses to it. The individual is apprised of the importance of cognitions and the possibility of changing them. Goals of the therapy will be elucidated.

The second stage of stress inoculation is skill acquisition and rehearsal. Here the individual is taught specific coping skills. One such skill will probably involve cognitive restructuring. The aim is to modify negative thoughts and beliefs so that positive ones emerge. Changes in self-verbalizations (for example, statements made to oneself concerning appraisals and expectations) will probably be used in the endeavor. Attempts will be made to change irrational thought patterns.

Finally, a stage of application and follow-through is reached. The individual confronts the stress situation and attempts to use the material learned in the first two stages. It may be necessary to introduce the stressor in a graduated manner. Sometimes the stressor is actually present, sometimes it is imagined, and sometimes role playing is used. In any case, the aim is to have reduced deleterious, negative aspects of the stress encounter.

Context

Interest in cognitive factors in stress may be viewed as part of a change in psychology that began in the late 1950's and the 1960's. While not monolithic in orientation, American psychology had been dominated by a view that held that only behavior was scientifically meaningful. Mind and its associated attributes, for example, cognitions, were to be excluded from psychology. Influences from both within and without the field began to turn psychologists away from this view. By the 1960's, cognitive psychology had emerged, and the field has been increasingly accepted. The interface between cognition, emotion, and stress could now be legitimately studied.

Some psychologists did not wait until cognitive psychology was in full flower, however; the years immediately following World War II saw publications concerned with psychological aspects of stress in men serving in the military, and later in post-service observations. Cognitive factors were explicitly and implicitly included in the analyses. These included appraisal and coping processes.

Not until the 1940's did "stress" become an important part of psychology's lexicon. Relevant material was studied, but usually under the rubric of arousal and emotion. Neither was there much in the way of formal and explicit concern with the concept of appraisal. Perhaps the first systematic treatment of the concept appears in Magda B. Arnold's *Emotion and Personality* (1960). Appraisal processes play a major role in this two-volume work on feelings and emotion. Influential, too, was the report by Stanley Schachter and Jerome Singer in 1962 purporting to show that the same symptoms of physiological arousal could be associated with different emotions, depending on the interpretation of circumstances by the feeling individual. Although controversial, the investigation accelerated attention to the importance of attributions for emotional experience. As a result of such work, psychologists could not ignore cognitive components in their conceptions of feeling and emotion. This attitude must have affected workers in the field of stress, for one cannot separate completely the topics of stress and emotion.

Cognitive appraisal theory entered the language of stress in deliberate fashion with the work of Richard S. Lazarus and his colleagues in the early 1960's. In 1966, Lazarus published his landmark book *Psychological Stress and the Coping Process*, in which his views on both the biological and psychological aspects of stress were spelled out and his appraisal theory was expounded. Eighteen years later, in collaboration with Susan Folkman, he updated his thoughts in *Stress, Appraisal, and Coping* (1984). Without question, these books and other of Lazarus' publications have been instrumental in establishing the critical importance of cognitive factors, including appraisal processes, in considerations of stress, coping, and, incidentally, emotion.

It is now clear that appraisal processes are integral to an understanding of how a potential stressor will affect a person and how the person will respond. Appraisal processes are of importance not only in common reactions but also in explaining individual differences in response. Concern with cognitive appraisal will lead to a better understanding of the stress encounter and will probably aid in developing better techniques to help people cope with stress.

Bibliography

Arnold, Magda B. "Perennial Problems in the Field of Emotion." In *Feelings and Emotions: The Loyola Symposium*, edited by Magda B. Arnold. New York: Academic Press, 1970. Although it is challenging reading for the general reader, this chapter is an excellent short presentation of Arnold's views on appraisal as well as other developments in the field.

Grinker, Roy Richard, and John P. Spiegel. *Men Under Stress.* Philadelphia: Blakiston, 1945. A relatively nontechnical study of psychological trauma resulting from combat stress. A classic of its kind, the book rests on case studies. Reference is made to the importance of emotional and mental determinants of anxiety, the latter determinant expressly being associated with an appraisal process. The general philosophical viewpoint is psychodynamic (that is, Freudian), and the book ends with some historically interesting social speculations.

Lazarus, Richard S. *Psychological Stress and the Coping Process.* New York: McGraw-Hill, 1966. A very important and influential book, perhaps the first to offer a comprehensive treatment of psychological stress and coping. While an excellent critical review of much of the early work on stress and related topics, its coverage of the literature is somewhat selective, and Lazarus' views are forcefully put. Written for a professional audience, but largely accessible to the motivated layperson.

Lazarus, Richard S., and Susan Folkman. *Stress, Appraisal, and Coping.* New York: Springer, 1984. Cognitive (including appraisal) approaches and coping had become major interests since Lazarus' 1966 book. The aims here are similar to those of that work; once again, there is a critical review of a very extensive, though selected, literature, and a presentation of cognitive appraisal and coping theory to a multidisciplinary audience. Of interest to the general reader.

Meichenbaum, Donald. *Stress Inoculation Training.* New York: Pergamon Press, 1985. A treatment manual designed to teach practitioners the rationale and applicability of this cognitive behavioral treatment and instruct them in how to use it for stress reduction and training. The writing is so clear (and even enjoyable) that the nonprofessional should have little trouble with the material. Includes an impressive reference list.

Samuel B. Schnitzer

Cross-References

Cognitive Therapy, 586; Coping Strategies: An Overview, 706; Emotion: Cognitive and Physiological Interaction, 881; Emotion and Attribution Theory, 921; Health Psychology, 1139; Stress: Behavioral and Psychological Responses, 2397; Theories of Stress, 2432; Stress and Reappraisal, 2438; Stress Prediction and Control, 2458; Stressors, 2471.

THE CONCEPT OF STRESS

Type of psychology: Stress
Fields of study: Coping; critical issues in stress; stress and illness

The stress response consists of physiological arousal, subjective feelings of discomfort, and the behavioral changes people experience when they confront situations that they appraise as dangerous or threatening. Because exposure to extreme situational or chronic stress causes emotional distress and may impair physical functioning, it is important to learn effective stress coping strategies.

Principal terms
   COGNITIVE APPRAISAL: an assessment of the meaningfulness of an event to an individual; events that are appraised as harmful or potentially harmful elicit stress
   EMOTION-FOCUSED COPING: minimizing negative emotions elicited by a stressor by using techniques such as relaxation and denial and paying little attention to the stressor itself
   LEARNED HELPLESSNESS: motivational, cognitive, and emotional deficits resulting from exposure to a stressor that is perceived to be uncontrollable
   PROBLEM-FOCUSED COPING: minimizing negative emotions elicited by a stressor by changing or avoiding the stressor
   STRESSOR: an event that is appraised as dangerous or threatening and that elicits a stress response

Overview

In the past, the term "stress" designated both a stimulus (a force or pressure) and a response (adversity, affliction). More recently, it has usually been used to denote a set of changes that people undergo in situations that they appraise as threatening to their well-being. These changes involve physiological arousal, subjective feelings of discomfort, and overt behaviors. The terms "anxiety" and "fear" are also used to indicate what people experience when they appraise circumstances as straining their ability to cope with them.

The external circumstances that induce stress responses are called stressors. Stressors have a number of important temporal components. Exposure to them may be relatively brief with a clear starting and stopping point (acute stressors) or may persist for extended periods without clear demarcation (chronic stressors). Stressors impinge on people at different points in their life cycles, sometimes occurring "off time" (at times that are incompatible with personal and societal expectations of their occurrence) or at a "bad time" (along with other stressors). Finally, stress may be induced by the anticipation of harmful circumstances that one thinks one is likely to confront, by an ongoing stressor, or by the harmful effects of stressors already encountered. All these factors affect people's interpretations of stressful events, how they deal with them, and how effective they are at coping with them.

Although there are some situations to which almost everyone responds with high levels of stress, there are individual differences in how people respond to situations. Thus, though most people cringe at the thought of having to parachute from an airplane, a substantial minority find this an exciting, challenging adventure. Most people avoid contact with snakes, yet others keep them as pets. For most people, automobiles, birds, and people with deep voices are largely neutral objects, yet for others they provoke a stress reaction that may verge on panic.

The key concept is cognitive appraisal. Situations become stressors for an individual only if they are construed as threatening or dangerous by that individual. As demonstrated in a study of parachuters, by psychologists Walter D. Fenz and Seymour Epstein, stress appraisals can change markedly over the course of exposure to a stressor, and patterns of stress arousal differ as a function of experience with the stressor. Fenz and Epstein found that fear levels of veteran jumpers (as evaluated by a self-report measure) were highest the morning before the jump, declined continuously up to the moment of the jump, and then increased slightly until after landing. Fear levels for novice jumpers, in contrast, increased up to a point shortly before the jump and then decreased continuously. For both groups, the peak of stress occurred during the anticipatory period rather than at the point of the greatest objective danger (the act of jumping).

Stress reactions are measured in three broad ways: by means of self-report, through behavioral observations, and on the basis of physiological arousal. The self-report technique is the technique most commonly used by behavioral scientists to evaluate subjective stress levels. The State Anxiety Scale of the State-Trait Anxiety Inventory, developed by psychologist Charles Spielberger, is one of the most widely used self-report measures of stress. Examples of items on this scale are "I am tense," "I am worried," and "I feel pleasant." Subjects are instructed to respond to the items in terms of how they currently feel.

Self-report state anxiety scales may be administered and scored easily and quickly. Further, they may be administered repeatedly and still provide valid measures of momentary changes in stress levels. They have been criticized by some, however, because they are face valid (that is, their intent is clear); therefore, people who are motivated to disguise their stress levels can readily do so.

Overt behavioral measures of stress include direct and indirect observational measures. Direct measures focus on behaviors associated with stress-related physiological arousal such as heavy breathing, tremors, and perspiration; self-manipulations such as nail biting, eyeblinks, and postural orientation; and body movement such as pacing.

Speech disturbances, both verbal (for example, repetitions, omissions, incomplete sentences, and slips of the tongue) and nonverbal (for example, pauses and hand movements), have been analyzed intensively, but no single measure or pattern has emerged as a reliable indicant of stress. Another way in which people commonly express fear reactions is by means of facial expressions. This area has been studied by psychologists Paul Ekman and Wallace V. Friesen, who concluded that the facial features that take on the most distinctive appearance during fear are the eyebrows (raised and drawn together), the eyes (open, lower lid tensed), and the lips (stretched back).

Indirect observational measures involve evaluating the degree to which people avoid feared objects. For example, in one test used by clinical psychologists to assess fear level, an individual is instructed to approach a feared stimulus (such as a snake) and engage in increasingly intimate interactions with it (for example, looking at a caged snake from a distance, approaching it, touching it, holding it). The rationale is that the higher the level of fear elicited, the earlier in the sequence the person will try to avoid the feared stimulus. Other examples include asking claustrophobics (people who are fearful of being closed in) to remain in a closed chamber as long as they can and asking acrophobics (people who fear heights) to climb a ladder and assessing their progress.

Physiological arousal is an integral component of the stress response. The most frequently monitored response systems are cardiovascular responses, electrodermal responses, and muscular tension. These measures are important in their own right as independent indicants of stress level, and in particular as possible indices of stress-related diseases.

Applications

The concept of stress has been used to help explain the etiology of certain diseases. Diseases that are thought to be caused in part by exposure to stress or poor ability to cope with stress are called psychophysiological or psychosomatic disorders. Among the diseases that seem to have strong psychological components are ulcers and coronary heart disease. The role of stress in ulcers was highlighted in a study by Joseph V. Brady known as the "executive monkey" study. In this study, pairs of monkeys were yoked together in a restraining apparatus. The monkeys received identical treatment except that one member of each pair could anticipate whether both of them would be shocked (he was given a warning signal) and could control whether the shock was actually administered (if he pressed a lever, the shock was avoided). Thus, one monkey in each pair (the "executive monkey") had to make decisions constantly and was responsible for the welfare of both himself and his partner. Twelve pairs of monkeys were tested, and in every case the executive monkey died of peptic ulcers within weeks, while the passive member of each pair remained healthy. This experiment was criticized because of flaws in its experimental design, but it nevertheless brought much attention to the important role that chronic stress can play in the activation of physiological processes (in this case, the secretion of hydrochloric acid in the stomach in the absence of food) that can be damaging or even life threatening.

Although being in the position of a business executive who has to make decisions constantly can be very stressful, research indicates that it may be even more damaging to be exposed to stress over long periods and not have the opportunity to change or control the source of stress. People and animals who are in aversive situations over which they have little or no control for prolonged periods are said to experience "learned helplessness." This concept was introduced by psychologist Martin E. P. Seligman and his colleagues. In controlled research with rats and dogs, he and his colleagues demonstrated that exposure to prolonged stress that cannot be controlled produces emotional, motivational, and cognitive deficits. The animals show signs of depression and withdrawal, they show little ability or desire to master their environment, and their problem-solving ability suffers.

Learned helplessness has also been observed in humans. Seligman refers to Bruno Bettelheim's descriptions of some of the inmates of the Nazi concentration camps during World War II, who, when faced with the incredible brutality and hopelessness of their situation, gave up and died without any apparent physical cause. Many institutionalized patients (for example, nursing home residents and the chronically ill) also live in environments that are stressful because they have little control over them. Seligman suggests that the stress levels of such patients can be lowered and their health improved if they are given maximum control over their everyday activities (such as choosing what they want for breakfast, the color of their curtains, and whether to sleep late or wake up early).

Research findings have supported Seligman's suggestions. For example, psychologists Ellen Langer and Judith Rodin told a group of elderly nursing home residents that they could decide what they wanted their rooms to look like, when they wanted to go see motion pictures, and with whom they wanted to interact. A second comparable group of elderly residents, who were randomly assigned to live on another floor, were told that the staff would care for them and try to keep them happy. It was found that the residents in the first group became more active and reported feeling happier than those in the second group. They also became more alert and involved in different kinds of activities, such as attending movies and socializing. Further, during the eighteen-month period following the intervention, 15 percent of the subjects in the first group died, whereas 30 percent of the subjects in the second group died.

Altering people's perception of control and predictability can also help them adjust to transitory stressful situations. Studies by psychologists Stephen Auerbach, Suzanne Miller, and others have shown that for people who prefer to deal with stress in active ways (rather than by avoiding the source of stress), adjustment to stressful surgical procedures and diagnostic examinations can be improved if they are provided with detailed information about the impending procedure. It is likely that the information enhances their sense of predictability and control in an otherwise minimally controllable situation. Others, who prefer to control their stress by "blunting" the stressor, show better adjustment when they are not given detailed information.

Context

Physiologist Walter B. Cannon was among the first scientists to describe how people respond to stressful circumstances. When faced with a threat, one's body mobilizes for "fight or flight." One's heart rate increases, one begins to perspire, one's muscles tense, and one undergoes other physiological changes to prepare for action—either to confront the stressor or to flee the situation.

Physician Hans Selye examined the fight-or-flight response in more detail by studying physiological changes in rats exposed to stress. He identified three stages of reaction to stress, which he collectively termed the general adaptation syndrome (GAS). This includes an initial alarm reaction, followed by a stage of resistance, and finally by a stage of exhaustion, which results from long-term unabated exposure to stress and produces irreversible physiological damage. Selye also brought attention to the idea that not only clearly aversive events (for example, the death of a spouse or a jail sentence) but also events that appear positive (for example, a promotion at work or meeting new friends) may be stressful because they involve changes to which people must adapt. Thus, these ostensibly positive events (which he called eustress) will produce the nonspecific physiological stress response just as obviously negative events (which he called distress) will.

How an individual cognitively appraises an event is the most important determinant of whether that event will be perceived as stressful by that person. Psychologist Richard S. Lazarus has delineated three important cognitive mechanisms (primary appraisals, secondary appraisals, and coping strategies) that determine perceptions of stressfulness and how people alter appraisals. Primary appraisal refers to an assessment of whether a situation is neutral, challenging, or potentially harmful. When a situation is judged to be harmful or threatening, a secondary appraisal is made of the coping options or maneuvers that the individual has at his or her disposal. Actual coping strategies that may be used are problem focused (those that involve altering the circumstances that are eliciting the stress response) or emotion focused (those that involve directly lowering physiological arousal or the cognitive determinants of the stress response). Psychologists have used concepts such as these to develop stress management procedures that help people control stress in their everyday lives.

Bibliography

Brady, Joseph Vincent. "Ulcers in Executive Monkeys." *Scientific American* 199 (October, 1958): 95-98. This article describes a classic series of studies in which monkeys subjected to psychological stress in a laboratory apparatus developed gastrointestinal lesions.

Lazarus, Richard S., and Susan Folkman. *Stress, Appraisal, and Coping.* New York: Springer, 1984. Lazarus and Folkman review the history and development of the concepts of stress and coping. The book, which is organized around their cognitive appraisal theory of emotion, includes sections on coping and health and adaptation, and on approaches to stress management.

Rodin, Judith. "Managing the Stress of Aging." In *Coping and Health,* edited by Seymour Levine and Holger Ursin. New York: Plenum Press, 1980. In this chapter, Rodin emphasizes that stress produced by the perception of loss of personal control is particularly prevalent among the elderly. She describes interventions and coping-skills training techniques that have been useful in enhancing the sense of control and reducing the stress levels of institutionalized older people.

Seligman, Martin E. P. *Helplessness: On Depression, Development, and Death.* San Francisco: W. H. Freeman, 1975. Seligman describes how being placed in a situation in which one is powerless to influence important outcomes produces "learned helplessness" and associated stress and depression. Many examples from studies with animals and humans are given. Ways of combating learned helplessness by giving people progressively greater control are also described.

Stephen M. Auerbach

Cross-References

Coping Strategies: An Overview, 706; General Adaptation Syndrome, 1068; Adaptation to Stress, 2390; Stress: Behavioral and Psychological Responses, 2397; Effects of Stress, 2417; Theories of Stress, 2432; Stress Prediction and Control, 2458; Stressors, 2471.

EFFECTS OF STRESS

Type of psychology: Stress
Fields of study: Critical issues in stress; stress and illness

Stress causes both biological and psychological changes that can profoundly affect the life and health of a person; among them are strong effects on both the nervous and hormonal systems.

Principal terms

AROUSAL: the state of awareness, excitability, and activity of the organism

AUTONOMIC NERVOUS SYSTEM: the part of the nervous system traditionally viewed as being concerned with involuntary, largely unconscious control of the viscera

BEHAVIORAL DESPAIR: the appearance of floating immobility in rats during a forced swim test; it may reflect a state analogous to depression in humans

GENERAL ADAPTATION SYNDROME (GAS): an attempt at adaptation to stress that uses means invoked by those stressors that have general effects on the body

HOMEOSTASIS: a term referring to the idea that the body tries to maintain steady states, that is, to maintain internal conditions within relatively narrow limits

LEARNED HELPLESSNESS: the hypothesized result of experience in which behavior performed seems to bear no relationship to the appearance of a stressor

NONSPECIFIC COMPONENTS OF STRESS: a syndrome of responses that will occur regardless of the particular nature of the stressor

SPECIFIC COMPONENTS OF STRESS: a syndrome of responses that are specific to the nature of the stressor

STRESSOR: an environmental or other event capable of causing stress

Overview

Some responses to stress are specific to the nature of the stressor. Consider the case of hot weather: The living organism, made very warm, will take steps to cool down. Examples of these steps include sweating, dilation of blood vessels in the skin, and, in some animals, panting. Behaviorally, too, people will act to enhance cooling. They will remove clothing, seek cooler environments, or try to create cooler environments, as with air conditioning. All these mechanisms will act to cool the body, particularly by enhancing both evaporation (as in sweating) and radiation (infrared radiation is emitted by a heated body).

High temperatures can induce other adaptive mechanisms that are of psychological and behavioral impact. One feels drowsy in hot weather because of reduced cardiac output and blood pressure. One tends to eat less. These are all effective measures, as muscular activity and digestion of solid food involve chemical activity that generates heat. On the other hand, one drinks more to replenish body fluids lost through sweating. Hot weather is a stressor; it causes discomfort. Atmospheric temperatures can reach a point at which, without special care, the body's ordinary defenses are inadequate to the challenge. Dangerous heat stroke can occur.

The body attempts to keep its temperature within a relatively narrow range. This is an example of homeostasis, the maintenance of steady and optimal levels of function within the body. Some stresses involve upset of homeostasis; the effects will include attempts to restore the optimal state.

The term homeostasis was coined by the physiologist Walter B. Cannon. Cannon significantly influenced later thinking on homeostasis and on the nonspecific aspects of stress as well. Suppose an organism is forced by a threat to make a decision as to whether to fight or flee. Associated with this situation are widespread physiological changes. These would include an increase in heart rate, an increase in blood supply to the muscles, and a decrease in gastrointestinal activity (although in extreme fear, a person may have an involuntary emptying of the bladder and rectum). The most striking part of the response will be the release of hormones by the medulla of the adrenal gland, the gland's innermost part. Most of that secretion will consist of the hormone epinephrine (commonly known as adrenaline).

These effects reflect function of the autonomic nervous system (ANS), augmented by adrenal secretions. The ANS is a part of the nervous system that is very much concerned with maintenance of homeostasis. Activation particularly of its sympathetic division is important to coping with emergency situations, although some responses reflect the functioning of the parasympathetic division. The latter division is primarily responsible for day-to-day functioning.

Current interest in stress owes much to Hans Selye. For Selye, the hormones of the adrenal medulla, perhaps interacting with what he called "conditioning" factors (differences in heredity, previous experience, diet, and so on), still reflected a somewhat specific response that served to modify the stress response. That response is a nonspecific one, reacting to nonspecific demands on the body; that is, it will occur no matter what the nature of the stressor. The stress response consists of three effects. There is increased activity by the cortex, the outer layer, of the adrenal gland. The most important hormones (in this context) secreted by the cortex are steroids, important for metabolism and control of inflammation. The major corticoid of this type in humans is cortisol (hydrocortisone). The second part of the triad is a reduction in size of structures and in materials associated with immune function. Finally, bleeding, deep ulcers are found in the gastrointestinal tract. This triad later becomes incorporated into Selye's broader view of the attempt of the body to deal with stress—the general adaptation syndrome (GAS).

Stress can directly or indirectly affect almost all, if not all, the organ systems of the body; an example of an indirect effect is the exacerbation of a preexisting condition such as asthma. Another topic of concern is the interrelationships among the myriad effects. While not completely neglecting them, however, early researchers did tend to neglect topics that eventually came to the fore. For example, a number of writers have focused on the positive effects of stress. While too much arousal, another aspect of stress in this context, can disrupt performance, a certain amount is probably necessary for optimal performance in a task. If stress can be defined in terms of "wear and tear" on the body, as Selye and others define it, then certainly vigorous and extended running can produce stress. Yet the euphoric "runner's high" can result from this stress. It is possible that the "high" results from the secretion of the morphinelike compounds that are secreted by the body under certain conditions, the endorphins. At any rate, stress can produce positive and even needed emotions.

Increasing emphasis has been placed on the psychological concomitants of stress. It has been reported that people showing considerable anxiety, hostility, and depression tend to report high levels of feelings of stress. There may be an interaction between personality characteristics and tendencies to respond in particular ways to stressful life experiences. To some extent, for example, a pessimistic "explanatory style," to use Martin E. P. Seligman's term, may reflect life experiences that induce expectations that the individual will not be able to cope successfully with threatening situations.

In the extreme, stress can apparently induce a psychological state requiring clinical intervention. Thus, there have been repeated attempts to tie stress to clinical depression. Perhaps the perceived inability to cope with stress will, in some individuals, yield not merely a relatively mild pessimism but rather a severe depressive state. Similarly, particular life experiences, usually subsumed under the rubric "stress," may be necessary for the appearance of schizophrenia, even in individuals genetically disposed to the disorder.

The effects of stress may remain long after the particular stressor has disappeared. Development of ulcers may begin not during the time of the stress experience but shortly thereafter. There is evidence that after undergoing a stressful experience, people are less able to perform optimally in a variety of tasks. This may be especially true for tasks requiring considerable cognitive involvement. Stress, then, can have a wide variety of biological and psychological effects. Some of these effects can be viewed as acute, lasting perhaps no longer than the life of the stressor; others can be termed chronic, lasting well beyond the time when the stressor has disappeared.

Applications

Given ethical considerations that limit the experimental treatments that can be applied to humans, research on animals that can yield useful information about stress and depression would be very desirable. The search for an appropriate model has been pursued for some time. The model to be described here is not without its critics, yet a coherent story does emerge, if the interpretation of experimental results by a number of investigators proves correct.

The Wistar-Kyoto (WKY) strain of laboratory rat was produced in the course of developing a strain prone to hypertension. (The Wistar-Kyoto strain does not show such a tendency.) There is considerable evidence, however, thanks largely to the work of William Paré, that WKY rats tend to be more emotional than a number of other strains of rat. The strain is also more likely to demonstrate "behavioral despair" in testing, a characteristic possibly analogous to depression. The test situations leading to these reactions are ones that are stressful to the animals. The results of this experimentation support the belief that, even at the animal level, individual differences in personality play a role in how an organism will react in stressful situations.

Earlier, reference was made to a possible association between depression and a person's self-perception of an inability to cope with stress. Martin E. P. Seligman and his associates suggested that an individual may learn to be helpless. While since modified considerably, the initial development of the "learned helplessness" model of depression rested on experimentation with dogs. Using a procedure similar to that employed by Seligman and his coworkers, William Paré studied learned helplessness in WKY and other strains of rats. That procedure requires that the animal first be subjected to a series of inescapable electric shocks. These shocks are far from life-threatening, but they are clearly uncomfortable. The animals are then introduced to an apparatus in which they can escape the shock readily by moving from one side of the enclosure to the other. Ordinarily, the animal can even avoid the shock altogether by learning to move during a warning signal that precedes the shock. Research has shown that animals, including WKY rats, that are not subjected to inescapable shocks first can learn to escape efficiently and even avoid the shocks, given the opportunity. Given the prior experience, however, avoidance and escape performance are detrimentally affected in the test situation. Presumably, the animal has learned to be helpless; it has become convinced that nothing it can do will allow it to escape the shocks.

While all strains studied by Paré seem to learn this "lesson," WKY rats appear especially sensitive to the experimental contingencies. The results support the role of learned helplessness in the genesis of depression. Even if one is reluctant to attribute such cognitions to rats, the findings do indicate that learning is involved in the response to stress and that, at the very least, this learning is influenced by the emotional proclivities of the organism.

Differences among various strains of rats regarding somatic functioning may have implications for reactions to stress among humans. WKY rats, for example, are more likely to develop extensive ulceration in the stomach than are a number of other strains when subjected to a variety of stress procedures that can produce ulcers. These findings provide another bit of evidence that there may be a genetic contribution to depression and to responses to stressors. The response may involve a syndrome of possible reaction.

Animal studies are useful in teaching about stress and its effects. The primary focus for most psychologists, however, remains the human being. As useful as they may be, investigations of animals cannot take the place of research on humans. A variety of techniques have been used to study the reactions of people to stress. One investigation, reported by Ronald Glaser and a number of coworkers, involved the kind of situation most people have faced. Medical students volunteered to serve in an investigation into the effects of stress on immune system functioning. Blood was taken from the students shortly after returning from spring vacation, six weeks before final examinations. Another sample was taken during the week of the examinations. In addition, students supplied information relating to severity of feelings of distress, recent health changes, medication, and sleep patterns. Comparisons were made between measures taken before the examination period and ones taken during the period.

As might be expected, much more distress was reported during the examination period than just after spring break. An increase in sleep loss also occurred. During the final examination week, interferon produced in response to a standard test procedure was less than what would be expected. Interferon, which really refers to a family of proteins, exerts a variety of effects, among which is the production of natural killer (NK) cells. These cells are important in fighting viral infections and tumors. Associated with the decrease in ability to manufacture interferon during the stressful examination period was a reduction in NK-cell count and activity.

The findings of this research join a growing body of evidence that stress can have dire effects on health. In this particular investigation, the students did not report ill health. Earlier work by Glaser and his associates did suggest some health effects caused by immunosuppression during examinations. The reduction in NK cell activity, too, suggests that defense against certain kinds of cancer can be compromised by fairly common stressors. There is reason to believe that immune reactivity is suppressed in certain groups of depressed individuals; there is also evidence that higher levels of depression are associated with increased risk of cancer. There has even been discussion of a Type C personality (a personality type susceptible to cancer), among whose characteristics is responding to stress with depression and hopelessness.

Context

Concern with stress can arguably be said to have entered biological and psychological science with the research and writings of the American physiologist Walter B. Cannon. In the early years of the twentieth century, he began publishing his work on hunger, thirst, and emotion. Some years later, he coined the term homeostasis and discussed the importance of autonomic nervous system activity in the management of steady states in the body. While ideas about "nervous stress" and "nervous tension" were current, Cannon did not initially use the term in his writings. Eventually, he did write about "great emotional stress" and the "stress and strains of homeostasis." His earlier writings indicate no great awareness of an association between stress and medical problems. By 1942, however, he was writing on "voodoo death"—the inducement, through beliefs, of such an intense state of stress that the individual dies.

In 1936, the Canadian physiologist Hans Selye began reporting his work. He argued that every disease state has both a specific component and a nonspecific one reflecting the operation of stress. The original triad of reactions to stress becomes the "alarm reaction" of the general adaptation syndrome (GAS), reflecting the disruption of homeostasis. Following this initial reaction, an attempt is made to defend against the problem, followed by, perhaps, severe difficulties if the attempt at adaptation fails.

Selye helped change many ideas about health. He suggested that a faulty GAS can lead to "diseases of adaptation." These can include allergies, headaches, ulcers, and cardiovascular disorders. One may be able to work with the aforementioned conditioning factors to develop "nonspecific therapies" to build resistance to the deleterious effects of stress. Selye suggested that it may even be possible to design techniques that would promote homeostasis by promoting adaptive responses. These views at the very least support the arguments for a holistic approach to medicine (that is, treating the whole person), are congruent with ideas about helping the body to help itself, and encourage wellness orientations (healthy life-styles and emphasis on prevention of illness).

Selye's writings were very influential in popularizing the concept of stress. He and Cannon were instrumental in establishing what might be called the physiologic view of stress. In this view, stress, while it may lead to difficulties, is a normal and repeated concomitant of living. A different tradition, which might be called the psychiatric view, emphasized the deleterious effects of stress: If possible, stress is to be reduced and even avoided, for it leads to maladaptive physiological and psychological effects. To a greater or lesser degree, the physiologic tradition also touched on psychological factors. Psychology, while having views of its own, has been profoundly influenced by both approaches. Beginning in the 1940's and 1950's, stress came more and more to be incorporated into thinking about conditions such as arousal, anxiety, and tension.

Over time, too, there has been increasing recognition in psychology and psychiatry of the importance of psychological factors in medicine. This recognition was actually first formalized in the 1930's with the development of the field of psychosomatic medicine, which was initially dominated by psychoanalytically oriented psychiatrists. In the 1970's, one began to hear of behavioral medicine, an interdisciplinary endeavor, and health psychology, which emphasized the role of the psychologist. By around 1980, formalization of these fields had taken place. A central concern in all these fields is stress and its effects. Many medical problems are produced by, exacerbated by, or otherwise influenced by stress. A critical concern is how best to cope with stress so as to avoid or lessen its most deleterious effects. Such efforts will no doubt continue. Important, too, will be efforts to understand how the myriad effects of stress interact to produce medical problems.

Bibliography

Cannon, Walter B. *The Wisdom of the Body.* Reprint. New York: W. W. Norton, 1963. The word "stress" does not appear in the index, and some usage is archaic (such as "adrenin" for the primary hormone of the adrenal medulla), but this book represents Cannon's classic statement on homeostasis for professional and general readers. The edition cited here is a paperback edition of a 1939 expansion of the work first published in 1932. Brief mention is made of Cannon's ideas on emotions. He speculates on the extension of homeostasis to social concerns. A book still cited by psychologists and biologists.

Constantinides, P. C., and Niall Carey. "The Alarm Reaction." *Scientific American* 180 (March, 1949): 20-23. A short article by two researchers in Selye's institute that remains of interest. Discusses examples of the research generated by explorations of the GAS and notes the work's medical importance. The writing, while not simple, is aimed at the nonspecialist.

Green, Judith Alyce, and Robert Shellenberger. *The Dynamics of Health and Wellness: A Biopsychosocial Approach.* Fort Worth: Holt, Rinehart and Winston, 1991. A general and very clinically oriented text in health psychology, in which stress occupies an important place. Parts 2 and 3 consist of eight chapters centered on stress and its effects. Less formal and conventional in tone than most texts. Invites the reader to participate actively in measuring and managing stress. Part 3 is especially interesting, as it contains some clinically explicit material on the management of stress.

Seligman, Martin E. P. *Learned Optimism.* New York: Random House, 1990. The idea here is that if one can learn to be helpless and pessimistic, then one can learn to be optimistic and more adaptive, too. Also contains some interesting information on learned helplessness, including how Seligman came upon the concept.

Selye, Hans. *The Stress of Life.* New York: McGraw-Hill, 1956. While at times this is highly technical, Selye did try to write a book that would be understandable (at least in part) to the nonprofessional reader; he even offers suggestions as to how best to read the book. Represents the definitive statement on the general adaptation syndrome and its implications. Rather philosophical at the end.

Taylor, Shelley E. *Health Psychology.* 2d ed. New York: McGraw-Hill, 1991. Another general text in health psychology, aimed primarily at the undergraduate college student. Accessible to the layperson. A comprehensive text that covers much more than stress. A mark of the topic's importance, however, is that of the approximately 525 pages in the body of the text, about 155 pages are expressly devoted to the topic of stress and coping. A number of other pages deal with closely related material. Contains an extensive glossary and reference list.

Samuel B. Schnitzer

Cross-References

Emotion and Stress, 941; General Adaptation Syndrome, 1068; Adaptation to Stress,

STRESS: PHYSIOLOGICAL RESPONSES

Type of psychology: Stress
Fields of study: Biology of stress; critical issues in stress; stress and illness

The human body contains a number of regulatory mechanisms that allow it to adapt to changing conditions. Stressful events produce characteristic physiological changes that are meant to enhance the likelihood of survival. Because these changes sometimes present a threat to health rather than serving a protective function, researchers seek to determine relations between stressors, their physiological effects, and subsequent health.

Principal terms

FIGHT-OR-FLIGHT RESPONSE: a sequence of physiological changes, described by Walter B. Cannon, that occur in response to threat and prepare the organism to flee from or fight the threat

GENERAL ADAPTATION SYNDROME: a physiological process by which the organism responds to stressors and attempts to reestablish homeostasis; consists of three stages: alarm, resistance, and exhaustion

HOMEOSTASIS: the tendency of the human body to strive toward an optimal or balanced level of physiological functioning

PARASYMPATHETIC NERVOUS SYSTEM: a branch of the nervous system responsible for maintaining or reestablishing homeostasis

STRESS RESPONSE: the physiological, emotional, cognitive, and/or behavioral changes that result from a stressful event, including increased heart rate, anxiety, confused thinking, and/or avoidance behaviors

STRESSOR: any psychological or physical event that produces the physiological, emotional, cognitive, and/or behavioral changes characteristic of a stress response

SYMPATHETIC NERVOUS SYSTEM: a branch of the nervous system that is responsible for activating the fight-or-flight response

Overview

Although the term "stress" is commonly used (if not overused) by the general population to refer to various responses to events that individuals find taxing, the concept involves much more. For centuries, scientific thinkers and philosophers have been interested in learning more about the interactions between the environment (stressful events), emotions, and the body. Much is now known about this interaction, although there is still much left to discover. In the late twentieth century, particularly, much has been learned about how stressful events affect the activity of the body (or physiology); for example, it has been established that these physiological responses to stressors sometimes increase the risk of development or exacerbate a number of diseases. In order best to understand the body's response to stressful events (or stressors), the general sequence of events and the specific responses of various organ systems must be considered.

Almost all bodily responses are mediated at least partially by the central nervous system: the brain and spinal cord. The brain takes in and analyzes information from the external environment as well as from the internal environment (the rest of the body), and it acts to regulate the activities of the body to optimize adaptation or survival. When the brain detects a threat, a sequence of events occurs to prepare the body to fight or to flee the threat. Walter B. Cannon, in the early twentieth century, was the first to describe this "fight-or-flight" response of the body. It is characterized by generalized physiological activation. Heart rate, blood pressure, and respiration increase to enhance the amount of oxygen available to the tissues. The distribution of blood flow changes to optimize efficiency of the tissues most needed to fight or flee: Blood flow to the muscles, brain, and skin increases, while it decreases in the stomach and other organs less important for immediate survival. Increased sweating and muscle tension help regulate the body's temperature and enhance movement if action is needed. Levels of blood glucose and insulin also increase to provide added energy sources, and immune function is depressed. Brain activity increases, resulting in enhanced sensitivity to incoming information and faster reactions to this information.

Taken together, these physiological changes serve to protect the organism and to prepare it to take action to survive threat. They occur quite rapidly and are controlled by the brain through a series of neurological and hormonal events. When the brain detects a threat (or stressor), it sends its activating message to the rest of the body through two primary channels, the sympathetic nervous system (SNS) and the pituitary-adrenal axis. The SNS is a branch of the nervous system that has multiple, diffuse, neural connections to the rest of the body. It relays activating messages to the heart, liver, muscles, and other organs that produce the physiological changes already described. The sympathetic nervous system also stimulates the adrenal gland to secrete two hormones, epinephrine and norepinephrine (formerly called adrenaline and noradrenaline), into the bloodstream. Epinephrine and norepinephrine further activate the heart, blood vessels, lungs, sweat glands, and other tissues.

Also, the brain sends an activating message through its hypothalamus to the pituitary gland, at the base of the brain. This message causes the pituitary to release hormones into the bloodstream that circulate to the peripheral tissues and activate them. The primary "stress" hormone released by the pituitary gland is adrenocorticotropic hormone (ACTH), which in turn acts upon the adrenal gland to cause the release of the hormone cortisol. The actions of cortisol on other organs cause increases in blood glucose and insulin, among many other reactions.

In addition to isolating these primary stress mechanisms, research has demonstrated that the body secretes naturally occurring opiates—endorphins and enkephalins—in response to stress. Receptors for these opiates are found throughout the body and brain. Although their function is not entirely clear, some research suggests that they serve to buffer the effects of stressful events by counteracting the effects of the SNS and stress hormones.

One can see that the human body contains a very sophisticated series of mechanisms that have evolved to enhance survival. When stressors and the subsequent physiological changes that are adaptive in the short run are chronic, however, they may produce long-term health risks. This idea was first discussed in detail in the mid-twentieth century by physiologist Hans Selye, who coined the term "general adaptation syndrome" to describe the body's physiological responses to stressors and the mechanisms by which these responses might result in disease. Selye's general adaptation syndrome involves three stages of physiological response: alarm, resistance, and exhaustion. During the alarm stage, the organism detects a stressor and responds with SNS and hormonal activation. The second stage, resistance, is characterized by the body's efforts to neutralize the effects of the stressor. Such attempts are meant to return the body to a state of homeostasis, or balance. (The concept of homeostasis, or the tendency of the body to seek to achieve an optimal, adaptive level of activity, was developed earlier by Walter Cannon.) Finally, if the resistance stage is prolonged, exhaustion occurs, which can result in illness. Selye referred to such illnesses as diseases of adaptation. In this category of diseases, he included hypertension, cardiovascular disease, kidney disease, peptic ulcer, hyperthyroidism, and asthma.

Selye's general adaptation syndrome has received considerable attention as a useful framework within which to study the effects of stressors on health, but there are several problems with his theory. First, it assumes that all stressors produce characteristic, widespread physiological changes that differ only in intensity and duration. There is compelling evidence, however, that different types of stressors can produce very different patterns of neural and hormonal responses. For example, some stressors produce increases in heart rate, while others can actually cause heart rate deceleration. Thus, Selye's assumption of a nonspecific stress response must be questioned. Also, Selye's theory does not take into account individual differences in the pattern of response to threat. Research during the later twentieth century has demonstrated that there is considerable variability across individuals in their physiological responses to identical stressors. Such differences may result from genetic or environmental influences. For example, some studies have demonstrated that normotensive offspring of hypertensive parents are more cardiovascularly responsive to brief stressors than individuals with normotensive parents. Although one might conclude that the genes responsible for hypertension have been passed on from the hypertensive parents, these children might also have different socialization or learning histories that contribute to their exaggerated cardiovascular reactivity to stressors. Whatever the mechanism, this research highlights the point that individuals vary in the degree to which they respond to stress and in the degree to which any one organ system responds.

Applications

Coinciding with the scientific community's growing acknowledgment that stressful events have direct physiological effects, much interest has developed in understanding the relations between these events and the development and/or maintenance of specific diseases. Probably the greatest amount of research has focused on the link between stress and heart disease, the primary cause of death in the United States. Much empirical work also has focused on gastrointestinal disorders, diabetes, and pain (for example, headache and arthritis). Researchers are beginning to develop an understanding of the links between stress and immune function. Such work has implications for the study of infectious disease (such as flu and mononucleosis), cancer, and acquired immune deficiency syndrome (AIDS).

A number of types of research paradigms have been employed to study the effects of stressors on health and illness. Longitudinal studies have identified a number of environmental stressors that contribute to the development or exacerbation of disease. For example, one study of more than four thousand residents of Alameda County, California, spanning two decades, showed that a number of environmental stressors such as social isolation were significant predictors of mortality from all causes. Other longitudinal investigations have linked stressful contexts such as loud noise, crowding, and low socioeconomic status with the onset or exacerbation of disease.

A major drawback of such longitudinal research is that no clear conclusions can be made about the exact mechanism or mechanisms by which the stressor had its impact on health. Although it is possible, in the Alameda County study, that the relationship between social isolation and disease was mediated by the SNS/hormonal mechanisms already discussed, individuals who are isolated also may be less likely to engage in health care behaviors such as eating healthy diets, exercising, and maintaining preventive health care. Thus, other research paradigms have been used to try to clarify the causal mechanisms by which stressors may influence particular diseases. For example, laboratory stress procedures are used by many scientists to investigate the influence of brief, standardized stressors on physiology. This type of research has the advantage of being more easily controlled. That is, the researcher can manipulate one or a small number of variables (for example, noise) in the laboratory and measure the physiological effects. These effects are then thought to mimic the physiological effects of such a variable in the natural environment.

This research primarily is conducted to ask basic questions about the relations between stressors, physiology, and subsequent health. The findings also have implications, however, for prevention and intervention. If a particular stressor is identified that increases risk of a particular disease, prevention efforts could be developed to target the populations exposed to this stressor. Prevention strategies might involve either modifying the stressor, teaching people ways to manage more effectively their responses to it, or both.

During the last two or three decades, applied researchers have attempted to develop intervention strategies aimed at controlling the body's physiological responses to stress. This work has suggested that a number of stress management strategies can actually attenuate physiological responsivity. Most strategies teach the individual some form of relaxation (such as deep muscle relaxation, biofeedback, hypnosis, or meditation), and most of this work has focused on populations already diagnosed with a stress-related disease, such as hypertension, diabetes, or ulcer. The techniques are thought to produce their effects by two possible mechanisms: lowering basal physiological activation (or changing the level at which homeostasis is achieved) and/or providing a strategy for more effectively responding to acute stressors to attenuate their physiological effects. Research has not proceeded far enough to make any statements about the relative importance of these mechanisms. Indeed, it is not clear whether either mechanism is active in many of the successful intervention studies. While research does indicate that relaxation strategies often improve symptoms of stress-related illnesses, the causal mechanisms of such techniques remain to be clarified.

Context

The notion that the mind and body are connected has been considered since the writings of ancient Greece. Hippocrates described four bodily humors (fluids) that he associated with differing behavioral and psychological characteristics. Thus, the road was paved for scientific thinkers to consider the interrelations between environment, psychological state, and physiological state (that is, health and illness). Such considerations developed most rapidly in the twentieth century, when advancements in scientific methodology permitted a more rigorous examination of the relationships among these variables.

In the early twentieth century, as noted already, Walter Cannon was the first to document and discuss the "fight or flight response" to threatening events. He also reasoned that the response was adaptive, unless prolonged or repeated. In the 1940's, two physicians published observations consistent with Cannon's of an ulcer patient who had a gastric fistula, enabling the doctors to observe directly the contents of the stomach. They reported that stomach acids and bleeding increased when the patient was anxious or angry, thus documenting the relations between stress, emotion, and physiology. Shortly after this work was published, Selye began reporting his experiments on the effects of cold and fatigue on the physiology of rats. These physical stressors produced enlarged adrenal glands, small thymus and lymph glands (involved in immune system functioning), and increased ulcer formation.

Psychiatrists took this information, along with the writings of Sigmund Freud, to mean that certain disease states might be associated with particular personality types. Efforts to demonstrate the relationship between specific personality types and physical disease endpoints culminated in the development of a field known as psychosomatic medicine. Research, however, does not support the basic tenet of this field, that a given disease is linked with specific personality traits; thus, psychosomatic medicine has not received much support from the scientific community. The work of clinicians and researchers in psychosomatic medicine paved the way for late twentieth century conceptualizations of the relations between stress and physiology. Most important, biopsychosocial models that view the individual's health status in the context of the interaction between his or her biological vulnerability, psychological characteristics, and socio-occupational environment have been developed for a number of physical diseases.

Future research into individual differences in stress responses will further clarify the mechanisms by which stress exerts its effects on physiology. Once these mechanisms are identified, intervention strategies for use with patients or for prevention programs for at-risk individuals can be identified and implemented. Clarification of the role of the endogenous opiates in the stress response, for example, represents an important dimension in developing new strategies to enhance individual coping with stressors. Further investigation of the influence of stressors on immune function should open new doors for prevention and intervention, as well.

Much remains to be learned about why individuals differ in their responses to stress. Research in this area will seek to determine the influence of genes, environment, and behavior on the individual, elucidating the important differences between stress-tolerant and stress-intolerant individuals. Such work will provide a better understanding of the basic mechanisms by which stressors have their effects, and should lead to exciting new prevention and intervention strategies that will enhance health and improve the quality of life.

Bibliography

Craig, Kenneth D., and Stephen M. Weiss, eds. *Health Enhancement, Disease Prevention, and Early Intervention: Biobehavioral Perspectives.* New York: Springer, 1990. Includes, among other chapters of interest, an excellent chapter by Neal Miller (the "father of biofeedback") on how the brain affects the health of the body.

Feist, Jess, and Linda Brannon. *Health Psychology: An Introduction to Behavior and Health.* Belmont, Calif.: Wadsworth, 1988. Written for undergraduate students. A very readable overview of the field of health psychology. Provides the reader with chapters on stress and health, and various stress-related diseases.

Fuller, M. G., and V. L. Goetsch. "Stress and Stress Management." In *Behavior and Medicine,* edited by Danny Wedding. New York: Mosby-Year Book, 1990. Provides an overview of the field, focusing particularly on the physiological response to stress.

Jacobson, Edmund. *You Must Relax.* New York: McGraw-Hill, 1934. A rare classic which may be available in the special collections section of the library. Jacobson is considered the father of modern relaxation training. This book is worth seeking for the pictures of Jacobson's patients after undergoing his relaxation procedure as well as for Jacobson's thoughtful insights.

Ornstein, Robert, and D. S. Sobel. "The Brain as a Health Maintenance Organization." In *The Healing Brain: A Scientific Reader,* edited by Robert Ornstein and Charles Swencionis. New York: Guilford Press, 1990. Discusses the body's responses to stressors from an evolutionary perspective.

Selye, Hans. *The Stress of Life*. New York: McGraw-Hill, 1956. A thoroughly readable account of Selye's work and thinking about stress and health. Available at most bookstores, a must for those interested in learning more about stress.

Virginia L. Goetsch
Kevin T. Larkin

Cross-References

Biofeedback and Relaxation, 416; Emotion and Stress, 941; Meditation and Relaxation, 1499; Adaptation to Stress, 2390; Effects of Stress, 2417; Stress and the Endocrine System, 2445; Stress and the Nervous System, 2452; Stress Prediction and Control, 2458; Stress-Related Diseases, 2464.

THEORIES OF STRESS

Type of psychology: Stress
Field of study: Critical issues in stress

Stress generally involves emotional and physiological responses to circumstances which an individual views as threatening. Most theories of stress claim that stress involves the interaction between problems people face and their resources for dealing with them. A wide range of theories emphasize either physiological responses, environmental circumstances, cognitions, personal coping skills, personal characteristics, or some combination of these factors.

Principal terms
> FIGHT-OR-FLIGHT RESPONSE: the physiological response that occurs when a person is exposed to an emotionally arousing stimulus; it includes increases in heart rate, blood pressure, and respiration
> GENERAL ADAPTATION SYNDROME: the three-stage response of the body to stress that was proposed by Hans Selye; the three stages are the alarm reaction, resistance stage, and exhaustion stage
> HARDINESS: the concept developed by Suzanne Kobasa which maintains that illness in the face of potentially stressful events is dependent on the three factors of control, commitment, and challenge
> STRESS: a state involving emotional and physiological responses to circumstances which a person perceives as potentially threatening
> STRESS APPRAISAL: the three-step process proposed by Richard S. Lazarus in which potentially stressful situations are evaluated; the three steps are primary appraisal, secondary appraisal, and reappraisal
> TYPE A PERSONALITY: a personality type, describing individuals who are driven, competitive, high-strung, impatient, time urgent, intense, and easily angered, which some researchers have associated with increased risk of heart disease
> TYPE B PERSONALITY: a personality type, describing individuals who are relaxed, calm, patient, and not easily angered, which has often been associated with a low risk of heart disease

Overview

The first important theorist who attempted to account for stress was Walter B. Cannon. He claimed that the sympathetic nervous system is activated by signals from the brain when a person is exposed to an emotionally arousing stimulus. This produces a series of physiological reactions which include increases in heart rate, blood pressure, and respiration. This "fight-or-flight" response prepares the person for potential vigorous physical activity. According to Cannon, the confrontation with an arousing stimulus produces both the feelings and physiological reactions which are associated with stress. While the contributions of Cannon were important, they did not take into consideration the role played by psychological and behavioral factors in the overall stress response.

The work of Cannon paved the way for the efforts of the most renowned stress theorist, Hans Selye. He has claimed that stress is nonspecifically induced and can be caused by diverse stimuli. It does not matter if the event is a major disaster, an uncooperative colleague, or a disobedient child. The important point to remember is that if the event is stressful for a person, the person's bodily reaction remains the same. Selye has labeled the body's response to stress the general adaptation syndrome (GAS). This process occurs in three stages. Stage one is the alarm reaction, during which the body activates in order to handle the perceived danger at hand. This activation resembles Cannon's fight-or-flight response. Blood is diverted toward the skeletal muscles in order to prepare them for action. The second phase of the general adaptation syndrome is the resistance stage. During this stage, the person either adapts to or resists the source of stress. The longer this stage lasts, the greater is the danger to the person. If the individual accepts the source of stress as a necessary part of life, the stressor may persist indefinitely. The person then gradually becomes more susceptible to a wide range of stress-related problems and diseases including fatigue, headaches, ulcers, hypertension, certain forms of cancer, and cardiovascular disease. These are but a few of the physical problems which are potentially related to stress. The third stage is the exhaustion stage. This demonstrates the finite nature of the body's ability to battle or adapt to stress. If the stressor is extremely intense and persists over a long period of time, the exhaustion stage sets in, and the risk of emotional and physical problems increases. In Selye's system, the precise nature of the source of the stress is unimportant. The reaction is hypothesized to be the same in the face of physiological and psychological stressors.

Cannon and Selye clearly focus on stress as a biological response of the person to a wide range of stimuli. Selye emphasizes the nonspecific nature of the stress response. This position has been criticized by John Mason, who maintains that while the general adaptation syndrome does exist, responses are different to diverse stimuli. He views stress as dependent upon emotional responses to situations. It is the nature of a person's emotional response that will play an important role in the probability that stress will lead to disease. People who are not psychologically aware of the existence of a potentially stressful event are least likely to experience a stress response. Mason believes that Selye's approach is too simplistic and does not provide ample opportunities to explain why some people develop stress-related disorders and others do not.

The theories of Cannon and Selye emphasize biological factors, while Mason's theory is typically described as an interactionist approach to stress. The psychological approach to stress is best represented by the work of Richard S. Lazarus. He claims that the key to a stress response cannot be found in either the nature of a specific stressful event or the person's response to that event. Rather, the most important factors are cognitive ones. Lazarus believes that it is the person's perception of an event that is crucial. This perception involves a combination of the person's perception of the potential danger of an event and his or her perceived ability to cope with that event. Stress will occur in those circumstances in which the person perceives that he or she does not have the ability or resources needed to cope with the situation.

Clearly, an important factor within the stress equation provided by Lazarus is appraisal of the situation. Along with his colleague Susan Folkman, Lazarus has described three types of appraisal of a potentially stressful situation. The first to occur is the primary appraisal. When a person is exposed to a new event such as a spouse returning to work, the situation can be judged as irrelevant, positive, or potentially stressful. The key to the stress is the person's appraisal of the situation, rather than the situation itself. Next in the appraisal process is the secondary appraisal. It is at this point that the person determines his or her ability to control, handle, or cope with the new situation. During this process, the person examines potential options for dealing with an event which has been judged as potentially stressful. This is followed by an analysis of his or her ability to make use of one or more of these options and a consideration of the success potential of each option, that is, whether the person is likely to be successful in making this option work for himself or herself. The final type of appraisal is reappraisal. During this process, the person reevaluates the stressful potential of a situation based on access to new thoughts and information. This can lead to an increase or decrease in stress. For example, the man who might have been mildly stressed by his wife's return to work may experience a decrease in stress as the family finances improve and he learns that many domestic tasks which he must now perform are less noxious than he originally thought. On the other hand, his stress may increase if he determines that he has less free time and that the cost of babysitters has removed the potential for financial improvement associated with his wife's return to work outside the home.

Whether they support a biological, interactionist, or psychological approach to stress, all theorists agree that stress has the capability of increasing the risk of suffering various forms of illness. In addition, many theorists believe that important relationships exist between stress, personality, and susceptibility to disease. These issues will now be addressed in an effort to demonstrate how some of the potential dangers of stress can be minimized.

Applications

Potentially stressful events occur in everyone's life. Many people, however, never develop stress-related symptoms and illnesses. This may result in part from issues pertaining to life-style and personality. One interesting approach to this problem has been provided by Suzanne Kobasa. She has found that several personality factors are helpful in people's efforts to avoid illness in the face of stress. These factors are control, commitment, and challenge. When faced with difficult events, one can view the situation either as hopeless or as one over which one has a degree of control.

Suppose that someone is notified that the factory in which he works is going to close in three years. While it is normal initially to treat the news with shock and disappointment, it is the worker's long-term response which is critical. On the one hand, he can continue to report for work during the next three years and commiserate with his colleagues. He can make the statement that the factory is going to close and there is nothing he can do about it. This response is likely to lead to gradual increases in stress and susceptibility to illness. On the other hand, he could take control of the situation by looking for other work, entering a job retraining program, or returning to school on a part-time basis. This approach is likely to decrease his risk of stress-related illness.

The second factor, commitment, involves one's dedication to and involvement in people, activities, institutions, and oneself. Some people have nowhere to turn in the presence of a stressful event. They have no friends, family ties have been severed, and they are loners who have no goal in life other than to wake up the next morning. These individuals will find it extremely difficult to cope with a stressful event such as the death of a parent or loss of a job. They may feel that they have nowhere to turn in the face of adversity because they have worked hard at removing the types of support systems that are helpful in times of stress. These people are highly susceptible to those illnesses that are associated with stress. Conversely, a person with many friends, strong family ties, and a sense of purpose in life will be better able to cope with significant stress.

The final factor, challenge, relates to a person's view of changes in his or her life. For example, a secretary who is transferred from one department at work to another, and who views this change as presenting interesting and new challenges, is likely to remain healthy. If the new position is seen as a threat which should be avoided at all costs, however, illness may be just around the corner. The three factors of control, commitment, and challenge make up an overall factor known as hardiness. The person who maintains high levels of these three factors has a high level of hardiness and is not a likely candidate for stress-related illnesses.

Perhaps the most talked-about and researched personality factor that has been related to stress is the Type A personality. The Type A person is one who is always on the go and is extremely driven. He or she walks fast, talks fast, is impatient with others, and is easily angered. The Type A person is a workaholic who measures life in numbers. He or she is concerned about money earned and saved, hours worked, praise received, and clients served. He or she always has a sense of time urgency. The Type B person is just the opposite. He or she is the relaxed and easygoing person who never seems in a hurry to do anything.

Research on the topic of the Type A personality, spearheaded by Meyer Friedman and Ray Rosenman, has traditionally maintained that the Type A personality is associated with increased stress and, more important, an increased risk of heart disease. This finding has been supported in at least forty research studies. For many years, the notion that Type A behavior was a risk factor for heart disease was taken for granted by many health professionals; however, several studies have failed to support this relationship. Researchers have attempted to account for these discrepancies. The mystery appears to have been solved in that it has been discovered that not all Type A behaviors are associated with increased risk of heart disease. The key factors appear to be anger and hostility. It is those Type A persons who are angry and hostile who are likely to convert potentially stressful situations into disease. The best advice that can be given to the typical Type A angry person is to learn to respond to situations without anger. This does not mean that anger which is felt should be held inside. Rather, the person should learn to respond to situations with feelings and emotions other than anger.

The key factor in looking at applications to theories of stress is coping. People must learn to cope with situations in ways which do not lead to increased stress and increased risk of disease. The good news is that many such strategies have proved to be very effective in helping people deal with those potentially stressful situations that seem to occur in the lives of everyone.

Context

Unlike most areas within psychology, the study of stress is basically limited to the twentieth century. As early as 1914, Walter B. Cannon claimed that the sympathetic nervous sytem is activated by signals from the brain when a person is exposed to an emotionally arousing stimulus. This results in increases in heart rate, blood pressure, and perspiration and prepares the individual for significant physical activity. Cannon's work was limited in that the role of behavioral and psychological factors in the stress response was ignored; however, his research paved the way for the most famous theorist in the field, Hans Selye. Selye maintained that the body responds similarly to a wide range of stressors. He labeled this three-stage response the general adaptation syndrome. Selye's emphasis on the nonspecific, biological aspects of stress led to the formulation of many theories of stress and countless research efforts.

Theories of stress began to play a more important role within psychology as the potential relationships between stress and illness were systematically investigated. The most important findings in this area related to heart disease. Investigators such as cardiologists Ray Rosenman and Meyer Friedman claimed that known risk factors for heart disease failed to account for a substantial percentage of existing cases of coronary heart disease. They hypothesized that people who have a Type A personality experience the type of long-term stress which is associated with an increased risk of developing heart disease. More recent research has focused on one Type A characteristic, anger, as the crucial aspect of the connection between the Type A personality and heart disease. It appears that angry people experience a type of stress which is particularly damaging to the cardiovascular system.

The work of pioneers such as Cannon, Selye, Rosenman, and Friedman has opened up many new avenues of research related to stress and stress management. The potential role of stress in a wide range of diseases including cancer is currently being explored. It can be anticipated that the future will bring to light many new and unexpected relationships between stress and health.

Bibliography

Dembroski, T. M., J. M. MacDougall, J. A. Herd, and J. L. Shields. "Perspectives on Coronary-Prone Behavior." In *Cardiovascular Disorders and Behavior*, edited by David S. Krantz, Andrew Baum, and Jerome S. Singer. Vol. 3 in *Handbook of Psychology and Health*. Hillsdale, N.J.: Lawrence Erlbaum, 1983. An extremely thorough work on the status of Type A behavior and its relationship to health in general and heart disease in particular. Includes a look at the history of the concept and ways of establishing the existence of a Type A behavior pattern, and evaluates existing research in the field.

Goldberger, Les, and Shlomo Breznitz, eds. *Handbook of Stress: Theoretical and Clinical Aspects.* New York: Free Press, 1982. Provides articles which emphasize both psychological and physiological aspects of stress. Includes material on coping with stress as well as on treatment approaches to stress and stress-related disorders.

Kobasa, Suzanne C. "Stressful Life Events, Personality, and Health: An Inquiry into Hardiness." *Journal of Personality and Social Psychology* 37 (January, 1979): 1-11. The original groundbreaking study which attempted to determine why some people develop stress-related illnesses while others do not. It was in this study that Kobasa determined that the key factors which protected some individuals from stress-related illnesses are control, commitment, and challenge. Excellent reading for any audience.

Lazarus, Richard S., and Susan Folkman. *Stress, Appraisal, and Coping.* New York: Springer, 1984. Provides a thorough analysis of Lazarus' views on stress. Includes his comments on the three types of appraisal and approaches to coping with stress. An excellent book which provides thorough research support for the theoretical positions which are taken.

Selye, Hans. *The Stress of Life.* New York: McGraw-Hill, 1956. The classic book in the field. Includes Selye's original analysis of stress and his development of the general adaptation syndrome. Also includes a thorough analysis of the proposed relationships between stress and various forms of disease.

Lawrence A. Fehr

Cross-References

Emotion and Stress, 941; General Adaptation Syndrome, 1068; Stress: Behavioral and Psychological Responses, 2397; Stress: Cognitive Appraisals, 2404; The Concept of Stress, 2411; Effects of Stress, 2417; Stress and Reappraisal, 2438; Stress-Related Diseases, 2464; Stressors, 2471.

STRESS AND REAPPRAISAL

Type of psychology: Stress
Field of study: Coping

Reappraisal is a form of coping in which people either deny realities, perceive realities in a positive light, or hold unsupported beliefs. This form of emotional coping may be valuable in relieving distress, but in some situations it can have the cost of delaying or halting the search for problem-focused coping.

Principal terms
   DOWNWARD SOCIAL COMPARISON: self-evaluation accomplished by comparing oneself to someone who is lower on some relevant dimension
   ILLUSIONS: beliefs that are unsupported by evidence or require perceiving facts in a particular, positive light
   PRIMARY APPRAISAL: the search for information regarding whether a problem exists and, if so, the nature of the problem
   REAPPRAISAL: an internally motivated search for information which will support a less stressful appraisal
   SECONDARY APPRAISAL: the search for information regarding coping resources, effectiveness of those resources, and ability to enact coping techniques
   STRESS: the judgment that a problem exceeds one's available resources, resulting from a primary appraisal of the problem and a secondary appraisal of the coping resources
   STRESSOR: the problem; the internal or external force that meets or exceeds one's resources

Overview

Richard S. Lazarus, one of the pioneers in stress research and one of its most prolific writers, defines stress as a relationship between the person and the environment that is appraised by the person as reaching (or exceeding) the limits of that person's resources and thereby endangering his or her well-being.

As is clear in this definition, the person's appraisal of the situation determines whether the situation is stressful and, if so, the level of stress. The experience of stress is a result of both the situation and the person's appraisal of the situation, which is affected by cognitive factors such as expectations, fear, and self-esteem.

Lazarus' model of stress includes two types of appraisal: primary and secondary. In primary appraisal, the person is trying to evaluate whether there is a problem and, if so, the nature of the problem. If primary appraisal indicates that there is a problem, secondary appraisal begins; the person tries to determine what, if anything, can be done about the problem. This is a complex process and includes an evaluation of what coping options are available, the likelihood of the success of the options, and the person's ability to use the coping techniques effectively. As the situation continues and new information is available, new primary and secondary appraisals are conducted. Together, primary and secondary appraisals determine the degree of stress that is experienced.

Since the stress experienced by people is partially determined by their appraisals of the situation and their resources, one way to lessen stress is to change those appraisals. This form of coping seems to be both prevalent and effective. Lazarus defines what he calls defensive reappraisal as an effort to reinterpret the past more positively, or to deal with present harms or threats by perceiving them in ways that are less harmful or threatening. Rather than being part of the primary and secondary appraisal cycle that is activated by external forces such as new information, defensive reappraisal arises from internal processes such as fear.

One type of defensive reappraisal is denial, which is rejecting some reality. An example of denial might be someone with cancer refusing to believe the illness might be life-threatening. Denials may differ in several ways. One way is in their scope. Partial denial is a tentative suspension of belief, rather than a complete one as is seen in full denial, that allows the person to become aware of or act on the denied reality if it is necessary that he or she do so. Another way in which denials can differ is in their target. Some denials are denials of facts, while others are denials of implications. For example, to deny that one's spouse has died is a denial of fact; to accept this fact but deny that one's life will be changed in any way is a denial of implication. Yet another target of denial is one's emotions. Someone undergoing stress might accept the fact of the stressor and its implications as well, but deny the emotional impact of these realities.

Lazarus believes that there are both costs and benefits associated with denial. Whether the costs will outweigh the benefits depends on several factors. Chief among these is whether there is some action that the person undergoing stress can take to relieve the stressor. If so, denial will be primarily destructive. For example, denying the symptoms of a heart attack will prevent seeking medical help. When there is no action to be taken, however, denial may help relieve the distress associated with stress. Another important factor is the timing of the denial. Denial can be beneficial at an early stage of coping, when the person's resources are insufficient to use more problem-focused coping. This is especially true in cases of health-related stress. The target of the denial also influences its costs and benefits. Denying emotional distress has little benefit; the person still feels distress despite the denial. Denying the fact of the stressor may be difficult and subject to disconfirmation. Especially when used in the early stages of stress, denial of implications may be the most beneficial form of denial. While leaving the person free to act and make decisions on the stressor, such denial allows him or her to delay facing all the negative aspects at once. Finally, because it also allows the stressed person to take action, partial denial involves lower costs than full denial.

Shelley Taylor has also investigated appraisal and coping. She proposes that what she calls illusions allow people to buffer against both present setbacks and future threats. Unlike denial, illusions do not necessarily contradict known facts. Illusions are beliefs that are unsupported by facts or that require looking at the facts in a particular, positive light. Taylor argues that three illusions are particularly important in adjustment to threatening events: meaning, mastery, and self-esteem.

The search for meaning often involves trying to determine the cause of the stressor. Because causal attributions help people to understand, predict, and control their environment, they assist in coping with stress. Although in some situations a cause for the stressor can be pinpointed, often that is not possible; in these cases, attributing the stressor to a particular cause is an illusion.

Because a threatening event can involve a frightening loss of one's sense of control over one's body and one's life in general, regaining mastery in this area is beneficial to adjustment. Often this sense of control is illusory. For example, patients with a life-threatening illness may try strategies that have no research support. Although these efforts may be medically ineffective, they may be psychologically effective if they help the patient regain a sense of control.

Threat of harm can damage one's self-esteem. People tend to use illusions such as self-serving attributional biases even in normal circumstances, so their use under stress is to be expected. One common bias is to remember one's past as being less happy in order to perceive the present as an improvement. Another bias used by people undergoing stress to foster self-enhancement is downward social comparison. Social comparison is measuring oneself against another person. Downward social comparison involves choosing someone who is less fortunate overall or less fortunate on some particular dimension as a comparison person. Clearly, this leads to favorable comparisons and results in enhanced self-esteem.

One possible problem with illusions is that they might be disconfirmed by new information. Taylor proposes that people hold multiple cognitions concerning causation, control, and self-esteem and that if one cognition is disconfirmed, the person shifts to another cognition. From her viewpoint, which is supported by others' research, humans are amazingly adaptive, self-protective, and able to function well in the face of adversity.

Applications

Stress and reactions to stress have been popular topics of research by health psychologists, physiological psychologists, and social psychologists. Although some laboratory research has been conducted with animals and humans, most of the research in this area has been field research. This research has ranged from studies of blood chemistry to studies of cognitive factors and has investigated stressors such as the loss of a child or spouse, natural and artificial disasters, war, and health problems.

In Taylor's research on illusions, she and her colleagues Rosemary Lichtman and Joanne Wood conducted extensive interviews with seventy-eight women with breast cancer. It was from this research that she developed the concepts of cognitive adaptation and the benefit of illusions.

Although the true cause or causes of their breast cancer were unknown and un-knowable, 95 percent of the women who were interviewed attributed their cancer to a particular event or factor or to multiple events or factors. The fact that so many people held beliefs that were counter to the known facts or at best unsupported by facts may be an indication of this illusion's effectiveness. Furthermore, many women either chose a cause which was in the past and therefore no longer a threat (a blow to the breast or a stressful situation such as a failed marriage) or identified a cause which they could control, such as diet, which then served two purposes: decreased threat and increased control.

The belief that they are in control of their lives appears to be quite strong in cancer patients—so strong, in fact, and so tenuously based that it seems to be il-lusory. Two-thirds of the breast cancer patients who were interviewed believed that they had some personal control over the course or recurrence of their cancer, and one-third believed they had a large amount of control. Of the one-third who believed they did not personally have control over their cancer, some believed that it could be controlled by their doctor or by medical treatment. Belief in either one's own control or a doctor's control was associated with better adjustment than lack of these beliefs. Many patients also regained a sense of control over their lives by controlling some aspect of their lives or treatment rather than the cancer itself. For example, 92 per-cent of the women who underwent chemotherapy developed strategies to attempt to control the side effects. In other research, conducted in laboratory settings, giving people control over a stressor (usually a loud noise) helped them cope. The sense of control these women developed when confronted with breast cancer may have served the same purpose.

To explore the issue of self-esteem enhancement, researchers asked the patients about their adjustment. Part of the "data" that the women used as a basis for these evaluations was obtained through downward social comparison. Only two of the women reported that they were coping somewhat worse than other cancer patients; the rest reported that they were doing as well as or somewhat better than others. The women often constructed hypothetical others to compare themselves to, saying that "some women" were devastated and that they themselves were coping better. They also chose dimensions on which to compare themselves; Taylor concludes that ev-eryone is better off than someone else as long as the right dimension is chosen. For example, older women often compared themselves to younger women, and women who had less extensive surgery compared themselves to those who had more exten-sive surgery. These comparisons allowed for self-esteem enhancement for everyone, regardless of her circumstances.

Although Lazarus' ideas about denial are less detailed than Taylor's concept of illusions, much of what her interviewees report could be explained using Lazarus' terms. For example, one could describe the tendency for patients to make causal attributions and strive for a sense of control as partial denials of the reality of un-known causes and lost control. Despite the differences in language, it is clear that Taylor's cognitive adaptation theory and Lazarus' ideas about the benefits of denial have much in common. It is also clear that they do not directly contradict one another; the types of denial (to use Lazarus' terms) that Taylor finds to be beneficial are the types that Lazarus would expect to be beneficial: denial of implications and partial, flexible denial.

Context

The history of the study of stress and cognitive appraisals of stress is linked to the history of the field of health psychology, which in turn is linked to the development of applied psychology. For the first sixty years after its inception as a separate discipline in the nineteenth century, psychology was almost exclusively an academic discipline. It was involved in questions about the nature of human thought and memory. Virtually all psychologists were teachers first and researchers second, and few worked in nonacademic settings.

World War I offered psychology the opportunity to be applied outside the laboratory. One of the biggest new areas was the application of psychology to military recruitment. Psychologists developed group tests of intelligence and measures of emotional stability for the military. After the war, this expertise was used in education and social agencies. Over time, and helped in large part by the huge numbers of people whose lives were disrupted by World War II, the testing movement developed into what is known as clinical psychology.

As the first applied area of psychology, clinical psychology gave birth to a number of other applied specialities, including health psychology. A number of factors were important in the development of health psychology, including clinical psychologists' struggle for inclusion on insurance policies, a vigorous public debate about establishing a national health insurance, and research indicating that behaviors such as smoking had an effect on physical health. These factors contributed to a climate in which health and especially preventive health measures were frequently discussed in the media, in hospitals, in homes, and in psychological laboratories. In 1973, the American Psychological Association's Task Force on Health Research found that more than five hundred psychologists were doing research that was related to physical health and concluded that psychology could be beneficial to the health-care field in at least three areas: susceptibility to illness, adaptation or adjustment to illness, and preventive medicine. In 1979, the American Psychological Association established a division of health psychology. Today, most stress researchers identify themselves as health psychologists or social psychologists interested in health issues.

Although the concept of stress is an ancient one, theory and research about stress and coping gained popularity only relatively recently. Early stress models in the 1950's and 1960's emphasized both physiological aspects of stress and drive-reduction models, which propose that humans prefer a steady state and that stress was uncomfortable because it disturbed that state.

In the 1970's, profound change occurred in psychology: Cognition, which had been largely ignored for sixty years during psychology's behaviorist period, was once again an acceptable topic for research. This cognitive revolution changed stress research as well. It was during this time that cognitive factors such as appraisal were introduced into stress research.

The study of reappraisal coping techniques such as denial and illusions is a relatively new, and promising, area of research. As stress researchers learn more about coping, they will be able to help those who work with people under stress learn or improve coping techniques. Given the relationship between stress and coping and both physical and mental health, this is a valuable area of psychological research.

Bibliography

Folkman, Susan, Charles E. Schaefer, and Richard S. Lazarus. "Cognitive Processes as Mediators of Stress and Coping." In *Human Stress and Cognition: An Information Processing Approach*, edited by Vernon Hamilton and David M. Warburton. New York: John Wiley & Sons, 1979. Introduces the concepts of primary and secondary appraisal, and includes an interesting discussion of the role of emotion and stress. Assumes some background in psychology, so beginning readers might find this chapter difficult; a good resource for a more advanced reader.

Kessler, Ronald C., Richard H. Price, and Camille B. Wortman. "Social Factors in Psychopathology: Stress, Social Support, and Coping Processes." In *Annual Review of Psychology* 36. Stanford, Calif.: Annual Reviews, 1985. Reviews the research on life stress and vulnerability, and includes a section on group differences such as sex differences. An excellent starting place for someone interested in stress and health in general. Assumes some background in psychology, but the article is so clear that even relative beginners should find it useful.

Lazarus, Richard S. "The Costs and Benefits of Denial." In *Stress and Coping: An Anthology*, edited by Alan Monat and Richard S. Lazarus. New York: Columbia University Press, 1977. This excellent article includes a brief discussion of research that can be interpreted using the framework of denial, but it is largely a theoretical piece. After the interesting but slightly tangential section on denial in literature, Lazarus carefully explains the costs and benefits associated with the different forms of denial.

Monat, Alan, and Richard S. Lazarus, eds. *Stress and Coping: An Anthology.* 3d ed. New York: Columbia University Press, 1991. All three editions of this anthology are useful resources, but this one is particularly good, including articles by Hans Selye and Norman Cousins and an excellent article by Salvatore Maddi and Suzanne Kobasa on how to rear a hardy, stress-resistant child. Most of the articles are free of obscure terms and are appropriate for students of all levels.

Taylor, Shelley E. "Adjustment to Threatening Events: A Theory of Cognitive Adaptation." *American Psychologist* 38, no. 11 (1983): 1161-1173. Describes cognitive adaptation theory and the research that was instrumental in its development. Although written for a scientific audience, this article is a wonderful example of how to convey both data and sophisticated insight in clear, simple language that is suitable for students of all levels.

Brynda Holton

Cross-References

Coping: Social Support, 700; Coping Strategies: An Overview, 706; Adaptation to Stress, 2390; Stress: Behavioral and Psychological Responses, 2397; Stress: Cognitive Appraisals, 2404; Effects of Stress, 2417; Theories of Stress, 2432.

STRESS AND THE ENDOCRINE SYSTEM

Type of psychology: Stress
Fields of study: Biology of stress; endocrine system; stress and illness

Hormones and their actions on both behavior and physiology are of critical importance in understanding the body's response to stress; hormones not only profoundly influence biological and behavioral coping mechanisms but also reflect the nature and effectiveness of these coping mechanisms.

Principal terms

AUTONOMIC NERVOUS SYSTEM: the division of the peripheral nervous system that regulates basic, automatically controlled life processes such as cardiovascular function, digestive function, and genital function

ENDOCRINOLOGY: the study of the nature and the role of hormones in biological systems

GLUCOCORTICOID HORMONES: hormones of the outer or cortical layers of the adrenal gland, such as cortisol, which inhibit immune/inflammatory function and are involved in the metabolism of glucose

HORMONE: a chemical released by a cell which acts on another cell, usually, but not always, at some distance from the originating cell

NEUROENDOCRINE: a term used to denote interactions between the nervous system and hormones

NEUROTRANSMITTER: a chemical that allows one neuron to direct information to an adjacent neuron

PITUITARY-ADRENOCORTICAL AXIS: the hormone system that is composed of corticotropin-releasing hormone from the hypothalamus, adrenocorticotropic-releasing hormone from the pituitary gland, and glucocorticoids from the adrenocortex

PSYCHOBIOLOGY: the study of the interactions between biological and psychological processes

STRESS: the demands, including the appraisal of threat, placed on an organism (rather than the response of the organism to those demands)

Overview

Early twentieth century interest in the relationships between hormones and stress stemmed from an attempt to understand the biology of fear and stress. Physiologist Walter Cannon presented the classical formulation known as the "fight-or-flight" response. According to this concept, the sympathetic nervous system is responsible for mobilization of the body to respond to a crisis. During times of fear, anxiety, or emotion the sympathetic nervous system becomes engaged to inhibit digestion and reproduction in favor of preparation of the body to undertake the explosive muscular action necessary for fight or flight. The hormones involved in the mediation of sympathetic activity include norepinephrine, which serves as the neurotransmitter for the sympathetic nervous system, and epinephrine, which is a hormone secreted by the adrenal medulla (the inner core of the adrenal gland) into the general circulation.

Hans Selye provided the foundational work underlying many late twentieth century concepts of the role of neuroendocrine function during stress. Selye suggested that environmental stressors produced a unitary, nonspecific response which includes the activation of the pituitary-adrenocortical axis in what he termed the "general adaptation syndrome." This syndrome has three phases: alarm, resistance, and exhaustion. The alarm reaction engages the autonomic nervous system and the adrenal medulla to resist a stressor during the fight-or-flight reaction. The second stage, resistance, recruits the pituitary-adrenocortical axis and other coping mechanisms to permit the organism to adapt to continuing demands caused by a stressor. The third stage, exhaustion, results when the organism depletes its adaptive resources and may result in the death of the organism.

According to Selye's original hypothesis, activation of the pituitary-adrenocortical axis is elicited by any external stimulus. Subsequent research has demonstrated that activation of the pituitary-adrenocortical axis is not unitary and nonspecific. Consider the range of stimuli that activate this hormonal axis as reflected by fluctuations in the concentration of glucocorticoids in the plasma or urine: surgery; rowing a boat; running a marathon; hospitalization; and the anticipation of surgery, a college examination, or exhausting exercise. Additionally, the release of glucocorticoids adapts very rapidly and is most evident in novel situations. Furthermore, events such as exposure to heat and cold have been shown to produce opposite effects on the release of glucocorticoids. Exposure to heat reduces glucocorticoids, whereas exposure to cold increases glucocorticoids. One of the major problems in studying the effects of stress is to separate the effects of psychological stress from the effects of physical stress. Successful separation of these kinds of stress requires that research subjects be unaware of an impending physical stress in order to exclude psychological factors that elicit the release of hormones. It appears that the early twentieth century notion of nonspecific effects of stress arose from the failure of researchers to separate anticipation, a psychological component, from what appeared to be purely physical stressors. It is apparent that the psychological component of anticipation most likely accounted for the uniform responses to stress found in the early work.

The most-studied hormonal response to stress is the activation of the pituitary-adrenocortical axis. Cortisol is released following surgery, during prolonged, exhausting exercise, and during exposure to heat. In addition, cortisol is released in anticipation of surgery, exhausting exercise, college tests, and parachute jumps; during the viewing of provocative films; upon admission to a hospital; and when relocating one's residence. This response is not found in all individuals undergoing the same provocative stimulus and adapts readily. For example, cortisol release in response to parachute jumping diminishes with experience; the greatest change in cortisol is found during initial jumps. One conclusion to be drawn from these findings is that novelty or uncertainty are necessary for activation of the pituitary-adrenocortical axis. Furthermore, this axis appears to be responsive to social contexts such as aggression, dominance, and social support. In short, it appears that the pituitary-adrenocortical axis is activated in situations that are novel or where the organism lacks control and/or support. Furthermore, this system is suppressed in situations which are repetitive or where coping mechanisms and/or support is adequate.

Although not as well studied, several other hormones are also known to be responsive to stress. Growth hormone has been found to be released by the pituitary gland in response to surgery, cardiac catheterization, electroconvulsive shock therapy, physical exercise, college examinations, viewing violent or sexually arousing films, and anticipation of physical exercise. While growth hormone release often parallels that of cortisol, it appears that it requires a more intense stimulus to release growth hormone than to release cortisol. Prolactin is also released by the pituitary gland as a result of surgery, pelvic examinations, motion sickness, college examinations, and parachute jumping. As was the case with growth hormone, release of prolactin requires a more intense stimulus than does release of cortisol.

As with the hormones already discussed, levels of epinephrine and norepinephrine increase rapidly when an organism is confronted by stimuli that are threatening, distressing, or novel. The release of epinephrine and norepinephrine does not appear to adapt with repeated exposure to these situations and may reflect the need to maintain vigilance and effort. Stress also increases the concentration of endogenous opiates (for example, endorphins) in the plasma, producing what is known as stress-induced analgesia. These hormones may be released by the pituitary gland and/or the adrenal medulla and modify sensitivity to pain. It is interesting that a variety of stressful stimuli, including surgery and childbirth, are accompanied by an increase in endorphins and that the greater the level of endogenous endorphin after surgery, the less morphine is required to control pain.

Finally, unlike the hormones already described, levels of testosterone fall during stressful events ranging from prisoners awaiting execution to soldiers undergoing basic training in the military and other physical and psychological stresses. Psychological stress also appears to be capable of disrupting ovulation and menstrual cycles in women, probably through disruption of gonadotropic hormones secreted by the pituitary gland.

Applications

Monitoring of stress-induced release of hormones may have at least three important applications. First, it may serve as an index for evaluating the adequacy of one's coping mechanisms when exposed to threatening situations. For example, Edward Sachar studied the correlation between levels of glucocorticoid and the course of acute psychosis. He noted that when turmoil was high there was an increased release of glucocorticoids; however, when patients were either in a phase of recovery or a phase of psychotic equilibrium which indicated lower levels of distress, glucocorticoids were lower. This suggests that the psychosis operates defensively to minimize emotional distress and that glucocorticoids come into play only when the defenses are not working. Other studies have shown that parents of children who were dying of leukemia showed either of two responsive patterns. They were either extremely agitated and demonstrative, showing little release of glucocorticoids, or were quieter and had elevated glucocorticoids. The quieter individuals appeared to have coped with their child's illness by using denial. The fact of their children's imminent death challenged this denial, which in turn led to the activation of the pituitary-adrenocortical axis. Therefore, it appears that release of glucocorticoids serves as an important index of the failure of defenses when coping with a crisis.

Second, hormonal release may allow the body to defend itself against some of the unwanted effects often associated with stress. For example, many studies indicate the release of endogenous opioids in anticipation of pain, a phenomenon known as stress-induced analgesia. Consider the number of people who become injured during a sporting contest but fail to "discover" the injury until after the event has ended. The most dramatic evidence for this stress-induced analgesia comes from reports that pain is often absent from soldiers who suffer mutilating injuries on the battlefield. Furthermore, there is considerable evidence that stress-induced hormones such as adrenocorticotropic hormone and vasopressin improve attention and memory in humans as well as in nonhuman animals. This modulation of memory may serve an adaptive function for individuals when confronted with similar situations in the future. Findings such as these indicate that hormonal responses not only are important as an index of the integrity of coping processes but also may reflect the alteration of sensory thresholds and memories that serve as part of normal adaptation to stress and determine the availability of coping responses in similar situations in the future.

Third, hormones released during stressful events may be a causative or contributory link in the development of illness. There is considerable evidence that immune function is altered during stress and that factors such as controllability contribute to these changes. For example, about 20 percent of the population experience allergic disorders, and the hypersensitivity of immune function is clearly influenced by family conflict and emotional arousal. It is interesting that one of the factors underlying the release of glucocorticoids is lack of control over a situation or failure of coping mechanisms to alleviate stress. Bereavement, depression, unemployment, marital discord, and caring for disabled relatives have been shown to be associated with immunosuppression. Additionally, considerable attention has been focused upon the connections among immune function, hormones, and the course of cancer. For example, it seems clear that the progression of cancer is linked with stress but the link with the initiation of cancer is less clear. Therefore, clear description and understanding of the relationships between hormones and immune function allow a more clear description of the course of physical illnesses, such as cancer and viral infections and their treatment. As glucocorticoids suppress immune function, many researchers have made the case that glucocorticoids are important in modulating the course of illnesses. Hormones such as epinephrine, norepinephrine, endogenous opioids, and neuropeptide Y have also been shown to be important in the modulation of immune function.

Context

Claude Bernard defined the process of adaptation whereby organisms become more independent of their environment by developing complex ways of stabilizing their internal environment. This process is known as homeostasis. Charles Darwin's *The Expression of the Emotions in Man and Animals* (1872) sparked interest in the study of emotional behavior. Otto Loewi demonstrated that nerves released chemical neurotransmitters that regulate heart rate by showing that stimulation of the vagus nerve released both a substance which slowed and a substance which speeded the rate of a second denervated heart. These substances later became termed acetylcholine and norepinephrine, respectively. These were among several early formulations that provided the foundation for Walter Cannon to describe the fight-or-flight response associated with adrenomedullary stimulation and for Hans Selye to describe the role of the pituitary-adrenocortical axis in the general adaptation syndrome. These developments set the stage for later theorizing about the role of hormones in emotion, stress, and adaptation.

The first theories relating stress and coping mechanisms to disease arose from the psychoanalytic formulations of Franz Alexander. Although his specific speculations on the relationship between personality and illness failed to be confirmed by later research, his ideas were instrumental in guiding work which has contributed to the understanding of the psychobiological processes involved in the etiology of disease.

Psychobiology is the field of study that broadly links behavior, autonomic physiology, endocrinology, immunology, genetics, and neurology in an attempt to understand the nature of human functioning. As a result of the determination of the structure of hormones and of the development of the ability to measure hormones both accurately and in minute quantities, there exists a better understanding of the important role that hormones perform in the modification of behavior. Hormones interact with neural function to mediate sensation, perception, memory, stress, emotion, aging, development, and disease. The term "psychoneuroendocrinology" has been coined to cover the broad interface between hormones, the nervous system, and behavior.

As a result of the interplay among all the forces mentioned above, the role of biology as it influences behavioral processes and the role of behavior as it influences biological processes is better understood. The emergence of the neurosciences has put psychobiology in an intensive, yet broadly defined, context that should allow more complete descriptions of the interactions among hormones, the brain, and behavior. This context will allow more specific questions to be asked. For example, given similar environmental pressures, why do some individuals develop disease states while others do not? What, specifically, is the pathway from a given environmental stress to the development of an illness such as cancer or hypertension? How may the etiology or course of diseases be altered to allow better outcomes? It is known that emotional turmoil in the family alters the regulation of insulin in individuals who have diabetes mellitus; how might psychological and interpersonal processes be incorporated into the functioning of the family as an integral aspect of treatment plans for diabetes mellitus? Furthermore, there are now synthetic hormones which are more long lasting and more potent than the parent hormone from which they were developed. For example, there is a form of vasopressin which restores normal fluid and electrolyte regulation for individuals with diabetes insipidus (people who either do not secrete vasopressin from the pituitary gland or who are insensitive to its effects on the kidney) without also altering cardiovascular function. Compounds such as this may offer the exciting possibility of providing safer and more specific drugs for intervention in disease processes and behavior modification than are now available. The interplay between stress and hormones offers a key to a better prediction and understanding of both success and failure of coping mechanisms and their link to wellness as well as dysfunction.

Bibliography

Cannon, Walter B. *Bodily Changes in Pain, Hunger, Fear, and Rage.* Boston: Charles T. Branford, 1929. The classical formulation of the fight-or-flight response. Cannon's formulations provided the impetus for the study of the interaction between stress and the autonomic nervous system.

Gray, Jeffrey Allan. *The Psychology of Fear and Stress.* Cambridge, England: Cambridge University Press, 1987. A thorough discussion of the psychological and physiological factors underlying fear and stress. Gray not only describes the various behavioral and biological processes necessary to understand fear and stress but also discusses their implications for human function.

Levine, Seymour. "Psychoneuroendocrinology of Stress: A Psychobiological Perspective." In *Psychoendocrinology,* edited by F. Robert Brush and Seymour Levine. San Diego, Calif.: Academic Press, 1989. A relatively short chapter which clearly makes the case that hormonal activation during stress is related to psychological processes such as expectancy. A good review of the effects of stress on the release of glucocorticoids (but has limited coverage of other hormones).

Selye, Hans. *The Stress of Life.* New York: McGraw-Hill, 1956. Although Selye's formulation of the nonspecific activation of the pituitary-adrenocortical axis is dated, this is the classic text that provided momentum for the study of hormones and stress.

Veith-Flanigan, Jane, and Curt A. Sandman. "Neuroendocrine Relationships with Stress." In *Stress: Psychological and Physiological Interactions,* edited by Susan R. Burchfield. Washington, D.C.: Hemisphere Publishing, 1985. A very broad, psychologically based discussion of the interactions of hormones and stress. Suggests multiple levels of interaction among hormones, behavior, and stress. Other chapters in this book also describe related aspects of the biology and psychology of stress.

Wilson, Jean D., and Daniel W. Foster. *Williams Textbook of Endocrinology.* Philadelphia: W. B. Saunders, 1985. A comprehensive textbook of endocrinology. Although very technical, most chapters in the text are clearly written and provide thorough description of the stress-related hormones in individual chapters and a discussion of hormones and stress in chapter 20.

Bill E. Beckwith

Cross-References

The Adrenal Gland, 136; Emotion and Stress, 941; The Endocrine System, 966; General Adaptation Syndrome, 1068; Hormones and Behavior, 1189; The Pituitary Gland, 1829; Effects of Stress, 2417; Stress: Physiological Responses, 2425; Stress and the Nervous System, 2452; Stress-Related Diseases, 2464.

STRESS AND THE NERVOUS SYSTEM

Type of psychology: Stress
Field of study: Biology of stress

Stress is the result of the body's response to a demand. The response, which takes place through the nervous system, stimulates activity in many parts of the body; this activity helps a person to fight or escape when in a dangerous situation. Extended stress can create imbalances in nervous system functioning and can contribute to illness and death.

Principal terms

CENTRAL NERVOUS SYSTEM: the nerves and brain tissue located within the bones of the skull and spinal cord

EPINEPHRINE: a chemical released by the adrenal glands in response to stressful stimuli that increases heart rate and output; also called adrenaline

GLUCOCORTICOIDS: hormones produced by the adrenal glands which increase the tone of heart muscle and blood vessels, prevent inflammation, and reduce the production of new antibody proteins

HORMONE: a chemical that creates general or long-term change in the action of organs; hormones are carried by the blood

IMMUNE RESPONSE: the body's response to invasion by disease-producing organisms; proteins (antibodies) which mark the unwanted cells for destruction are produced

NOREPINEPHRINE: a chemical released by the adrenal glands in response to stressful stimuli that narrows blood vessels in the gut and bladder; also called noradrenaline

PERIPHERAL NERVOUS SYSTEM: all the nerves located outside the bones of the skull and spinal cord

STRESS RESPONSE: the body's response to a demand

STRESSOR: anything that produces a demand on the body

Overview

Stressors in the environment affect people first through their action on the nervous system. The nervous system is responsible for allocation of the body's resources and the control of all the body's actions. Different parts of the nervous system are responsible for different parts of one's response to stressors, and much of what is commonly referred to as a stress response is the result of high levels of arousal in the sympathetic nervous system.

The two major divisions of the nervous system are the central and peripheral nervous systems. The central nervous system consists of the brain and the spinal cord. The peripheral nervous system consists of the somatic and autonomic nervous systems and includes all the nerves outside the skull and spinal column. The autonomic nervous system also has two divisions, the parasympathetic and sympathetic. The central nervous system determines whether something that a person senses is considered a threat. A sudden noise or a quick movement may startle one and begin an arousal response, but if one looks and sees that there is nothing of which to be afraid, arousal levels quickly return to normal. If, on the other hand, one compares the event with memories of threatening situations and finds similarities, these thoughts can maintain arousal for long periods of time until one feels safe again.

How a person thinks about an event plays a large part in determining what he or she feels. Imagine the responses of an ordinary person, "Bob." A bat flies past Bob's head. The bat can be seen as a threat particularly if Bob has been watching a vampire film and thinks it is a vampire bat, or the bat can be seen as a small harmless animal which can be ignored.

The brain is the most important part of the central nervous system. Different areas of the brain control different functions of the body, but not all behaviors take place in response to stress. The brain interprets the sights, sounds, smells, tastes, and touches of a person's experience. The limbic system, a group of structures in the brain, contributes to emotional response to stressors. Within the limbic system are structures such as the amygdala, which is important in the experience of aggression and fear; and the hypothalamus, which influences the other structures of the brain and the endocrine system. The hypothalamus, through its influence on the pituitary gland, can send chemical messages (hormones) through the bloodstream to any part of the body.

Within a second or two after Bob's brain receives information about the bat, Bob's hypothalamus releases a hormone. This begins a series of actions which include raising blood pressure by narrowing arteries. The adrenal glands are stimulated to release glucocorticoids, epinephrine (also known as adrenaline), and norepinephrine (noradrenaline). As these chemicals circulate throughout the body, they create changes similar to those created by the arousal of the sympathetic nervous system. The glucocorticoids assist in the release of glucose from the liver, decrease inflammation, and inhibit the production of proteins needed by the immune system to resist disease. Heart rate and strength are increased by epinephrine. Norepinephrine causes blood vessels in the gut and kidney to constrict, making more blood available to the brain and muscles.

At the same time, other aspects of the limbic system are activated. The limbic system also has connections to the cortex of the brain. The cortex is responsible for the more complex activities of the brain, such as thought, speech, and memory. The limbic system is involved in recognizing the bat, deciding how Bob feels about its presence, and beginning a course of action.

The central nervous system controls the functions of the peripheral nervous system. The peripheral nervous system consists of the somatic and autonomic nervous systems. The somatic nervous system is responsible for sensory information coming into the brain from the environment. The somatic nervous system also controls the muscles which move the body. Somatic nerves carry information about the location of the bat and the position of the body to Bob's brain. They also carry messages to the muscles in Bob's arms to allow a net to be swung at the bat, or muscles in the mouth and vocal cords to allow a scream for help. People learn to control the somatic nerves which move these muscles without too much difficulty.

The autonomic nervous system is just as important and just as active, but people seldom learn to have conscious control over autonomic activities. The autonomic nervous system controls the muscles that make up the heart and circulatory system and maintains blood circulation throughout the body without any conscious effort. It also controls the organs responsible for digestion of food (the stomach and intestines) and elimination of wastes (bowel and bladder).

The autonomic nervous system, like the peripheral nervous system, has two divisions which work together by having the opposite influence on many major organs. The parasympathetic nervous system is active in the digestion of food and excretion of waste products. It also helps to regulate a steady resting heart rate. The sympathetic nervous system inhibits parasympathetic activity and reduces gastric acid secretion, salivation, and intestinal motion; it pulls resources away from the everyday activity of digestion.

The sympathetic nervous system becomes more active when a person needs to deal with a threatening situation. It prepares a person to fight an enemy or to flee from a dangerous situation. When the sympathetic nervous system is aroused, the pupils of the eyes dilate, letting in more light; the lungs expand and breathing is more rapid, making it possible to take in more oxygen; stored red blood cells are released from the spleen to carry the increased oxygen supply; sweat glands become more active, helping to cool an active body; and skin becomes less sensitive to pain, making it possible to continue fighting when injured. An inconvenient consequence of sympathetic activity is the relaxation of the sphincter muscles which close the bladder and bowel. For a wild animal, the loss of fluid and waste products makes it easier to run or fight. For a human being wearing clothing, the same sympathetic nervous system response can be inconvenient and embarrassing.

Epinephrine and norepinephrine, released by the adrenal glands, have some of the same effects as the sympathetic nervous system. The adrenal glands have an advantage in that they can function over a longer period of time than the small nerves and can continue the defensive readiness for days or months.

Applications

When stress results in the arousal of the nervous system, a person becomes more effective in dealing with many types of threat. Arousal may also cause problems when the body's response and the necessary actions do not correspond. Arousal of the sympathetic nervous system when an animal is threatened has an evolutionary advantage, as survival in a wild environment is made more likely when fighting efficiency is improved. This stress response does not always help a person to be more effective in dealing with the types of problems that modern people must face. When someone is threatened by a boss or a difficult task, response to the threat is more likely to require calm, thoughtful action than physical attack.

A man nervously waiting to make a speech may find it harder to speak when his mouth is dry as a result of the decreased salivation produced by sympathetic arousal. Increased sweating when being introduced to a future father-in-law can make hands clammy. A political argument during dinner can disrupt normal digestive functioning and create an upset stomach. Frequent trips to the bathroom to urinate may be necessary immediately before an important event. Athletes continue to play with injuries and risk further damage, only noticing the pain when the competition is over and arousal levels drop.

When the stressful incident does not last very long, the unwanted consequences of sympathetic nervous system arousal are usually little more than inconvenient. When the stressful incident continues for a long period of time, however, or when many stressors appear close together, the damaging effects of chronic stress can be seen.

When sympathetic nervous system arousal reduces blood supply to the stomach, it reduces the stomach's ability to produce its protective mucus lining. Only a few stressful hours may be enough to allow the digestive acids to destroy the muscle tissue of the stomach, causing an ulcer. Increased heart rate and pumping capacity are useful when arousal levels are high and physical activity increases the muscles' need for oxygen and glucose. High blood pressure over an extended period of time, however, makes it more likely that blood vessels in the brain will break, causing a stroke.

A normally functioning body has a strong immune system that can eliminate most disease-producing organisms, even before a person feels sick. When the immune system is not working well because of sympathetic arousal and an excess of glucocorticoids, the microorganisms in the body continue to grow and reproduce, and the symptoms of illness are more likely to appear. If the immune system is too weak to respond at all as a result of too many stressors or stress that has lasted too long, it is even possible to die from a disease that would normally be controlled by the body's defenses.

When the sympathetic arousal response to stress is extended, processes associated with growth and reproduction can also slow down. The depression of thyroid activity can inhibit growth. Puberty may be delayed, and menstrual cycles may be irregular or cease entirely. Reduction in testosterone in males may reduce the production of sperm and may reduce sexual drive and aggressive behavior.

Context

Hans Selye published a book called *The Stress of Life* in 1956; it significantly changed the way that psychologists understand stress and its relationship to illness. Selye proposed that all stressors are essentially the same thing. Any challenge or change that placed a demand on the body could be a stressor. Physical threats, such as extreme heat or cold, strenuous physical exertion, poisons, illness, and sleep loss, are stressors. Emotional stressors produce fear, excitement, or anger as well as the nervous-system responses related to stress. Even positive events such as a party or moving to a new town can create the physiological arousal associated with stress. Selye called this arousal response the general adaptation syndrome (GAS).

Selye predicted that extreme stress and long-term exposure to stress of any kind would make illness more likely. Thomas Holmes and Richard Rahe created the Life Scale of Recent Events which allows measurement of the number of stressful events experienced in the last year and assigns point values which reflect the potential severity of the stress. People with high scores have been found to be more likely to have a serious illness at some point in the two years following the stressful events. More recent studies have emphasized the negative consequences of the stressful event and whether the event was seen as threatening. The same event may make some people more likely to become ill, while others seem to be unaffected or strengthened by stressors.

Investigation of the effects of stress is important in the understanding of psychosomatic illness. Thoughts, feelings, and how a situation is understood can play an important role in producing physical change in the body. Increased understanding of the effects of stress on the nervous system has also led to a wide variety of treatments for stress-related illness, including biofeedback and relaxation training, exercise programs, cognitive therapies (which attempt to change the way one thinks about stressful events), and drug therapies. All these approaches attempt to step in at some stage in the reaction to stress and reduce the physiological arousal associated with stress and the problems caused by excess arousal.

Even when stressors are the same, the stress response in an individual is not always predictable. Differences in the ways people's bodies work and the way people interpret or cope with stressors can change their response. The nervous system's response to stressors is complex, but researchers are beginning to understand how stress can change people's bodies and how it can make them stronger. With further work, further reduction of the damaging effects of stress should become possible.

Bibliography

Bloom, Floyd E., and Arlyne Lazerson. *Brain, Mind, and Behavior.* 2d ed. New York: W. H. Freeman, 1988. Written to accompany the Public Broadcasting Service television series *The Brain.* Provides a clear description of the function of the nervous system, with many excellent illustrations. The section on stress describes many of the basic studies which have contributed to an understanding of the relationship between stress and the nervous system.

Charlesworth, Edward A., and Ronald G. Nathan. *Stress Management: A Comprehensive Guide to Wellness.* New York: Atheneum, 1984. Begins with an easy-to-understand description of the effects of stress on the nervous system. Most of the book covers assessment of the sources of stress in one's life and suggests how its negative effects can be reduced. Includes Holmes and Rahe's "social readjustment rating scale," as well as excellent and easy-to-follow instructions on relaxation.

Goliszek, Andrew G. *Breaking the Stress Habit.* Winston-Salem, N.C.: Carolina Press,

1987. Includes a more detailed description of the physiology of the stress response, questionnaires which allow one to examine one's own problems, and suggestions for the reduction of stress-related problems.

Holmes, Thomas H., and Minoru Masuda. "Psychosomatic Syndrome: When Mothers-in-Law or Other Disasters Visit, a Person Can Develop a Bad, Bad Cold. Or Worse." *Psychology Today* 5 (April, 1972): 71. An easy-to-understand summary of Holmes's work on the relationship between stress (in the form of life events) and illness.

Monat, Alan, and Richard S. Lazarus, eds. *Stress and Coping: An Anthology.* New York: Columbia University Press, 1977. This collection of articles and book excerpts is more technical than many of the other sources given here. Includes brief articles by many of the major researchers investigating stress response. Topics range from Selye's theory to examination of social factors in stress to religion and voodoo death.

Selye, Hans. *The Stress of Life.* New York: McGraw-Hill, 1956. An introduction to the theory relating stressors to physiological responses. Less complex than some of the more recent books, yet provides a good description of the relationship between stress and the body. Appropriate for a high school or college student with some understanding of basic biology and biological terminology.

Susan J. Shapiro

Cross-References

The Autonomic Nervous System, 362; The Central and Peripheral Nervous Systems, 494; General Adaptation Syndrome, 1068; Adaptation to Stress, 2390; Effects of Stress, 2417; Stress: Physiological Responses, 2425; Stress and the Endocrine System, 2445; Stress-Related Diseases, 2464; Stressors, 2471.

STRESS PREDICTION AND CONTROL

Type of psychology: Stress
Field of study: Coping

Foreknowledge of stress and various forms of control over potential or pending stressors affects the negative psychological and physiological effects of those stressors. The ability to predict and exercise some form of control over stressors is a useful and necessary addition to effective coping repertoires.

Principal terms
AVERSIVE: unpleasant, threatening, and/or painful
COGNITIVE: of or relating to thoughts or ideas
CONDITIONED: learned through the process of conditioning by association or through trial and error
HYPOTHESIS: a theoretical assumption or guess that is subject to proof or disproof
NONCONTINGENCY: nondependency or absence of any relationship between two variables
PSYCHOPHARMACOLOGICAL: pertaining to chemicals or drugs that have effects on mental states
STIMULUS: any action or situation that elicits a response; can be internal (thoughts, feelings) or external (people, events, sounds)
STRESSOR: a stimulus that produces a state of psychological or physiological tension

Overview

Stress is a ubiquitous phenomenon in human life. Though it may in some cases be beneficial, attention is ordinarily drawn to its negative effects. In that regard, stress is both a psychological and physiological response to aversive life events, situations, and stimuli, as well as to an accumulation of or overexposure to mundane stimuli or common hassles. Because of the primary or secondary role of stress in most medical and psychological pathology, stress management and coping exact considerable attention from both professionals and laypeople.

With rare exceptions, everyone faces—at some time or another in their lives—the necessity of experiencing a stressor that is unavoidable, such as the need to leave home for the first time, taking a crucial test for which one is unprepared, or undergoing a painful or life-threatening medical procedure. Most people would agree that being able to predict the onset and intensity of such stressors seems to make them somehow more tolerable. Prediction allows people to make defensive preparations, to develop new coping methods, and to brace themselves for the ordeal to come. As a matter of fact, prediction is apparently so important that humans would prefer to suffer a painful stressor immediately rather than tolerate an uncertain postponement.

In two 1966 studies, Pietro Badia and his colleagues found that humans given a choice of being shocked immediately or with a variable amount of delay showed a distinct preference for getting it over with immediately. If humans or animals must tolerate a delay in experiencing something stressful and unpleasant, it would appear that both prefer some sort of signal preceding and announcing that stressor. Badia and his colleagues demonstrated, for example, that rats not only preferred signaled shocks but also were willing to tolerate longer and more intense shocks, providing they were announced.

According to Russell G. Geen, two hypotheses have been proposed to account for the signal preferences. The first is the preparatory-response hypothesis, which suggests that the signal sets off automatic or conditioned anticipatory defense reactions, making the stressor more tolerable. The second is the safety-signal hypothesis, which proposes that the signal makes the intervening time until stressor onset more tolerable. Both hypotheses emphasize the notion that stressor predictability provides people with a sense of control that serves to moderate stress effects.

Humans are able to tolerate life better when they have, or believe they have, a fair amount of control over their day-to-day lives. Knowing what is happening is preferable to being in the dark, having a strategy or defense ready is preferable to being unprepared, and being able to avoid or terminate a stressor is better than sitting there and suffering. In 1973, James R. Averill described behavioral, cognitive, and decisional methods of stress control. He first delineated two kinds of behavioral control: self-regulation and stressor modification. With self-regulation, people can choose to self-administer the inescapable stressor, or they can choose when and/or where to suffer the stressor. Research has shown that humans prefer to self-administer painful stimuli such as electric shocks, a finding that mirrors the relatively common tendency for people to want, for example, to remove their own splinter.

Stressor modification, on the other hand, involves being able to escape, avoid, or reduce the aversiveness of the stressor. A number of studies have demonstrated, for example, that subjects who know that they have the means to terminate a stressor suffer less physical stress than subjects who believe that they have no control. Note that it is the individual's belief in his or her ability to control and not the actual exercise of control that appears to reduce the stress.

Frequently, however, people are powerless to self-regulate or modify a stressor. In those cases, information about the stressor can provide people with a sense of control through the use of cognitive processes. Cognitive processes can moderate or minimize the effects of stressors in several possible ways. For example, detailed prescience of a stressor allows the individual to focus on less harmful or threatening aspects of the stressor or to think about the stressor differently (to see it as a challenge rather than a threat). In addition, one can tolerate a stressor better by knowing the nature of the discomfort the stressor will cause and how the stressor will materialize. Research is generally supportive of the idea that having information about an otherwise uncontrollable stressor allows people to rid themselves of uncertainty about the stressor and to eliminate any stress resulting from that uncertainty.

Decision control has to do with the individual's perception that he or she is free to choose between alternative stressors. Despite how distasteful any two or three alternative aversive events may be, the freedom to choose between them tends to reduce the overall level of stress. Having choices—even unpleasant choices—gives one a sense of control and acts to moderate stress. On the other hand, the effects of a perceived loss or absence of control can result in reactance (a struggle to gain control) or, at the other extreme, a form of learned helplessness (a surrender to the stressor and all of its effects).

Applications

Stress prediction and control lends itself to a wide variety of mundane applications as well as to broader social and individual issues, such as crowding, learned helplessness, and individual differences in stress proneness.

In the physician's or dentist's office, many things take place that are stressful to the uninformed or timid soul. For example, an individual who is about to undergo his or her first root canal procedure may find the pending event threatening and consequently stressful. Stress in this case results from uncertainty about the qualitative effects of the procedure, expectations of pain and discomfort, and feelings of lack of control. Technology and training provide the contemporary dentist with the means to minimize pain and discomfort and to describe accurately the sensations associated with various aspects of the procedure. Such information provides the basis for cognitive control and a reduction in the overall level of stress. When behavioral control is impossible, information can become the instrumentality of control.

In general, humans seem to have a need for control, even in the absence of clearly identifiable stressors. A perceived lack of control in the face of ambient nonnoxious stimuli can also be stressful. How the individual responds to perceived lack of control forms the basis for the discussion of such phenomena as crowding, learned helplessness, and the Type A coronary stress-prone pattern.

As the earth's population increases, the effect of crowding on human behavior becomes a matter of increasing concern. There is a prevalent—but not universally held—view that crowding is stressful. There is, however, no consensus about the reasons for the stressfulness of crowding.

Those who study crowding generally agree that density is a necessary, but not sufficient, factor in crowding. Crowding is therefore regarded as a subjective aversive feeling that may or may not be related to objective density. Two hypotheses tie density to crowding. The first hypothesis suggests that feelings of crowding happen when density is perceived to constrain behavior, such as when heavy freeway traffic blocks freedom of movement. This loss of freedom is a threat to behavioral and decisional control that results in negative affect or stress.

The second hypothesis is that the individual feels crowded when the near presence of others is unpleasantly arousing or overstimulating. When overaroused, the individual suffers impaired coping and decision-making capabilities. Again, the perception of crowding is subjective and is often mitigated by situational or cultural norms.

For example, the density one comfortably sustains at the well-attended football game would likely be intolerable in one's own living room. Thus situational density norms moderate the feeling of loss of control, which, as suggested earlier, tends to be inherently stressful.

Elevators provide natural settings for studying the effects of crowding. There are many behavioral indicators of the increasing discomfort people suffer as the elevator fills to capacity. People stand facing the door with eyes cast downward, fixed straight ahead, or focused on the elevator floor indicator as if exercising some form of psychokinesis. Occupants generally attempt to maintain some semblance of interpersonal spacing, however crowded the elevator becomes. Only the individuals standing by—and commanding—the control panels manifest something different in the way of behavior as they press the buttons. Indeed, in 1978, Judith Rodin and her colleagues found that elevator occupants who stand away from elevator controls report feeling more crowded, more aroused, and less in control.

Generally speaking, when individuals perceive a loss of control in the face of an imminent stressor, there is an attempt to adjust or cope with the stressor (for example, to reestablish control by running away from it). There are times, however, when the means of regaining control is not manifest—when there is no apparent way to cope. In the absence of any control, the individual may develop a sense of helplessness that causes him or her to suffer the stressor and its effects. Sometimes after repeated instances of an inability to control outcomes, the individual may develop the belief that he or she is incapable of coping, even in cases where the means of control exist. This generalization of one's inability to control and to suffer whatever the stressor has to hand out is called "learned helplessness."

That learned helplessness exists is probably not arguable. Depressed patients often manifest an unreasonable resignation to whatever might go wrong. Some people attribute the passivity of Jews in Nazi extermination camps to the phenomenon of learned helplessness. Some evidence, however, tends to suggest that learned helplessness in the face of stressors of any kind is not so much the result of noncontingency between behavior and outcomes as it is a function of personality and attributional style.

Some humans carry on a mighty struggle for control of themselves and their surroundings, while others manifest no such need. People who manifest the competitive, hostile, impatient, and aggressive characteristics that typify the Type A coronary stress-prone pattern seem, according to David Glass, to react to threats to their control and freedom with vigorous actions to regain their sense of command. If the Type A person's struggle to regain control is unsuccessful, frustration, exhaustion, and a drastic decrease in attempts to control will follow. Repeated failure at attempts to control robs Type A people of their motivation and renders them helpless.

Context

According to Charles Spielberger, the term "stress" is a Latin derivative that was "first used during the 17th century to describe distress, oppression, hardship, and adversity." In the eighteenth and nineteenth centuries, the meaning of stress changed to that of some pressure or force acting on a physical object or person resulting in some form of strain, possibly the basis for the colloquial phrase "stress and strain." During the nineteenth century, speculation about the connection between stress and illness began, but it was not until the early twentieth century that professionals, such as the distinguished Canadian physician Sir William Osler, began to make the connection between stress, worry, and heart disease.

The massive contemporary interest in stress, its ill effects, and its management, including prediction and control, found its impetus in the work of physician and researcher, Hans Selye. In 1936, Selye described a systematic and progressive physiological reaction to unremitting stressors that he called the general adaptation syndrome (GAS) or the biologic stress syndrome. Selye's work highlights the human body's innate defensive response to perceived threats, whether physical or psychological, internal or external.

Much has been learned about the details of the physiological stress reaction since 1936, especially about the role of the sympathetic nervous system and hormones. This acquired knowledge has led to the discovery of psychopharmacological agents (for example, tranquilizers) that control, relieve, or combat the physical and mental effects of stress. Such remedies, however, require medical prescription and supervision, do not eliminate or affect stress at its origins, and provide only symptomatic relief.

Increasing attention has therefore been given to nonchemical means of controlling or eliminating stress and its effects. Such means include relaxation techniques, lifestyle changes, biofeedback techniques, and the development of behavioral, cognitive, and decisional controls over stressors. Researchers have also investigated other possible influential factors, such as individual differences in stress vulnerability or proneness as well as individual differences in stress perception.

Stress prediction and control as a means of softening or eliminating stress will be a continuing subject of research and individual stress management development for the foreseeable future. The effects of relaxation techniques and stress prediction and control on stress effects accentuate the human potential for self-prevention, control, and healing of stress effects. Maximizing and mastering this human potential has highly beneficial portents for health, happiness, and the lowering of health care costs.

Bibliography

Averill, James R. "Personal Control over Aversive Stimuli and Its Relationship to Stress." *Psychological Bulletin* 80, no. 4 (1973): 286-303. Original presentation of author's descriptive hypothetical scheme for behavioral, cognitive, and decisional control of stressors.

Geen, Russell G. "The Psychology of Stress." In *Personality: The Skein of Behavior.* St. Louis: C. V. Mosby, 1976. Survey of research relating to helplessness, uncertainty, stress, and control.

Geen, Russell G., William W. Beatty, and Robert M. Arkin. "Stress and Motivation." In *Human Motivation: Physiological, Behavioral, and Social Approaches.* Boston: Allyn & Bacon, 1984. Addresses stress prediction and control, including principal applications to such phenomena as crowding and learned helplessness.

Goldberger, Leo, and Shlomo Breznitz, eds. *Handbook of Stress: Theoretical and Clinical Aspects.* New York: Free Press, 1982. Comprehensive compendium of articles by noted researchers of stress processes, stressors, treatment, management, and support.

Spielberger, Charles Donald. *Understanding Stress and Anxiety.* New York: Harper & Row, 1979. Stress manual by a stress researcher and specialist. Discusses what stress is, what its sources are, and how to adjust to and live with others.

Ronald G. Ribble

Cross-References

Coping Strategies: An Overview, 706; Crowding, 744; Adaptation to Stress, 2390; Stress: Behavioral and Psychological Responses, 2397; Stress: Cognitive Appraisals, 2404; Effects of Stress, 2417; Theories of Stress, 2432; Stressors, 2471.

STRESS-RELATED DISEASES

Type of psychology: Stress
Field of study: Stress and illness

As a person experiences stress, physical responses occur that have been associated with a host of physical diseases. Understanding the stress-disease relationship, including how to control and lower stress levels, is important in maintaining a healthful life.

Principal terms
> BIOFEEDBACK: a procedure in which one's biological functions are monitored and immediately fed back to the person so that control over these functions can be learned
> GENERAL ADAPTATION SYNDROME: a general pattern of biological reactions to stressors consisting of three stages—the alarm stage, the resistance stage, and the exhaustion stage
> LOCUS OF CONTROL: beliefs concerning the sources of power over one's life; persons who believe they can generally control the direction of their lives have an internal locus of control, and those who believe that their lives are influenced more by fate have an external locus of control
> STRESSOR: the agent, circumstance, or demand that causes stress
> TYPE A PERSONALITY: a set of personality characteristics that includes impatience, competitiveness, hostility, cynicism, and a sense of constant pressure
> TYPE B PERSONALITY: a set of personality characteristics that includes low levels of impatience, competitiveness, hostility, and cynicism, and a more relaxed, easygoing attitude toward life

Overview

The term "stress," as it is used in the field of psychology, may be defined as the physical or psychological disturbance an individual experiences as a result of what that individual perceives to be an adverse or challenging circumstance. Four observations concerning this definition of stress should be made. First, stress is what the individual experiences, not the circumstance causing the stress (the stressor). Second, individuals differ in what they perceive to be stressful. What may be very stressful for one individual may not be at all stressful for another. Hans Selye, the researcher who did more than anyone else to make the medical community and the general population aware of the concept and consequences of stress, once noted that, for him, spending the day on the beach doing nothing would be extremely stressful. This difference in people's perceptions is behind the familiar concept that events do not cause stress. Instead, stress comes from one's perception or interpretation of events.

Third, stress occurs in response to circumstances that are seen as negative, but stress may also arise from challenging circumstances, even positive ones. The well-known Social Readjustment Rating Scale developed by Thomas Holmes and Richard Rahe includes both positive and negative life events. A negative event, such as the death of a spouse, is clearly stressful; however, marriage, generally viewed as a positive life event, can also be stressful. Fourth, stressors can lead to stress-related disturbances that are psychological, physiological, or both. The psychological response is rather unpredictable. A given stressor may result in one individual responding with anger, another with depression, and another with a new determination to succeed.

The physiological response is more predictable. Beginning in the 1930's, Selye began studying the human response to stressors. Eventually he identified what he termed the general adaptation syndrome (GAS) to describe the typical pattern of physical responses. Selye divided the GAS into three stages: alarm, resistance, and exhaustion.

The first stage begins when an individual becomes frightened, anxious, or even merely concerned. The body immediately undergoes numerous physical changes to cope with the stressor. Metabolism speeds up. Heart and respiration rates increase. The hormones epinephrine, norepinephrine, and cortisol are secreted. Sugar is released from the liver. The muscles tense. Blood shifts from the internal organs to the skeletal musculature. These and a host of other changes are aimed at helping the body cope, but the price paid for this heightened state of arousal typically includes symptoms such as headache, upset stomach, sleeplessness, fatigue, diarrhea, and loss of appetite. The body's increase in alertness and energy is accompanied by a lowered state of resistance to illness.

Obviously, people cannot remain in the alarm stage for long. If the stressor is not removed, the body enters the resistance stage—a stage which may last from minutes to days or longer. During this stage, the body seeks to adapt to the stressor. The physical changes that occurred during the alarm stage subside. Resistance to illness is actually increased to above-normal levels. Because the body is still experiencing stress, however, remaining in this stage for a long period will eventually lead to physical and psychological exhaustion—the exhaustion stage.

Selye has noted that over the course of life, most people go through the first two stages many, many times. Such is necessary to adapt to the demands and challenges of life. The real danger is found in not eliminating the stressor. During the exhaustion stage, the body is very vulnerable to disease and in extreme cases may suffer collapse and death. Although newer research has found subtle differences in the stress response, depending on the stressor involved, the basic findings of Selye have continued to be supported. Moreover, specific illnesses are caused or promoted by stress.

For many years Americans have been aware of the relationship between stress and heart disease. The biochemical changes associated with stress lead to higher blood pressure, an increased heart rate, and a release of fat into the bloodstream. If the fat is completely consumed by the muscles through physical activity (for example, defending oneself from an attacker), no serious health consequences follow. If, however, a person experiences stress without engaging in physical activity (a more common scenario in Western culture), the fat is simply deposited on the walls of the blood vessels. As these fatty deposits accumulate, life is threatened.

The work of two cardiologists, Meyer Friedman and Ray Rosenman, is of particular importance to a discussion of heart disease and stress. Friedman and Rosenman demonstrated, based originally on personal observation and subsequently on clinical research, that there is a personality type that is particularly prone to heart disease. The personality type that is at the greatest risk was found to be one which is highly stressed—impatient, hostile, hard-driving, and competitive. They termed this a Type A personality. The low-risk person, the Type B personality, is more patient, easygoing, and relaxed.

Numerous studies have examined health based on the Type A–Type B concept. Virtually all have supported Friedman and Rosenman's conclusions. One major report, however, did not; subsequent analysis of that report and other research generally has indicated that the aspects of the Type A personality which are threatening to one's health are primarily the hostility, cynicism, and impatience, not the desire to achieve.

Stomach ulcers are another health problem long known to be caused or aggravated by stress. Stress leads to an increase in the production of digestive acids and pepsinogen. When pepsinogen levels are abnormally high, the lining of the stomach is destroyed. Research with laboratory rats has demonstrated that even rats, when placed under high levels of stress, produce additional pepsinogen and develop stomach ulcers. Thus, the adage sometimes spoken by gastroenterologists, "It's not what you eat, it's what eats you," has merit.

A newer area of research that is even more fundamental to understanding how stress is related to disease involves the immune system. As the physiological changes associated with stress occur, the immune system is suppressed. The immune system has two primary functions: to identify and destroy hazardous foreign materials called antigens (these include bacteria, viruses, parasites, and fungi) and to identify and destroy the body's own cells that have undergone changes associated with malignancy. Thus, if the immune system is suppressed, the body is less able to detect and defend against a host of diseases. An example of this effect again involves research with laboratory rats. One such investigation involved placing tumor cells in the bodies of rats. Some of the rats were then exposed to an abundance of stress. Those that were given this treatment were less resistant to the cancer. Their tumors were larger, and they developed sooner than those found in the "low-stress" rats.

As research continues, the number of specific diseases that can be linked to stress grows. A partial alphabetical listing of stress-related diseases and disorders for which recent research is available would include acne, asthma, cancers (many types), coronary thrombosis, diabetes mellitus, gastric ulcers, herpes simplex (types 1 and 2), human immunodeficiency virus (HIV) infection, infertility, migraine headache, mononucleosis syndrome, rheumatoid arthritis, streptococcal infection, stroke, systemic lupus erythematosus, and tuberculosis.

It should be emphasized that few, if any, of these physical problems are caused solely by stress. Many other factors influence risk, including genetic composition, gender, race, environmental conditions, nutritional state, and so forth. Nevertheless, stress is frequently an important factor in determining initial resistance as well as the subsequent course of a given disease.

Applications

Why is it that some individuals who appear to live with many stressors generally avoid physical and psychological illness? Understanding the answer to that question is important, because it can provide insight as to what the average person can and should do to lower stress levels. Dispositional factors (optimistic versus pessimistic, easygoing versus hard-driving, friendly versus hostile) are probably most important in determining one's stress level. The Type A-Type B research noted above is an example of research demonstrating the influence of dispositional factors.

Research with twins has found that temperament is largely inborn; however, any individual can choose to be more optimistic, generous, and patient. Norman Cousins is often cited as an example of a person who decided to change his outlook and mental state in order to preserve his life. He had read Selye's *The Stress of Life* (1956), which describes how negative emotions can cause physical stress and subsequent disease. Cousins, who had a rare and painful illness from which he was told he would likely never recover, decided that if negative emotions could harm one's health, then positive emotions could possibly return one's health.

As Cousins describes his experience in *Anatomy of an Illness as Perceived by the Patient* (1979), he left his hospital room for a more pleasant environment, began trading massive doses of drugs for television comedies and laughter, and decided to stop worrying. To the surprise of his medical team, his recovery began at once. Though this now-classic example is only anecdotal, the research on disposition and stress would support the assumption that Cousins' decision to change his mental state and stop worrying—not his avoidance of traditional medical care—was the truly important influence.

A related area of research has investigated how psychological hardiness helps people resist stress. Studies by Suzanne Kobasa and her colleagues examined business executives who all had an obvious abundance of stressors in their lives. In comparing those hardy individuals who handled the stressors well with the nonhardy individuals, the researchers found that the two groups differed in three important but basic ways.

The first was commitment. Stress-resistant executives typically possessed a clear sense of values. They had clear goals and a commitment to those goals. Less hardy executives were more likely to feel alienation. The second was challenge. The hardy executives welcomed challenges and viewed change rather than stability as the norm in life. Their less healthy counterparts viewed change with alarm. The third factor was control. The hardy executives felt more in control of their lives. This aspect of Kobasa's research overlaps with research conducted since the 1960's involving a concept known as the "locus of control." People with an internal locus of control are those individuals who believe they are influential rather than powerless in controlling the direction of their lives. This area of research has also found that such a belief lowers stress.

Many years ago it was estimated that more than a thousand studies had been completed that examined the relationship between physical fitness and mental health. What has emerged from this heavily researched area is a clear conclusion: Exercise can lower stress levels. Though regular, sustained aerobic exercise is generally advocated, research has found that even something as simple as a daily ten-minute walk can have measurable beneficial effects. Why does exercise lower stress levels? There are several possible explanations—the increased production of neurotransmitters (such as the endorphins that influence mood), the emotional benefit of feeling more physically fit, and the benefit of distracting one's mind from immediate problems are commonly suggested; however, the research as to why exercise is beneficial is still inconclusive.

Another approach to reducing stress involves learning to evoke a physical "relaxation response," a term coined by Harvard Medical School cardiologist Herbert Benson. Benson became intrigued by the ability of some people who practice meditation to lower their blood pressure, heart rate, and oxygen consumption voluntarily. He discovered that the process is not at all mystical and can be easily taught. The process involves getting comfortable, closing the eyes, breathing deeply, relaxing muscles, and relaxing one's mind by focusing on a simple word or phrase.

Others are helped by using an electronic device which closely monitors subtle physiological changes. By observing these changes (typically on a monitor), a person can, for example, learn to slow down a heart rate. This is known as biofeedback training. Many other techniques and suggestions arising from research as well as common sense can lower stress. A strong social support system has been found to be very important; disciplining oneself not to violate one's own value system is essential. Even having a pet that needs love and attention has been found to lower stress.

Context

A general recognition that a relationship exists between mind and body is at least as old as the biblical Old Testament writings. In the book of Proverbs, for example, one reads, "A cheerful heart is good medicine,/ but a crushed spirit dries up the bones" (Proverbs 17:22). Hippocrates (460-377 B.C.), generally considered the "father of medicine," sought to understand how the body could heal itself and what factors could slow or prevent this process. He clearly perceived a relationship between physical health and what we now term "stress," though his understanding was shallow.

Several physiologists of the nineteenth century made contributions; however, it was not until the twentieth century that the classic studies of American physiologist Walter B. Cannon proved the link scientifically. Cannon and his student Phillip Bard began their analysis of stress and physiological arousal to disprove the idea espoused by others, that emotion follows physiological arousal.

Cannon found a variety of stressors that led to the release of the hormones adrenaline and noradrenaline (or, properly now, epinephrine and norepinephrine). Heat, cold, oxygen deprivation, and fright all led to hormonal changes as well as a number of additional physiological adaptations. Cannon was excited about this discovery and impressed with the body's remarkable ability to react to stressors. All these changes were aimed at preparing the body for what Cannon termed the "fight-or-flight" response. It was Selye's task to build on Cannon's work. His description of the reaction subsequently termed the general adaptation syndrome first appeared in a scientific journal in 1936. As knowledge of the stress concept began to spread, interest by the public as well as the research community increased.

Literally tens of thousands of stress research studies conducted throughout the world have been completed during the last half of the twentieth century. Of particular importance was the discovery by three American scientists that the brain produces morphinelike antistress substances. The discovery of these substances, named endorphins, won the 1977 Nobel Prize for the scientists involved and opened a whole new area of research.

The hope remains that someday an endorphin-type drug could be used to counter some of the unhealthy effects of stress, ensuring better health and longer lives. Better health and longer lives are available even today, however, for all people who are willing to make life-style changes based on current knowledge.

Bibliography

Brown, Barbara B. *Between Health and Illness.* Boston: Houghton Mifflin, 1984. One of many books available for the nonprofessional who simply wants an overview of stress and its consequences. This easy-to-read book is full of accurate information and practical suggestions.

Friedman, Meyer, and Diane Ulmer. *Treating Type A Behavior—and Your Heart.* New York: Knopf, 1984. This is an easily read book on preventing heart disease by changing one's life-style. Presents the results of a large research project and relates relevant research. The first author, Meyer Friedman, along with fellow cardiologist Ray Rosenman, also authored the classic *Type A Behavior and Your Heart* (New York: Alfred A. Knopf, 1974).

Managing Stress: From Morning to Evening. Alexandria, Va.: Time-Life Books, 1987. A very good introduction to understanding and managing stress. Written in clear, simple language and widely available, it provides an overview of the sources of stress, the physiological changes associated with stress, the effects of stress on the immune system, the way to assess one's own stress level, and suggestions for numerous approaches to managing stress. Full of illustrations and photographs. A weakness is that the book fails to address adequately the importance of dispositional factors, focusing too heavily on some stress-reduction techniques that few are likely to use.

Pelletier, Kenneth R. *Mind as Healer, Mind as Slayer.* New York: Dell Books, 1977. This well-known work examines how stress contributes to heart disease, cancer, arthritis, migraine, and respiratory disease. Sources of stress, evaluation of personal stress levels, profiles of unhealthy personality traits, and means of preventing stress-related diseases are addressed.

Selye, Hans. *The Stress of Life.* Rev. ed. New York: McGraw-Hill, 1976. Originally published in 1956, this is the most influential book ever written about stress. It focuses on the relationship between a stressful life and subsequent illness, but it is very technical. Those wanting a less difficult introduction to Selye's writings and work should read his *Stress Without Distress.*

_____. *Stress Without Distress.* New York: New American Library, 1975. Written by the pioneering researcher who discovered and named what is known as the general adaptation syndrome. Describes that syndrome and discusses how to handle stress so as not to suffer the physical declines that so often arise from excessive stress.

Timothy S. Rampey

Cross-References

Biofeedback and Relaxation, 416; Endorphins, 973; General Adaptation Syndrome, 1068; Adaptation to Stress, 2390; Stress: Behavioral and Psychological Responses, 2397; Stress: Physiological Responses, 2425; Stress and the Endocrine System, 2445; Stress and the Nervous System, 2452; Stressors, 2471; The Type A Behavior Pattern, 2597.

STRESSORS

Type of psychology: Stress
Fields of study: Coping; critical issues in stress; stress and illness

Stressors are the circumstances or events that cause stress—a "nonspecific" condition that may harm almost any part of a person. Stressors range from the catastrophic, such as the death of a loved one, to the seemingly harmless, such as getting a parking ticket; alone or in combination, all can harm a person in a general way that may not immediately be recognized.

> *Principal terms*
>
> COPING: effectively dealing with an event to reduce or eliminate the harm it might cause
>
> FIGHT-OR-FLIGHT RESPONSE: a set of related bodily responses, mediated by the autonomic nervous system, that prepare a person or animal for reacting to an emergency
>
> GENERAL ADAPTATION SYNDROME: a series of three responses—alarm, resistance, and exhaustion—that occur when a person faces stressors
>
> HASSLES: sometimes called "mini-stressors," these are minor problems that may lead to harm as they accumulate
>
> STRESS: the rate of wear and tear on a person (in Hans Selye's definition), determined by stressors, one's vulnerabilities, and the coping skills that one uses as protection

Overview

The term "stressor" became a part of psychology's vocabulary shortly after physician Hans Selye published *The Stress of Life* (1956), an extraordinarily popular book that caught the attention of thousands of people outside the medical community, including many psychologists. Much earlier, Walter Cannon had studied the "fight-or-flight" response—a set of bodily changes that occur when one faces an emergency. The fighting or running away puts heavy demands on an individual, but the response usually is of short duration, ending when the emergency does.

Selye focused attention on the long-term biological consequences of continually facing a wide range of perceived emergencies, or stressors; he was concerned with the bodily harm they can produce. The psychologists inspired by his ideas continued to look at bodily harm but went further, to study psychological harm as well. They also began attempts to measure the amount of stress produced by a number of circumstances and events that most people face. To understand the nature of stressors, one must have a working knowledge of the concept of "stress" as Selye conceived it. Defined by him as "the rate of wear and tear on the body," it represents general harm, often not repairable, that may be expected to lead to various specific symptoms, to hastened aging, and (in the extreme) to destruction of the body through death.

If a person is unlucky enough to break a leg in a skiing accident, the harm is specific. Crashing into a tree, for example, exerts enough force to break the bone, causing harm that is immediate and obvious to anyone. That same accident could, under certain circumstances, also produce the nonspecific harm called stress. For example, if the skiing-accident victim were a professional dancer or professional football player, the broken leg might put the person out of work. Being without expected income might force the person to file for bankruptcy, and the related circumstances might jeopardize the person's marriage and family life. Even in combination, such events will not break another bone, but as Selye demonstrated, they may set off a set of chemical changes in the body that produce, or at least activate, a variety of "diseases of adaptation." The unlucky skier may sometime later develop a stress-induced ulcer, asthma, the skin disease psoriasis, or a host of other diseases.

Stressors, then, do their harm indirectly and—to the naïve victim—unexpectedly or unpredictably. Although the person may be painfully aware of a stressor's presence, the ultimate consequences of experiencing it often remain obscure. Once a demanding situation has passed, a person may believe that by coping with it he or she has escaped its influence. Specific issues in the situation may have been successfully handled, but the stress it generated can remain. Selye speaks of "conditioning factors"—such as heredity, previous experience, and diet—that influence how a particular person will react to stress. The same stressors, present to the same degree, may lead to arthritis in one person, to high blood pressure in another, and to no harm at all in a third.

Very likely, folk wisdom has until recently been more concerned with stressors and their impact than have physicians or others who worked to explain and treat illness. Once naturalistic, scientific explanations of illness came into favor, specific and demonstrable cause-effect relationships were sought—often with great success. The fact that specific explanations allowed physicians to prevent or cure a particular disease was enough to divert attention from the wide-ranging effects of stressors. Yet sufferers themselves of what today would be considered stress-induced physical or mental illnesses very likely suspected that pressures, hard times, or whatever unpleasant long-term circumstances they were experiencing prior to the illness had "worn them down" so that it could strike.

Folk wisdom also has long recognized another aspect of stressors that can have both general practical value and specific medical value under the right conditions. A stressor can goad a person, either at the psychological or the physiological level, into effectively marshalling a defense against an already existing problem. If the problem is, for example, boredom with one's job, the threat of having to fight not to lose that job may make one work more effectively. If the problem is a chronic illness, such as rheumatoid arthritis, fighting off a modest new stressor may, at least temporarily, ease the pain from the illness.

Except when they can be used as weapons against a psychological or physiological problem, stressors are usually thought of as something to avoid. It would probably be more reasonable, however, to suggest that they could be controlled or balanced, one against another. In *The Stress of Life*, Selye presents a "stress quotient," a comparison of the amount of stress on one part of the body to the amount on the body as a whole. He argues that when one part is much more strongly affected than the others, the person needs diversion or that part will fail, disrupting the entire system. As grim, but telling, support for his recommendations, Selye states that in the many autopsies he performed as a physician, he never found a person who had truly died of old age—that is, of equal, incurable harm to the entire organism. Rather, he always found that the failure of one organ had destroyed the system and thereby killed the person.

Applications

The main application of the stressor concept today is as a guide to avoiding certain unpleasant circumstances and to balancing others, that cannot be avoided, with pleasant experiences in order to preserve mental and bodily health—and sometimes even life itself. Even without the insights provided by Selye and expanded upon by those following him, people have been aware of what are now labeled stressors and have tried to avoid some of them. Without being concerned about the fact that stressors create a nonspecific reaction—that is, one that endangers the person as a system, not simply one part of the person—or understanding that extended exposure to them is hastening wear and tear on their bodies, people have long recognized that many stressors are very uncomfortable, causing feelings ranging from vague discomfort to undeniable pain.

Many of the events now recognized as stressors, however, are not extremely noxious. Being burned is a stressor in addition to being the source of specific tissue damage, and people avoid dangerously hot things because of the pain associated with the specific damage. Being deeply dissatisfied with one's work is also a stressor, yet it does not carry with it pain comparable to being burned; many people remain in jobs they hate because they need the work or because the pay is better than for work that would please them more. Tolerating a single modest stressor because of the benefits associated with it may be a reasonable choice, but ignoring or tolerating a combination of stressors because no one of them is too aggravating is courting danger. Research begun by Richard Lazarus indicates that even very minor stressors, ones he terms "hassles," can accumulate, creating effects that rival those of major stressors.

Readers of Selye's works can recognize examples that fit them all too well and can use some of his recommendations to cope with the stressors involved. For example, Selye writes of the frustrations he found in many committee meetings; he confesses that when he could not avoid or escape them, he would disengage himself and "float," remaining there physically but not mentally or emotionally.

Many books and articles other than Selye's also offer explanations of the concept of stressors and advice about how to manage them. Often the first steps in managing stressors are to recognize which ones are present, and to what degree. For many people, identification and measurement have come from the often-published Social Readjustment Rating Scale, devised by Thomas Holmes and Richard Rahe. This scale assigns numerical values to various life changes that represent the stress level involved; a minor violation of the law, for example, is assigned a value of 11, whereas the death of a spouse has a value of 100. Most introductory college psychology texts contain the scale, giving students the opportunity to see what other people find stressful and to learn how their own experiences of these events compare with those of others. Learning that others with a level of stress comparable to one's own have suffered physical illness more often than those with lower levels can be a sobering but useful bit of information. Thoughtful individuals may be able to make at least a few changes in their life-styles to bring their own levels of stress within safe limits.

Organizations and businesses may be interested in reducing the stress levels of their members to increase satisfaction and decrease absenteeism. If industrial psychologists can identify circumstances within a corporation that serve as stressors, changing them may be well worth the effort and expense. If a psychologist can identify people within a corporation who are "stress carriers," teaching them how to behave differently may also be worth the effort. (A stress carrier is much like a person who, while not personally being ill with a disease, infects those nearby: While this person does not personally feel stress, his or her behavior creates stressors for others.)

A few cautions are needed regarding activities purported to reduce stressors, whether at the individual or organizational level, or whether on the physical or psychological level. Even when the activities are well-designed by knowledgeable people, they may be counterproductive. Modest, balanced stressors may help, rather than harm, those facing them, and their elimination may not be wise. Moreover, as the concept of stress has gained popularity, unscrupulous "experts" have appeared who claim to be able to reduce stress through various techniques—mostly methods that are expensive to the individuals or organizations who decide to implement them. Stress, and the stressors that create it, are real enough, but many proposed approaches to their reduction or management are not.

A very different application of the concept of stressors was made by early physicians to try to treat disorders otherwise beyond them: They would introduce physical stressors to capitalize on the curative effects of the body's defensive responses. Applying leeches to the skin or, especially, "bleeding" a person could trigger what Selye calls the "stage of resistance" in his general adaptation syndrome. It is unlikely, however, that those who carried out such practices included anything like stressors in the rationale for using them. Medical practice of today recognizes that producing mild stress or directly administering substances that the body naturally produces as a response to stress may prove beneficial. An example of the latter is the use of cortisone to reduce the inflammation of arthritis.

Activities that challenge people in unusual ways—for example, ones that expose sedate executives to the rigors of mountain climbing to build self-confidence in inter-personal relations—include many mild stressors, and often they achieve their spe-cific goals by generating the nonspecific stress response.

Context

Scientific psychology advances by producing discrete pieces of evidence and theo-retical frameworks to organize the pieces. Sometimes the production of pieces and the creation of frameworks keep pace with each other; sometimes they do not. When Selye began popularizing his ideas on stress and stressors, many pieces—bits of data, limited theories, specific practices—that seemed unrelated began to fall into place in the framework he provided.

Perhaps most important, his theorizing provided a broad, general explanation for "psychosomatic illnesses," cases of genuine physical disorders believed to arise from or be worsened by events in a patient's environment. For centuries, people accepted the notion that outside pressures could do inner damage, but the complexity of the relationship was troublesome. The same pressures seemed to cause different damage in different people. Moreover, different pressures seemed to cause the same dam-age—or none at all—in different people, or at different times. The idea that stress-ors impact the entire person and that the weakest link in that person's system is likely to be damaged was an elegantly simple and very useful framework.

On the other side of the coin, people for centuries have accepted the notion that challenges, both physical and mental, often strengthen a person. Selye's work dem-onstrated that the defenses created by a specific challenge (stressor) will spread throughout the body, often helping in areas far removed from that challenge.

Looking for a common denominator among the many circumstances that create psychological and physiological stress, Holmes and Rahe worked from the assump-tion that psychological stressors force people to make social readjustments. The au-thors prepared a list of circumstances ranging from catastrophic through probably innocuous, then had subjects rate them on a scale (with 100 points used for the most severe). On the basis of the mean ratings, they assigned life change unit (LCU) values to the circumstances. Their work introduced the interesting notion that pleas-ant events as well as unpleasant ones necessitating change would precipitate stress.

Holmes and Rahe's scale has been widely used, and the claim that people with higher scores are more vulnerable to illness has been very often supported. Their idea that a favorable readjustment (from winning a lottery or receiving a promotion at work, for example) could be as great a stressor as a miserable readjustment was only partly supported by other researchers, but it did suggest areas for other re-searchers to explore in fitting the pieces into the stressor jigsaw puzzle.

Lazarus and his colleagues questioned Holmes and Rahe's emphasis on high-value events from their scale—the death of a spouse, for example—as determiners of stress levels. They argued that extreme events tend also to be infrequent ones, while very modest stressors continually bombard everyone daily. The suggestion that "hassles" become powerful through their cumulative effect and the demonstration that they, like catastrophes, can be used to predict the onset of illness have added to the growing understanding of stress.

Bibliography

Brown, Barbara B. *New Mind, New Body: Biofeedback—New Directions for the Mind.* New York: Harper & Row, 1974. Chapter 8, "Blood Pressure: Blood Vessels and Social Tension," of this classic popular introduction to biofeedback clearly describes how people can make only mildly noxious stimuli into stressors and how psychosomatic illnesses can be learned. Suggests how the power of stressors can be reduced through biofeedback training. Should be available in most libraries.

Holmes, Thomas H., and Richard H. Rahe. "The Social Readjustment Rating Scale." *Journal of Psychosomatic Research* 11, no. 2 (1967): 213-218. A now-classic article describing a first attempt to catalog and measure stressors common in American society. The authors' work continues to be cited as an ingenious approach to quantifying stressors.

Kanner, Allen D., James C. Coyne, Catherine Shaefer, and Richard S. Lazarus. "Comparison of Two Modes of Stress Measurement: Daily Hassles and Uplifts Versus Major Life Events." *Journal of Behavioral Medicine* 4, no. 1 (1981): 1-39. Working from different assumptions from those of Holmes and Rahe, the authors focus not on major life events but on the ever-present minor challenges that people face; they look at the frustration that "hassles" produce. They argue that minor events have a cumulative effect that gives them real power.

Selye, Hans. *The Stress of Life.* New York: McGraw-Hill, 1956. Selye had been publishing on stress in medical journals for twenty years when this book appeared, granting him popular acclaim almost immediately. In places it is detailed and complex, but it is organized in such a way that almost anyone can read selected portions and understand most of the points. Clear and engaging, reflecting a zest for scholarship not often encountered. Should be found in most libraries.

Weiten, Wayne. *Psychology: Themes and Variations.* 2d ed. Pacific Grove, Calif.: Brooks/Cole, 1991. Since Selye's work on stress attracted the attention of psychologists, nearly all introductory texts have contained simplified discussions of it and of work by others that preceded and followed it. Weiten's text, likely to be found in many college bookstores, is one of the best: easy and interesting to read, yet strong in its coverage of scientific psychology. His chapter "Stress, Coping, and Health" is an excellent source of information.

Harry A. Tiemann, Jr.

Cross-References

STRUCTURALISM

Type of psychology: Origin and definition of psychology
Fields of study: Descriptive methodologies; experimental methodologies; methodological issues

Structuralism was the first formal scientific approach to studying the mind. Derived from associationist philosophy, it sought to define the primitive sensory elements of experience and determine the mental processes by which they combined into everyday consciousness. Structuralism anticipated modern cognitive psychology, but its use of introspection was problematic and prompted the development of several other important systems of defining psychology.

Principal terms
ASSOCIATIONISM: a theory of knowledge and meaning in which events leave traces (ideas) of their occurrence in the mind; these are linked on the basis of certain basic principles such as contiguity, similarity, differences, and contingency
INTROSPECTION: the process by which trained "observers" analyzed and reported on the context of their own conscious experience
PSYCHOPHYSICS: the application of specific methods of research and mathematical analysis to allow quantifying the magnitude of subjective sensory experience
REDUCTIONISM: an aspect of the scientific method which seeks to understand complex and often interactive processes by reducing them to more basic components and principles
STIMULUS ERROR: the tendency to report the content and nature of conscious experience in terms of complex past associations or processes rather than individual conscious elements

Overview

The central problem for philosophy can be summed up in a question: Is knowledge possible? Most people have reflected on the possibility that what they take to be "reality"—the contents of their daily conscious mental life—might be filled with false beliefs. One could misperceive, have hallucinations and delusions, be in a lifelong dream, or, for all one really knows, be a disembodied brain in a beaker in a laboratory.

The British associationist philosophers argued that human consciousness is initially underdeveloped, a "blank slate." It is able to grow, however, by the mental association, or tying together, of many simple sensory experiences. These sensory events were believed to be closely tied to activity in the nervous system as it responds to presumed real-world events. Sensations, like the bare physical states of the world, have no inherent meaning or organization—they are only the correlates of presumed physical states. Being states of consciousness, they are essentially unlike the physical events that prompted them. Nevertheless, when they combine in the mind, the phenomenon of a rationally understood, meaningful, rich, organized, coherent and continuous consciousness emerges.

Yet can one have any confidence that this consciousness is really like the world? After all, since its contents, taken individually, are without meaning, the mind somehow has to create the appearance of causality, organization, space, time, and even the subjective continuity of being the person one seems to be. To get around this problem, Plato was forced to postulate that people are born with their knowledge. The great eighteenth century German philosopher Immanuel Kant argued that while all knowledge was not innate, the organizing principles were. For Kant, these mental phenomena were too ephemeral ever to be the stuff of science: They did not exist in space, came and went before they could be fully observed, and did not seem to be quantifiable.

Two nineteenth century German scientists changed this skeptical view. Ernst Weber, a physiologist in Leipzig, was able to show a consistent mathematical relationship between the size of changes in the strength of a physical stimulus, relative to its absolute intensity, and how a person's sensation of it changed. A few years later, his colleague, physicist Gustav Fechner, was able to extend Weber's finding into a general mathematical principle that showed a lawful relationship between physical stimulation and mental sensory intensity. It was, and continues to be, obscure exactly how mental phenomena are related to physical events, but the discovery of these and several other lawful regularities between mental and physical states led another German physiologist, Wilhelm Wundt, to conclude that they might really be two aspects of the same thing. Therefore, scientific study of the mind was possible. To accomplish this end, he proposed to add to Fechner's psychophysical methods a system of his own.

Wundt's scientific training led him to see complex phenomena as made up of simpler, elemental states much as a chemist sees innumerable compounds made of just over a hundred chemical elements. This reductionistic approach is characteristic of the foundation period of any science, and Wundt determined to apply it to the mind. He argued that one could reduce the complexity (and thus Kant's complaints of the "ephemerality" and "non-quantifiability") of consciousness by reducing it to a set of basic states and the laws of their combination. In other words, he sought to determine the associative structure of consciousness scientifically. Wundt built many types of apparatus to help present stimuli under controlled conditions, and he meticulously trained graduate students as observers to report cautiously and attentively on their own consciousness via introspection. He was the first to call this process experimental psychology.

The term "structuralism," however, awaited the coming to America of one of Wundt's most influential students, Edward Bradford Titchener. Titchener was an Englishman who studied with Wundt for two years and then took a position at Cornell University. Titchener, like Wundt, saw psychology as the study of mental events such as sensation, emotion, memory, and imagination. The primary goal of psychology was to determine the way these elemental processes combine to form the structure of mind. While this quest could be aided by seeing how mental phenomena are paralleled by nervous system events, chemistry and physics were not part of psychology; further physical reductionism was left to the biologists and physicists. Similarly, since the introspective study of mental phenomena could, for Titchener, only be done by highly trained normal adults, psychology could not study the minds of other animals, the mentally ill, or children.

While the application of the scientific method to the study of the mind marked the beginning of modern psychology, Titchener's attempt to adhere rigidly to his program in America was difficult. While Wundt had been more open to the issues of conscious acts or process representing the functions of the mind, Titchener's research focused mainly on mental contents and elements. This relative exclusion of the dynamic, purposive, self-modifying aspects of behavior and attention drew severe criticism from great American philosopher-scientists such as William James and John Dewey. They emphasized the Darwinian adaptive function of mental processes such as learning, attention, and individual abilities. Additional doubt concerning the viability of structural decomposition came from the bias caused by the special training required of observers. This bias led them to see what the theory said they should see, changed the nature of what was introspected, and was even the cause of an intolerable lack of agreement between observers whose training had differed.

Furthermore, Sigmund Freud had sparked a great scientific interest in the unconscious, just as Charles Darwin had inspired scientific interest in the adaptive function served by the mental processes of animals. Was not much of what determined the accessible content of consciousness itself unconscious and therefore unintrospectable? Plagued both with doubts and with new quests, American psychologists rejected Titchener's approach, which he formally labeled structuralism, and replaced it with a fuller definition of psychology that allowed the study of mental processes and their purposes, animals, the unconscious, the mentally ill, and children. The practical data of such a science would, psychologists believed, be applicable to therapy, education, and even business. Programs dedicated to the new American psychology, which Titchener labeled functionalism, started in the early twentieth century at the University of Chicago and Columbia University and grew quickly.

Applications

Titchener's approach to experimental psychology is not irrelevant to contemporary psychology or even to the conduct of one's personal life. For Titchener, the major problem for the scientific (reductionistic) study of the mind was the tendency for an observer to report mental events in terms that confused or combined information that he or she knew from prior experience about the "true" nature of the stimulus with the immediate experience of the stimulus. Titchener called this combining of objective and subjective views the stimulus error.

If one is reading a reference book, for example, and is asked what one is experiencing at that moment, one might simply respond, "a book." Although this answer is obviously correct, it also commits the stimulus error. The term "book" has rich associative meanings derived from past experience. One's report of "bookness" probably has aspects of many of these experiences—for example, how books are made, what they feel like, the color and graphic composition of the pages, emotions such as the joy of learning new things or the anxiety of studying material about which one might be tested, and perhaps memories of similar reference books. These and many other things make up the meaning of "book" but are not the individual sensations that one is directly experiencing.

To report those sensations, one would have to use terms that have little associative meaning—terms as elemental as possible. Thus, one might say, "I see a rectangular solid measuring 20 × 40 centimeters, having hundreds of black line segments averaging 1.5 millimeters in any direction on its white surface, which has a matte texture," and so on, for quite some time. Consider what happens when a customer asks the clerk at a delicatessen counter for a certain weight of sliced meat. The findings of Weber and Fechner show that two pounds does not, in terms of immediate sensory experience, feel twice as heavy as one pound. Similarly, three pounds feels much less than three times one pound. Nevertheless, experienced deli workers frequently come astonishingly close to slicing the precise weight desired. They accomplish this by combining their considerable past experience of the feel of the different weights of food with associated scale readings. This provides a rich context of "weight meaning" that is attached to the raw sensory information. In other words, by committing Titchener's "stimulus error," they become phenomenally accurate.

The issue here is basic to psychology and philosophy. What one learns associatively about the world often results in the formation of abstract, generalized concepts that are much truer to the way the world is and how it affects one than the elemental experiences one has in any given situation. Which, then, is the "real" world: the various individual sensations, memory images, and emotions that make up a book or the unanalyzed whole instantaneous comprehension of bookness? Although one might be tempted to reply that it is the latter, keep in mind that eyewitness testimony is often suspect because it can be severely distorted by one's prior experiences; one sees what one expects to see rather than what is actually there.

Thus, structuralism is a reminder that there are various points of view that one can take, some emphasizing immediate sensory experience, some emphasizing the activation of complex networks of associative memory, and still others stressing the physical nature of the stimulus world and the consequent activity in the observer's nervous system. The failure of structuralism to prevail as the one and only psychology should be kept in perspective: To date, although there have been other major theories of the mind, the relationship between the physical world, sensation, and a person's subjective, coherent self remains scientifically and philosophically intractable. Perhaps the best application to be made of this fact is to realize that there may be no single "correct" point of view. Instead, one should try to understand the nature of one's subjective experience as such. Yet one should also juxtapose this effort with the equally important attempt to see oneself and others as beings in a natural world and universe which may be seen as not having any point of view.

Context

Although Edward Bradford Titchener was responsible for the fully articulated research program called structuralism, he was carrying forward (and carrying to America) the psychology of Wilhelm Wundt. Wundt founded the structuralistic tradition by combining the key elements of associationistic philosophy, reductionistic science, and the successes of psychophysics. He was led to do this because he was poised at a crucial juncture in intellectual history when the force of each of these ideas was strong. Collectively, and perhaps without his realizing it, they shaped his view that psychology was the scientific analysis of experience. Wundt's psychology was a turning point in that it rejected purely philosophical and often metaphysical approaches to understanding the mind and championed the experimental method. In turn, Titchener's narrow vision of structuralism fell on infertile intellectual soil in America. This occurred because there was a new intellectual atmosphere created by Darwinism, pragmatism (the practical philosophy of John Dewey), the holistic view of mind put forth by William James, the influence of Freud (and his American advocate, developmental psychologist Granville Stanley Hall), and a growing number of scientists that wanted to study the minds of animals. These intellectual forces combined to create the psychology of functionalism.

Functionalism was plagued by accusations of being "unscientific," subjective, and mentalistic by the behaviorial psychologist John B. Watson. The Watsonian tradition produced the school of behaviorism and its most famous standard-bearer, B. F. Skinner. This extreme form of objective reductionism produced a valuable technology, but it ultimately failed to yield a workable explanation of the undeniable fact of subjective points of view in the natural world. More recent approaches to the mind have combined the study of cognitive content and abilities (as Wundt and Titchener advocated), neuropsychology, and computer modeling of cognitive function. Thus the importance of the objective study of mental phenomena and their subjective components that, in structuralism, marked the birth of modern psychology remains an inescapable part of any realistic view of the natural world.

Bibliography

Boring, Edwin Garrigues. *A History of Experimental Psychology.* New York: Century, 1929. Few historians have undertaken a history of psychology. One of the finest early psychologists, Edwin Boring, came the closest to being a true and creative historian of the new science. An enduring and incisive work, scholarly but readable. Boring's contribution to historiography was his brilliant explication of how the intellectual climate of the times, the *Zeitgeist*, was responsible for the development of new and even great ideas.

Bringmann, Wolfgang G., and Ryan D. Tweney, eds. *Wundt Studies.* Toronto, Canada: C. J. Hogrefe, 1980. This volume brings together a number of key articles that represent a renaissance of interest in the legacy of Wundt and structuralism. Until the time around the publication of this work, Wundt was often seen as responsible only for the misbegotten attempt to use introspective reductionism that prompted the later "workable" systems. Here one may see both the problems with and the considerable positive influence of Wundt's contribution.

Heidbreder, Edna. *Seven Psychologies.* New York: Century, 1933. Heidbreder's book remains the most readable introduction to the major "schools" of psychology up to and including behaviorism. Although the book is dated, the insight, humanity, and beauty of her narrative writing make this a classic. One can read this work as one would a novel. The discussion of structuralism is particularly fine.

Schultz, Duane P., and Sydney Ellen Schultz. *A History of Modern Psychology.* 4th ed. San Diego: Harcourt Brace Jovanovich, 1987. Refined, readable, and biographically based, this is one of the best introductions to the history of psychology available. It has narrative flow rather than definitions and enumerations, and includes key passages from original sources. The structuralism chapter has a particularly felicitous excerpt (more than ten pages) from Titchener's 1909 work, *A Text-Book of Psychology.*

Watson, Robert Irving, Sr., and Rand B. Evans. *The Great Psychologists.* 5th ed. New York: HarperCollins, 1991. Watson was one of the best proponents of the biographical approach to the history of psychology. He argues forcefully for the recognition of the individual genius that often characterized the pioneering efforts of the psychologists of his title. His great writing, zeal, and intimate knowledge of the material bring it alive. The discussion of each of the men discussed in this article is fascinating and easily readable. One learns much about philosophy as well.

John Santelli

Cross-References

Behaviorism: An Overview, 401; Cognitive Psychology: An Overview, 572; Functions of Consciousness, 656; Functionalism, 1055; Psychology Defined, 1945; Psychophysical Scaling, 1963; Sensation and Perception Defined, 2207.

STUTTERING

Type of psychology: Psychopathology
Field of study: Childhood and adolescent disorders

Stuttering is the most common speech disorder among adolescents and adults, and it has profound consequences for self-esteem. Its origins appear in early childhood, as a result of both biological influences and learning processes; modern therapy most often focuses on the latter.

Principal terms

COMMUNICATION ENVIRONMENT: the complex interactions whereby all spoken communication takes place; includes verbal and nonverbal responses of listeners

DESENSITIZATION TECHNIQUES: speech therapy techniques used to treat stuttering with the aim of increasing tolerance for speech disrupters such as interruptions

DISTRACTION TECHNIQUES: speech therapy techniques used to treat stuttering in which the speaker is distracted from the speech effort by a competing activity

LEARNING THEORY: a broad theory which assumes that behavior is a result of learning in a particular environment; it can be applied to stuttering

NEUROSIS: a psychological disorder whose primary symptoms and causes are related to anxiety or internal conflict

PSYCHOANALYST: a psychotherapist who adheres to theories specifically influenced by Sigmund Freud, strongly emphasizing the role of unconscious conflict in producing observed behavior

PSYCHOTHERAPY: any of a number of techniques aimed at relieving psychological disorders, most often by providing support and promoting self-awareness

SPEECH DISRUPTERS: aspects of the communication environment which are found to aggravate stuttering in an individual, such as interruption and pressure to hurry

STUTTERING: a speech disorder characterized by an unusual frequency of verbal disfluencies, accompanied by tension associated with speaking

VERBAL DISFLUENCIES: interruptions in speech rhythms found in all speakers, including pauses, nonwords such as "uh," and repetitions of words or syllables

Overview

All people sometimes hesitate when they speak, or repeat the starting sound or syllable of a word when they are nervous. These are examples of normal verbal disfluencies. Stutterers are different from normal speakers primarily because of the frequency of their problem, not because their speech problem is by itself unusual. Stuttering is a problem of the timing and rhythms of speech, not of articulation. Thus, it is quite different from other common speech defects. It is also the most common speech problem to affect teens or adults.

Stuttering is a universal phenomenon, affecting people of every society and language group on earth. It is about four times as common in boys as in girls. It typically begins in the preschool years (almost always before age six) and, unless outgrown by adolescence, becomes progressively more pronounced. As the problem worsens, the stutterer is likely to show other, related behavior problems such as nervous twitches or slapping himself when trying to stop stuttering. Self-esteem usually suffers; teens, especially, are self-conscious about this speech problem. This can lead to avoidance of speaking or to more pronounced social withdrawal.

There are several possible causes of stuttering. Scientists do not seek to know which of these causes is "correct"; for different stutterers, different causes may apply. In addition, in any individual case, more than one cause may be relevant. For example, stuttering tends to run in families, suggesting a genetic contribution. This contribution may only make an individual more likely to develop the stuttering problem, given the right (or wrong) circumstances. About the only cause which has been ruled out is imitation. There is no evidence that stuttering develops from a child's exposure to another stutterer.

A variety of physical differences between stutterers and nonstutterers have been investigated, with all aspects of the mouth and airways involved in speech production taken into account. Hearing problems should be considered, although stuttering is actually less common among the deaf. Nevertheless, partial hearing losses can influence confidence in learning to speak, and, in fact, the onset of the stuttering problem often corresponds with the earliest use of sentences. In the treatment of any speech defect, a check for hearing problems is an important preliminary step. Brain damage can also lead to stuttering, although this is not the usual cause.

While stress certainly aggravates stuttering for a stutterer, it is not usually the cause of the speech disorder. Most stuttering problems develop gradually, and parents typically cannot pinpoint when the problem began. Extremely stressful events have, however, been known to cause stuttering directly.

Most stuttering probably develops gradually during the time when children are beginning to speak in sentences and engage in conversation. As stated earlier, everyone shows verbal disfluencies; young children are even more likely to do so. Wendell Johnson argues that the difference between stuttering and nonstuttering preschoolers is not in the children, but in the perceptions of their parents. By overreacting to normal disfluencies, parents may impair a young child's self-confidence, instigating a truly vicious cycle: Low self-confidence creates more disfluency, which further lowers self-confidence. The cycle continues until the child is, in fact, a "stutterer."

The difficulty with this line of reasoning is that it imposes an unfair burden of guilt on the parents. In effect, concerned parents are accused of causing the problem by expressing their concern. While parental behavior may contribute to stuttering, most experts believe that the evidence on genetics and the preponderance of boys among stutterers suggest a physical contribution as well. Moreover, treatment of speech disorders is most effective when begun early, and the social impact of stuttering makes early treatment even more critical; thus, parents of stutterers may not know whether they will do more harm by calling attention to the problem (thus making it worse) or by ignoring it.

The best advice to parents is patient but watchful concern. First, it is important to remember that all speakers show disfluencies, and show more of them under stress. The child learning to speak may require patience from the adult listener. Parents should not pressure a child who is attempting to express what, to the child, may be a complex idea. Parents should not finish a child's sentences. If a child's stuttering problem does not disappear with time, if it appears without obvious stressful circumstances, or if accompanying nervous behaviors develop, it is time to seek help. Patience and lack of pressure are that much more important with a diagnosed stutterer. The most helpful role for the parent at this point is to provide unconditional emotional support and to cooperate with the therapist.

Current approaches to the treatment of stuttering emphasize controlling the problem rather than eliminating it. Stutterers are often advised to slow down their speaking and simply to stop and take a deep breath if stuttering begins. They may be advised to sigh before any speech attempt. Therapy is also concerned with self-esteem problems and with the social avoidance of stutterers, treating these as results, not causes, of stuttering.

Stutterers often develop their own control techniques. Some find, for example, that singing is easier than talking and take advantage of this to modify the pitch of their speech when a problem occurs. The best advice may simply be to do whatever works for any individual.

Applications

The decision to treat or not treat stuttering is complicated by the similarity of speech between early stutterers and nonstutterers and by the resulting difficulty in pinpointing the origin of the problem. Edward G. Conture has pointed out that therapists deal both with parents who are overconcerned about normal disfluency and with parents who are underconcerned about a real problem. Moreover, Conture has noted, the nature of treatment depends considerably on the age of the stutterer.

Younger stutterers offer the best hope for treatment, before the complications created by social stigma occur or worsen. On the other hand, they present greater problems in diagnosis, as well as a need to counsel parents who are themselves experiencing stress related to the stuttering. For example, parents of stutterers frequently have great difficulty looking at their child when the child stutters. They feel their child's pain, but their own pained response may not be helpful. Additionally, young children may not understand instructions for speech exercises or may lack the patience to practice techniques. Teens are better able to cooperate with the activities of speech therapy, which involve following directions and practice. On the other hand, they may be uncooperative for a number of reasons: past negative therapy experience, fear of peer reactions to being in speech therapy, and normal adolescent resistance to adults.

Adult stutterers have the least likelihood of overcoming the problem but are highly motivated (although they also may have had bad experiences with past therapy efforts) and have the freedom to structure their own environments. This last point is important, because a stutterer's relationship with parents often is a complication for younger stutterers. The adult's greater freedom—not only from parents but also from peer pressure—can make psychotherapy for self-esteem problems more successful. On the other hand, the adult continues to face a tremendous social stigma, which can even take the form of job discrimination. Moreover, stuttering by this time has become ingrained as part of a stutterer's identity and is thus more resistant to change.

Specific speech therapy techniques are varied. Distraction techniques aim to distract the stutterer from the speech problem. They have their basis in the fact that self-consciousness about speech aggravates stuttering. One example that has been used is asking the stutterer to speak while crawling on the floor. These techniques most often provide only temporary success. One obvious problem is that it is hard to generalize the use of such methods to real-life situations.

Desensitization techniques focus on training the stutterer to deal with situations that provoke stuttering. This requires analyzing all situations that produce stuttering (such as interruptions or being asked to hurry one's speech). After a stress-free therapy environment is created, the "speech disrupters" are reintroduced one at a time, with the aim of strengthening the individual's tolerance for disruption.

Therapy is most effective when parents are involved. They are very important for their role in promoting self-esteem. They may require counseling themselves, both to deal with their own frustrations and to understand the impact of their own and others' reactions on the stuttering child. In addition, they are the most important members of the child's communication environment. The parents' roles, not only in their responses to the child's speech but also in their own manner of speaking with the child, largely structure that environment. It has been found, for example, that when parents slow down their own speech to a stuttering child, the child's stuttering is reduced.

The individual's self-esteem is central to effective therapy. Psychotherapy frequently deals with the psychological damage created by the stigma of stuttering. There are also many books on stuttering, many with a focus on self-help. Several authors advise stutterers of the needs, first, to increase their self-confidence, and second, to refrain from avoiding social interaction. For example, Wendell Johnson specifically emphasizes concentrating on one's "normal" speech instead of on one's stuttering. The idea is that the stutterer's overconcern with stuttering has served to maintain and worsen the problem.

A common tactic in the self-help literature is to cite famous stutterers. Jock A. Carlisle has composed an impressive list, including Moses, Aristotle, Thomas Jefferson, Winston Churchill, Charles Darwin, and Marilyn Monroe. Many famous stutterers have been known for their writing, and some have sufficiently coped to allow public speaking or even acting. This success may help to inspire a stutterer; it should at least enhance a stutterer's self-esteem to know that stutterers have succeeded in such a variety of fields. Self-confidence is the common thread, whether a result of self-help, speech therapy, psychotherapy, or unconditional parental support.

Context

Descriptions of the treatment of stuttering can be found throughout recorded history. Charles Van Riper has listed several of the prescientific approaches, some dating to ancient Greece and Rome: speaking with pebbles in the mouth (an ancient use of a distraction technique), exorcism, hot substances applied to the tongue, and bloodletting. The beginning of the modern era saw the development of tongue exercises and even surgery that deformed the tongue.

In the late nineteenth century, stuttering was for the first time described as a neurosis, or disorder caused by anxiety. This theme was elaborated by twentieth century psychoanalysts in their treatment of stutterers; through the first half of the twentieth century, the psychoanalytic view dominated theoretical views and treatment of stuttering. According to this view, stuttering is the result of an unconscious conflict between the desire to speak and a preference to remain silent. The obvious tension experienced by stutterers, as well as their avoidance of speaking, supported this interpretation.

While some therapists remain influenced by psychoanalytic views, most contemporary therapists view the observed tension to be a result of, not the cause of, stuttering. They are more influenced by learning theory—that is, they view stuttering as the result of a process of learned reactions to specific environmental influences. Johnson's research on the similarities between preschool stutterers and nonstutterers, along with the differences among those same children's parents' perceptions, strongly supports this interpretation. Most theorists and therapists also accept the role of genetic disposition in determining who is more likely to develop a stuttering disorder. In this view, therapy relies on re-learning on the part of the stutterer and on control of the communication environment, especially the speech and reactions of the parents. Psychotherapy remains important not because psychological problems are seen as the cause of stuttering but because they appear to result from stuttering—from the social stigma involved as well as from the frustrations in communicating with others.

The recent shift in views may in part be attributed to the growing role in research of people who themselves have or have had a stuttering problem. Charles Van Riper was such an individual, and he devoted his entire career to research and treatment of stuttering. The value of his personal experience is found in his own solution: He became fluent when he stopped trying to hide his problem. Stuttering is a learned speech problem, with tremendous emotional consequences; stutterers are simply normal people coping with this problem.

Bibliography

Carlisle, Jock Alan. *Tangled Tongue: Living with a Stutter.* Toronto: University of Toronto Press, 1985. A comprehensive review of the causes of and treatments for stuttering, written by a stutterer. Besides general information for and identification with the reader, it provides useful appendices on self-help and consumer organizations as well as organizations involved in stuttering therapy and research.

Conture, Edward G. *Stuttering.* Englewood Cliffs, N.J.: Prentice-Hall, 1990. A basic text aimed at speech therapy students. Emphasis is on evaluation and treatment, highlighting important treatment differences related to the age of the stutterer. Includes a wealth of clinical examples throughout and a full case study in an appendix.

Glauber, I. Peter. *Stuttering: A Psychoanalytic Understanding.* New York: Human Sciences Press, 1982. Presents the psychoanalytic view of stuttering as the result of unconscious conflicts. Not the dominant view, but one that should be considered for a full understanding of stuttering. The first of two parts presents the basic interpretation. The second part requires more familiarity with psychoanalytic concepts and concerns.

Johnson, Wendell. *Stuttering: And What You Can Do About It.* Minneapolis: University of Minnesota Press, 1961. Aimed at parents of stutterers; very readable as well as comprehensive. Johnson presents his own research comparing stuttering and nonstuttering children as well as their parents, and he emphasizes the importance of parental expectations as well as the child's self-concept in both the cause and treatment of stuttering.

Sheehan, Joseph Green, et al. *Stuttering: Research and Therapy.* New York: Harper & Row, 1970. Contains separately authored chapters from a variety of perspectives, including personality, sociology, physiology, and development. The chapter "Historical Approaches," by Charles Van Riper, is especially interesting, both as a history of ideas about and treatments for stuttering and because Van Riper, himself a former stutterer, is perhaps the most renowned researcher on stuttering.

Starkweather, C. Woodruff. *Fluency and Stuttering.* Englewood Cliffs, N.J.: Prentice-Hall, 1987. Aimed at speech therapy students. Presents a readable and thorough summary of current research, with a particular sensitivity to the variability of the problem and to problems in defining stuttering. Coverage of the development of the disorder discusses contributions of both nature and nurture.

Nancy E. Macdonald

Cross-References

Language: The Developmental Sequence, 1387; Language and Cognition, 1401; Psycholinguistics, 1918; Self-Esteem, 2188; Speech Disorders, 2342.

SUBSTANCE ABUSE: AN OVERVIEW

Type of psychology: Psychopathology
Fields of study: Biological treatments; nervous system; substance abuse

Substance abuse is the use of any substance in amounts or frequencies that violate social, personal, or medical norms for physical or behavioral health; these substances are often addictive.

Principal terms

DEPENDENCE: the presence of withdrawal signs when use of a substance is discontinued

HALLUCINOGENS: drugs that can alter perception, including LSD, PCP, peyote, psilocybin, and possibly marijuana

INHALANTS: volatile drugs, including glue, gasoline, propellants, and some anesthetics

OPIATES: substances derived from the opium poppy, including morphine, heroin, codeine, and Demerol

SEDATIVES/HYPNOTICS: nonopiate substances that cause a slowing of behavioral arousal, including alcohol, tranquilizers, and barbiturates

SELF-MEDICATION: a theory that substance abuse is a form of self-treatment in order to alleviate measured or perceived pain/dysphoria

STIMULANTS: drugs that cause behavioral and/or physiological stimulation, including amphetamine, cocaine, and their respective derivatives; caffeine; nicotine; and some antidepressants

TOLERANCE: the need for greater amounts of a substance over time in order to achieve a previous effect

Overview

Substance abuse is studied in psychology from personality, social, and biological perspectives. Social and personality studies of the substance abuser have produced theories with four principal themes: The abuser displays inability to tolerate stress, immaturity in the form of inability to delay gratification, poor socialization, and/or environmental problems. Biological theories of substance abuse maintain that at least two major factors can result in abusive disorders: the need to relieve some form of pain and the seeking of pleasure or euphoria. Pain is broadly defined as any feeling of dysphoria. Because both pain and euphoria can be produced by psychosomatic or somatopsychic events, these two biological categories can subsume most of the stated nonbiological correlates of substance abuse.

There are several forms of substance abuse, including chronic abuse, intermittent abuse (sprees), active abuse that involves drug seeking, and passive abuse that involves unintentional repeated exposure to drugs. In each case, abuse is determined by a physical or psychological reaction or status that violates accepted professional or personal health norms.

Substance abuse may or may not involve the development of tolerance or physical dependence and may or may not result in easily detectable symptomatology. Tolerance, the need for greater amounts or more frequent administration of a substance, can develop over time or can be acute. In addition, the amount of a substance needed to produce tolerance varies widely among drugs and among individuals. Similarly, the withdrawal signs that indicate dependence need not be the same among individuals and are not always obvious, even to the abuser. Thus, an individual can be an "invisible" abuser.

There are several types of abused substances, and some of these are not typically viewed as problematic. Major categories include sedatives/hypnotics, such as alcohol; opiates, such as heroin; stimulants, including cocaine and caffeine; inhalants, such as nitrous oxide ("laughing gas"); and hallucinogens, including phencyclidine (PCP or "angel dust"). Food is an example of a substance not usually considered a substance of abuse, but it has definite abuse potential.

The experience of pain or the seeking of euphoria as causes of substance abuse can be measured physically or can be perceived by the individual without obvious physical indicators. The relative importance of pain and euphoria in determining the development and maintenance of substance abuse requires consideration of the contributions of at least five potential sources of behavioral and physical status: genetic predisposition, dysregulation during development, dysregulation from trauma at any time during the life span, the environment, and learning. Any of these can result in or interact to produce the pain or feelings of euphoria that can lead to substance abuse.

The key commonality in pain-induced substance abuse is that the organism experiences pain that it does not tolerate. Genetic predisposers of pain include inherited diseases and conditions that interfere with normal pain tolerance. Developmental dysregulations include physical and behavioral arrests and related differences from developmental norms. Trauma from physical injury or from environmental conditions can also result in the experience of pain, as can the learning of a pain-producing response.

Several theories of pain-induced substance abuse can be summarized as self-medication theories. In essence, these state that individuals abuse substances in order to correct an underlying disorder that presumably produces some form of dysphoria. Self-medication theories are useful because they take into account the homeostatic (tendency toward balance) nature of the organism and because they include the potential for significant individual differences in problems with pain.

Relief from pain by itself does not account entirely for drug use that goes beyond improvement in health or reachievement of normal status and certainly cannot account entirely for drug use that becomes physically self-destructive (an exception occurs when pain becomes more motivating than the need to preserve life). Thus, the desire for euphoria is also studied. This type of substance abuse can be distinguished from the possible pleasure produced by pain relief because it does not stop when such relief is achieved.

Euphoria-induced substance use, or pleasure seeking, is characteristic of virtually all species tested. The transition from pleasurable use to actual abuse is also widespread, but often limited in other species when life-threatening conditions are produced. Some theorists have proposed that pleasure seeking is an innate drive not easily kept in check even by socially acceptable substitutes. Thus, euphoria-induced substance abuse is conceived of as pleasure seeking gone awry. Other theorists believe that euphoria-induced substance abuse is related to biological causes such as evolutionary pressure. For example, some drug-abuse researchers believe that organisms that could eat rotten, fermented fruit (partly alcohol) may have survived to reproduce when others did not.

Applications

Laboratory studies of the biological bases of substance abuse involve clinical (human) and preclinical (animal) approaches. Such research has demonstrated that there are areas of the brain that can provide powerful feelings of euphoria when stimulated, indicating that the brain is primed for the experience of pleasure. Direct electrical stimulation of some areas of the brain, including an area first referred to as the medial forebrain bundle, produced such strong addictive behaviors in animals that they ignored many basic drives including those for food, water, mating, and care of offspring.

Later research showed that the brain also contains highly addictive analgesic and euphoriant chemicals that exist as a normal part of the neural milieu. Thus, the brain is also predisposed to aid in providing relief from pain and has coupled such relief in some cases with feelings of euphoria. It is not surprising, therefore, that substance abuse and addictive behaviors can develop so readily in so many organisms.

The effects of typical representatives of the major categories of abused substances can be predicted. Alcohol, a sedative/hypnotic, can disrupt several behavioral functions. It can slow reaction time, movement, and thought processes and can interfere with needed rapid eye movement (REM) sleep. It can also produce unpredictable emotionality, including violence. Abusers of alcohol develop tolerance and dependence, and withdrawal can be life-threatening. Heroin, an opiate, has analgesic (pain-killing) and euphoriant effects. It is also highly addictive, but withdrawal seldom results in death. Marijuana, sometimes classified as a sedative, sometimes as a hallucinogen, has many of the same behavioral effects as alcohol. Stimulants vary widely in their behavioral effects. Common to all is some form of physiological and behavioral stimulation. Some, such as cocaine and the amphetamines (including crystal methamphetamine, or "ice"), are extremely addictive and seriously life-threatening and can produce violence. Others, such as caffeine, are relatively mild in their euphoriant effects. Withdrawal from stimulants, especially the powerful forms, can result in profound depression. Hallucinogens are also a diverse group of substances that can produce visual, auditory, tactile, olfactory, or gustatory hallucinations, but most do so in only a small percentage of the population. Some, such as PCP, can produce violent behavior, while others, such as lysergic acid diethylamide (LSD), are not known for producing negative emotional outbursts. Inhalants usually produce feelings of euphoria, but they are seldom used by individuals beyond the adolescent years.

It is noteworthy that some of the pharmacological effects of very different drugs are quite similar. Marijuana and alcohol affect at least three of the same brain biochemical systems. Alcohol can become a form of opiate in the brain following some specific chemical transformations. These similarities raise an old question in substance abuse: Is there a fundamental addictive mechanism common to everyone that differs only in the level and nature of expression? Older theories of drug-abuse behavior approached this question by postulating the "addictive personality," a type of person who would become indiscriminately addicted as a result of his or her personal and social history. With advances in neuroscience have come theories concerning the possibility of an "addictive brain," which refers to a neurological status that requires continued adjustment provided by drugs. This is a modification of self-medication theories.

An example of the workings of the addictive brain might be a low-opiate brain that does not produce normal levels of analgesia or normal levels of organismic and behavioral euphoria (joy). The chemical adjustment sought by the brain might be satisfied by use or abuse of any drug that results in stimulation of the opiate function of the brain. As discussed above, several seemingly unrelated drugs can produce a similar chemical effect. Thus, the choice of a particular substance might depend both on brain status and on personal or social experience with the effects and availability of the drug used.

The example of the opiate-seeking brain raises at least two possibilities for prevention and treatment, both of which have been discussed in substance-abuse literature: reregulation of the brain and substitution. So far, socially acceptable substitutes or substitute addictions offer some promise, but reregulation of the dysregulated brain is still primarily a hope of the future. An example of a socially acceptable substitute might be opiate production by excessive running, an activity that can produce some increase in opiate function. The success of such a substitution procedure, however, depends upon many variables that may be quite difficult to predict or control. The substitution might not produce the required amount of reregulation, the adjustment might not be permanent, and tolerance to the adjustment might develop. There are a host of other possible problems.

Context

Use and probable abuse of psychoactive substances date from the earliest recorded history and likely predate it. Historical records indicate that many substances with the potential for abuse were used in medicinal and ceremonial or religious contexts, as tokens in barter, for their euphoriant properties during recreation, as indicators of guilt or innocence, as penalties, and in other practices.

Substance abuse is widespread in virtually all countries and cultures, and it can be extremely costly, both personally and socially. There is no doubt that most societies would like to eliminate substance abuse, but current practices have been relatively unsuccessful in doing so. It is obvious that economic as well as social factors contribute both to abusive disorders and to the laws regulating substance use, and possibly create some roadblocks in eliminating abuse.

In psychology, the systematic and popular study of substance abuse became most extensive during the period when such abuse was most popular, the 1960's and 1970's. Research into psychological, social, environmental, therapeutic, and some biological aspects of abuse proliferated during these years, and the reasons proposed to explain abuse disorders were almost as numerous as the authors proposing them. During the early 1980's, drug-abuse research experienced a somewhat fallow period, but with discoveries of the brain mechanisms involved in many disorders, a resurgence has occurred. Many disorders previously thought to be the result of nonbiological factors are now known to have strong neural determinants. Both psychosomatic and somatopsychic events affect the nervous system, and the resurgence of brain-oriented research reflects this understanding.

Future research on substance abuse is likely to focus on more of the biological determinants and constraints on the organism and to try to place substance-abuse disorders more in the contexts of biological self-medication and biological euphoria. Many people erroneously consider biological explanations of problematic behaviors to be an excuse for such behaviors, not an explanation. In fact, discoveries regarding the neural contributions to such behaviors are the basis on which rational therapies for such behaviors can be developed. Recognizing that a disorder has a basis in the brain can enable therapists to address the disorder with a better armamentarium of useful therapeutic tools. In this way, simple management of such disorders can be replaced by real solutions to the problems created by substance abuse.

Bibliography

Jaffe, Jerome H. "Drug Addiction and Drug Abuse." In *Goodman and Gilman's the Pharmacological Basis of Therapeutics*, edited by Alfred Goodman Gilman, Louis S. Goodman, et al. 7th ed. New York: Macmillan, 1985. A standard reference for students interested in an overview of the pharmacological aspects of selected addictive drugs. Of greater interest to those interested in pursuing the study of substance abuse from a neurological and physiological perspective.

Julien, Robert M. *A Primer of Drug Action*. 5th ed. New York: W. H. Freeman, 1988. An introductory treatment of types and actions of many abused and therapeutic substances. A useful, quick reference guide for psychoactive effects of drugs used in traditional pharmacological therapy for disorders and of abused substances. Contains good reference lists and appendices that explain some of the anatomy and chemistry required to understand biological mechanisms of substance abuse.

Leavitt, Fred. *Drugs and Behavior.* 2d ed. New York: John Wiley & Sons, 1982. Inclusive coverage from a psychological perspective of the effects of drugs on many types of behaviors. Includes sections on licit and illicit drugs, theories of drug use and abuse, prevention and treatment, and development of drugs. Important because it considers the effects of drug use on a large range of behaviors and physical states and because it presents a relatively integrated view of biopsychological information on drugs.

Ray, Oakley Stern, and Charles Ksir. *Drugs, Society, and Human Behavior.* 4th ed. St. Louis: Times Mirror/Mosby, 1987. A good text for the newer student of substance abuse who not only wishes to understand the substances and their biological significance but also is interested in current methods of prevention and treatment. Of special interest are the interspersed history and comments regarding the social aspects of abused substances.

United States Department of Health and Human Services. *Drug Abuse and Drug Abuse Research: The First in a Series of Triennial Reports to Congress.* Rockville, Md.: National Institute on Drug Abuse, 1984. An excellent summary of research on selected substances of abuse. The rest of the series should also be of great interest to the reader interested in substance-abuse research. The strength of this series is the understandable language and style used to convey recent research. Treatment, prevention, and specific drug research are summarized, and a well-selected reference list is provided for each chapter.

United States Department of Health and Human Services. *Theories on Drug Abuse: Selected Contemporary Perspectives.* Edited by Dan J. Lettieri, Mollie Sayers, and Helen Wallenstein Pearson. Rockville, Md.: National Institute on Drug Abuse, 1980. An older but good compendium of theoretical positions related to the question of substance abuse. Theories covered include the gamut of empirical and nonempirical thought concerning the predisposition to, development of, maintenance of, and possible termination of abuse disorders. Perspectives are biological, personal, and social. Of interest are a quick guide to theory components and an extensive list of references.

Rebecca M. Chesire

Cross-References

Addictive Personality and Behaviors, 102; Alcoholism, 213; The Codependent Personality, 534; Endorphins, 973; Motivation: Opponent Process Theory, 1611; Neurotransmitters, 1673; Optimal Arousal Theory, 1721.

SUDDEN INFANT DEATH SYNDROME

Type of psychology: Developmental psychology
Fields of study: Coping; infancy and childhood

Sudden infant death syndrome is the main cause of death in infants after the neonatal period and a phenomenon that is presently an unsolved puzzle to both research workers and clinicians. Inexplicable to stricken families, it is often a psychological tragedy with which it is difficult to cope; it presents a challenge for clinicians and counselors.

Principal terms
APNEA: a transient cessation of respiration
BRONCHOSPASM: a spasm of one or more of the major breathing tubes of the lung
HYPOXIA: a deficiency in oxygen
PETECHIAE: small spots on body surfaces caused by hemorrhages
PHARYNX: the section of the digestive tract that extends from the nasal cavity to the larynx (or voice box)
POSTMORTEM EXAMINATION: a medical examination after death, usually an autopsy
POSTNATAL PERIOD: the period soon after birth
SELF-IMAGE: the self as the individual pictures or imagines it
SYNDROME: a group of symptoms that collectively characterize a physical or psychological disease

Overview

Sudden infant death syndrome (SIDS), also called "crib death" in the United States and "cot death" in Great Britain and other parts of the world, is presently an unsolved dilemma. It is a tragedy that frustrates researchers, families, and psychological counselors and causes extreme stress in afflicted families. SIDS was defined in 1969 as the sudden death of any infant, unexpected from its medical history and unexplained, because a thorough postmortem examination fails to demonstrate an adequate cause of death.

Victims of sudden infant death syndrome typically die while unattended—presumably while asleep—and they are therefore found dead after being left for a nap or for the night. Most SIDS episodes occur during a narrow time period, beginning a week after birth, peaking at twelve weeks after birth, and virtually stopping around week thirty-six after birth. This temporal distribution of SIDS is very different from that of other major causes of infant death, which occur most frequently within the first month after birth. In fact, death within the appropriate time period helps to classify infant death as SIDS.

SIDS is purportedly an ancient disease, described anecdotally even in biblical times. For centuries, however, it was attributed to accidental overlying (smothering) by the afflicted child's mother or wet nurse, or to infanticide. Beginning in the nineteenth century—and continuing well into the twentieth century—the problem came to be attributed to suffocation caused by such things as an enlarged thymus gland, bedclothing, or even pet cats stealing an infant's breath while sleeping with it. While these early explanations have proved to be unfounded, there is still no widely accepted explanation for SIDS.

In the United States, the incidence of the syndrome is about two deaths per thousand live births, so it is estimated that between seven thousand and ten thousand American children die of the disease every year. This represents a significant portion of all infant deaths and about 30 percent of all deaths of children under one year old; therefore, SIDS merits serious consideration. In Canada, the problem is of similar relative magnitude. Even in the underdeveloped countries of the world, where the number of infant deaths is much higher, the toll of SIDS on afflicted families is considerable.

One of the factors that make SIDS so difficult to cope with is the fact that it is entirely unpredictable and therefore impossible to prevent. Adding to this is the fact that even very extensive postmortem examination of SIDS victims gives no solid, absolute answers about the overall basis for SIDS deaths. Moreover, study of the problem is virtually impossible to carry out in the standard ways: There are no living patients to examine, there is no widely accepted animal model to use as a test base, and there is no appropriate high-risk population that has been clearly defined for particularly close examination.

As to the last item, epidemiologic study has shown several potentially useful things. First, SIDS is quite rare during the first week of life, the period in which most infant deaths occur. In addition, several countries (New Zealand, for example) have an exceptionally high incidence of SIDS, while others (such as Scandinavia) have a very low incidence of the syndrome. Furthermore, SIDS strikes blacks and Eskimos at rates near triple that seen in Caucasians. Also, the children of teenage mothers, uneducated members of the lower socioeconomic groups of society, and drug addicts are very susceptible to the syndrome.

Many avenues of possible SIDS origin have been explored, including examination of the course of pregnancies ending in SIDS, the effects of premature birth, examination of the lives of SIDS infants, all pathology related to SIDS, alterations of respiratory control factors, enzymology, hormone levels, the possibility of bronchospasm or apnea, and cardiac problems. Yet reliable, objective clinical markers for SIDS have not been obvious. Therefore, there is no indication that a breakthrough is imminent in understanding SIDS, and solving the enigma of its basis will take considerable work. However, as Laura Hillman has pointed out, a bright spot does exist—the fact that there are now many SIDS researchers who have the experience to recognize any clues that come up and to use the scientific method to produce a solution to the disease.

Applications

The question of whether there is anything that serves as a marker for sudden infant death syndrome has been asked by many who study the problem, by others who have suffered the loss of a child to the syndrome, and by those who provide psychiatric and psychological counseling to the families involved. Though it is not clearly helpful, there is one thing—interthoracic petechiae—that is seen in 80 percent of all SIDS victims.

These petechiae, which are attributed to the violent action of the heart, are proposed to be attributable to upper airway obstruction and have led to the suggestion by a number of SIDS researchers that this is the area of infant health that should be investigated thoroughly to facilitate the development of a more complete understanding of the cause of SIDS. Aspects viewed as particularly valuable to these efforts include careful examination of abnormalities in the size and development of the upper airway, pharynx, tongue, and other anatomic structures that are viewed as being potential mediators of SIDS; identification of consequences of upper respiratory infections which could facilitate respiratory collapse, leading to the petechiae; and elucidation of the involvement of sleep apnea, observed in a number of SIDS cases and in many infants viewed as having nearly succumbed to SIDS.

It has been proposed, by Henry Krous, that as to petechiae, "delineation of their pathogenesis and their significance may lead to effective screening or monitoring systems, allowing earlier attempts at therapeutic intervention." In addition, Krous pointed out that a number of hypoxic markers, first identified by Richard L. Naeye and later studied by both Naeye's group and many other researchers, may be useful, "since there is good evidence that many SIDS victims suffer prenatal and postnatal growth failure, and occasionally subtle growth disturbances."

The consequences of SIDS are extremely difficult for afflicted parents; it may lead to extreme stress and destructive effects on their self-images that, in some cases, may never go away, and it may produce major familial disruption that clinicians and counselors find very difficult to handle. For example, in a case history described by Maria Valdes-Dapena, the SIDS victim was a fifty-five-day-old child who was being breast fed and was described as being essentially healthy and happy. On the night of her death, the baby had a mild case of bronchitis and had experienced trouble getting to sleep. A bit after midnight, the exhausted mother left her husband alone with the baby and slept to 5:30 A.M.

On awakening, she found her husband asleep and the baby dead. After this extreme trauma, and in spite of many assurances—including those from clergymen—that the baby had died of SIDS and that there was nothing that they could have done, these parents believed that they were to blame. Long after the death of the child, the parents still reiterated that their lives would never be the same.

According to John Defrain, Jacque Taylor, and Linda Ernst, in *Coping with Sudden Infant Death* (1982), the usual level of parental grief after a SIDS death is very intense, and it requires an average of three years for afflicted parents to regain their previous levels of personal happiness. In that source, one mother is quoted as saying,

"I've learned to accept that my baby is gone, but I don't think I'll ever get over it." Mothers are not the only ones hurt; fathers grieve too, and they often resent the fact that they are expected to "tough out" SIDS. For example, Defrain and coworkers quoted one husband as saying, "I was expected to go back to work . . . and function as if nothing had happened. My tender defense emotions quickly turned into a feeling of hostility toward society in general." With this in mind, perhaps it is not surprising that it is estimated that more than half of SIDS couples eventually end their marriages by divorce.

Other aspects of SIDS trauma that should be considered include how friends and relatives may best interact with SIDS parents, how SIDS parents may best let other children know what happened to their missing sibling, what to do about having another baby, and the type of psychological support needed by SIDS families.

Context

Many researchers believe that SIDS has occurred throughout history. As late as the seventeenth and eighteenth centuries, considerable social stigma and even harsh punishment of parents (especially mothers) accompanied sudden infant death. Even at the end of the nineteenth century, much of the stigma remained. For example, William Butler Yeats, the great Irish poet and playwright, wrote "The Ballad of Moll Magee" about an Irish mother's remorse at the sudden death of her infant. Throughout this ballad, Moll Magee bemoans her fate and her shortcomings as a mother. In addition, she endures the scornful reactions of others to her baby's death.

Despite the tremendous suffering of the parents of SIDS victims—often culminating in divorce—organized efforts at dealing with the syndrome and the psychological problems left in its wake did not begin until the 1960's. As already mentioned, SIDS was not even defined until 1969. According to Valdes-Dapena, it was in the 1960's that cooperation between parents and well-known physicians launched organizations that led to the National Sudden Infant Death Syndrome Foundation in the United States and to similar foundations in other countries.

Continued effort by grief-stricken, socially conscious parents of SIDS victims also produced the 1974 SIDS Act. As a consequence of the law, funds began to be available for regional centers that performed autopsies on SIDS victims and counseled SIDS families, attempting to help them cope with their grief.

By the late 1970's, psychological counseling programs were being widely established that increased coping and stress management by SIDS families. In many locations, SIDS autopsies are performed at no cost; parents are informed quickly about postmortem examinations. Many nursing and counseling options are available. Perhaps even more important, public awareness of SIDS has increased, and much of the social stigma attached to sudden infant death has begun to disappear. Useful efforts along such lines are exemplified by the book by Defrain, Taylor, and Ernst, in which the authors provide a psychological lifeline for parents and other SIDS family members, as well as a text of use both to the general public interested in psychosocial impacts of the syndrome and to SIDS counselors. A final, valuable quote from the book states that "the course of life for parents who lose a baby to SIDS is altered forever. . . . They slowly and painfully acquire new insights into the limits of their power." The efforts of medical research may someday do away with SIDS; meanwhile, the work of psychologists will aid parents in coping with the grief and stress that follow SIDS.

Bibliography

Corr, Charles A., Helen Fuller, Carol Ann Barnickol, and Donna M. Corr, eds. *Sudden Infant Death Syndrome: Who Can Help and How.* New York: Springer, 1991. A very useful resource for SIDS family members, professional and lay helpers, and all those wanting to learn about SIDS. Divided into a review of SIDS characteristics and research, effects of SIDS on family members, guidelines for helping them, and resources for such families. Many references are included.

Culbertson, Jan L., Henry F. Krous, and R. Debra Bendell, eds. *Sudden Infant Death Syndrome: Medical Aspects and Psychological Management.* Baltimore: The Johns Hopkins University Press, 1988. This text, with many references, touches many bases. Its chapters—by specialists—deal with the epidemiology, pathology, proposed mechanistics, and possible origins of SIDS. Consideration of the psychological aspects of SIDS loss are also covered, including loss, grieving reactions, family responses, and development of a National SIDS Foundation.

Defrain, John D., Jacque Taylor, and Linda Ernst. *Coping with Sudden Infant Death.* Lexington, Mass.: Lexington Books, 1982. This book is concerned with the responses of families to SIDS—their stress and coping. Deals with parental responses to SIDS, concerns about what to tell other children, fears about the possibility of having another child after SIDS strikes, and identification of support for SIDS parents; provides a parents' questionnaire that helps parents to identify how they are coping with their loss. Well written and educational.

International Research Conference on the Sudden Infant Death Syndrome. *Sudden Infant Death Syndrome.* Edited by J. Tyson Tildon, Lois M. Roeder, and Alfred Steinschneider. New York: Academic Press, 1983. Contains the presentations of more than a hundred contributors at the 1982 International SIDS Conference in Baltimore. Many important areas, including endocrinology, cardiology, respiratory relationships, sleep involvement, airway physiology, and identification of at-risk infants, are included. This technical text provides much information and extensive references.

Naeye, Richard L. "Sudden Infant Death." *Scientific American* 242 (April, 1980): 56-62. This simple but concise article covers considerable ground about SIDS, including possible origins, some epidemiology, pathological aspects, and symptomology. The writing style is informative, geared to the general reader, and replete with useful references.

Sanford S. Singer

Cross-References

Coping: Social Support, 700; Coping Strategies: An Overview, 706; Couples Therapy, 718; Death and Dying: Theoretical Perspectives, 763; Emotion and Stress, 941; Reflexes in Newborns, 2072; Separation, Divorce, and Family Life: Adult Issues, 2220.

SUICIDE

Type of psychology: Psychopathology
Field of study: Depression

Suicide is the intentional taking of one's own life; roughly twelve per 100,000 Americans commit suicide annually. Suicide rates are higher for males than females and increase with age; risk for suicide also increases with clinical depression, so suicide may be considered the most severe consequence of any psychological disorder.

Principal terms
> ALTRUISTIC SUICIDE: a suicide that occurs in response to societal demands; introduced by Émile Durkheim as one of the three basic types of suicide
> ANOMIE: the experience of alienation or disorientation following a major change in one's social relationships
> EGOISTIC SUICIDE: a suicide that occurs because of insufficient ties between the individual and society
> EPIDEMIOLOGICAL RESEARCH: the study of the frequency of a condition in a population and its relationship to characteristics of the population
> PSYCHOLOGICAL AUTOPSY: an attempt to determine the reasons for suicide, through interviewing the victim's friends and family members and examining personal records
> SUICIDAL GESTURE: an apparent attempted suicide, the primary purpose of which is to call attention to oneself in order to gain sympathy or assistance

Overview

Suicide is the intentional taking of one's own life. Psychologists have devoted much effort to its study, attempting to identify those at greatest risk for suicide and to intervene effectively to prevent suicide.

Sociologist Émile Durkheim introduced what has become a well-known classification of suicide types. Altruistic suicides, according to Durkheim, are those that occur in response to societal demands (for example, the soldier who sacrifices himself to save his comrades). Egoistic suicides occur when the individual is isolated from society and so does not experience sufficient societal demands to live. The third type is the anomic suicide. Anomie is a sense of disorientation or alienation which occurs following a major change in one's societal relationships (such as the loss of a job or the death of a close friend); the anomic suicide occurs following such sudden and dramatic changes.

Research supports Durkheim's ideas that suicide is associated with social isolation and recent loss. Many other variables, both demographic and psychological, have also been found to be related to suicide. Numerous studies have shown that the following demographic variables are related to suicide: sex, age, marital status, employment status, urban/rural dwelling, and race. Paradoxically, more females than males attempt suicide, but more males than females commit suicide. The ratio in both cases is about three to one. The difference between the sex ratios for attempted and completed suicide is generally explained by the fact that males tend to employ more lethal and less reversible methods than do females (firearms and hanging, for example, are more lethal and less reversible than ingestion of drugs).

Age is also related to suicide. In general, risk for suicide increases with increasing age; however, even though suicide risk is higher in older people, much attention has been devoted to suicide among children and adolescents. This attention is attributable to two factors. First, since 1960, there has been an increase in the suicide rate among people under twenty-five years of age. Second, suicide has become one of the leading causes of death among people under twenty-one, whereas suicide is surpassed by many illnesses as a cause of death among older adults. Other demographic variables are related to suicide. Suicide risk is higher for divorced than married people. The unemployed have a higher suicide rate than those who are employed. Urban dwellers have a higher suicide rate than rural dwellers. Caucasians have a higher suicide rate than African Americans.

In addition to these demographic variables, several psychological or behavioral variables are related to suicide. Perhaps the single best predictor of suicide is threatening to commit suicide. Most suicide victims have made some type of suicide threat (although, in some cases, the threat may be veiled or indirect, such as putting one's affairs in order or giving away one's belongings). For this reason, psychologists consider seriously any threat of suicide. A related index of suicide risk is the detailedness or clarity of the threat. Individuals who describe a suicide method in detail are at greater risk than those who express an intent to die but who describe the act only vaguely. Similarly, the lethality and availability of the proposed method provide additional measures of risk. Suicide risk is higher if the individual proposes using a more lethal method and if the individual has access to the proposed method.

Another useful indicator of suicide risk is previous suicide attempts. People who have made prior attempts are at higher risk for suicide than people who have not. The lethality of the method used in the prior attempt is a related indicator. An individual who survives a more lethal method (a gunshot to the head) is considered at higher risk than one who survives a less lethal attempt (swallowing a bottle of aspirin).

Suicide risk is associated with particular behavioral or psychological variables: depression, isolation, stress, pain or illness, recent loss, and drug or alcohol use. These factors may help explain why certain of the demographic variables are related to suicide. For example, people who are unemployed may experience higher levels of stress, depression, and isolation than people who are employed. Similarly, divorced people may experience more stress and isolation than married people. The elderly may experience more isolation, depression, and pain or illness than younger people.

Although the demographic and psychological variables summarized above have been found to be related to suicide, the prediction of suicide remains extremely difficult. Suicide is a statistically rare event; according to basic laws of probability, it is very difficult to predict such rare occurrences. What happens in actual attempts to predict suicide is that, in order to identify the "true positives" (individuals who actually attempt suicide), one must accept a very large number of "false positives" (individuals who are labeled suicidal but who in fact will not attempt suicide).

Applications

Several methods have been used to study the psychology of suicide. Epidemiological research determines the distribution of demographic characteristics among suicide victims. Another method is to study survivors of suicide attempts. This enables psychologists to examine intensively their psychological characteristics. A third method is to analyze suicide notes, which may explain the individual's reasons for suicide. A final method is the psychological autopsy. This involves interviewing the victim's friends and family members and examining the victim's personal materials (such as diaries and letters) in an attempt to identify the psychological cause of the suicide.

Although all these approaches have been widely used, each has its limitations. The epidemiological method focuses on demographic characteristics and so may overlook psychological influences. Studying survivors of suicide attempts has limitations because survivors and victims of suicide attempts may differ significantly. For example, some suicide attempts are regarded as suicidal gestures, or "cries for help," the intent of which is not to die but rather to call attention to oneself to gain sympathy or assistance. Thus, what is learned from survivors may not generalize to suicide victims. The study of suicide notes is limited by the fact that, contrary to popular belief, most suicide victims do not leave notes. For example, in a study of all suicides in Los Angeles County in a single year, psychologists Edwin Shneidman and Norman Farberow found that only 35 percent of the males and 39 percent of the females left notes. Finally, the psychological autopsy is limited in that the victim's records and acquaintances may not shed light on the victim's thought processes.

In 1988, Harry Hoberman and Barry Garfinkel conducted an epidemiological study to identify variables related to suicide in children and adolescents. They examined death records in two counties in Minnesota over an eleven-year period for individuals who died at age nineteen or younger. Hoberman and Garfinkel examined in detail the death records of 225 suicide victims. They noted that 15 percent of their sample had not been identified as suicides by the medical examiner, but had instead been listed as accident victims or as having died of undetermined causes. This finding suggests that official estimates of suicide deaths in the United States are actually low.

Consistent with other studies, Hoberman and Garfinkel found that suicide was related to both age and sex. Males accounted for 80 percent of the suicides, females for only 20 percent. Adolescents aged fifteen to nineteen years composed 91 percent of the sample, with children aged fourteen and under only 9 percent. In addition, Hoberman and Garfinkel found that a full 50 percent of the sample showed evidence of one or more psychiatric disorders. Most common were depression and alcohol and drug abuse. Finally, Hoberman and Garfinkel found that a substantial number of the suicide victims had been described as "loners," "lonely," or "withdrawn." Thus, several of the indicators of suicide in adults also are related to suicide in children and adolescents.

Psychiatrist Aaron Beck and his colleagues developed the Hopelessness Scale in 1974 to assess an individual's negative thoughts of self and future. In many theories of suicide, an individual's sense of hopelessness is related to risk for suicide. Beck and others have demonstrated that hopelessness in depressed patients is a useful indicator of suicide risk. For example, in 1985, Beck and his colleagues reported a study of 207 patients who were hospitalized because of suicidal thinking. Over the next five to ten years, fourteen patients committed suicide. Only one demographic variable, race, differed between the suicide and nonsuicide groups: Caucasian patients had a higher rate of suicide (10.1 percent) than African-American patients (1.3 percent). Of the psychological variables assessed, only the Hopelessness Scale and a measure of pessimism differed between suicide victims and other patients. Patients who committed suicide were higher in both hopelessness and pessimism than other patients. Beck and his colleagues determined the Hopelessness Scale score which best discriminated suicides from nonsuicides. Other mental health professionals can now use this criterion to identify those clinically depressed patients who are at greatest risk for suicide.

Several approaches have been developed in efforts to prevent suicide. Shneidman and Farberow developed what may be the most well-known suicide-prevention program, the Los Angeles Suicide Prevention Center. This program, begun in 1958, helped popularize telephone suicide hotlines. Staff members are trained to interact with individuals who are experiencing extreme distress. When an individual calls the center, staff members immediately begin to assess the caller's risk for suicide, considering the caller's demographics, stress, life-style, and suicidal intent. Staff members attempt to calm the caller, so as to prevent an immediate suicide, and to put the person into contact with local mental health agencies so that the individual can receive more extensive follow-up care.

Psychologists William Fremouw, Maria de Perczel, and Thomas Ellis published a useful guide for those who work with suicidal clients. Among their suggestions are to talk openly and matter-of-factly about suicide, to avoid dismissing the client's feelings or motives in a judgmental or pejorative way, and to adopt a problem-solving approach to dealing with the client's situation.

Suicide-prevention programs are difficult to evaluate. Callers may not identify themselves, so it is difficult to determine whether they later commit suicide. Still, such programs are generally thought to be useful, and suicide-prevention programs similar to that of Shneidman and Farberow have been developed in many communities.

Context

Suicide is one of the most extreme and drastic behaviors faced by psychologists. Because of its severity, psychologists have devoted considerable effort to identifying individuals at risk for suicide and to developing programs that are effective in preventing suicide.

Psychological studies of suicide have shown that many popular beliefs about suicide are incorrect. For example, many people erroneously believe that people who threaten suicide never attempt suicide; that all suicide victims truly wish to die; that only the mentally ill commit suicide; that suicide runs in families; and that there are no treatments that can help someone who is suicidal. Because of these and other popular myths about suicide, it is especially important that psychological studies of suicide continue and that the results of this study be disseminated to the public.

Suicide risk increases in clinically depressed individuals. In depressed patients, suicide risk has been found to be associated with hopelessness: As one's sense of hopelessness increases, one's risk for suicide increases. Since the 1970's, Beck's Hopelessness Scale has been used in efforts to predict risk for suicide among depressed patients. Although the suicide rate has been relatively stable in the United States throughout the 1900's, the suicide rate of young people has increased since the 1960's. For this reason, depression and suicide among children and adolescents have become major concerns of psychologists. Whereas childhood depression received relatively little attention from psychologists before the 1970's, psychologists have devoted considerable attention to this condition since then. Much of this attention has concerned whether biological, cognitive, and behavioral theories of the causes of depression and approaches to the treatment of depression, which were originally developed and applied to depressed adults, may generalize to children.

In the 1980's, psychologists developed several innovative programs that attempt to identify youths who are depressed and experiencing hopelessness, and so may be at risk for suicide; evaluations and refinements of these programs will continue.

Bibliography

Durkheim, Émile. *Suicide.* Reprint. Glencoe, Ill.: Free Press, 1951. In this work, originally published in 1897, Durkheim introduced his classification system of suicide types—altruistic, egoistic, and anomic suicides—and examined the relationship of suicide to isolation and recent loss.

Fremouw, William J., Maria de Perczel, and Thomas E. Ellis. *Suicide Risk: Assessment and Response Guidelines.* New York: Pergamon Press, 1990. This book presents useful guidelines, based on both research and clinical practice, for working with suicidal individuals.

Hawton, Keith. *Suicide and Attempted Suicide Among Children and Adolescents.* Beverly Hills, Calif.: Sage Publications, 1986. This work overviews research results concerning the causes of youth suicide and treatment programs for suicidal youngsters.

Holinger, Paul C., and J. Sandlow. "Suicide." In *Violent Deaths in the United States,* edited by Paul C. Holinger. New York: Guilford Press, 1987. This chapter presents epidemiological information on suicide in the United States, from 1900 to 1980. It also addresses demographic variables and their relationship to suicide.

Lann, Irma S., Eve K. Moscicki, and Ronald Maris, eds. *Strategies for Studying Suicide and Suicidal Behavior.* New York: Guilford Press, 1989. This book examines the various research methods used to study suicide. Considers the relative strengths and weaknesses and offers examples of each method.

Lester, David, ed. *Current Concepts of Suicide.* Philadelphia: Charles Press, 1990. A useful overview of research results on the possible causes of suicide and on programs designed both to prevent suicide and to treat suicidal patients.

Peck, Michael L., Norman L. Farberow, and Robert E. Litman, eds. *Youth Suicide.* New York: Springer, 1985. A useful overview of the psychological influences on youth suicide and on the treatment and prevention programs that have been used with suicidal youths.

Shneidman, Edwin S., Norman L. Farberow, and Robert E. Litman. *The Psychology of Suicide.* New York: Science House, 1970. This is a collection of articles, some of which are now regarded as classics in the study of suicide.

Stengel, Erwin. *Suicide and Attempted Suicide.* Rev. ed. Harmondsworth, England: Penguin Books, 1973. This classic work summarizes the demographic and psychological variables that were known at the time to be associated with suicide.

Michael Wierzbicki

Cross-References

Abnormality: Biomedical Models, 39; Abnormality: Cognitive Models, 46; Bipolar Disorder, 422; Clinical Depression, 521; Depression: Theoretical Explanations, 789; Psychoactive Drug Therapy, 1891; Teenage Suicide, 2527.

SURVEY RESEARCH:
QUESTIONNAIRES AND INTERVIEWS

Type of psychology: Psychological methodologies
Fields of study: Descriptive methodologies; experimental methodologies; methodological issues

Psychologists use survey research techniques including questionnaires and interviews to evaluate specific attitudes about social or personal issues, and to find out about people's behaviors directly from those people. Questionnaires are self-administered and in written form; interviews consist of the psychologist asking questions of the respondent. There are strengths along with limitations for both of these data collection methods.

Principal terms

ATTITUDES: a person's thoughts and beliefs about something in the world or about him- or herself

DEMOGRAPHICS: statistical features of populations, such as age, income, race, and marital status

INTERVIEW: a Data collection technique involving one-to-one verbal communication, either face-to-face or by means of a telephone, between the interviewer and respondent

POPULATION: all people in a definable group

QUESTIONNAIRE: a data collection technique in which the questions are in written format and the respondents write down their answers

RESPONDENT: a person (subject) who provides answers to a questionnaire or in an interview

SAMPLE: the number of people who participate in a study and are part of a population

SURVEY RESEARCH: the collection of data from people by means of questionnaires or interviews

Overview

Survey research is common in both science and daily life. Most everyone in today's society has been exposed to survey research in one form or another. Researchers ask questions about the political candidate one favors, the television programs one watches, the soft drink one prefers, whether there should be a waiting period prior to purchasing a handgun, and so on.

There are many ways to obtain data about the social world; among them are observation, field studies, and experimentation. Two key methods for obtaining data—questionnaires and interviews—are survey research methods. Most of the social research conducted or published involves these two data collection devices.

In general, when using survey methods, the researcher gets information directly from each person (or respondent) by using self-report measurement techniques to ask people about their current attitudes, behaviors, and demographics, in addition to past experiences and future goals. In questionnaires, the questions are in written format and the subjects write down their answers. In interviews, there is one-to-one verbal communication, either face-to-face or by means of a telephone, between the interviewer and respondent. Both techniques are flexible and adaptable to the group of people being studied and the particular situation. Both can range from being highly structured to highly unstructured.

Questionnaires can be completed in groups or self-administered on an individual basis. They can also be mailed to people. They are generally less expensive than conducting interviews. Questionnaires also allow greater anonymity of the respondents. One drawback is that a questionnaire requires that the subjects understand exactly what the questions are asking. Also, there may be a problem of motivation with the filling out of questionnaires, because people may get bored or find it tedious to fill out the forms on their own. The survey researcher must therefore make sure that the questionnaire is not excessively long.

In contrast, with an interview there is a chance that the interviewer and subject will have good communication and that all questions will be understood. Telephone interviews are less expensive than face-to-face interviews; still, questionnaires tend to be less costly. In an interview, the respondent is presented with questions orally, whereas in the questionnaire, regardless of type or form, the respondent is presented with a written question. Each data collection device has pros and cons. The decision to use questionnaires versus interviews would basically depend on the purpose of the study, the type of information needed, the size of the sample, the resources for conducting the study, and the variable(s) to be measured. Overall, the interview is probably the more flexible device of the two.

When creating a questionnaire, the researcher must give special thought to writing the specific questions. Researchers must avoid questions that would lead people to answer in a biased way, or ones that might be easily misinterpreted. For example, the questions "Do you favor eliminating the wasteful excesses in the federal budget?" and "Do you favor reducing the federal budget?" might well result in different answers.

Questions are either closed- or open-ended, depending on the researcher's choice. In a closed-ended question, a limited number of fixed response choices are provided to subjects. With open-ended questions, subjects are able to respond in any way they like. Thus, a researcher could ask a person "Where would you like a swimming pool to be built in this town?" versus "Which of the following locations is your top choice for a swimming pool to be built in this town?" The first question allows the person to provide any answer; the second provides a fixed number of alternative answers from which the person must choose. Use of closed-ended questions is a more structured approach, allowing greater ease of analysis because the response alternatives are the same for everyone. Open-ended questions require more time to analyze and are therefore more costly. Open-ended questions, however, can provide valuable insights into what the subjects are actually thinking.

A specialized type of interview is the clinical, or therapeutic, interview. The specific goal of a particular clinical interview depends on the needs and the condition of the particular individual being interviewed. There is a distinction between a therapeutic interview, which attempts both to obtain information and to remedy the client's problem, and a research interview, which attempts solely to obtain information about people at large. Because the clinical interview is a fairly unstructured search for relevant information, it is important to be aware of the factors that might affect its accuracy and comprehensiveness. Research on hypothesis confirmation bias suggests that it is difficult to search for unbiased and comprehensive information in an unstructured setting such as the clinical interview. In the context of the clinical interview, clinicians are likely to conduct unintentionally biased searches for information that confirms their early impressions of each client. Research on self-fulfilling prophecies suggests a second factor that may limit the applicability of interviews in general. This research suggests that the interviewer's expectations affect the behavior of the person being interviewed, and that respondents may change their behavior to match the interviewer's expectations.

Applications

Knowing what to believe about research is often related to understanding the scientific method. The two basic approaches to using the scientific method, the descriptive and the experimental research approaches, differ because they seek to attain different types of knowledge. Descriptive research tries to describe particular situations; experimental research tries to determine cause-and-effect relationships. Independent variables are not manipulated in descriptive research. For that reason, it is not possible to decide if one thing causes another. Instead, survey research uses correlational techniques, which allow the determination of whether behaviors or attitudes are related to one another and whether they predict one another. For example, how liberal a person's political views are might be related to that person's attitudes about sexuality. Such a relationship could be determined using descriptive research.

Survey research, as a widely used descriptive technique, is defined as a method of collecting standardized information by interviewing a representative sample of some population. All research involves sampling of subjects. That is, subjects must be found to participate in the research whether that research is a survey or an experiment. Sampling is particularly important when conducting survey research, because the goal is to describe what a whole population is like based on the data from a relatively small sample of that population.

One famous survey study conducted in the mid-1930's was the interviewing done by Alfred Kinsey and his colleagues. Kinsey studied sexual behavior. Until that time, most of what was known about sexual behavior was based on what biologists knew about animal sex, what anthropologists knew about sex among natives in non-Western, nonindustrialized societies, or what Freud learned about sexuality from his emotionally disturbed patients. Kinsey and his colleagues were the first psychological researchers to interview volunteers about their sexual behaviors. The research was hindered by political investigations and threats of legal action against them. In spite of the harassment encountered by the scientists on the project, the Kinsey group published *Sexual Behavior in the Human Male* in 1948 and *Sexual Behavior in the Human Female* in 1953. The findings of the Kinsey group have benefited the public immensely. As a result, it is now known that the majority of people (both males and females) interviewed by the Kinsey group masturbated at various times, but that more males than females said they masturbated. Data collected by the Kinsey group on oral-genital sexual practices have allowed researchers to discover that, since the 1930's, attitudes toward oral-genital sex have become more positive. Their research also shocked the nation with the discovery that the majority of brides at that time were not virgins.

When scientific sampling techniques are used, the survey results can be interpreted as an accurate representation of the entire population. Although Kinsey and his associates helped to pave the way for future researchers to be able to investigate sexual behaviors and attitudes, there were some problems with the research because of its lack of generalizability. The Kinsey group research is still the largest study of sexual behavior ever completed. They interviewed more than ten thousand people; however, they did not attempt to select a random or representative sample of the population of the United States, which meant that the responses of middle-class, well-educated Caucasians were overrepresented. There is also a problem with the accuracy of the respondents' information, because of memory errors, exaggerations, or embarrassment about wanting to tell an interviewer personal, sensitive information. Despite these limitations, the interviewing conducted by Kinsey and associates made great strides for the study of sexuality and great strides for psychology in general.

When research is intended to reveal very precisely what a population is like, careful sampling procedures must be used. This requires defining the population and sampling people from the population in a random fashion so that no biases will be introduced into the sample. In order to learn what elderly people think about the medical services available to them, for example, a careful sample of the elderly population is needed. Obtaining the sample only from retirement communities in Arizona would bias the results, because these individuals are not representative of all elderly people in the population.

Thus, when evaluating survey data, a researcher must examine how the responses were obtained and what population was investigated. Major polling organizations such as the Gallup organization typically are careful to obtain representative samples of people in the United States. Gallup polls are frequently conducted to survey the voting public's opinions about the popularity of a presidential candidate or a given policy. Many other surveys, however, such as surveys that are published in popular magazines, have limited generalizability because the results are based on people who read the particular magazine and are sufficiently motivated to complete and mail in the questionnaire. When *Redbook*, for example, asks readers to write in to say whether they have ever had an affair, the results may be interesting but would not give a very accurate estimate of the true extent of extramarital sexual activity in the United States. An example of an inaccurate sampling technique was a survey by *Literary Digest* (a now defunct magazine) sampling almost ten million people. The results showed that Alfred Landon would beat Franklin D. Roosevelt by a landslide in the 1936 presidential election. Although it was large, the sample was completely inaccurate.

Context

One of the earliest ways of obtaining psychological information using descriptive techniques was through clinical interviewing. The early interviews conducted by Sigmund Freud in the late 1800's were based on question-and-answer medical formats, which is not surprising, considering that Freud was originally a physician. Later, Freud relied on the less structured free-association technique. In 1902, Adolf Meyer developed a technique to assess a client's mental functioning, memory, attention, speech, and judgment. Independent of the style used, all the early clinical interviews sought to get a psychological portrait of the person, determine the source of the problem, make a diagnosis, and formulate a treatment. More detailed studies of interviews were conducted in the 1940's and 1950's to compare and contrast interviewing styles and determine how much structure was necessary. During the 1960's, much research came about as a result of ideas held by Carl Rogers, who emphasized the interpersonal elements he thought were necessary for the ideal therapeutic relationship; among them are warmth, positive regard, and genuineness on the part of the interviewer.

In the 1800's and early 1900's, interviews were used mainly by psychologists who were therapists helping people with problems such as fear, depression, and hysteria. During that same period, experimental psychologists had not yet begun to use survey research methods. Instead, they used introspection to investigate their own thought processes. For example, experimental psychologist Hermann Ebbinghaus gave himself lists of pronounceable nonsense syllables to remember; he then tested his own memory and attempted to improve it methodically. Many experimental psychologists during this period relied upon the use of animals such as dogs and laboratory rats to conduct behavioral research.

As mentioned above, one of the first attempts by experimental psychologists to study attitudes and behaviors by means of the interview was that of the Kinsey group in the 1930's. At about that same time, Louis Thurstone, an experimental social psychologist, formalized and popularized the first questionnaire methodology for attitude measurement. Thurstone devised a set of questionnaires, or scales, that have been widely used for decades. He is considered by many to be the "father" of attitude scaling. Soon thereafter, Rensis Likert made breakthroughs in questionnaire usage with the development of what are known as Likert scales. A Likert scale provides a series of statements to which subjects can indicate degrees of agreement or disagreement. Using the Likert technique, the respondent answers by selecting from predetermined categories ranging from "strongly agree" to "strongly disagree." It is fairly standard to use five categories (strongly agree, agree, uncertain, disagree, strongly disagree), but more categories can be used if necessary. An example of a question using this technique might be, "Intelligence test scores of marijuana users are higher on the average than scores of nonusers." The respondent then picks one of the five categories mentioned above in response. Likert scales have been widely used and have resulted in a vast amount of information about human attitudes and behaviors.

Bibliography

Berdie, Douglas R., and John F. Anderson. *Questionnaires: Design and Use.* Metuchen, N.J.: Scarecrow Press, 1974. Provides extensive, detailed information that guides the reader through the process of questionnaire creation. Also helps the novice learn how to administer a questionnaire correctly.

Bordens, Kenneth S., and Bruce B. Abbott. *Research Design and Methods: A Process Approach.* Mountain View, Calif.: Mayfield, 1988. Places the techniques of surveys, interviews, and questionnaires for collecting data in the context of conducting research as a process from start to finish. A well-received textbook in psychology.

Converse, Jean M., and Stanley Presser. *Survey Questions: Handcrafting the Standardized Questionnaire.* Beverly Hills, Calif.: Sage, 1986. Provides explicit, practical details which would be of use to a person who needs to put together a questionnaire for any of a variety of reasons. Stresses the art of questionnaire creation.

Cozby, Paul C. *Methods in Behavioral Research.* 4th ed. Mountain View, Calif.: Mayfield, 1989. Examines the importance of survey research in the context of conducting experiments and doing research in psychology in general. Allows the reader to understand the research process from a broader perspective.

Kidder, Louise H., and Charles M. Judd. *Research Methods in Social Relations.* 5th ed. New York: Holt, Rinehart and Winston, 1986. A popular book whose writing style is exceptionally clear. Offers thorough information that introduces the reader to the process of doing research in psychology, including how to get an idea for a research topic, how to collect the information, how to be ethical with subjects, and how to report the results. Detailed information is provided on questionnaires and interviews.

Stewart, Charles J., and William B. Cash, Jr. *Interviewing Principles and Practices.* 3d ed. Dubuque, Iowa: Wm. C. Brown, 1982. A "hands-on" introduction to interviewing which provides practical suggestions and tips along with background information.

Deborah R. McDonald

Cross-References

SYNAPTIC TRANSMISSION

Type of psychology: Biological bases of behavior
Field of study: Nervous system

A neuron transmits chemical or electrical signals to other cells and controls their functions through an intercellular space called synaptic cleft. Synaptic transmission is a key to understanding various normal and abnormal behavioral and physiological phenomena as well as the effects of various neuroactive drugs.

Principal terms
AGONIST: a chemical compound which has the same effects as a neurotransmitter or enhances its effects
ANTAGONIST: a compound which blocks or reduces the effects of a neurotransmitter
NEUROPSYCHOPHARMACOLOGY: the study of the relationship among behavior, neuronal functioning, and drugs
NEUROTRANSMITTER: a chemical signal released by a neuron to "talk" to other cells, resulting in cellular changes
RECEPTOR: a protein molecule embedded in the postsynaptic membrane with which neurotransmitter molecules act to initiate chemical and electrical events in a receiving cell
SYNAPTIC CLEFT: an intercellular space—2 to 30 nanometers wide, between a neuron and its target cell—through which a neuron communicates with another cell
SYNAPTIC TRANSMISSION: the transfer of signals from a neuron to other cells through the synaptic cleft
VESICLE: a spherical or oval-shaped bubble with a diameter of 30 to 160 nanometers found inside a presynaptic terminal; contains molecules of a neurotransmitter

Overview

Transmission refers to the transferring of signals from a source to a receiving end through or across a medium. Synaptic transmission specifically refers to the transferring of a signal from a neuron (a nerve cell) across a space called the synaptic cleft to a target cell. The nerve impulse is generated in the cell body of the neuron and is related to the movement of sodium ions across the cell membrane of the axon (the axon is an extension of the neuron cell body). This impulse is known as an action potential. When the impulse reaches the axon terminal, this presynaptic signal either remains as an electrical signal or is converted to a chemical signal; either way, it is then transmitted through this space and exerts an influence on the target cell. The "synapse" contains three areas: the presynaptic terminal, the synaptic cleft, and the postsynaptic membrane.

Physical activity and behavior involve neuronal activities and the resulting contractions and relaxations of many muscles. The winking of an eye, for example, involves the control of contraction and relaxation of eyelid muscles. The axon terminals of the motor neurons must synapse with the eyelid muscles. A synapse between neuron and muscle cells is called a neuromuscular junction. The axon terminal releases a neurochemical that acts on the receptors embedded in the cell membrane of the postsynaptic muscle cells, resulting in muscle contraction. The synaptic area is a key to the control of neural effects; most chemicals that affect the nervous system vary physiological and behavioral responses at this site.

Two distinct modes of synaptic transmission have been delineated, one electrical and the other chemical. At an electrical synapse, the presynaptic current spreads across the intercellular gap to the target cell. In order for this spreading to occur, a low-resistance pathway is required; this is achieved by a close apposition of cells with a gap of about 2 nanometers (one nanometer is one-billionth of a meter). This type of coupling is called a gap junction. Unlike in chemical transmission, in electrical transmission an impulse in the presynaptic terminal is transmitted to the postsynaptic terminal with little attenuation (lessening) and with no time delay. Electrical synapses are very common in the nervous systems of invertebrates, lower vertebrates, and embryonic animals.

At a chemical synapse, the gap is about 20 to 30 nanometers. The high resistance does not allow spreading of the presynaptic current to the postsynaptic current to occur. Upon arrival of impulses, a presynaptic terminal releases chemicals termed neurotransmitters. These molecules then diffuse through the cleft and interact with receptors, complex protein molecules embedded in the postsynaptic membrane. The neurotransmitter molecules are stored in vesicles. The wall of the vesicle becomes fused to the presynaptic membrane because of the influx of calcium ions upon arrival of the impulse; this results in release of the molecules. The interaction between neurotransmitter and receptor results in certain electrical and chemical events in the target cell. In chemical transmission, the signals are attenuated, and the process takes more time than electrical transmission—about 0.3 millisecond, which is termed the synaptic delay. Neurotransmitters secreted by the presynaptic terminals include acetylcholine, dopamine, epinephrine, norepinephrine, serotonin, certain amino acids (gamma-aminobutyric acid, glutamate, glycine, aspartate), and many peptides.

Neurons come in various shapes and possess varying numbers of branches. Basically, however, each consists of the dendrites, the soma (cell body), and the axon. Synapses are classified in terms of the nature of the presynaptic terminal and the postsynaptic end. The presynaptic terminal is usually an axon; however, it has been found that dendrites may communicate with other dendrites directly at a synapse termed a dendrodendritic synapse. Three types of synapses between neurons are axodendritic, axosomatic, and axoaxonic. An axodendritic synapse couples an axon terminal to a dendrite of another neuron and usually produces a depolarization or excitatory postsynaptic potential (EPSP). An axosomatic synapse couples an axon terminal to the soma of another neuron, and it may produce a hyperpolarization or inhibitory postsynaptic potential (IPSP) as well as an EPSP. An axoaxonic synapse couples an axon terminal to another axon terminal, which results in reduction of EPSP in the target neuron of the second neuron, so the net effect is inhibitory. When an axon terminal is coupled to a muscle cell or a glandular cell, the synapse is called a neuromuscular junction or a neuroeffector junction. The EPSP occurring in the muscle is called end-plate potential. When the sum of those potential changes reaches the threshold of firing, an action potential is generated, resulting in a propagating impulse or muscular contraction.

Applications

The release of a neurotransmitter substance, the binding of neurotransmitter molecules to receptors, and the termination of neurotransmitter activities are among the key considerations in understanding the regulation of the effects of the nervous system. The synthesis and storage (in vesicles) of these substances are also important. The magnitude and duration of many physiological and behavioral responses are jointly determined by various neuronal effects. Neuroactive drugs are crucial tools, and various ones manipulate different phases of transmission, synthesis, storage, release, binding, and termination of neurotransmitters. These drugs may be used to study the functions of various neurochemicals as well as to control synaptic transmission for therapeutic purposes.

Neuroactive drugs and chemicals are classified in terms of their facilitating or inhibitory effects. Agonists are those that enhance the effects of a neurotransmitter; antagonists inhibit the effects. For example, curare, a compound extracted from a vine by South American Indians for use as an arrow poison to paralyze animals, is an antagonist of the neurotransmitter acetylcholine at the neuromuscular junction. Curare interferes with synaptic transmission at this junction, resulting in muscle paralysis.

A lock-and-key analogy is often employed to explain how synaptic transmission works. The neurotransmitter molecule represents the key, and the receptor molecule represents the lock. Just as the correct key is needed to open the lock on a door, the appropriate chemical "key" is needed to start the effect. The molecular lock has the recognition site and the active site as well as the support structure, just as the door has the keyhole with specific notch configurations, as well as other parts. A neurotransmitter may be able to open several different locks, termed receptor subtypes, which are named for the chemical compounds specific to each subtype. (In this sense, a neurotransmitter is like a submaster key that will fit several doors, while a subtype-specific compound is the key for only one door.) The neurotransmitter acetylcholine, for example, acts on two receptor subtypes—nicotinic and muscarinic. The nicotinic receptor is so named because it reacts specifically to nicotine, a substance found in tobacco. This receptor subtype is found in the smooth and cardiac muscles; the muscarinic subtype, on the other hand, is abundant in the brain.

Nicotine and muscarine, in other words, each affect only one subtype, but acetylcholine affects both; thus, acetylcholine and nicotine are both nicotinic receptor agonists, and acetylcholine and muscarine are both muscarinic receptor agonists. To return to the example of curare, it is a subtype-specific blocker that acts on the nicotinic receptor to block the effect of acetylcholine, causing paralysis of the skeletal muscles. Chemical variants of curare are used clinically to cause muscle relaxation before surgery.

Atropine is a muscarinic receptor blocker, so the cholinergic effects that are mediated by this subtype are antagonized. This drug is used to reduce motion sickness, to induce pupillary dilation for retinal examination, and to fight the sickening effects of certain gases used in chemical warfare. It is because those gases often involve cholinergic agonists that atropine is an appropriate antidote. There are many other compounds that can affect cholinergic effects through interfering with the release, receptor binding, and termination mechanisms. For example, the venom of the black widow spider facilitates the release of acetylcholine, whereas botulinum food poison inhibits its release. Physostigmine, a compound obtained from the Calabar bean in West Africa, enhances acetylcholine effects. Physostigmine is used to treat glaucoma and to help control the forgetfulness of Alzheimer's disease patients.

The potency and efficacy of a drug are presumably related to the degree of fit between the drug molecule and the receptor molecule; a potent drug is one with a good fit to a receptor or subtype. The pharmaceutical industry is constantly working to synthesize variants of neurotransmitters and neuroactive compounds to make the effects of the drug both potent and specific, thus reducing undesirable side effects.

Since acetylcholine in the brain is known to be related to learning and memory, and since Alzheimer's disease involves memory loss, it is theorized that the disease may involve cholinergic subfunctioning. Indeed, cholinergic neurons have been found to be lacking in Alzheimer's patients' brains. Thus, drugs that could alleviate the symptoms are cholinergic agonists of various kinds, such as physostigmine, and various cholinomimetics, drugs that mimic acetylcholine. Many cholinomimetics are so-called nootropic drugs, compounds that may be able to improve learning, memory, and cognitive functions. Dopamine, another neurotransmitter in the brain, has been found to be involved with the hallucinations and delusions of schizophrenics, and dopamine antagonists are used as antipsychotic drugs. Amphetamine is known to induce those psychotic symptoms; this type of drug promotes the release of dopamine.

Furthermore, a lack of dopamine activity has been linked to the symptoms of Parkinson's disease, so anti-Parkinson's drugs tend to be dopamine agonists. Depression has been found to be related to reduced activity of norepinephrine in the brain, so some antidepressants are norepinephrine agonists. Morphine is a well-known pain reducer; in the body, there are chemically similar compounds known as endorphins (from "endogenous morphine"). They are released by neurons within the spinal cord, resulting in a reduction of the release of the neurotransmitter (called substance P) related to pain signaling, thus suppressing pain. Arousal is known to be related to acetylcholine and norepinephrine in the brain; dreaming has also been related to norepinephrine. The action of the tranquilizer Valium (diazepam), the most commonly prescribed drug in the United States, is related to the activity of an inhibitory neurotransmitter, gamma-aminobutyric acid. Neuropsychopharmacology is the area of study that explores the relationships among neurophysiology, neuroanatomy, and pharmacology. Neurotransmission is an important key to discovering these relationships. Beyond the importance of such research efforts, however, it must also be remembered that behavior, both normal and abnormal, is inextricably related to the effects of synaptic transmission.

Context

In the earliest years of the twentieth century, neurotransmission was thought to be solely electrical. The discovery of the synaptic cleft, however, made neuroscientists wonder whether an electrical current could jump a gap of this magnitude. The chemical hypothesis of neurotransmission was then proposed, although it was not until 1921 that convincing evidence of chemical transmission was obtained. Otto Loewi, a German physiologist, electrically stimulated the parasympathetic vagus nerve of a frog and recorded the effect on the frog's heart. He then transferred the liquid from the stimulated heart to an unstimulated frog heart and observed that the recipient heart reacted as if it were stimulated. The effect of the vagal stimulation—decreasing the heart rate—was transferred to the unstimulated heart via the liquid from the stimulated heart. This transferral could only occur if the electrical stimulation of the vagus had resulted in the release of a chemical into the heart and this chemical was transferred to the new heart, thus inducing the same effect. Loewi called this substance *Vagusstoff*, since it was released from the vagus nerve. Later chemical analysis revealed the substance to be acetylcholine, the first neurotransmitter to be identified.

No fewer that fifty neurotransmitter substances have been identified, and researchers are still discovering new ones. In order to classify a substance as a neurotransmitter, a scientist needs to show that it fulfills a number of conditions. The substance (referred to as a putative neurotransmitter) should be found in the presynaptic terminals. Exogenous applications of the substance should mimic the effect of endogenously released substance when the presynaptic neurons are electrically stimulated. The drug effect should be the same as the effect of exogenously applied substance and as the effect of endogenously released transmitter substance. A mechanism must exist for the synthesis of the substance in the presynaptic neuron. A mechanism must also exist for the termination of the transmitter activity of the substance. As can be seen, it is not an easy task to identify and define a new neurotransmitter substance.

The United States Public Health Service proclaimed the 1990's to be the "decade of the brain." The synthesis of drugs that may be related to brain functions is an area of intense research activity. Neuropsychopharmacological studies test the effects of various compounds; the new compounds are also used to test for specific neuronal bases of brain functions. New drugs not only increase the possibilities for controlling neuronal function but also reduce the undesirable side effects of drug therapy by making the effects specific to receptor subtypes. Better, more effective drugs will undoubtedly continue to be produced.

Bibliography

Adelman, George, ed. *Encyclopedia of Neuroscience.* 2 vols. Boston: Birkhäuser, 1987. A very comprehensive source of information on neuroscience. Eleven topics cover the synapsis specifically.

Feldman, Robert Simon, and Linda F. Quenzer. *Fundamentals of Neuropsychopharmacology.* Sunderland, Mass.: Sinauer Associates, 1984. This is a popular text addressing much information related to drugs and behavior. It covers major neurochemical systems in terms of how the synthesis, release, and fate of each neurotransmitter may be controlled by various neuroactive compounds, and it looks at the ensuing behavioral changes.

Julien, Robert M. *A Primer of Drug Action.* 4th ed. New York: W. H. Freeman, 1985. This paperback book describes how synaptic transmission can be manipulated by drugs to affect physiological and psychological responses. Historical episodes about drugs and coverage of various "street" compounds make this interesting reading.

Kuffler, Stephen W., John G. Nicholls, and A. Robert Martin. *From Neuron to Brain.* 2d ed. Sunderland, Mass.: Sinauer Associates, 1984. The authors are well-known researchers; Kuffler was a respected teacher in neurophysiology from Harvard University. This widely used neuroscience text covers historical and modern approaches to neurophysiology in general and synaptic transmission in particular.

Shepherd, Gordon M. *Neurobiology.* 2d ed. New York: Oxford University Press, 1988. The author is an authority in sensory physiology at Yale University. The text covers the nervous system from molecular to system levels, with synaptic transmission regarded as a major link.

Siegel, George J., Bernard W. Agranoff, R. Wayne Albers, and Perry B. Molinoff, eds. *Basic Neurochemistry.* 4th ed. New York: Raven Press, 1989. The book covers forty-eight topics, each discussed by one or more authoritative researchers in the respective fields. Thirteen topics are under "Synaptic Function," covering the major neurotransmitter systems. Useful as a text or reference source; it has a helpful glossary and an index.

Sigmund Hsiao

Cross-References

The Autonomic Nervous System, 362; The Central and Peripheral Nervous Systems, 494; Inhibitory and Excitatory Impulses, 1296; Neural and Hormonal Interaction, 1648; Neurons, 1661; Neurotransmitters, 1673; Reflexes, 2066.

TASTE AVERSION AND LEARNING THEORY

Type of psychology: Learning
Fields of study: Biological influences on learning; instrumental conditioning;
Pavlovian conditioning

Taste aversion occurs when an animal or person eats a food, becomes ill, and subsequently develops a distaste for the food that motivates avoidance. Most often considered a form of Pavlovian conditioning, taste aversion learning has several unusual characteristics that have made it an important topic in the literature of learning theory.

Principal terms
AVOIDANCE CONDITIONING: learning in which certain behaviors come not to be emitted because they produce aversive consequences or in which behaviors are emitted because they avoid such consequences
EQUIPOTENTIALITY: in Pavlovian conditioning, the idea that any stimulus paired with an effective unconditioned stimulus will come to elicit a conditioned response with equal facility
INSTRUMENTAL CONDITIONING: learning in which the consequences of a behavior determine whether the behavior is repeated
INTERSTIMULUS INTERVAL: in Pavlovian conditioning, the time between the conditioned stimulus and the unconditioned stimulus
PAVLOVIAN CONDITIONING: learning in which a neutral (conditioned) stimulus comes to elicit a conditioned response through pairing with an unconditioned stimulus that elicits an innate unconditioned response
PREPAREDNESS: the idea that, through evolution, animals have been genetically prepared to learn certain things important to their survival

Overview

When an animal eats a food, especially one with which it has had little experience, and then becomes ill, the food acquires a nauseating or aversive quality and will subsequently be avoided. This phenomenon is called bait shyness, food aversion, or, most commonly, taste aversion, although the odor and sometimes even the sight of the food also become aversive.

When confronted with a new food, rats will investigate it thoroughly by sniffing. If the odor is unfamiliar, and familiar food is available elsewhere, the rats may pass by the novel food without eating it. If sufficiently hungry, the rats may sample the new food by nibbling at it and then withdrawing to wait for adverse effects. If none occurs, the new food may be accepted, but if the rats become ill the food will be avoided; even the trails or runways where the new food is located may be abandoned. This cautiousness toward novel foods makes rats notoriously difficult to poison.

Taste-aversion learning has been construed both as instrumental avoidance learning and as Pavlovian conditioning. Clearly, elements of both are involved. Development of the aversion itself, in which the food takes on a negative motivational quality, is seen by most learning theorists as Pavlovian conditioning. Subsequent avoidance of the food is learned by instrumental conditioning.

In development of the aversion, the smell or taste of the food clearly serves as the conditioned stimulus; however, there has been some confusion in the literature as to what constitutes the unconditioned stimulus in taste-aversion conditioning. In a typical experiment, rats are presented with water that contains a distinctive flavor, such as saccharin or almond extract. After drinking the flavored water, the rats are treated in some way that makes them ill. Illness treatments have been as diverse as X-ray irradiation and spinning on a turntable, but the preferred method is injection of a toxic drug such as lithium chloride or apomorphine. As a result of the treatment-produced illness, the rats subsequently avoid the flavored water.

Most frequently, "illness" is cited as the unconditioned stimulus in these experiments, but one also sees references to "poisoning" or to the "illness treatment" in this regard. These latter references actually make more sense and are more consistent with other research in which a drug treatment (the unconditioned stimulus) is seen as producing an innate drug effect (the unconditioned response).

In 1927, Ivan Pavlov described experiments with morphine and apomorphine in which the drug injection, the drug itself, or "changes in the internal environment due to alteration in the composition of the blood" were construed as the unconditioned stimulus. The drug effects, including salivation, nausea, vomiting, and sleep, were construed as unconditioned responses. Pavlov even described an experiment in which tying off the portal vein led to development of an aversion to meat in dogs because of buildup in the blood of toxic substances derived from the digestion of the meat. The implication was that the smell and taste of meat were conditioned stimuli and the toxins (or the alterations in blood chemistry) were unconditioned stimuli.

In taste-aversion conditioning, the smell or taste (and sometimes the sight) of food serves as the conditioned stimulus. This stimulus signals the presence of a toxin, which acts as the unconditioned stimulus by altering body chemistry, which in turn produces nausea, illness, or vomiting, the unconditioned response. Through conditioning, nausea or "aversion" develops as the conditioned response to presentation of the taste, smell, or sight of the food. This aversion then motivates an instrumental avoidance response; that is, because of the conditioned aversion, the animal does not eat the food.

Taste aversion plays an important adaptive role in the everyday life of animals, especially those that eat a diversity of foods. Food preferences are learned early in the lives of such animals—they eat what they see their mothers eating or, even earlier, they come to prefer foods with flavors encountered previously in mothers' milk. To cope with a variable environment, however, animals must often adopt a new food. Animals with no mechanism for learning to accept safe foods while rejecting toxic ones would soon perish.

Nor is taste aversion learning seen only in laboratory animals. Humans, too, learn food aversions quickly and convincingly. Martin E. P. Seligman, a prominent learning theorist, has supplied his own autobiographical account of taste aversion learning. Six hours after eating filet mignon flavored with sauce Béarnaise, Seligman became violently ill with the stomach flu. "The next time I had sauce Béarnaise, I couldn't bear the taste of it," he relates. He did not, however, develop an aversion to the steak, to the white plates from which it had been eaten, or to the opera that he attended during the six-hour interstimulus interval.

Seligman's experience exemplifies several peculiarities of taste-aversion learning that have made it an important topic in the literature of learning theory: A strong conditioned response develops in a single learning trial, the conditioned response develops even when the conditioned and unconditioned stimuli are separated by long interstimulus intervals, the aversion develops selectively to some stimuli but not to others, and the conditioned response is irrational in the sense that it is not much affected by conscious knowledge that the food was not tainted or is not likely to be tainted in the future.

Applications

In nature, taste-aversion learning is a common event. Animals that do not specialize on one or a few foods must be able to reject toxic foods. Rats especially have a problem in this regard, since they do not vomit and therefore cannot expel poisons once they have ingested them. When rats have access to many foods, their behavior is marvelously adapted to detecting toxins. They eat only one or two different food types at a time and may eat these exclusively for days. Then they shift to concentration on another food type. If illness develops, the rats know immediately which type of food is probably to blame and subsequently avoid it. If the rats had eaten a variety of foods all the time, such discrimination would not be possible.

Human infants may adopt a similar strategy when allowed to eat without supervision. In the 1920's, Clara Davis gave infants the opportunity to eat any of a variety of nutritious foods, none of which alone supplied a balanced diet. The infants specialized on one or two foods for days at a time before shifting to another food. Although daily diets were certainly not nutritionally balanced, the infants did, over the long run, eat a balanced, healthy diet. The behavior of one infant was particularly interesting. This child voluntarily consumed cod-liver oil, a vile-tasting fluid usually rejected by children. This child, however, was suffering from vitamin D deficiency, and the cod-liver oil supplied the necessary vitamin. After the deficiency was eliminated, the infant stopped eating cod-liver oil and never went back to it.

The idea that the infant's behavior may be related to taste learning was shown by Paul Rozin, who found that rats fed a thiamine-deficient diet subsequently chose a food laced with thiamine supplements even though thiamine itself is tasteless. The rats apparently were able to use the taste of the food as a discriminative stimulus for its nutritive properties. Thus, the phenomenon is the opposite of taste-aversion learning—the development of specific hungers for foods with nutritive qualities, foods that promote health or recovery from illness. Anecdotal reports suggest that humans sometimes also suddenly develop tastes for foods that contain needed nutrients.

Thus, taste aversion is apparently only one side of the story of food selection and rejection in nature. Both appetitive and avoidance behaviors can be predicated on taste cues. In some cases, these behaviors are innate responses to the taste. Bitter tastes usually indicate the presence of toxic alkaloids and are often rejected by young animals that have had no prior experience with them. Human infants do the same. In other cases, the response to taste cues must be learned. Thus, specific hungers and taste aversions both represent examples of appropriate behaviors that are cued by discriminative taste stimuli.

Lincoln Brower has described a classic example of taste-aversion learning in nature. Blue jays, he noted, typically avoid preying on monarch butterflies. If hungry enough, however, jays will take and eat monarchs. The caterpillars of these butterflies eat milkweed, which contains a poison to which the butterflies are immune but birds are not. Enough of the poison remains concentrated in the tissues of adult monarchs to make a bird that eats one quite sick. The jays subsequently reject monarchs after a brief taste, and eventually the distinctive orange and black insects are rejected on sight.

In more applied settings, Carl Gustavson and John Garcia have described the use of taste-aversion conditioning in wildlife management. On the western ranges where large flocks of sheep are left relatively unprotected, ranchers often face the threat of predation of coyotes, wolves, and mountain lions. One response has been wholesale shooting and poisoning of these wild predators, but this is less than an ideal solution. Gustavson and Garcia found that predators, such as coyotes, that scavenge a lamb carcass laced with a sublethal dose of lithium chloride will subsequently develop a strong aversion to lamb and may even avoid areas where lamb and sheep are grazing. The authors proposed a scheme for reducing predation on sheep using taste-aversion conditioning that would drastically reduce the need for shooting and the use of indiscriminate lethal poisons.

In humans, many medical conditions are accompanied by loss of appetite and weight loss. Although this is often attributable to chemical changes within the body, it can also be caused by taste-aversion learning. Ilene Bernstein investigated the loss of appetite, or anorexia, that frequently accompanies cancer chemotherapy and found that, in all likelihood, it was attributable to aversive conditioning caused by the cancer medications, which often induce nausea and vomiting. Bernstein and her colleague, Soo Borson, investigated other anorexic syndromes and found the same possibility. In an important review article published in 1986, they proposed that taste-aversion learning may play a significant role in such conditions as cancer anorexia, tumor anorexia, anorexia nervosa, and the anorexias that accompany clinical depression and intestinal surgery.

On the other hand, taste-aversion learning is intentionally induced in some types of aversion therapy for maladaptive behaviors. Alcoholics are sometimes given a drug called Antabuse (disulfiram) that interferes with alcohol metabolism in the liver. Drinking alcohol after taking this drug results in a very unpleasant illness that conditions an aversion to alcohol. Subsequently, the taste, smell, or even the thought of alcohol can induce nausea. Cigarette smoking has been treated similarly.

Context

Before 1966, psychologists believed that learning obeyed the law of equipotentiality. In Pavlovian conditioning, the nature of conditioned and unconditioned stimuli was seen as unimportant—if they were paired appropriately, learning would occur with equal facility for any stimulus pair. In instrumental conditioning, psychologists believed that any reinforcer would reinforce any behavior.

Equipotentiality had been challenged. Ethologists insisted that each species of animal is unique in what it learns, that learning is an evolutionary adaptation, and that species are not interchangeable in learning studies. Nikolaas Tinbergen, in *The Study of Instinct* (1951), wrote of the innate disposition to learn. Keller and Marian Breland, who trained animals for commercial purposes, discovered that animals drifted toward species-specific food-related behaviors when their arbitrary instrumental responses were reinforced with food.

In 1966 John Garcia, Robert Koelling, and Frank Ervin published their research on taste-aversion learning. In an article called "Relation of Cue to Consequence in Avoidance Learning," they described an experiment in which rats received aversive consequences for licking water from a drinking spout. In the "tasty water" condition of the experiment, the water was flavored with saccharin, while in the "bright-noisy water" condition, licking the spout activated a flashing lamp and a clicking relay. Half the animals from each condition were made sick after drinking. The other half received a mild but disruptive electric shock after licking the spout. In the tasty water condition, animals that were made sick, but not those that were shocked, avoided drinking. In the bright-noisy water condition, animals that were shocked, but not those that were made sick, avoided drinking. Thus, light and noise were easily associated with shock, and taste was easily associated with illness, but the contrary associations were much more difficult to establish.

In a second article, called "Learning with Prolonged Delay of Reinforcement," Garcia, Ervin, and Koelling demonstrated that taste aversion developed even when the taste and illness treatment were separated by seventy-five minutes. Learning with such prolonged delays had been regarded as impossible, and it could not be reproduced in shock-avoidance experiments. These results were quickly replicated in other laboratories. Similar effects were demonstrated in other types of learning experiments, including traditional avoidance paradigms and even in mazes and Skinner boxes. The fact that something was wrong with traditional learning theory and equipotentiality was soon evident.

The doctrine of prepared learning replaced equipotentiality. Preparedness is the idea that evolution equips animals to learn things that are important to their survival. Examples of prepared learning already existed in the literature, but until 1966 their significance was not widely recognized among psychologists. Ethologists, however, pointed to studies of imprinting, food recognition, song learning, and place learning in a variety of animals, all illustrating prepared learning. Psychologists quickly included language learning and the learning of some phobias under the umbrella of preparedness. It was even proposed that human cognition evolved to cope with widely divergent situations that require unprepared learning. Taste-aversion learning, however, which is strongly prepared apparently even in humans, seems relatively immune to such ratiocination.

Bibliography

Bernstein, Ilene L., and Soo Borson. "Learning Food Aversion: A Component of Anorexia Syndromes." *Psychological Review* 93, no. 4 (1986): 462-472. A review of some of the issues relevant to development of clinically significant food aversions in humans. The authors discuss tumor anorexia, cancer anorexia, anorexia nervosa, and anorexia following intestinal surgery. Technical, but interesting and important.

Bolles, Robert C. *Learning Theory*. New York: Holt, Rinehart and Winston, 1975. One of the most concise and readable textbooks on learning theory, it reads almost like a mystery story in places. Details learning theory both before and after the discovery of the Garcia effect and includes a discussion of learning in its evolutionary context. Chapter 9 is almost entirely on taste aversion and its implications.

Braveman, Norman S., and Paul Bronstein, eds. *Experimental Assessments and Clinical Applications of Conditioned Food Aversions*. New York: New York Academy of Sciences, 1985. This is volume 443 in the Annals of the New York Academy of Sciences, and it reprints papers presented at a 1984 conference. Many of the articles, by experts in the field, deal with the medical relevance of food aversions in humans. Many of the articles are quite technical, but some are accessible to the general reader with some background.

Brower, Lincoln Pierson. "Ecological Chemistry." *Scientific American* 220 (February, 1969): 22-29. An excellent and enjoyable description of taste-aversion learning in nature. Brower describes how birds become averted to insects, such as monarch butterflies, that feed on plants containing chemical toxins. Some of the evolutionary implications of this phenomenon are discussed.

Gustavson, Carl R., and John Garcia. "Pulling a Gag on the Wily Coyote." *Psychology Today* 8 (August, 1974): 68-72. Very entertaining article describing the research on averting wild predators to sheep as a way of limiting predation on ranchers' herds without destroying the predators themselves. The authors convincingly show that shooting and poisoning coyotes are unnecessary and undesirable.

Seligman, Martin E. P., and Joanne L. Hager, eds. *Biological Boundaries of Learning*. New York: Appleton-Century-Crofts, 1972. Almost a history of the revolution in learning theory brought about by taste aversion, this volume contains reprints of and commentaries on many of the original research articles, including those by

Garcia cited in the text. Difficult in places but necessary reading for a complete understanding.

William B. King

Cross-References

Avoidance Learning, 375; Defense Reactions: Species-Specific, 775; Pavlovian Conditioning: Acquisition, Extinction, and Inhibition, 1757; Pavlovian Conditioning: Theoretical Foundations, 1764; Preparedness and Learning, 1866.

TEENAGE SUICIDE

Type of psychology: Developmental psychology
Field of study: Adolescence

Teenage suicide is a profoundly tragic and unsettling event. The rise in adolescent suicide has been so dramatic since the 1960's that it cannot be ignored as a passing problem; attention has been directed toward gaining insight into the myths, causes, warning signs, treatments, and preventive measures of adolescent suicide.

Principal terms
BEHAVIORAL PSYCHOLOGY: a school of psychology that studies only observable and measurable behavior
COGNITIVE LIMITATIONS: a lack of development in mental activities such as perception, memory, concept formation, reasoning, and problem solving
COGNITIVE PSYCHOLOGY: a school of psychology devoted to the study of mental processes; behavior is explained by emphasizing the role of thoughts and individual choice regarding life goals
DEPRESSION: a psychological disorder characterized by lowered self-esteem, feelings of inferiority, and sadness
PSYCHODYNAMIC ORIENTATION: psychotherapeutic thinking that is based loosely on the theories of Freud and his theory of psychoanalysis
SUICIDE: self-destruction in which the victim clearly intended to kill himself or herself; the act must be successful
SUICIDE ATTEMPT: a situation in which the individual commits a life-threatening act that does not result in death; the act must have the intent or give the appearance of actually jeopardizing the person's life

Overview

The statistics on teenage suicide are shocking. Suicide is the fifth leading cause of death for those under age fifteen, and it is the second leading cause of death for those ages fifteen to twenty-four. Perhaps even more disturbing are the statistics regarding the classification of attempted suicides. Although it is difficult to determine accurately, it is estimated that for every teenager who commits suicide there are approximately fifty teenagers who attempt to take their own lives. According to John Santrock, as many as two in every three college students has thought about suicide on at least one occasion.

According to Linda Nielson, the dramatic increase in youth suicide is primarily a result of the change in the male suicide rate. From 1970 to 1980, male suicides increased by 50 percent, with only a 2 percent increase among females. Females attempt suicide at higher rates than males but are less successful in actually dying.

Males are much more likely to use violent and lethal methods for trying to kill themselves, such as shooting or hanging. Females are more likely to use passive means to commit suicide; the use of drugs and poisons, for example, is more prevalent among females than males.

As alarming as these figures may be, it should be noted that suicide is still very rare among the young. The National Center for Disease Control has estimated that suicide claims the lives of only 0.0002 percent of all adolescents. Nevertheless, preventing suicide would save thousands of adolescent lives each year. The problem of suicide is complex, and studying it has been especially difficult because suicidal death is often denied by both the medical professional and the victim's family. The whole subject of suicide is carefully avoided by many people. As a result, the actual suicide rate among adolescents may be significantly higher than the official statistics indicate.

There are no simple answers to explain why adolescents attempt suicide, just as there are no simple solutions that will prevent its occurrence; however, researchers have discovered several factors that are clearly related to this drastic measure. These include family relations, depression, social interaction, and the adolescent's concept of death.

Family factors have been found to be highly correlated with adolescent suicide. A majority of adolescent suicide attempters come from families in which home harmony is lacking. Often there is a significant amount of conflict between the adolescent and his or her parents and a complete breakdown in communications. Many suicidal youths feel unloved, unwanted, and alienated from the family. Almost every study of suicidal adolescents has found a lack of family cohesion.

Most adolescents who attempt suicide have experienced serious emotional difficulty prior to their attempt. For the majority, this history involves a significant problem with depression. The type of chronic depression that leads some adolescents to commit suicide is vastly different from the occasional "blues" most people experience from time to time. When depression is life-threatening, adolescents typically feel extremely hopeless and helpless, and believe there is no way to improve their situation. These feelings of deep despair frequently lead to a negative self-appraisal in which the young person questions his or her ability to cope with life.

Further complicating the picture is the fact that clinically depressed adolescents have severe problems with relating to other people. As a result, they often feel isolated, which is a significant factor in the decision to end one's life. They may become withdrawn from their peer group and develop the idea that there is something wrong with society. At the same time, they lack the ability to recognize how their inappropriate behavior adversely affects other people.

Another factor that may contribute to suicidal thoughts is the adolescent's conception of death. Because of developmental factors, a young person's cognitive limitations may lead to a distorted, incomplete, or unrealistic understanding of death. Death may not be seen as a permanent end to life and to all contact with the living; suicide may be viewed as a way to punish one's enemies while maintaining the ability to observe their anguish from a different dimension of life. The harsh and unpleasant reality of death may not be realized. Fantasy, drama, and "magical thinking" may give a picture of death that is appealing and positive. Adolescents' limited ability to comprehend death in a realistic manner may be further affected by the depiction of death in the songs they hear, the literature they read, and the films they watch. Frequently death is romanticized. Often it is presented in euphemistic terms, such as "gone to sleep" or "passed away." At other times it is trivialized to such an extent that it is the stimulus for laughter and fun. Death and violence are treated in a remarkably antiseptic fashion.

Applications

Suicide is a tragic event for both the victim and the victim's family. It is also one of the most difficult problems confronting persons in the helping professions. In response, experts have focused their attention on trying to understand better how to prevent suicide and how to treat those who have made unsuccessful attempts to take their own lives.

It is believed that many suicides can be prevented if significant adults in the life of the adolescent are aware of various warning signals that often precede a suicide attempt. Most adolescents contemplating suicide will emit some clues or hints about their serious troubles or will call for help in some way. Some of the clues are easy to recognize, but some are very difficult to identify.

The adolescent may display a radical shift in characteristic behaviors related to academics, social habits, and relationships. There may be a change in sleeping habits; adolescents who kill themselves often exhibit difficulty in falling asleep or maintaining sleep. They are likely to be exhausted, irritable, and anxious. Others may sleep excessively. Any deviation from a usual sleep pattern should be noted. The individual may experience a loss of appetite with accompanying weight loss. A change in eating habits is often very obvious.

A pervasive feeling of hopelessness or helplessness may be observed. These feelings are strong indicators of suicide potential. Hopelessness is demonstrated by the adolescent's belief that his or her situation will never get better. It is believed that current feelings will never change. Helplessness is the belief that one is powerless to change anything. The more intense these feelings are, the more likely it is that suicide will be attempted. The adolescent may express suicidal thoughts and impulses. The suicidal adolescent may joke about suicide and even outline plans for death. He or she may talk about another person's suicidal thoughts or inquire about death and the hereafter. Frequently, prized possessions will be given away. Numerous studies have demonstrated that drug abuse is often associated with suicide attempts. A history of drug or alcohol abuse should be considered in the overall assessment of suicide potential for adolescents.

A variable that is often mentioned in suicide assessment is that of recent loss. If the adolescent has experienced the loss of a parent through death, divorce, or separation, he or she may be at higher risk. This is especially true if the family is significantly destabilized or the loss was particularly traumatic. A radical change in emotions is another warning sign. The suicidal adolescent will often exhibit emotions that are uncharacteristic for the individual. These may include anger, aggression, loneliness, guilt, grief, and disappointment. Typically, the emotion will be evident to an excessive degree.

Any one of the above factors may be present in the adolescent's life and not indicate any serious suicidal tendency; however, the combination of several of these signs should serve as a critical warning and result in some preventive action.

The treatment of suicidal behavior in young people demands that attention be given to both the immediate crisis situation and the underlying problems. Psychologists have sought to discover how this can best be done. Any effort to understand the dynamics of the suicidal person must begin with the assumption that most adolescents who are suicidal do not want to die. They want to improve their lives in some manner, they want to overcome the perceived meaninglessness of their existence, and they want to remove the psychological pain they are experiencing.

The first step in direct intervention is to encourage talking. Open and honest communication is essential. Direct questions regarding suicidal thoughts and/or plans should be asked. It simply is not true that talking about suicide will encourage a young person to attempt it. It is extremely important that the talking process include effective listening. Although it is difficult to listen to an individual who is suicidal, it is very important to do so in a manner that is accepting and calm. Listening is a powerful demonstration of caring and concern.

As the adolescent perceives that someone is trying to understand, it becomes easier to move from a state of hopelessness to hope and from isolation to involvement. Those in deep despair must come to believe that they can expect to improve. They must acknowledge that they are not helpless. Reassurance from another person is very important in this process. The young person considering suicide is so overwhelmed by his or her situation that there may seem to be no other way of escape. Confronting this attitude and pointing out how irrational it is does not help. A better response is to show empathy for the person's pain, then take a positive position which will encourage discussion about hopes and plans for the future.

Adolescents need the assurance that something is being done. They need to feel that things will improve. They must also be advised, however, that the suicidal urges they are experiencing may not disappear immediately, and that movement toward a better future is a step-by-step process. The suicidal young person must feel confident that help is available and can be called upon as needed. The adolescent contemplating suicide should never be left alone.

If the risk of suicide appears immediate, professional help is indicated. Most desirable would be a mental health expert with a special interest in adolescent problems or in suicide. Phone-in suicide prevention centers are located in virtually every large city and many smaller towns, and they are excellent resources for a suicidal person or for someone who is concerned about that person. In order to address long-term problems, therapy for the adolescent who attempts suicide should ideally include the parents. Family relationships must be changed in order to assist the young person in feeling less alienated and worthless.

Context

Suicide has apparently been practiced to some degree since the beginning of recorded history; however, it was not until the nineteenth century that suicide came to be considered a psychological problem. Since that time, several theories which examine the suicidal personality have been developed.

Émile Durkheim was one of the first to offer a major explanation for suicidal behavior. In the late nineteenth century he conducted a now-classic study of suicide and published his book *Le Suicide: Étude de sociologie* (1897; *Suicide: A Study in Sociology*, 1951). He concluded that suicide is often a severe consequence of the lack of group involvement. He divided suicide into three groupings: egoistic, altruistic, and anomic suicides.

The egoistic suicide is representative of those who are poorly integrated into society. These individuals feel set apart from their social unit and experience a severe sense of isolation. He theorized that people with strong links to their communities are less likely to take their lives. Altruistic suicide occurs when individuals become so immersed in their identity group that group goals and ideals become more important than their own lives. A good example of this type of suicide would be the Japanese kamikaze pilots in World War II: They were willing to give up their lives in order to help their country. The third type, anomic suicide, occurs when an individual's sense of integration in the group has dissolved. When caught in sudden societal or personal change that creates significant alienation or confusion, suicide may be viewed as the only option available.

Psychologists with a psychodynamic orientation explain suicide in terms of intrapsychic conflict. Emphasis is placed on understanding the individual's internal emotional makeup. Suicide is viewed as a result of turning anger and hostility inward. Sigmund Freud discussed the life instinct versus the drive toward death or destruction. Alfred Adler believed that feelings of inferiority and aggression can interact in such a way as to bring a wish for death in order to punish loved ones. Harry Stack Sullivan viewed suicide as the struggle between the good me, bad me, and not me.

Other areas of psychology offer different explanations for suicidal behavior. Cognitive psychologists believe that suicide results from the individual's failure to utilize appropriate problem-solving skills. Faulty assessment of the present or future is also critical and may result in a perspective marked by hopelessness. Behavioral psychologists propose that past experiences with suicide make the behavior an option which may be considered; other people who have taken their lives may serve as models. Biological psychologists are interested in discovering any physiological factors that are related to suicide. It is suggested that chemicals in the brain may be linked to disorders which predispose an individual to commit suicide.

Research in the area of suicide is very difficult to conduct. Identification of those individuals who are of high or low suicidal risk is complex, and ethical considerations deem many research possibilities questionable or unacceptable. Theory construction and testing will continue, however; the crisis of adolescent suicide demands that research address the causes of suicide, its prevention, and treatment for those who have been unsuccessful in suicide attempts.

Bibliography

Friedman, Myra. *Buried Alive: The Biography of Janis Joplin.* New York: William Morrow, 1973. A powerful biography of a famous rock singer who died of a heroin overdose. It poignantly describes how insecurity and acute loneliness played a significant role in her death. An interesting and informative book which is appropriate for adolescents and adults. Contains photographs.

Hyde, Margaret O., and Elizabeth Held Forsyth. *Suicide: The Hidden Epidemic.* New York: Franklin Watts, 1978. A book written for grades nine through twelve. Discusses the misconceptions of suicide, self-destructive patterns, and motivation theories. Includes a chapter that specifically addresses teenage suicide. Contains a list of suicide prevention centers located across the nation.

Klagsbrun, Francine. *Too Young to Die.* 3d ed. New York: Pocket Books, 1984. An excellent book that combines scientific research with practical examples in a manner that is easy to comprehend. Discusses myths, causes, and prevention of suicide; offers concrete suggestions for talking to a suicidal person. Includes a list of hotlines and suicide prevention centers.

Peck, Michael L., Norman L. Farberow, and Robert E. Litman, eds. *Youth Suicide.* New York: Springer, 1985. Provides a comprehensive overview of adolescent suicide. Written especially for the individual who is interested in working with suicidal youth, but an excellent resource for all who want to increase their understanding of this topic. Contains information on the psychodynamics of suicide, the impact of social change, the role of the family, and intervention strategies.

Petti, T. A., and C. N. Larson. "Depression and Suicide." In *Handbook of Adolescent Psychology*, edited by Vincent B. Van Hassett and Michel Herson. New York: Pergamon Press, 1987. A well-written chapter that makes the complicated factors involved in depression and suicide accessible to the general audience. The authors discuss the causes of both depression and suicide, as well as how the two are related. Addresses how to help the suicidal adolescent. Very readable and informative.

Doyle R. Goff

Cross-References

Adolescence: Cognitive Skills, 118; Clinical Depression, 521; Community Psychology, 618; Coping: Social Support, 700; Death and Dying: Theoretical Perspectives, 763; Depression: Theoretical Explanations, 789; Identity Crises: Erikson, 1255; Suicide, 2501.

TEMPERATURE

Type of psychology: Sensation and perception
Field of study: Auditory, chemical, cutaneous, and body senses

Thermoreceptors are specialized to detect a particular physical change in the environment—the flow of heat, detected as a change in temperature—and to convert this information into nerve impulses that can be integrated and processed by the central nervous system to allow an appropriate compensating response.

Principal terms

ADAPTATION: a drop in nerve impulses generated by a receptor over time when the intensity of a stimulus remains constant

CIRCADIAN TEMPERATURE RHYTHM: a daily variation of internal body temperature of about 0.6 degree Celsius

COLD THERMORECEPTOR: a type of thermoreceptor that is active in thermoreception between about 5 and 43 degrees Celsius, and acts as a pain receptor above about 45 degrees

HYPERTHERMIA: an uncontrolled rise in body temperature above 37 degrees Celsius

HYPOTHALAMUS: a brain structure containing the center that detects and regulates internal body temperature

HYPOTHERMIA: an uncontrolled fall in body temperature below 37 degrees Celsius

PYROGEN: a substance released by bacteria or body cells that can induce fever

THERMORECEPTOR: a sensory receptor specialized for detection of changes in the flow of heat

WARM THERMORECEPTOR: a type of thermoreceptor that is active between about 30 and 50 degrees Celsius

Overview

Humans have thermoreceptors that can detect the flow of heat energy. These specialized sensory receptors can detect the flow of heat, which is detected as a change in temperature, and convert this information into nerve impulses. Conversion into nerve impulses places the information into a form that can be processed by the central nervous system, allowing a compensating response, if required, to be initiated.

Humans and other mammals have two kinds of thermoreceptors. One type, called the warm thermoreceptor, becomes active in sending nerve impulses when the body surroundings or an object touched reaches temperatures above 30 degrees Celsius. Nerve impulses from the warm thermoreceptors increase proportionately in frequency as the temperature rises to about 43 degrees Celsius; past this temperature, impulses from the warm thermoreceptors drop proportionately in frequency until they become inactive at about 50 degrees Celsius.

The second type of thermoreceptor becomes active in generating nerve impulses at temperatures below about 43 degrees Celsius. Nerve impulses from these receptors, called cold thermoreceptors, increase proportionately as temperatures fall to about 25 degrees Celsius. Below this temperature, the frequency of nerve impulses generated by the receptors drops proportionately; as temperatures fall to about 5 to 10 degrees Celsius, activity of the cold thermoreceptors falls to zero. The activity of cold and warm thermoreceptors overlaps between temperatures of about 30 and 40 degrees Celsius. Within this range, the sensation of heat or cold results from an integration in the brain of nerve impulses generated by both cold and warm receptors.

At temperatures below about 15 degrees and above about 45 degrees Celsius, pain receptors become active and increase proportionately in activity as temperatures rise or fall beyond these levels. There is a narrow range of overlap of the limits of pain receptors and thermoreceptors, so that temperatures between about 5 and 15 degrees Celsius are felt as both cold and pain (or as "freezing cold") and temperatures between about 43 and 50 degrees Celsius are felt as both heat and pain (or "burning hot"). Temperatures beyond the 5-degree and 50-degree limits for the thermoreceptors stimulate only the pain receptors and are felt primarily or exclusively as pain. Curiously, the cold receptors become active as pain receptors as the temperature rises above about 45 degrees Celsius. The dual activity of the cold thermoreceptors may account for the fact that freezing cold and burning heat may produce a similar sensation.

Both types of thermoreceptors adapt quickly as the temperature stabilizes. Adaptation refers to the fact that as a stimulus is maintained at a constant level, the nerve impulses generated by a receptor drop in frequency. In effect, the receptor undergoes a reduction in sensitivity if the stimulus remains constant. If the stimulus changes, the receptor again generates nerve impulses at a frequency proportional to the intensity of the stimulus. The ability of receptors to adapt makes them sensitive to a change in stimulus, which is often the factor of greatest importance to an appropriate response.

The rapid adaptation of thermoreceptors is part of common experience. In going from the outdoors into a warm room on a cold day, one immediately detects the warmer temperature and has a resultant strong sense of a temperature change. After a few minutes, one no longer notices the temperature difference, as one's thermoreceptors adapt and reduce their generation of nerve impulses. If the temperature of the room changes by only a degree or so, however, the generation of impulses by the thermoreceptors increases again, and one becomes aware of the change.

Thermoreceptors also show strong spatial summation. If only a very small region of the body is stimulated, one has difficulty discerning whether a temperature change has been experienced, or even whether the stimulus is hot or cold. As the surface area stimulated increases, impulses arriving in the brain from thermoreceptors are summed, so that perception of the change increases proportionately. If only a square centimeter of skin is stimulated by a warm or cold probe, for example, one might not be able to detect a temperature change smaller than about 1 degree Celsius. If the entire body surface is stimulated, as in total immersion in water, one becomes exquisitely sensitive to changes in temperature. Summation of information from all surface thermoreceptors may allow detection of temperature changes as small as a hundredth of a degree Celsius.

Thermoreceptors in humans are most numerous at the body surface, where they are located immediately under the skin. Each thermoreceptor can detect temperature changes over an area of about 1 millimeter in diameter. Cold thermoreceptors occur in greater numbers at the body surface than warm receptors—depending on the body region, there may be as many as three to ten cold thermoreceptors for each warm thermoreceptor. Thermoreceptors of both types are particularly densely distributed in the skin of the tongue and lips. In these regions, there may be as many as twenty to thirty or more thermoreceptors per square centimeter of surface. About a third as many thermoreceptors occur in the skin of the fingertips. In other parts of the body surface, only a few thermoreceptors occur per square centimeter.

Although the locations of cold and heat receptors can be pinpointed on the body surface by touching the skin with a warm or cold probe, it has proved difficult to detect particular structures responsible for thermoreception. One group of cold thermoreceptors, however, has been identified as branched nerve endings that terminate near the inner surfaces of cells in the skin. Presumably, other cold thermoreceptors and the warm thermoreceptors are little more than naked nerve endings that cannot be distinguished from pain and some touch receptors, which have a similar appearance.

Little is understood about the physical and chemical mechanisms underlying thermoreception; however, it is considered likely that the reception mechanism depends on increases and decreases in chemical reaction rates in the receptor cells as the temperature rises and falls. In general, chemical reaction rates approximately double for each 10-degree increase in temperature or are halved for each 10-degree fall. Thermoreceptors probably respond to these increases or decreases in chemical reaction rates rather than directly detecting the changes heat flow responsible for changes in temperature. The thermoreceptors responsible for detecting heat are also sensitive, to some degree, to chemicals. This explains why spices such as red peppers give the sensation of heat when placed on the tongue or rubbed into the skin. Other chemicals, such as menthol, feel cold on the tongue or skin.

Applications

Thermoreception has two primary functions in warm-blooded animals such as humans. One is detection of extreme temperatures, so that a person can respond to avoid tissue damage by burning or freezing. The second is maintenance of normal body temperature of 37 degrees Celsius.

Maintenance of body temperature involves both conscious and automated responses.

At temperatures not too far above and below the range of comfort (about 22 to 24 degrees Celsius), one feels consciously warm or cool and responds by one or more voluntary methods to decrease or increase skin temperature, such as donning or removing clothing. The automated responses maintaining body temperature are complex and involve a variety of systems. Changes in internal temperature are detected by thermoreceptors in the body interior, particularly in the hypothalamus. The thermoreceptors of the hypothalamus are extremely sensitive to shifts from the normal body temperature of 37 degrees Celsius. If such changes occur, the hypothalamus triggers involuntary responses that adjust body temperature.

If the internal body temperature rises above 37 degrees, sweat glands in the skin are stimulated to release their secretion, which evaporates and cools the body surface. Heat loss is also promoted by dilation of the peripheral vessels, which increases blood flow to the body surface. Blood cooled at the surface is carried to the body interior by the circulatory system, where it removes heat from internal regions and causes a drop in body temperature. In addition to these cooling mechanisms, release of thyroxin from the thyroid gland is inhibited. The resulting reduction in the concentration of this hormone in the circulation slows the rate at which body cells oxidize fuel substances and diminishes the amount of heat released by these reactions in the body.

If the internal body temperature falls below 37 degrees Celsius, a series of automated responses with opposite effects are triggered. Peripheral blood vessels contract, reducing the flow of blood to the body surface. The output of thyroxin from the thyroid gland increases; the increased thyroxin concentration stimulates body cells to increase the rate at which fuel substances are oxidized to release heat within the body. Although the effect of the response in humans is not pronounced, a drop in internal temperature also stimulates contraction of small muscles at hair roots over the body. The contraction, which is felt as "goose bumps," raises body hairs and increases the dead-air space at the surface of the body. If the drop in internal temperature becomes more extreme, shivering caused by rhythmic contractions of voluntary muscles is induced. Shivering increases body temperature through the heat released by the muscular contractions.

The hypothalamus has been identified as the region of the brain regulating body temperature through observations of the effects of injuries and electrical stimulation. Damage to the hypothalamus can inhibit such temperature-regulating responses as sweating and dilation or constriction of peripheral blood vessels. Conversely, experimental electrical stimulation of the hypothalamus can induce the regulatory responses. These observations indicate that the primary temperature-regulating center of the hypothalamus is in its anterior or preoptic region. The automated responses triggered by the hypothalamus in addition to conscious responses allow humans to maintain an almost constant body temperature in the face of a wide variety of environmental conditions. These combined automated and conscious responses allow humans to survive and remain active in a wider range of environmental conditions than any other animal.

The body temperature maintained by the thalamus is not actually set perfectly and constantly at 37 degrees. For most persons, the internal body temperature varies over a range of about 0.6 degree, with the lowest temperatures in the early morning and the highest point at about four to six in the afternoon. This daily variation in body temperature is called the circadian temperature rhythm.

Although the body temperature is normally set at 37 degrees, the set point can be adjusted upward to produce fever as a part of the body's response to infection by invading organisms. Raising the body temperature above 37 degrees results from the same automated responses that normally raise internal temperatures—shivering, constriction of peripheral blood vessels, and an increase in the rate of metabolic reactions.

Several types of bacteria secrete substances that can directly stimulate the hypothalamus to raise its set point and induce fever. Substances of this type, capable of inducing fever, are termed pyrogens. Other substances derived through the breakdown of infecting bacteria, or from substances released through the breakdown of body tissues in disease, particularly fragments of some body proteins, can indirectly trigger the hypothalamus to raise its set point. These substances are engulfed by certain types of white blood cells, including macrophages. On engulfing the breakdown substances, the white blood cells release a powerful pyrogen, interleukin-1. This substance stimulates the secretion of a type of hormone, the prostaglandins, which in turn induces the hypothalamus to raise its temperature set point above 37 degrees. The advantage that fever provides to the body in fighting infection is unclear. Aspirin and corticosteroids are able to reduce fever by inhibiting the secretion of prostaglandins.

Context

When the body's ability to regulate temperature is exceeded, resulting in extreme hyperthermia or hypothermia, the results can be extremely serious. Fevers above about 41 to 42 degrees Celsius, or about 106 to 108 degrees Fahrenheit, can cause severe or fatal damage if the body temperature is not quickly lowered by treatments such as water or alcohol sponging of the skin. The high temperatures injure or kill body cells, particularly in the brain, liver, and kidneys, and cause internal bleeding. Damage to brain cells from extremely high fever is essentially irreversible and may cause permanent impairment or even death within minutes.

Under some conditions, as on hot and humid days, or when the body is immersed in hot water, the normal physiological reactions regulating body temperature are ineffective and body temperature may rise uncontrollably. If the air temperature rises above about 38 degrees Celsius on days in which the humidity approaches 100 percent, for example, temperature regulation by sweating and dilation of peripheral blood vessels is ineffective. Under such conditions, internal body temperature may rise to damaging levels, particularly if physical exercise is attempted. The resulting reaction, known as hyperthermia or heat stroke, may include dizziness and abdominal distress or pain in milder cases; more severe heat stroke may produce delirium or even death. Hyperthermia differs fundamentally from fever in that the set point of the hypothalamus remains at 37 degrees. Another difference is that the circadian temperature rhythm is maintained during fever, but not in hyperthermia. In addition to high environmental heat and humidity, hyperthermia may also be caused by cocaine and psychedelic drugs.

Low environmental temperatures can also exceed the body's capacity to regulate its internal temperature. Heat loss attributable to accidental or intentional immersion in ice water, for example, induces a steady drop in internal body temperature that cannot be effectively reversed by shivering, constriction of peripheral blood vessels, or increases in chemical reaction rates. The effects of extreme cold in lowering body temperature are magnified by impairment of the regulatory function of the hypothalamus. At body temperatures below about 34 degrees Celsius, the function of the hypothalamus in temperature regulation becomes severely impaired. Shivering usually stops below 32 degrees. At internal temperatures below about 28 degrees Celsius, the temperature regulation centers of the hypothalamus cease to function entirely. Below this temperature, internal body temperature falls rapidly, breathing slows greatly or arrests, and the heart may develop an irregular beat or stop beating entirely. Death follows quickly if breathing or the heartbeat stops. Any fall of body temperature below 35 degrees is known as hypothermia.

For some surgical procedures, body temperature is deliberately reduced by administering a drug that inhibits activity of the hypothalamus. The body is then immersed in ice water or surrounded by cooling blankets until internal temperatures reach levels of 30 degrees or below. At these temperatures, the heart can be stopped temporarily without significant damage to the brain or other body tissues. Induced reduction of body temperatures in this manner is routinely used in heart surgery.

Bibliography

Berne, Robert M., and Matthew N. Levy, eds. *Physiology.* 2d ed. St. Louis: C. V. Mosby, 1988. Chapter 9, "The Somatosensory System," in this standard college physiology text outlines the anatomy and physiology of the cells and nerve tracts in the spinal column and brain involved in the sensation of temperature and other body sensations. Although the text is intended for students at the college level, it is clearly written and should be accessible to high school readers.

Coren, Stanley. *Sensation and Perception.* New York: Academic Press, 1979. This simply written text provides an easily understood discussion of the senses, sensory cells, and the routes traveled by sensory information through the spinal cord to the brain. A clear and interesting description is provided of the basics of perception in the cerebral cortex.

Guyton, Arthur C. *Textbook of Medical Physiology.* 7th ed. Philadelphia: W. B. Saunders, 1986. Chapter 50, "Somatic Sensations II: Pain, Visceral Pain, Headache, and Thermal Sensations," in this readable and clearly written text includes an excellent discussion of thermoreceptors, the role of the hypothalamus in regulation of body temperature, and medical implications of fever, hyperthermia, and hypothermia. Chapter 48, "Sensory Receptors and Their Basic Mechanisms of Action," provides a general description of the structure and function of receptors. Although intended for college and medical students, the text can be easily understood by readers at the high school level.

Milne, Lorus Johnson, and Margery Milne. *The Senses of Animals and Men.* New York: Atheneum, 1962. A simple and entertaining survey of the senses and their importance in humans and other animals. Written for a popular audience, the book provides interesting and thought-provoking comparisons between the sensory systems of humans and other animals.

Schmidt-Nielsen, Knut. *Animal Physiology, Adaptation, and Environment.* 4th ed. New York: Cambridge University Press, 1990. This standard college text, by one of the greatest animal physiologists, provides a deeply perceptive comparison of sensory systems in humans and other animals. Chapters 6 and 7 describe temperature effects and temperature regulation. The text is remarkable for its lucid and entertaining descriptions of animal physiology.

Stephen L. Wolfe

Cross-References

The Central and Peripheral Nervous Systems, 494; Neurons, 1661; Pain, 1727; Sensation and Perception Defined, 2207; Sensory Modalities and Stimuli, 2214; Signal Detection Theory, 2271; Touch and Pressure, 2578.

TESTING: HISTORICAL PERSPECTIVES

Type of psychology: Intelligence and intelligence testing
Fields of study: Ability tests; intelligence assessment

Current psychological tests have been historically influenced by French research-ers, who emphasized clinical observation; by German researchers, who emphasized experimentation; by British researchers, who were interested in individual differ-ences; and by American researchers, who have been more pragmatic in their ap-proach.

Principal terms
GENIUS: a person who shows a high degree of ability, often intellectual, sometimes creative, and sometimes in a very specific field
INDIVIDUAL DIFFERENCES: differences between persons in psychological aspects such as personality, intelligence, and motivation
REACTION TIME: the time it takes for a person to respond to a specific stimulus
SENSORY: having to do with the senses, such as sight, hearing, smell, taste, or touch
TEST: any instrument or device used to assess an individual along a particular dimension

Overview

Tests are an intrinsic part of people's lives. They are tested as children to deter-mine when they will enter school and how much they will learn in school. They are tested as young adults to determine whether they should receive a high school di-ploma, whether they should enter college, how much they can learn, or whether they can participate in some specialized training. People are tested if they seek admission to law school or medical school, if they want to practice a profession, and if they want to work for a specific company or show proficiency in a particular talent.

Tests have been used for quite some time. In China around 2000 B.C., public offi-cials were examined regularly and were promoted or dismissed on the basis of these examinations. The direct historical antecedents of testing go back slightly more than one hundred years and reflect contributions made by many individuals representing four historical traditions: the French clinical tradition, the German scientific tradi-tion, the British emphasis on individual differences, and the American practical orientation.

The French clinical tradition emphasized clinical observation. That is, the French were very interested in the mentally ill and mentally retarded, and a number of French physicians wrote excellent descriptions of patients they had studied. They produced very perceptive and detailed descriptions, or case studies, and thereby contributed the notion that the creation of a test must be preceded by careful observations of the real world. To develop a test to measure depression, for example, one must first carefully observe many depressed patients. The French also produced the first practical test of intelligence: Alfred Binet, a well-known French psychologist, in 1905 devised the Binet-Simon test (with Théodore Simon) to be used with French schoolchildren in order to identify those who were retarded and hence needed specialized instruction.

A second historical trend that affected testing was the scientific approach promulgated by German scientists in the late 1800's. Perhaps the best-known name in the field was Wilhelm Wundt, who is considered to be the founder of experimental psychology. He was particularly interested in reaction time, the rapidity with which a person responds to a stimulus. To study reaction time, Wundt and his students carried out systematic experimentation in a laboratory, focused mostly on sensory functions such as vision, and developed a number of instruments to be used to study reaction time. Although Wundt was not interested in tests, his scientific approach and his focus on sensory functions did influence later test developers, who saw testing as an experiment in which standardized instructions needed to be followed and strict control over the testing procedure needed to be exercised. They even took the measurement of sensory processes such as vision to be an index of how well the brain functioned, and therefore of how intelligent the person was.

Whereas the Germans were interested in discovering general laws of behavior, and were trying to use reaction time as a way of investigating the intellectual processes that presumably occur in the brain, the British were more interested in looking at individual differences. The British viewed these differences not as errors, as Wundt did, but as a fundamental reflection of evolution and natural selection, the ideas that had been given a strong impetus by the work of Charles Darwin. In fact, it was Darwin's cousin, Sir Francis Galton, who is said to have launched the testing movement on its course. Galton studied eminent British men and became convinced that intellectual genius was fixed by inheritance: One was born a genius rather than trained to be one. Galton developed a number of tests to measure various aspects of intellectual capacity, tested large numbers of individuals who visited his laboratory, and developed various statistical procedures to analyze the test results.

It was in the United States, however, that psychological testing really became an active endeavor. In 1890, psychologist James McKeen Cattell wrote a scientific paper and for the first time used the phrase "mental test." In this paper, he presented a series of ten tests designed to measure a person's intellectual level. These tests involved procedures such as the subject's estimating a ten-second interval, and measurement of the amount of pressure exerted by the subject's grip. Cattell had been a pupil of Wundt, and these tests reflected Wundt's heavy emphasis on sensory abilities. The tests were administered to Columbia University students, since Cattell was a professor there, to see if the results predicted grade point average. They did not; nevertheless, the practice of testing students to predict their college performance was born.

Lewis Terman, a professor at Stanford University, took the French test that Binet had developed and created a new, English version, called the Stanford-Binet test; thus, intelligence testing became popular in America. When World War I started in 1917, there was a great need in the military to screen out recruits whose intellectual capabilities were too limited for military service, as well as a need to identify recruits who might be given specialized training or admitted to officer training programs. Several tests were developed to meet these needs and, when the war was over, became widely used in industry and schools. By World War II, testing had become quite sophisticated and widespread and was again given an impetus by the need to make major decisions about military personnel in a rapid and efficient manner. Thus, not only intellectual functioning but also problems of adjustment, morale, and psychopathology all stimulated interest in testing.

As with any other field of endeavor, advancements in tests were also accompanied by setbacks, disputes, and criticisms. In the late 1930's and early 1940's, for example, there was a rather acrimonious controversy between researchers at Iowa University and at Stanford University over whether the intelligence quotients (IQs) of children could be increased through enriched school experiences. In the 1960's, tests were severely criticized, especially the multiple-choice items used in tests to make admission decisions in higher education. Many books were published that attacked testing, often in a distorted and emotional manner. In the 1970's, intelligence tests again came to the forefront, in a bitter controversy about whether whites are more intelligent than blacks. Many school districts eliminated the administration of intelligence tests, both because the tests were seen as tools of potential discrimination and because of legal ramifications.

Tests are still criticized and misused, but they have become much more sophisticated and represent a useful set of tools that, when used appropriately, can help people make more informed decisions.

Applications

In the everyday world, there are a number of decisions that must be made daily. For example, "Susan" owns a large manufacturing company and has openings for ten lathe operators. When she advertises these positions, 118 prospective employees apply. How will Susan decide which ten to hire? Clearly, she wants to hire the best of the applicants, those who will do good work, who will be responsible and come to work on time, who will follow the expected rules but also be flexible when the nature of the job changes, and so on. She would probably want to interview all the applicants, but it may be physically impossible for her to do so since it would require too much time, and perhaps she may realize that she does not have the skills to make such a decision. An alternative, then, would be to test all the applicants and to use the test information with other data, such as letters from prior employers, to make the needed decision. A test, then, can be looked upon as an interview, but one that is typically more objective, since the biases of the interviewer will be held in check; more time effective, since a large number of individuals can be tested at one sitting, whereas interviews typically involve one candidate at a time; more economical, since a printed form will typically cost less than the salary of an interviewer; and, usually, more informative, since a person's results can be compared to the results of others, whereas one's performance in an interview is a bit more difficult to evaluate.

In fact, historically, most tests have been developed because of pressing practical needs: the need to identify schoolchildren who might benefit from specialized instruction, the need to identify army recruits with special talents or problems, or the need to identify high school students with particular interest in a specific field such as physics. As testing has grown, the applications of testing have also expanded. Tests are now used to provide information about achievement, intellectual capacity, potential talents, career interests, motivation, and hundreds of other human psychological concerns. Tests are also developed to serve as tools for the assessment of social or psychological theories; for example, measures of depression are of interest to social scientists investigating suicide, while measures of social support are useful in studies of adolescents and the elderly.

Another way of thinking about tests is that a test represents an experiment. The experimenter, in this case usually a psychologist or someone trained in testing, administers a set of carefully specified procedures and just as carefully records the subject's responses or performance on these procedures. Thus, a psychologist who administers an intelligence test to a schoolchild is interested not simply in computing the child's IQ but also in observing how the child goes about solving new problems, how extensive the child's vocabulary is, how the child reacts to frustration, the facility with which the child can solve word problems versus numerical problems, and so on. While such information could be derived by carefully observing the child in the classroom over a long period of time, using a specific test procedure not only is less time-consuming but also allows for a more precise comparison between a particular child's performance and that of other children.

There are, then, at least two ways, not mutually exclusive, of thinking about a test. Both of these ways of thinking are the result of the various historical emphases: the French emphasis on the clinical symptoms exhibited by the individual, the German emphasis on the scientific procedure, the British interest in individual differences, and the American emphasis on practicality—"Does it work, and how fast can I get the results?"

To be sure, tests are only one source of information, and their use should be carefully guided by a variety of considerations. In fact, psychologists who use tests with clients are governed by two very detailed sets of rules. One set has to do with the technical aspects of constructing a test, with making sure that indeed a particular test has been developed according to scientific guidelines. A second set has to do with ethical standards, ensuring that the information derived from a test is to be used carefully for the benefit of the client.

Because the use of tests does not occur in a vacuum, but rather in a society that has specific values and expectations, that emphasizes or denies specific freedoms, and in which certain political points of view may be more or less popular, the use of tests is often accompanied by strong feelings. For example, in the 1970's, Americans became very concerned about the fact that subsequent classes of high school seniors who were taking the Scholastic Aptitude Test (SAT) for entrance into college were performing less well. From 1963 to 1977, the average score on the SAT verbal portion declined by about 50 points, and the average score on the SAT mathematics section declined by about 30 points. Rather than seeing the SAT as simply a nationwide "interview" that might yield some possibly useful information about a student's performance at a particular point in time, the SAT had become a goal in itself, a standard by which to judge all sorts of things, including whether high school teachers were doing their job.

Context

Tests play a major role in most areas of psychology, and the history of psychological testing is in fact intertwined with the history of psychology as a field. Psychology is defined as the science of behavior, and tests are crucial to the experimentation that is at the basis of that science. Especially with human subjects, studies are typically carried out by identifying some important dimension, such as intelligence, depression, concern about one's health, or suicide ideation, and then trying to alter that dimension by some specific procedure, such as psychotherapy to decrease depression, education to increase health awareness, a medication designed to lessen hallucinations, and so on. Whether the specific procedure is effective is then assessed by the degree of change, typically measured by a test or questionnaire.

Psychology also has many applied aspects. There are psychologists who work with the mentally ill, with drug abusers, with college students who are having personal difficulties, with spouses who are not getting along, with business executives who wish to increase their leadership abilities, or with high school students who may not be certain of what career to pursue. All these situations can involve the use of tests, to identify the current status of a person (for example, to determine how depressed the person is), to make predictions about future behavior (for example, to determine how likely it is that a person will commit suicide), to identify achievement (for example, to assess how well a person knows elementary math), or to identify strengths (for example, to gauge whether someone is a people-oriented type of person)—in other words, to get a more objective and detailed portrait of the particular client.

The wide and growing use of computers has also affected the role of tests. Tests can be administered and scored by computer, and the client can receive feedback, often with great detail, by computer. Computers also allow tests to be tailored to the individual. Suppose, for example, a test with one hundred items is designed to measure basic arithmetic knowledge in fifth-grade children. Traditionally, all one hundred items would be administered, and each child's performance scored accordingly. By using a computer, however, a test can present only selected items, with subsequent items being present or absent depending on the child's performance on the prior item. If, for example, a child can do division problems quite well, as shown by his or her correct answers to more difficult problems, the computer can be programmed to skip the easier division problems.

Clearly, tests are here to stay. The task is to use them wisely, as useful but limited tools to benefit the individual rather than facilitate political manipulations.

Bibliography

Anastasi, Anne. *Psychological Testing*. 6th ed. New York: Macmillan, 1988. An excellent though somewhat technical introduction to psychological testing. Often required reading for students of psychology. Chapter 1 gives an overview of the history of psychological testing.

Ballard, Philip Boswood. *Mental Tests*. London: Hodder & Stoughton, 1920. A fascinating little book, written for schoolteachers, that covers the development of mental tests, the measurement of intelligence, and school-related activities such as reading, spelling, and arithmetic. Gives the English translation of the Binet-Simon test of intelligence, as well as a number of tests the author developed. Should be read for historical context; most of the book's contents are clearly outdated, but certainly give a flavor of what testing was like in the 1920's.

Garrett, Henry Edward, and Matthew R. Schneck. *Psychological Tests, Methods, and Results*. New York: Harper & Brothers, 1933. A textbook for courses in psychological testing as given in the 1930's. The authors, in their preface, thank Anne Anastasi, who was later to write her own textbook, which became number one in the field. It is interesting to note that the Garrett and Schneck book begins with a chapter on the measurement of physical and sensory capacities such as height, strength of grip, lung capacity, and pulse rate, whereas today's texts would not consider these to be "mental" capacities. Again, a book to be read in its historical context.

OSS Assessment Staff. *Assessment of Men: Selection of Personnel for the Office of Strategic Services*. New York: Rinehart, 1948. A fascinating book that describes the Office of Strategic Services (the OSS, the forerunner of the Central Intelligence Agency) program during World War II to select potential spies and saboteurs.

Sokal, Michael M., ed. *Psychological Testing and American Society, 1890-1930*. New Brunswick, N.J.: Rutgers University Press, 1987. This book had its genesis in a symposium given in 1984 at the 150th national meeting of the American Association for the Advancement of Science. Consists of eight chapters, written by seven different authors, which place testing in a historical perspective. For example, chapter 2 talks about James McKeen Cattell and how his tests came to be.

Wise, Paula Sachs. *The Use of Assessment Techniques by Applied Psychologists*. Belmont, Calif.: Wadsworth, 1989. Introduces the reader to the ways in which assessments are conducted in real settings by professional psychologists, especially clinical, counseling, organizational, and school psychologists. Well written, with a minimum of technical detail and many examples. Covers assessment in its broad aspects, rather than simply discussing psychological testing.

George Domino

Cross-References

Ability Testing: Individual and Group, 1; Bias in Ability Tests, 7; Ability Tests: Design and Construction, 13; Ability Tests: Reliability, Validity, and Standardization, 21; Ability Tests: Uses and Misuses, 27; Intelligence: Definition and Theoretical Models, 1328; Intelligence Tests, 1341; Interest Inventories, 1349; Race and Intelligence, 2031.

THIRST

Type of psychology: Motivation
Fields of study: Endocrine system; motivation theory; physical motives

Thirst, along with hunger, is one of the basic biological drives; it motivates humans to drink in order to ensure their survival.

Principal terms

ANTIDIURETIC HORMONE (ADH): a hormone secreted by the pituitary gland that increases water retention

CELLULAR DEHYDRATION THIRST: thirst caused by the loss of water from the cells

DRIVE: the motivational tension that causes a certain behavioral response in order to fulfill a need

HYPOTHALAMUS: a portion of the brain that is involved in the regulation of thirst and hunger

HYPOVOLEMIC THIRST: a loss of water from the extracellular fluid surrounding the cells and/or from the blood

MOTIVATION: factors that help to direct certain aspects of behavior

Overview

The range of human motivation is quite broad in controlling behaviors. Motivation can be defined as a condition that energizes and directs behavior in a particular manner. Different aspects of motivation can be attributed to instinctive behavior patterns, the need to reduce drives, or learned experiences.

Thirst is one of many biologically based motivational factors; among other such factors are those that involve food, air, sleep, temperature regulation, and pain avoidance. Biologically based motivational factors help humans and other organisms to maintain a balanced internal environment. This is the process of homeostasis. Deviations from the norm, such as hunger, excessive water loss, and pain, will cause an organism to seek out whatever is lacking.

Biologically based motivational factors, such as thirst, have been explained by the drive-reduction theory proposed by Clark Hull in 1943. The lack of some factor, such as water or food, causes the body to feel unpleasant. This is turn motivates one to reduce this feeling of unpleasantness, thus reducing the drive. Thirst is considered what is called a primary drive. Primary drives, which are related to biologically based needs such as hunger, thirst, and sleepiness, energize and motivate one to fulfill these biological needs, thus helping the body to maintain homeostasis. Secondary drives fulfill no biological need.

One may wonder what it is that makes one thirsty and how one knows when one has had enough to drink. Seventy-five percent of a human's weight is water. The maintenance of water balance is an ongoing process. In an average day, a person will lose approximately 2.5 liters of water; 60 percent of the water loss occurs through urination, 20 percent is lost through perspiration, and the remainder is lost through defecation and exhalation from the lungs. These 2.5 liters of water must be replaced.

What is the stimulus that motivates one to drink when one is thirsty? The simplest hypothesis, which was proposed by Walter Cannon in 1934, is the dry-mouth hypothesis. According to Cannon, it is a dry mouth that causes one to drink, not the need for water. This hypothesis has not held up under scrutiny. Research has shown that neither the removal of the salivary glands nor the presence of excess salivation in dogs disrupts the animals' regulation of water intake. Studies have indicated that the amount of water consumed is somehow measured and related to the organism's water deficit. This occurs even before the water has been replaced in the person's tissues and cells. Thus, dry mouth is a symptom of the need for water.

When a human being's water intake is lower than its level of water loss, two bodily processes are set in motion. First, the person becomes thirsty and drinks water (provided it is available). Second, the kidneys start to retain water by reabsorbing it and concentrating the urine. Thus, the kidneys can conserve the water that is already in the body. These processes are set in motion by the central nervous system (CNS).

The CNS responds to two primary internal bodily mechanisms. One is cellular dehydration thirst, and the other is hypovolemic thirst (a change in the volume of water in the body). In order to understand these mechanisms, one must realize that the body contains two main supplies of water. One supply, the intracellular fluid, is in the cells; the other supply consists of the extracellular fluid surrounding the cells and tissues and the fluid in the circulatory system. Water moves between these two areas by means of a process called osmosis, which causes it to move from an area of higher concentration to an area of lower concentration.

A person who is deprived of water will experience cellular dehydration thirst as a result of water loss caused by perspiration and excretion through the urine. This increases the salt concentration in the extracellular fluid, thereby lowering the water concentration. Thus, the cells lose their water to the surrounding extracellular fluid. The increasing salt concentration triggers specialized osmoreceptors located in the hypothalamic region of the brain. Two events occur: First, drinking is stimulated; second, antidiuretic hormone (ADH) is secreted from the pituitary gland in the brain. The ADH helps to promote the reabsorption of water into the kidneys.

The second kind of thirst, hypovolemic thirst, occurs when there is a decrease in the volume of the extracellular fluid as a result of bleeding, diarrhea, or vomiting. This produces a decrease in the salt concentration of the extracellular fluid, which lowers the blood pressure, which in turn stimulates the kidney cells to release a chemical. Eventually, the thirst receptors in the hypothalamus are stimulated; these cause the organism to consume water. In addition, ADH is also secreted in this process, which promotes the conservation of water.

The regulation of water intake in humans is thus related to a number of factors and is quite complex. Though cellular dehydration thirst and hypovolemic thirst play a role, it appears that in humans peripheral factors such as dry mouth play an even larger role. Humans can drink rapidly, replacing a twenty-four-hour water deficit in two to three minutes. This occurs even before the cellular fluid has replaced the water, which takes approximately eight to twelve minutes.

Applications

Thirst is a strong motivational factor. The importance of replacing lost water is underscored by the fact that a person can survive for a month without food but for only several days without water. It appears that both thirst processes help to promote drinking. Researchers have estimated that 64 to 85 percent of the drinking following water loss is caused by cellular dehydration thirst. Hypovolemic thirst accounts for 5 to 27 percent of the drinking, and the remainder is caused by peripheral factors.

The two types of thirst are independent of each other. The receptors for both thirsts are located in the hypothalamic region of the brain, but they are at different locations. Research has shown that lesions in one region will have no effect on thirst regulation in the other region.

Although the motivation to drink in humans is under conscious control by peripheral factors, unconscious control does exert a large influence. A study of cellular dehydration thirst using goats showed that the injection of a saline solution that has a salt concentration of more than 0.9 percent salt (body fluids have a salt concentration of 0.9 percent salt) into the area in which the osmoreceptors are located will produce a drinking response within sixty seconds. Similar results have been found regarding hypovolemic thirst; injecting angiotensin II (a converted protein found in the blood) into the hypothalamus causes a drinking response. This occurs even in animals that are fully hydrated. These animals will consume in direct proportion to the amount of angiotensin II injected into the hypothalamus.

Diet can have a profound effect on water balance in humans. Eating salty foods will produce cellular dehydration thirst despite adequate fluid levels, because water will flow out of the cells into the extracellular fluid. In contrast, salt-free diets will produce hypovolemic thirst by causing water to flow into the cells. Other factors also cause thirst. As stated previously, diarrhea, vomiting, and blood loss will cause hypovolemic thirst as a result of the loss of extracellular fluid. Therefore, significant blood loss will cause a person to become thirsty.

Diseases can also have an impact on thirst. An interesting example of such a disease is diabetes. Diabetes is a condition in which the body cannot process blood glucose (a type of sugar) properly. Improper diet or medication can cause diabetic ketoacidosis, which causes the levels of glucose and ketone bodies (derivatives from fat) in the blood to rise. This creates a major shift in the water balance of the body. Water leaves the cells and enters the blood system, causing the volume of blood to increase. This extra fluid (along with potassium and sodium) is excreted from the body in the urine, which causes the body to suffer dehydration and triggers a tremendous thirst. Since fluid is lost from both cells and extracellular fluid, this causes both types of thirst. Excessive thirst is still a symptom of diabetes, but it has become rare as a result of education and improved treatment.

Thirst motivation also operates during exercise. In short-term exercise, thirst motivation does not come into play because the body usually maintains its temperature. During long-term exercise, however, water intake at intervals facilitates athletic performance by helping to maintain body temperature. The motivation to drink occurs as a result of sweating, which causes the salt concentration in the body to rise during exercise, thereby causing cellular dehydration thirst. Interestingly, voluntary thirst and peripheral factors do not motivate one to take in water during prolonged exercise in the heat until it is too late. Thus, coaches should insist that athletes drink water as they perform.

Context

Different theories of motivation have been used to explain the many types of behaviors seen in humans. The first theories tried to explain motivation in terms of instincts, which are inborn patterns of behavior, but instincts did not go very far in explaining behaviors.

It was not until Clark Hull proposed the drive-reduction theory of motivation in 1943 that instinct theory was replaced. Hull's theory suggested that humans are motivated to meet unmet biological requirements. One is motivated to drink when one's body contains insufficient water. This is called the thirst drive.

The drive-reduction theory appeared to explain some types of motivation—primarily those that are biologically based. Thirst is one such type of motivation. There are, however, problems with the drive-reduction theory. For example, a person at a party may eat or drink because he or she is urged to do so. In such a situation, a person who has no internal drive eats or drinks anyway. This is an external stimulus to eat or drink, a learned situation.

The theory that drinking is the result of a dry mouth has a long history; it can be credited to Hippocrates in the fourth century B.C. The theory was revived in the eighteenth century and adopted again in 1934 by Walter Cannon. Though this theory was not supported, research has shown that, at least in humans, peripheral factors such as dry mouth are involved in the thirst drive.

It was not until the 1950's that the roles of the hypothalamus and the osmoreceptors in thirst became well known. Alan Epstein studied thirst in the 1970's. The prevailing view is that, although cellular dehydration and hypovolemic thirst are usually present together, they are independent of each other. Epstein has called this the "double-depletion hypothesis of thirst."

The role of biological drives is still undergoing study. Most biological drives are inborn, but the expression of these behaviors can be altered by learning. Though the thirst drive can be explained by the drive-reduction theory, the importance of drives is still advancing and being redefined. Ever-increasing information from the area of physiological psychology is making possible a better understanding of the role of the biological basis of behavior. Researchers are still a long way from a complete understanding of motivation and its biological basis.

Bibliography

Crooks, Robert L., and Jean Stein. "Motivation and Emotion." In *Psychology.* New York: Holt, Rinehart and Winston, 1988. This chapter reviews the process of motivation and drives, and it has a good section on hunger. The chapter may be a little advanced for the high school student, but it is nevertheless worth exploring.

Feldman, Robert S. "Motivation and Emotion." In *Understanding Psychology.* 2d ed. New York: McGraw-Hill, 1989. This easy-to-read chapter reviews motivation and has a good section on hunger, but it lacks a detailed account of thirst. Good simplified diagrams and figures.

Jorgensen, Caryl Dow, and John E. Lewis. *The ABCs of Diabetes.* New York: Crown, 1979. An informative book on diabetes in the form of a dictionary. Contains clear explanations and is very easy to read.

Levinthal, Charles F. "Chemical Senses and the Mechanisms for Eating and Drinking." In *Introduction to Physiological Psychology.* 3d ed. Englewood Cliffs, N.J.: Prentice-Hall, 1990. A very good chapter on the thirst drive. It is quite detailed, but the clarity of the writing makes it easy to read.

Mader, Sylvia S. *Biology.* 3d ed. Dubuque, Iowa: Wm. C. Brown, 1990. An easy-to-read introductory textbook on biology that provides a good background on hormones, water regulation, and kidney function, with many fine diagrams and figures. A good basis for understanding physiological psychology.

Lonnie J. Guralnick

Cross-References

THOUGHT: INFERENTIAL

Type of psychology: Cognition
Field of study: Thought

An argument is a process that takes assertions as inputs and produces conclusions as outputs; to go beyond the information given and get from the inputs to the outputs is to draw inferences. Formal inferences include deduction and induction. Inferential thought of a formal and informal nature is essential to both scientific reasoning and reasoning in daily life.

Principal terms
ARGUMENT: a set of statements (assertions) used to support a belief
ASSERTION: a statement that is a component of an argument
BELIEF: a high level of confidence that something is true
DEDUCTION: an inference in which the conclusion follows in a necessary way from the assertions
FORMAL LOGIC: a mathematical logic that has been formalized in propositional and predicate calculus and in other types of philosophical logic
INDUCTION: reasoning from the particular to the general
PRAGMATIC INFERENCES: inferences that are reasonable, considering world knowledge
PREMISE: another term for an assertion
PRESUPPOSITION: knowledge upon which one draws in order to understand an assertion
SYLLOGISM: a formal argument consisting of a major statement, a minor statement, and a conclusion

Overview

Psychologists are only beginning to understand how human thought processes operate, but there is no doubt that thinking is a critical skill. Reasoning is but one of many types of thought. Others include decision making and concept formation. Reasoning is unique in that it involves drawing inferences from current knowledge and beliefs. There are multiple components of reasoning, including the production and evaluation of arguments, the drawing of inferences, and the generation and testing of hypotheses.

The process of inference involves the exploration of alternatives, using evidence. Evidence is information that helps determine the degree to which a possibility achieves a goal. Basically, using inference, each possibility for choice is made stronger or weaker, considering that goal. The process can be done well or poorly. Without the ability to make inferences, there would not be any science, mathematics, or even laws.

Almost every statement a person says or writes leads the listener or reader to make inferences. A presupposition is knowledge upon which one draws in order to understand a statement or assertion. Once the assertion is understood, an inference can be drawn. Certain types of inferences, known as logical inferences, *must* follow from what was said. Logical inferences are, in a sense, demanded by the assertions. For example, the statement "Jack's heart problems forced his doctor to put him on a strict diet" logically implies that Jack was put on a diet.

There are two basic forms of formal, logical inference: induction and deduction. An induction is a judgment that something is probably true on the basis of experience. It involves generalization—that is, reasoning from a few to all, or from the particular to the general. People infer that they should avoid all bees, having only been stung by one or two up to that time. The inductive inference allows one to go beyond the data at hand and draw a useful conclusion (*all* bees will sting people) that cannot be proved, because it cannot be exhaustively tested. Induction can extend the content of the assertions at the cost of introducing uncertainty.

In contrast, deductive inference achieves absolute certainty, if performed correctly, at the cost of sacrificing innovation. It requires that two or more separate assertions be integrated in order to deduce a new assertion as a necessary consequence. Deductive inference deals with the validity, or form, of the arguments, providing methods and rules for restating given information so as to make what is implicit explicit. All valid deductive arguments reformulate knowledge already given in the assertions. They typically utilize key terms, such as quantifiers (such as "all," "some," "none"), connectives (such as "and," "or," "if-then"), and comparatives (such as "more," "less").

An experiment published in 1972 by John D. Bransford, J. Richard Barclay, and Jeffrey J. Franks illustrated that people could not distinguish sentences that were actually presented from inferences they made in the process of comprehending those sentences. Subjects saw sentences such as "Three turtles rested on a floating log and a fish swam beneath it." Subjects were then given memory tests to see if they recognized logically implied sentences such as "Three turtles rested on a floating log and a fish swam beneath them" that were new, so to speak, because they had not actually been seen by the subjects before the recognition test. A large number of the subjects claimed that they had seen the new sentences, which suggests that the logical inferences were formed and stored at the time when the original sentences were initially presented.

Not all inferences are demanded by formal logic, however; the majority of inferences are *invited* by the assertion, and they are known as pragmatic inferences. A pragmatic inference does not need to follow from an assertion, but rather is reasonable, considering world knowledge. For example, to say that "Albert and Rae were looking at wedding rings" in no way demands the inference that Albert and Rae are to be married; however, that inference is certainly reasonable, given what is known about the world. A large number of experiments have been reported which demonstrate that pragmatic inferences also are remembered as part of the original event.

As a further illustration, additional research by Bransford and other colleagues in 1973 presented subjects with sentences such as "John was trying to fix the birdhouse. He was pounding the nail when his father came out to watch him and to help him do the work." The assertions imply, but do not logically demand, that John was using a hammer. Subjects later falsely recognized the sentence "John was using a hammer to fix the birdhouse when his father came out to watch him and help him do the work." Just as with the logical inference, the pragmatic inference is usually remembered as if it had actually been presented.

Applications

Experimental investigations of thinking have revealed a wide range of shortcomings in human inference. Both deductive and inductive reasoning can go astray and produce incorrect conclusions, often either because one of the premises from which the conclusion was drawn is false or because the rules of deductive inference were violated. Many inferential judgments are based on imperfect information, and that means mistakes are unavoidable; however, the shortcomings are not simply errors. Instead, the ones that psychologists have identified involve the way in which information is used to draw the inference. For example, relevant information is sometimes ignored and sometimes relied upon too heavily. In addition, multiple pieces of information are often not combined as they should be.

In order to understand human communication, it is necessary to recognize the prevalence and power of inferential processing. Much of what is communicated is actually left unsaid. Speakers instead rely on listeners to draw appropriate inferences. The ability to communicate without explicitly saying everything one is trying to convey enormously increases efficiency; however, as with other thought processes, increased efficiency comes at the cost of increased error. Everyone occasionally says things in such a way that a listener will infer information that may not be quite accurate. To determine whether a speaker is actually being dishonest, the speaker's intentions need to be discovered, which is a difficult thing to do if the actual assertion is accurate. As a result, it is easy to mislead—either when sufficient information to evaluate an assertion is intentionally withheld or when care in drawing inferences is not taken.

Real-world situations such as advertising copy and courtroom testimony provide interesting examples. For example, the Federal Trade Commission was established to make decisions about what constitutes deceptive advertising, but deciding exactly what is deceptive is complex. The decision becomes especially difficult if a claim is not blatant, but instead is implied. Consider the following commercial: "Aren't you tired of sneezing and having a red nose throughout the winter? Aren't you tired of always feeling under the weather? Get through the entire winter without colds. Take NuPills as directed."

Notice that the commercial does not directly state that NuPills will get one through the entire winter without colds. The commercial only implies it. In order to test whether people can distinguish between asserted and implied claims, John Harris

(1977) presented people with a series of twenty fictitious commercials, half of which asserted claims and half of which implied claims. The subjects in the experiment were told to rate the claims as true, false, or of indeterminate truth value, based on the presented information. Some of the people made their judgments immediately after hearing each commercial, and others made their judgments after hearing all the commercials. Half the people were given instructions that warned them to take care not to interpret implied claims as asserted ones.

The results were that the subjects responded "true" more often to assertions than to implications, and instructions did help to reduce the number of implications accepted as true. Overall error rates, however, were high. Even in the group that gave an immediate judgment after hearing each commercial, people mistakenly accepted about half the implied statements as asserted ones. Finally, when the judgments were delayed until all commercials were presented, people accepted about as many implied statements as true as they did direct statements, even when they had been specifically warned about implied statements.

In the context of how information can be misleading in courtroom testimony, Elizabeth Loftus published an article in 1975 that described how she showed subjects ("witnesses") a film of a multiple-car accident. Immediately afterward, the witnesses completed a questionnaire that included questions such as "Did you see a broken headlight?" Half the witnesses, however, were given a question that was worded "Did you see *the* broken headlight?" When the word "the" is used, the question encourages the subject/witness to assume that there was a broken headlight and seems to be asking whether he or she happened to see it. The word "a" does not presuppose the existence of a broken headlight. Questions with "the" more often led to reports that the witness had seen the broken headlight than questions with "a." This was the case regardless of whether the object (a broken headlight) had actually appeared in the film. Thus, in a courtroom situation, attorneys can intentionally or inadvertently influence the memories of witnesses by using leading words that entail presuppositions in their questions, leading to inaccurate inferences.

Regardless of the source of the information, the elaborative nature of comprehension can be and is used to imply potentially inaccurate information. Yet through knowledge of influence, one can be in the position to protect oneself by directly questioning assertions and carefully analyzing one's own inferences.

Context

In ancient Greece, the philosopher Aristotle was the main creator of a formal inferential system. Historically, however, the scientific study of inference began fairly recently. Psychologists such as Robert S. Woodworth and S. B. Sells first began publishing articles in the 1930's on errors people made in the process of inferring conclusions. Woodworth and Sells were interested in how a reasoner's personal attitudes toward the conclusion of a syllogistic argument could bias the ability to draw inferences. They, along with other psychologists during the next three decades or so, studied formal inference and mainly looked at logical arguments called categorical syllogisms. As time passed, psychologists began to study other forms of deductive arguments and, later, inductive ones.

In 1962, Mary Henle encouraged psychologists to consider the difference between formal and practical reasoning. Henle attempted to clarify the heated controversy between the psychologists who thought formal logic was largely irrelevant to the thinking process, those who believed the mind contained a formal logic, and those who thought the mind contained other systems of logic that were more practical for day-to-day thinking. Henle pointed out that mathematical logic was never intended to be a direct description of how people think. For example, formal reasoning makes two demands not made in everyday reasoning. First of all, the reasoner must restrict the information to that contained in the premises. Second, the reasoner needs to discover the minimum commitments of the assertions as they are worded, which is not typical of ordinary comprehension. In ordinary comprehension, many inferences are invited that are unacceptable in formal deductive logic.

Linguists have also helped to promote research on inference. A long-standing question posed by linguists is how logic relates to actual conversation and argumentation. In conversation, most utterances have multiple functions. For example, the same utterance could be a description, a persuasion, an emotional expression, or even a warning. Numerous functions can arise, because the speaker may have one of a variety of intentions in mind when making the utterance.

It has been argued by Philip Johnson-Laird, in work he began publishing in 1978, that what subjects use to understand text is a mental model of the textual statements. He claims that people construct representations of models when they read a text. Rather than relying on formal logic in the interpretation of the material, Johnson-Laird believes, people manipulate the models they have formed. He thinks that the psychology of reasoning should describe the degree of competence that people display when it comes to inference, but that the mental processes underlying them— inferential performance—also need to be investigated. Given the increasing interest in the relationship of inference to linguistics, especially considering the applications that can be made in the area of artificial intelligence, such as getting computers to understand speech and to translate from one human language to another, the psychology of inferential thought will undoubtedly continue to be important research.

Bibliography

Baron, Jonathan. *Thinking and Deciding.* New York: Cambridge University Press, 1988. An excellent book that emphasizes the factors that keep people from thinking effectively and provides information to help the reader improve thinking and decision-making skills. The book is clearly written, but many of the ideas are complex. The author describes the role that thinking plays in relationship to learning, intelligence, and creativity.

Evans, Jonathan St. B. T. *Bias in Human Reasoning: Causes and Consequences.* Hillsdale, N.J.: Lawrence Erlbaum, 1989. Almost everyone interested in inferential thought should find this short book (slightly more than a hundred pages) a pleasure to read. The book is in an extended essay form. Classifies the types of bias and puts them in a general theoretical framework, while considering practical applications. Suggestions, based on research, are provided to help the reasoner avoid bias as much as possible. There are also suggestions for educators.

——————————. *The Psychology of Deductive Reasoning.* Boston: Routledge & Kegan Paul, 1982. The author reviews the available research in the area. He has published numerous journal articles on reasoning and is one of the top experts in the area of the psychology of reasoning. It is a thorough book, and the sections that address especially theoretical concerns can be skimmed over, if desired.

——————————, ed. *Thinking and Reasoning: Psychological Approaches.* Boston: Routledge & Kegan Paul, 1983. Contains eight chapters by a variety of experts in the area of inference. The chapters provide in-depth material on numerous aspects of inference, such as key logical rules, the influence of realistic content on reasoning, and thinking in general as a skill that involves the ability to draw inferences.

Nickerson, Raymond S. *Reflections on Reasoning.* Hillsdale, N.J.: Lawrence Erlbaum, 1986. This brief book is an adaptation of a report that the author prepared under a project sponsored by the National Institute of Education. It clearly describes reasoning and factors that can impede reasoning, and it provides practical chapters on how to improve one's own reasoning ability and how to use reasoning to win disputes of all kinds.

Deborah R. McDonald

Cross-References

Artificial Intelligence, 299; Cognitive Ability: Gender Differences, 540; Cognitive Development Theory: Piaget, 553; Concept Formation, 637; Decision Making as a Cognitive Process, 769; Intelligence Tests, 1341; Logic and Reasoning, 1471.

THOUGHT: STUDY AND MEASUREMENT

Type of psychology: Cognition
Fields of study: Cognitive processes; thought

The study of thought is probably as old as thought itself. Although the measurement of thought did not originate in psychology, cognitive psychology is primarily dedicated to the study and measurement of thought processes.

Principal terms
COGNITIVE PSYCHOLOGY: an area of study that investigates mental
    processes; areas within cognitive psychology include attention,
    perception, language, learning, memory, problem solving, and logic
EBBINGHAUS FORGETTING CURVE: an empirical demonstration that
    suggests that as time passes, memory performance decreases
HIGHER MENTAL FUNCTIONS: a phrase used to describe advanced thinking
    processes believed to be mostly limited to humans, such as reasoning,
    logic, decision making, problem solving, and language use
INFORMATION PROCESSING MODEL: a method of characterizing the
    processing of the human mind that finds the mind's approach similar
    to the basic processing of a computer
PARALLEL PROCESSING: a theory concerning how people scan information
    in memory that suggests the ability to comprehend simultaneously all
    the components in immediate memory
PERCENT SAVINGS: a formula developed by Hermann Ebbinghaus for the
    precise measure of memory and forgetting; the higher the percent
    savings, the less time Ebbinghaus had to spend rememorizing
    nonsense syllables he had forgotten
PERSONAL EQUATION: an equation developed by astronomers in the
    1800's that allowed them to account and compensate for individual
    differences in tracking the movement of stars across the sky
SERIAL PROCESSING: a theory concerning how people scan information
    in memory that suggests that as the number of items in memory
    increases, so does the amount of time taken to determine whether
    an item is present in memory
SUBTRACTION TECHNIQUE: a method developed by the Dutch physiologist
    Frans C. Donders to measure the various components of a complex
    cognitive task

Overview
Cognitive psychologists study many processes basic to human nature and everyday life. Mental processes are central to who people are, what they do, and how they

survive. In cognitive psychology, the study of thought necessitates its measurement. For example, much effort has been put forth in cognitive psychology to study how people understand and process information in their environment. One popular approach is to use the idea of a human information-processing system, analogous to a computer. Computers are information-processing devices that use very specific instructions to achieve tasks. A computer receives input, performs certain internal operations on the data (including memory operations), and outputs certain results. Cognitive psychologists often use the information-processing metaphor in describing human operations. People must "input" information from the environment; this process includes sensory and perceptual systems, the recognition of certain common patterns of information, and attention processes.

Once this information has entered the "system," a vast number of operations can be performed. Much of the work by cognitive psychologists has centered on the storage of information during this process—that is, on memory. While memory processes have been of interest since ancient times, it was not until the 1880's that scientists, notably Hermann Ebbinghaus, first systematically and scientifically studied memory. Scientists studying memory today talk about concepts such as short-term and long-term memory as well as about the distinction between episodic and semantic memory systems. The function of memory is essential to human thought and ultimately to the measurement of thought.

In terms of measuring what happens to incoming information, more than memory storage occurs; people manipulate these data. They make decisions based on the information available, and they have capabilities (often referred to as higher mental processes) that in many ways differentiate humans from other animals. Some of the functions commonly studied and measured include reasoning, problem solving, logic, decision making, and language development and use. The information-processing analogy is completed with the "output" of information. When a person is asked a question, the response is the output; it is based on the information stored in memory, whether those items be personal experiences, knowledge gained from books, or awareness of social customs. People do these things so effortlessly, day in and day out, that it is difficult to stop, appreciate, and comprehend how thoughts work. Psychologists have pondered these questions for many years and are only beginning to discover the answers.

Applications

Some of the earliest systematic studies of thought and the accompanying desire to measure it came from astronomy, not psychology or philosophy. From this beginning, Dutch physiologist Frans C. Donders set out specifically to measure a sequence of mental processes—thought—in the middle of the nineteenth century. His technique was simple yet elegant in its ability to measure how much time mental processes consume; the procedure developed by Donders is typically referred to as the subtraction technique.

The subtraction technique begins with the timing and measurement of a very basic task. For example, a person might be asked to press a button after hearing a tone. Donders realized that it was fairly easy to time accurately how long subjects took to perform this task. He believed that two cognitive (thought) processes would be operating: perception of the tone and the motor response of pressing the button. Once the time of this simple task was known, Donders would make the task more difficult. If a discrimination task were added, he believed, the time taken to complete the task would increase compared to the basic perception-motor response sequence. In this discrimination task, for example, Donders might tell a person to press the button only after hearing a high-pitched sound. That person is now faced with an added demand—to make a decision about pitch. Donders believed that with this discrimination stage, the processing of the information would require more mental effort and more time; he was right. More important, Donders could now measure the amount of extra thought required for the decision by subtracting the simple-task time from the discrimination-task time. In a general sense, Donders had a method for measuring thought.

Donders also had the ability to measure and manipulate specific components of the thought process. He even added another component to the sequence of tasks, what he called choice time. For example, the task could be changed so that for a high tone the subject should press the right button, and for a low tone, press the left button. By subtracting the discrimination time from this new choice time, he could estimate how long the added choice contributed to the overall thought process. Through these ingenious methods, Donders inspired generations of cognitive psychologists to study thought in terms of the time it takes to think.

The first recognized work done in psychology on the measurement of thought processes was Hermann Ebbinghaus' work on memory capacity and forgetting. Working independently in the 1880's in Germany, Ebbinghaus set out to study memory processes, particularly the nature of forgetting. Being the first psychologist to study the issue, he had no precedent as to how to proceed, so Ebbinghaus invented his own procedures for measuring memory. To his credit, those procedures were so good that they are still commonly used. Before describing his measurement of memory, Ebbinghaus made two important decisions about methods for studying memory. First, he studied only one person's memory—his own. He believed he would have better control over situational and contextual variables that way.

Second, Ebbinghaus decided that he could not use everyday words in his memory studies, because they might have associations that would make them easier to study. For example, if one were memorizing a poem, the story and the writing style might help memory, and Ebbinghaus was interested in a pure measure of memory and forgetting. To achieve this, Ebbinghaus pioneered the use of nonsense syllables. He used three-letter combinations of consonant-vowel-consonant so that the items were pronounceable but meaningless. Nonsense syllables such as "geb," "fak," "jit," "zab," and "buh" were used.

Ebbinghaus used a vigorous schedule of testing and presented himself with many lists of nonsense syllables to be remembered at a later time. In fact, he spent five years memorizing various lists until he published his seminal work on the topic, *Über das Gedächtnis* (1885; *Memory: A Contribution to Experimental Psychology,* 1913). He systematically measured memory by memorizing a list, letting some time pass, and testing himself on the list. He devised a numerical measurement for memory called percent savings. Percent savings was a measure of the degree of forgetting that occurred over time. For example, it might take him ten minutes to memorize a list perfectly. He would let forty-eight hours pass, then tell himself to recall the list. Forgetting occurs during that time, and only some items would be remembered. Ebbinghaus would then look at the original list and rememorize it until he knew it perfectly; this might take seven minutes or so. He always spent less time rememorizing the list. Said another way, there was some savings from the earlier experience forty-eight hours before. This percent savings was his measure of memory. The higher the percentage of savings, the more items remembered (or the less forgotten), and Ebbinghaus could remember the list in less time.

Ebbinghaus then varied the time between original list learning and later list recall. He found that percent savings drops over time; that is, the longer one waits to remember something, the less one saves from the prior experience, so the more time he had to spend rememorizing the list. Ebbinghaus found fairly good percent savings two or nine hours later, but percent savings dropped dramatically after two or three days. Plotted on a graph, this relationship looks like a downward sloping curve, and it is called the Ebbinghaus forgetting curve. Simply stated, it means that as time passes, memories become poorer. Although this effect is not surprising today, Ebbinghaus was the first (in 1885) to demonstrate this phenomenon empirically.

Another example of the work in the area of cognitive psychology comes from the studies of Saul Sternberg in the 1960's at Bell Laboratories. Sternberg examined how additional information in memory influences the speed of mental operations in retrieving information stored in memory. Sternberg's task was fairly simple. He presented people with a list of numbers; the list might range from one to six numbers. After the people saw this initial list, a single number (called a probe) was presented. People were asked to identify whether the probe number was on the initial list of numbers. The list might be "2935," for example, and the probe might be "3."

Sternberg's primary interest was in studying how the length of the initial list affected the time it took to make the required yes-or-no decision. Two possibilities typically emerge when people consider this problem. The concept called serial processing holds that the comparison of the probe to each number in the initial list takes up a little bit of time, so that the more items in the initial list, the longer the memory search takes. An alternative idea, parallel processing, suggests that people instantaneously scan all the items in the memory set, and the number of items in the initial list does not make a difference. Another way of saying this is that all the items are scanned at once, in parallel fashion. Sternberg found that people search their memories using the technique of serial processing. In fact, he was able to calculate precisely the amount of additional search time needed for each added item in the memory set—38 milliseconds (a millisecond is a thousandth of a second). Although the search may seem fast, even instantaneous, the more there is to think about, the more time it takes to think.

Context

The study of thought, and particularly its measurement, is a relatively recent development. For centuries, the thinking processes of humans were believed to be somewhat mystical, and certainly not available for scientific inquiry. Most philosophers were concerned more with the mind and its relationship to the body or the world than with how people think. The study of thought, although it was generally considered by the ancient Greek philosophers, did not merit serious attention until the emergence of the "personal equation" by astronomers and the realization that thought processes are indeed measurable and can be measured accurately and precisely.

The story of the first recorded measurements of thought begins with the royal astronomer to England, Nevil Maskelyne, and his assistant, David Kinnebrook, in 1794. Astronomers of the day were mostly concerned with stellar transits (measuring the movement of stars across the sky). Using telescopes and specialized techniques, the goal of the astronomer was to measure the time taken for a particular star to move across a portion of the telescopic field. Using a complicated procedure that involved listening to a beating clock and viewing the sky, astronomers could measure the transit time of a star fairly accurately, to within one-tenth or two-tenths of a second. These measurements were particularly important because the clocks of that period were based on stellar transits.

Maskelyne and Kinnebrook often worked together in recording the movement of the stars. While Kinnebrook had no problems during 1794, in 1795 Maskelyne began to notice that Kinnebrook's times varied from his own by as much as one-half of a second—considered a large and important difference. By early 1796, the difference between the astronomers' times had grown to eight-tenths of a second. This was an intolerable amount of error to Maskelyne, and he fired his assistant Kinnebrook.

About twenty years later, a German astronomer named Friedrich Bessel came across the records of these incidents and began to study the "error" in the differing astronomers' measurements. He believed that the different measurements were attributable in part to differences between people and that this difference was not necessarily an error. He found that even the most famous and reliable astronomers of the day differed from one another by more than two-tenths of a second.

This incident between Maskelyne and Kinnebrook, and its later study by Bessel, led to some important conclusions. First, measurements in astronomy would have to consider the specific person making the measurement. Astronomers even went to the lengths of developing what became known as the personal equation. The personal equation is a verified, quantified account of how each astronomer's thought processes worked when measuring stellar transits. In essence, the personal equation was a measurement of the thought process involved and a recognition of differences between people. Second, if astronomers differed in their particular thought processes, then many people differ in other types of thinking processes as well. Finally, and perhaps most important in the long run, this incident laid the groundwork for the idea that thought could be measured accurately and the information could be put to good use. No longer was thinking a mystical or magical process that was unacceptable for study by scientists.

It is from this historical context that the field of cognitive psychology has emerged. Cognitive psychology is chiefly concerned with the thought processes and, indeed, all the general mental processing of organisms (most often humans). The interests of a cognitive psychologist can be quite varied: learning, memory, problem solving, reasoning, logic, decision making, linguistics, cognitive development in children, and other topics. Each area of specialization continues to measure and examine how people think, using tasks and procedures as ingenious as those of Donders, Ebbinghaus, and Sternberg. The study and measurement of thought (or, more generally, the field of cognitive psychology) will continue to play an important and vital role. Not many questions are more basic to the study of human behavior than how people think, what processes are involved, and how researchers can scientifically study and measure these processes.

Bibliography

Anderson, John R. *Cognitive Psychology and Its Implications.* 3d ed. New York: W. H. Freeman, 1990. This text is a long-standing leader in the field of cognitive psychology. Provides a wonderful overview of the fundamental issues of cognitive psychology, including attention and perception, basic principles of human memory, problem solving, the development of expertise, reasoning, intelligence, and language structure and use.

Ashcraft, Mark H. *Human Memory and Cognition.* Glenview, Ill.: Scott, Foresman, 1989. A cognitive psychology textbook that heavily emphasizes the human information-processing metaphor. Arranged differently from Anderson's text, it too provides good coverage of all the basic areas of cognitive psychology.

Boring, Edwin G. *A History of Experimental Psychology.* 2d ed. Englewood Cliffs, N.J.: Prentice-Hall, 1950. This text is the foremost authority on the development and history of psychology up until 1950. Contains detailed accounts of the work of early philosophers and astronomers who contributed to the study of thought, and even contains an entire chapter devoted to the personal equation. This can be a difficult text to read, but it is the authoritative overview of the early history of psychology.

Lachman, Roy, Janet L. Lachman, and Earl C. Butterfield. *Cognitive Psychology and Information Processing: An Introduction.* Hillsdale, N.J.: Lawrence Erlbaum, 1979. One of the earliest texts that adequately captures the coming importance and influence of cognitive psychology. There are outstanding chapters that trace the influences of other disciplines and traditions on what is now known as cognitive psychology. Topic areas within the field are discussed as well.

Mayer, Richard E. *Thinking, Problem Solving, and Cognition.* 2d ed. New York:

W. H. Freeman, 1992. A book primarily dedicated to the topic of problem solving, which is unusual. The format is interesting and creative, covering the historical perspective of problem solving, basic thinking tasks, information-processing analysis, and implications and applications. The focus on thought and its measurement is seen throughout, especially in sections discussing mental chronometry.

Schultz, Duane P., and Sydney Ellen Schultz. *A History of Modern Psychology.* 4th ed. San Diego: Harcourt Brace Jovanovich, 1987. A readable and understandable treatment of the history of psychology. Touches on the importance of the contributions of the astronomers as well as Donders in the study and measurement of thought.

R. Eric Landrum

Cross-References

Artificial Intelligence, 299; Cognitive Maps, 566; Cognitive Psychology: An Overview, 572; Computer Models of Cognition, 631; Language and Cognition, 1401; Learning: Concept, Expectancy, and Insight, 1431; Logic and Reasoning, 1471; Memory: Empirical Studies, 1511; Thought Structures, 2565.

THOUGHT STRUCTURES

Type of psychology: Cognition
Field of study: Thought

Thought structures are the means by which the mind organizes ideas and information. The theories that have been developed to describe thought structures provide insights into the ways people come to understand each other and the world.

Principal terms
BEHAVIORISM: the theoretical approach that argues that the proper subject matter of psychology is observable behavior, not internal mental processes
FEATURE COMPARISON THEORY: a theory of thought structure which hypothesizes that concepts are mentally represented as lists of features or attributes
IMAGERY: mental representations based on the senses; visual images are the ones most often studied by cognitive psychologists
NATURAL CONCEPTS: a concept is a group of items that are perceived as similar in some respect; natural concepts are used in everyday life
PROPOSITIONS: mental representations based on the underlying structure of language; a proposition is the smallest unit of knowledge that can be stated
PROTOTYPE: a "best example" of a concept—one that contains the most typical features of that concept
SCHEMA (pl. SCHEMATA): an organized frame of knowledge about situations, behaviors, objects, and so forth
SCRIPTS: temporally organized schemas; representations of sequences of events

Overview

Cognitive scientists assume that human knowledge of the world is organized and that this organization provides the structure for human thoughts. Countless pieces of information are stored in people's long-term memories. This knowledge is organized so that one can remember it easily, draw reasonable inferences when one has only partial information, and comprehend new information in the light of what one already knows. Many models of the structure of thought have been proposed as scientists have grappled with the complexities of the mind. Debates have arisen about whether the basic structure of thought is quasi-linguistic (based on language), imagistic (based on images), or both. Allan Paivio, Roger Shepard, and Steven Kosslyn have been at the forefront of research demonstrating that imagery is a significant form of thought.

Researchers agree that imagery can help solve problems and that memories are often recalled in terms of images. Many say, however, that mental structures are basically quasi-linguistic propositions. This means that there is an underlying abstract linguistic form—like a basic grammar with "slots" for various subjects and objects—to all thought, not that thought itself is organized in a language such as French or English. Zenon Pylyshyn strongly argues that there is only one mental code, which is propositional. Images may be derived from propositions in much the same way that computers can generate pictures from programs that are written in a propositional computer language.

Models of the structure of quasi-linguistic thought have been designed for a variety of purposes. Some describe how concepts, words, and their meanings are organized in the mind. Others take as their basic unit propositions rather than single concepts, and still others describe broader structures that encompass entire sequences of events. An example of approaches at each of these levels of generality will be given below.

Eleanor Rosch has demonstrated that most natural concepts—those that people use in everyday life—do not have rigid definitions. Rather, members of a class of objects—for example, chairs—share a "family resemblance." Windsor chairs, recliners, and rocking chairs have similar characteristics but do not share the same properties. Most people, however, will agree on a "best example," or prototype, of a concept, and that prototype will be consulted when one is deciding whether a new object is an example of the concept. Rosch has demonstrated that concepts are organized into different levels, from the most general (for example, "chair") to the most specific ("authentic Louis XIV"). Basic-level categories, such as "rocking chair," are the ones that are most commonly used, since they provide clear identification but are not overdetailed.

The notion that one classifies new objects by comparing their features to previous examples of a concept is formalized in feature-comparison models of cognitive structure. These models hypothesize that when one attempts to decide whether a new object is an example of a concept, one first examines the overlap between the new object's features and the characteristic and defining features of the known concept. If the overlap is not great, the defining characteristics are examined in detail to determine the identity of the new object. For example, at first glance, penguins may not be thought of as birds, since flying, not swimming, is characteristic of most birds. Closer examination, however, reveals that penguins do possess hollow bones and feathers, features that define birds.

Network models of cognitive structure describe how concepts are related to one another. A network can be described as a "fishnet" of concepts intersected by lines of relationship. The network preserves the meaning of propositions, not particular words or word order. For example, the two sentences "Mary danced with Tom" and "Mary and Tom danced" would be represented by the same proposition. John Anderson's propositional network theory describes how viewing knowledge as a complex network of intersecting propositions can help to explain learning and memory. Learning is viewed as the addition of new information to a network. Remembering occurs when a cue activates (brings to awareness) a portion of a network; the activation can spread to other parts of the network.

Like network theory, schema theory accounts for broad bases of knowledge. Roger Schank has described how the particular types of schemata called scripts (temporally patterned events) allow people to form inferences. For example, people may be described as having a "going to the movies" script that includes choosing a film from those advertised in the newspaper, driving to the theater, buying a ticket, buying refreshments, finding a seat in the theater, watching the film, leaving the theater, and driving home. When a friend says that she went to the movies over the weekend, one can infer that she bought a ticket, found a place to sit, and so forth, without being explicitly told these details. Adults have schemata such as this for a great many everyday events and situations.

Applications

Models of the structure of thought have been used to explain many aspects of everyday thinking; three examples will be presented here. The spatial nature of imagery has been studied in the laboratory and can be applied to remembering things in everyday life. The idea of prototypes may explain how people categorize others and predict their behavior. Schema theory and propositional network theory can explain some aspects of how people comprehend written material.

In laboratory research, Steven Kosslyn has demonstrated the spatial nature of imagery. He had subjects memorize a simple map of an island with specific landmarks such as a tree, a hut, and a lake. When asked to travel mentally from one point to another and say when they "arrived," subjects took longer to respond to the travel to the more distant landmarks. These results suggest to Kosslyn that imagery is a distinct mental code, one that is organized in terms of spatial relationships.

Mental travel with imagery has been used as a powerful memory aid since ancient times. In the technique known as the method of loci, one uses imagery to "place" mentally what one wants to remember along a familiar route. For example, one might remember a shopping list containing the items milk, eggs, peanut butter, and apples by mentally walking through one's home, placing the milk on the sofa, the eggs on the dining table, the peanut butter on the bed pillow, and the apples on the kitchen counter. Once in the grocery store, mentally retracing the route through the home will help the shopper remember the items on the list. The method of loci is particularly useful in memorizing a series of items that have no inherent organization.

Psychologists interested in studying social relationships have used the idea that natural concepts are classified by their similarity to a prototype to explain how people categorize others. As people strive to make sense of their complex social world, some degree of categorization is probably inevitable. To bring order to the world, people make tentative predictions of how others will behave based on the types of persons they seem to be. For example, an employer needs to predict whether an applicant for a job would make a good employee. "Good employee" may be thought of as a natural concept. Examples of "good employees" have a resemblance to one another, but it may be difficult or impossible to give an all-encompassing definition of the concept. In such situations, the employer may decide whether to hire the applicant based on how similar that applicant seems to someone who has been a particularly good employee in the past—that person serving as the prototype or best example of the concept. Similarly, one may be more likely to pursue a friendship with an individual one has recently met if that individual resembles a particularly good friend.

The danger in such categorization is that, in addition to characteristics directly relevant to what one is trying to predict, the prototype will include other, irrelevant characteristics, such as race, age, and gender. The use of prototypes can inadvertently bias one's judgments about others and set the stage for discrimination.

Schema theory and propositional network theory partly explain how people comprehend material that they read. Language is often ambiguous, and understanding the context of a communication helps in deciphering its meaning. For example, the meaning of the statement "They are cooking apples" depends upon whether the context is defined as "apple identification" or "the activity of people in the kitchen." The order in which material is presented provides one type of context. Different types of writing typically are organized differently. Most stories, for example, describe a situation, introduce conflict, and resolve the conflict; a textbook often has an introduction, subsections introducing ideas and giving examples, and summaries. Knowledge of the schema for the type of material one is reading can enhance comprehension by allowing one to anticipate the type of information that will be presented next.

Propositional network theory also explains how readers grasp context and how that aids comprehension. According to John Anderson, a stimulus such as reading activates the portion of one's propositional network that is related to the material one is reading. This activation may include information that must be assumed in order to comprehend new information. For example, the statement "Christopher Columbus was not the first adventurer to explore the New World" assumes that the reader has at least a rudimentary knowledge of the traditional account of the discovery of the Americas. The activation of appropriate knowledge bases thus allows one to comprehend new information more easily by making related material available to memory. In this way, the more one knows about a topic, the more easily new material can be learned.

Context

Although attempts to describe the structure of the mind can be traced back at least as far as the ancient Greeks, contemporary models of the mind are a product of the cognitive revolution of the 1950's. At that time, behaviorism was on the wane, and researchers from a variety of disciplines saw hope in reconstructing psychology as the science of the mind rather than the study of behavior. The inspiration of much of this interest came from advances in computer science.

Computer science influenced the development of cognitive psychology and the study of mental structures in two ways. First, the computer serves as a metaphor for the mind. The information-processing approach views the input, storage, and output of the computer as analogous to functions in the human mind. Second, the computer can be used to test models of the mind. In artificial intelligence studies, cognitive scientists often strive to formulate theories that are explicit enough to be written as computer programs. If a program produces output that seems to draw conclusions, make inferences, or otherwise perform like a human, the theory gains credence. Propositional network, schema, and feature-comparison theories of mental structures have been tested by means of computer programs, and the results have contributed to increasingly sophisticated theoretical analyses.

The search to understand the mind is not exclusively the province of psychology. Philosophers, neuroscientists, linguists, and others have theorized about thought structures. Much speculation has surrounded the relationship between language and thought. In the 1970's, cross-cultural psychologist Eleanor Rosch (then Eleanor Heider) challenged the prevailing view that thought was dependent upon the specific language one used. She and anthropologists Brent Berlin and Paul Kay studied the Dani of New Guinea, among others, and concluded that concepts have universal mental structures. Concepts may be propositionally based, but they are not dependent upon the specifics of any individual language. Rosch's research later demonstrated the utility of thinking of concepts as having "fuzzy" boundaries and being typified by prototypes.

Philosophers and psychologists have wondered whether the mind can be studied scientifically, since it is internal and not accessible to traditional experimental manipulation. Some believe that the computer analogy is mistaken and the use of computers to test cognitive theories is unconvincing. According to philosopher Herbert Dreyfus, computer models are doomed to failure because human minds, unlike computers, are only partly rule governed. Others say that theories about thought structures often neglect the relationship between the mind and the physical and social environments. For example, Ulric Neisser argues that the proliferation of internal structural models has diverted scholars from what the mind is really about—apprehending and acting in the world—and Jerome Bruner points out that the construction of meaning is the product of an entire culture, not only an individual mind.

The scientific study of thought structures is in its infancy. In the years since the 1950's, however, the cognitive approach has revitalized and redirected most of mainstream scientific psychology and in doing so has influenced disciplines as diverse as education, philosophy, and business.

Bibliography

Anderson, John Robert. *Cognitive Psychology and Its Implications.* 2d ed. New York: W. H. Freeman, 1985. Much of this sophisticated cognitive psychology textbook is based on Anderson's propositional network theory. The chapter entitled "Meaning-Based Knowledge Representations" describes the specifics of this theory and discusses schema theory. The chapter entitled "Perception-Based Knowledge Representations" discusses imagery. Suggestions for further reading are provided at the end of each chapter.

Flanagan, Owen J., Jr. "Cognitive Psychology and Artificial Intelligence: Philosophical Assumptions and Implications." In *The Science of the Mind.* Cambridge, Mass.: MIT Press, 1984. A readable introduction to the central philosophical issues addressed by cognitive psychology. Discusses mental representation in terms of imagery and propositions, and reviews the ambitions and criticisms of artificial intelligence.

Gardner, Howard. *The Mind's New Science: A History of the Cognitive Revolution.* New York: Basic Books, 1985. An excellent review of the central issues, research, and criticisms of cognitive science. Parts 1 and 2 provide a historical account of cognitive science, including contributions from psychology, artificial intelligence, linguistics, anthropology, and neuroscience. Mental imagery and natural concepts are included in part 3.

Hunt, Morton M. *The Universe Within.* New York: Simon & Schuster, 1982. A very readable introduction to cognitive science; good for the beginning student. Chapter 3 discusses how information is stored in memory, chapter 5 discusses concepts, and chapter 9 discusses artificial intelligence.

Neisser, Ulric. "From Direct Perception to Conceptual Structure." In *Concepts and Conceptual Development: Ecological and Intellectual Factors in Categorization.* Cambridge, England: Cambridge University Press, 1987. Contains a number of sophisticated articles on concepts, following the Rosch model. This article, by the "father" of cognitive psychology, describes the development of concepts in children from the ecological perspective, arguing for the importance of the environment in specifying the concepts that a person develops.

Schank, Roger C. "Knowledge Structures." In *The Cognitive Computer.* Reading, Mass.: Addison-Wesley, 1984. A readable introduction to the issues, promises, and problems of the artificial intelligence approach to representing human minds. This chapter describes scripts and related models.

Susan E. Beers

Cross-References

Artificial Intelligence, 299; Cognitive Psychology: An Overview, 572; Computer Models of Cognition, 631; Concept Formation, 637; Long-Term Memory, 1479; Thought: Inferential, 2552.

THE THYROID GLAND

Type of psychology: Biological bases of behavior
Field of study: Endocrine system

The thyroid gland is responsible for the production of three hormones important for proper growth and development: thyroxine and triiodothyronine, which regulate the basal metabolic rate of the body, and calcitonin, which lowers blood calcium levels. Disorders associated with the thyroid may result from either underactivity (hypothyroidism) or overactivity (hyperthyroidism) of the gland.

Principal terms

ENDOCRINE GLANDS: secretory organs that produce hormones which are released directly into the blood

GOITER: an enlargement of the thyroid gland

HYPERTHYROIDISM: a disorder of the thyroid characterized by overactivity resulting in an increased output of thyroid hormones; symptoms include an increased metabolic rate, rapid heartbeat, and elevated body temperature

HYPOTHYROIDISM: a disorder of the thyroid characterized by underactivity of the gland; results in a lowered metabolic rate and body temperature

METABOLISM: the sum total of the chemical reactions that occur in the body

PITUITARY GLAND: the small endocrine gland located beneath the hypothalamus of the brain which regulates other endocrine glands through the production and release of hormones

THYROID-STIMULATING HORMONE: a hormone produced by the anterior pituitary gland which stimulates the production and secretion of thyroid hormones

THYROXINE: the major hormone produced and secreted by the thyroid gland; stimulates protein synthesis and the basal metabolic rate

Overview

The thyroid gland is the largest endocrine gland in the human body. It is located on the upper portion of the trachea (windpipe) near the junction between the larynx (voice box) and the trachea. The thyroid gland is made up of a right lobe and a left lobe, which are joined by a narrow band of tissue called the isthmus, which lies across the trachea.

The thyroid gland is classified as an endocrine gland because it is made up of epithelial cells which are specialized for the production and secretion of specific hormones. Hormones produced by endocrine glands are specialized organic molecules that regulate biological activity by affecting certain cells of the body called target cells. Once the hormones have been produced by the gland, they are released into the bloodstream and carried by the blood throughout the body. The target cells have receptors on their surfaces to which the hormones attach; attachment of the hormone initiates cellular activities that lead to the observed effects of the hormone on body processes.

Internally, the thyroid gland is composed of hollow groups of cells called follicles. The cells are bound together by connective tissue and surround an inner region which contains a protein substance called colloid. It is in the colloid that the hormones produced by the thyroid gland are stored until their release into the bloodstream. The thyroid gland is different from all other endocrine glands in this respect, since the other endocrine glands of the human body store their hormones within the cells of the gland.

The thyroid gland produces the hormones triiodothyronine (T_3), thyroxine (tetraiodothyronine or T_4), and calcitonin. Triiodothyronine and thyroxine contain iodine, which is obtained from the diet and actively taken up from the bloodstream by the follicle cells. Within the follicle cells, iodine is attached to an amino acid called tyrosine to form a molecule called monoiodotyrosine (MIT). A second iodine may then be attached to form diiodotyrosine (DIT). Thyroxine is produced by coupling 2 DIT molecules; triiodothyronine is produced by coupling an MIT with a DIT. The thyroid hormones thyroxine (T_4) and triiodothyronine (T_3) are then stored extracellularly in the colloid surrounded by the ball of follicle cells. Normally the thyroid produces 10 percent T_3 and 90 percent T_4.

The release of thyroid hormones is controlled by the anterior lobe of the pituitary gland, a small pea-shaped gland located at the base of the brain. The pituitary gland produces a hormone known as thyrotropin, or thyroid-stimulating hormone (TSH), which controls the production and secretion of the thyroid hormones. The release of TSH from the anterior pituitary is in turn regulated by thyrotropin-releasing hormone (TRH), a hormone produced by the hypothalamus. TRH is transported by way of a capillary system to the anterior pituitary, where it stimulates the release of TSH. TSH then travels via the bloodstream to the thyroid, where it stimulates the production and release of the thyroid hormones. When the thyroid is stimulated by TSH to secrete its hormones, T_3 and T_4 are taken into the follicle cells from the colloid by a process called endocytosis. T_3 and T_4 then enter the bloodstream from the follicle cells. While traveling in the bloodstream, the thyroid hormones are bound to thyroid-binding globulin (TBG), a plasma protein. Once the hormones reach the target cells, most of the T_4 is converted to T_3, indicating that T_3 is the major active form of the thyroid hormones at the cellular level.

The thyroid hormones influence the metabolic rate of the body primarily by controlling the rate of cell respiration. Most tissues of the body are responsive to the influence of these hormones; exceptions include the testes, uterus, spleen, and brain. T_3 and T_4 cause a calorigenic effect on the body—they promote oxygen usage and heat production by the tissues. They promote the synthesis of proteins from amino acids and stimulate the synthesis, mobilization, and degradation of lipids. Thyroid hormones increase the utilization of carbohydrates, promoting their breakdown and the subsequent release of energy, and they increase the rate by which glucose is absorbed from the intestine. T_3 and T_4 promote the uptake of glucose from the blood by adipose tissue and muscle, and stimulate a process known as gluconeogenesis, whereby carbohydrates are produced from non-carbohydrate molecules. The effects of thyroid hormones on carbohydrate metabolism are modified by other hormones, especially insulin, epinephrine, and norepinephrine.

Although normal quantities of thyroid hormone stimulate the production of proteins, excessive amounts cause muscle wasting and weakness, especially in the heart and eye muscles. High levels of T_3 and T_4 also cause an increase in the breakdown of lipids and a decreased amount of cholesterol and phospholipids in the blood plasma.

In addition to T_3 and T_4, the thyroid produces and secretes calcitonin. This hormone is produced by parafollicular cells, which are located adjacent to the thyroid follicle cell. Structurally, calcitonin is a polypeptide made up of a chain of thirty-two amino acids. When calcitonin is released into the bloodstream, it primarily affects bone cells, causing them to increase bone formation and suppress bone resorption. As a result, the amount of calcium and phosphate in the blood is lowered. Release of calcitonin is regulated by the amount of calcium ions in the blood plasma; when the concentration of calcium increases, calcitonin production and secretion by the thyroid is stimulated. Some hormones released by the digestive tract during the digestion and absorption of food also promote the secretion of calcitonin from the thyroid. This aids the body's conservation of calcium from the diet by preventing a rapid surge in the amount of calcium in the blood, which could lead to increased excretion of calcium in the urine by the kidneys.

Applications

Most functional disorders of the thyroid result either from underactivity (hypothyroidism) or overactivity (hyperthyroidism) of the cells of the gland. A thyroid disorder may develop at any time during a person's life, from a dietary deficiency, a disease, or problems in development. Hypothyroidism in infants results in a condition known as cretinism. Because T_4 stimulates protein synthesis, it is needed for the proper development of the skeleton and the central nervous system. Cretins are individuals characterized by abnormal bone formation, stunted growth, low body temperature, and retarded mental development. Infants suffering from an underactive thyroid can be treated successfully by the administration of thyroxine soon after birth, preferably before they are one month of age. If treatment is delayed, the mental retardation becomes permanent.

Hypothyroidism in adults is called myxedema. The disease develops slowly over a period of months or years. This condition is more common in women than in men and is characterized by swollen tissues, especially of the face, eyelids, tongue, and larynx, because of an accumulation of body fluid in the subcutaneous tissue. Other symptoms include a low metabolic rate, poor appetite, and abnormal sensitivity to cold. A person with an underactive thyroid also experiences physical sluggishness and weight gain.

In severe cases, hypothyroidism in the adult can lead to poor muscle tone, a slowing of mental processes, heart failure, and inability to maintain normal body temperatures. Myxedema coma is a rare condition that results from prolonged undiagnosed hypothyroidism; its symptoms include intense cold intolerance and sleepiness, followed by profound lethargy and unconsciousness. This serious condition can be caused by surgery, injury, exposure to cold, or illness and must be treated immediately with hormone injections. In most cases, however, with proper treatment, an underactive thyroid does not lead to a chronic or serious condition and the individual can lead a normal life.

Hypothyroidism is easily diagnosed through blood tests. It is characterized by low levels of T_4 and high levels of TSH from the pituitary gland as the pituitary tries to compensate for lack of hormones by overstimulating the underactive thyroid. Once the disease is diagnosed, oral administration of thyroid hormones begins, at first in small amounts, then gradually increasing to the proper level. Patients with myxedema must continue to take the medication for the rest of their lives.

Goiters (swelling of the thyroid gland) can result from various conditions. A simple goiter frequently affects people living in areas where the soil or water is deficient in iodine. Without sufficient iodine in the diet, the thyroid gland is unable to produce the proper amounts of T_3 and T_4. Because T_3 and T_4 normally exert an inhibitory effect on the production of TSH by the anterior pituitary through negative feedback, a deficiency of these hormones results in an excessive release of TSH. The thyroid gland is then overstimulated by TSH and enlarges into a goiter. Since the gland cannot make sufficient levels of hormones, symptoms of this condition are those of hypothyroidism. Symptoms of simple goiter can be alleviated by adding iodine to the diet.

Hyperthyroidism results in an excess of thyroid hormones acting on the tissues and is characterized by an elevated basal metabolism, rapid heartbeat, and elevated body temperature. Although the individual has an increased appetite and eats excessively, there may be a large loss of weight. A person with an overactive thyroid may be nervous or emotionally unstable and may suffer from insomnia. In addition, because of swelling in the tissues behind the eyes, the person's eyes are likely to protrude, a condition called exophthalmos. The thyroid may swell, producing a goiter. The type of goiter caused by an overactive thyroid is called a toxic goiter.

Most cases of hyperthyroidism are caused by Graves disease, a type of hyperthyroidism that results in an enlarged thyroid and an oversecretion of thyroxine. It is characterized by exophthalmos, increased heart and metabolic rates, and excessive sweating. Graves disease is a type of autoimmune disease that occurs when abnormal antibodies produced by the immune system act like TSH and overstimulate the thyroid.

Because anxiety can cause symptoms typical of an overactive thyroid, psychological causes for the symptoms must first be ruled out. Blood samples are analyzed for levels of TSH and high concentrations of thyroxine. In Graves disease, the thyroid takes up an increased amount of iodine; a radioactive iodine test can be used to establish the diagnosis, as a greater amount of radioactive iodine than normal will collect in the thyroid within the first twenty-four hours.

The nervous symptoms experienced by individuals with an overactive thyroid vary depending on the personality of the individual and the severity of the disease. In severe cases, the hyperthyroid patient suffers from emotional instability; it has been shown that such instability can indeed cause hyperthyroidism. The overactive thyroid promotes emotional and nervous irritability, with clinical symptoms varying from severe agitation to feelings of restlessness and apprehension.

Excessive thyroid secretion is believed to have profound effects on the autonomic nervous system, resulting in various symptoms of anxiety. Patients suffering from extreme cases of hyperthyroidism feel restless and jittery, and have feelings of impending disaster. Mood swings are common, and the patients are prone to tears. Speech is excitable and rapid, with changes in topic frequently occurring. The speed of thinking can increase to such a degree that patients complain that their ideas run together and they have lost control of their thoughts. As the severity of the disease increases, the patient can become confused, disoriented, and suffer from hallucinations.

Hyperthyroidism can be treated with oral drugs that suppress thyroid function; treatment requires a year or more. If the gland is very large, surgery may be required to remove part of it. In the case of Graves disease, eye surgery may be required to tack down the eyelids in order to protect the eyes or to reduce the amount of eye protrusion. A third alternative is to administer radioactive iodine by mouth, which destroys some thyroid cells. Since the radioactive iodine is only taken up by the thyroid, there is no danger to other tissue; thyroid activity will be reduced within six weeks. While the hormone levels are being brought under control, the symptoms can be decreased by drugs that block the effects of epinephrine, since high levels of T_3 and T_4 seem to cause an increased response to epinephrine.

Calcitonin may be a factor in the onset of several human disorders associated with abnormal calcium metabolism. Abnormal changes in blood calcium level, possibly caused by changes in calcitonin levels, sometimes follow thyroid surgery. Calcitonin is effective as a drug in cases of hypercalcemia, which may occur because of prolonged bed rest, osteoporosis, or overproduction of parathormone from the parathyroid glands.

Context

The thyroid gland has been important in both medical and nonmedical history since ancient times. The ancient Chinese of approximately 1600 B.C. are believed to have known of the beneficial effects of burnt sponge and seaweed for the treatment of goiter. By the Greek and Roman eras, goiter was well known, and there are some references to goiter being caused by problems with the drinking water. Chinese writings early in the Middle Ages mention that the thyroids of sheep were used therapeutically in cases of myxedema and goiter. Early surgical and medical procedures during the Middle Ages resulted from the older Chinese, Greek, and Roman practices.

The gland was first named the thyroid, meaning "oblong shield," in 1656 by Thomas Wharton. At the time, it was suggested that the purpose of the gland was to beautify the neck by filling in the areas around the larynx, especially in females. Other suggestions offered during the seventeenth century were that the gland served as a lubricating organ for the larynx, thus aiding speech, that it was a receptacle for the eggs of worms which reached the stomach via the esophagus to develop into adult worms, or that it served to prevent sudden increases in bloodflow to the brain.

By 1800, the gross anatomy of the thyroid was relatively well understood, and the study of its function had proceeded to the point where most physicians believed that it produced some type of internal secretion essential for health. The relationship between the thyroid and various body functions was studied by experimental thyroidectomy as early as 1827. In 1883, physicians became aware of the similarity between myxedema and associated symptoms which developed after successful removal of the thyroid. Thyroxine was first identified in 1896, and the effectiveness of this substance in relieving the symptoms of myxedema was demonstrated. The hormone was further purified by Edward C. Kendall in 1914.

The development of radioactive isotopes, beginning in 1934, greatly facilitated the study of iodine metabolism and thyroid function. Work with radioactive iodine made an enormous contribution to the knowledge of thyroid biochemistry and physiology and led to the discovery of T_3. Through the synthesis of thyroid hormones using radioactive iodine, the development of antithyroid drugs for treatment of hyperthyroidism was made possible. Further research involving the thyroid and its hormones led to increased understanding of the gland and its function.

Problems associated with the thyroid gland cause the most common type of hormonal disorders and affect a large number of people. Although hyperthyroidism can occur at any age, it is eight times more likely to occur in women than in men, and it is extremely rare in children. In the adult, the risks of an overactive thyroid vary; some individuals recover completely, and some experience recurrent episodes of the disorder. The effects of an overactive thyroid can be fatal if left untreated for many years. Elderly people with a history of high blood pressure or hardening of the arteries are at even greater risk because of the additional strain on the heart and circulation caused by the increased production of thyroid hormones.

Hypothyroidism can affect anyone, although it is most common in middle-age women. This condition is very rare at birth, occurring in only one in five thousand births. Routine blood samples taken at birth provide a means for detecting the disorder immediately; proper treatment leads to normal development of the child. In adults, hypothyroidism is unlikely to be fatal unless myxedema coma develops. Most individuals return to normal health within a few months after being treated for the underactive thyroid by the oral administration of drugs containing thyroid hormones.

The thyroid gland is an extremely important gland in the human body, particularly because of its effects on the basal metabolic rate. Although problems associated with the thyroid and the hormones it produces are fairly common, most of the disorders respond well to treatment and can be completely cured once they have been identified.

Bibliography

Fox, Stuart I. "The Endocrine System." In *Perspectives on Human Biology.* Dubuque, Iowa: Wm. C. Brown, 1991. This textbook is an excellent source for introductory biology information. Student aids such as chapter outlines, lists of objectives, and keys to pronunciation are included as well as clinical and practical applications of the material presented. Illustrations are outstanding.

Hole, John. "The Endocrine System." In *Human Anatomy and Physiology.* 3d ed. Dubuque, Iowa: Wm. C. Brown, 1984. Presents a well-organized discussion of the endocrine glands, including pertinent information on clinical aspects (such as pathological disorders) and laboratory techniques associated with each gland. The text is suitable for high school and college students, as the writing style is easy to read and rather informal.

Larson, David E., ed. *Mayo Clinic Family Health Book.* New York: William Morrow, 1990. Excellent text on human diseases and disorders; includes symptoms, diagnosis, treatment, and medication. The authors explain concepts clearly. Can be readily understood by high school and college students.

Lidz, Theodore. "Emotions and Mentation." In *The Thyroid: A Fundamental and Clinical Text,* edited by Sidney C. Werner and Sidney H. Ingbar. 3d ed. New York: Harper & Row, 1971. Compiles information regarding the thyroid from many diverse sources. The book is designed for clinical use as well as the basic science laboratory. The text is thorough and detailed and is more suitable for college students. Extensive reference sections are provided at the end of each chapter.

Spence, Alexander P., and Elliott B. Mason. "The Endocrine System." In *Human Anatomy and Physiology.* 3d ed. Menlo Park, Calif.: Benjamin/Cummings, 1987. The authors describe the glands of the endocrine system in this chapter of their introductory anatomy and physiology textbook. Discussions are thorough and written at a level suitable for high school and college students. Illustrations are excellent.

Spencer, Roberta Todd. *Patient Care in Endocrine Problems.* Philadelphia: W. B. Saunders, 1973. Provides basic knowledge in the health sciences and introduces the reader to the complexities of the endocrine system. Each chapter is devoted to a discussion of the anatomy and physiology of a particular gland and is complete with charts and photographs of individuals suffering from various disorders.

Debra Zehner

Cross-References

The Adrenal Gland, 136; The Autonomic Nervous System, 362; The Endocrine System, 966; Hormones and Behavior, 1189; Neural and Hormonal Interaction, 1648; The Pituitary Gland, 1829; Stress and the Endocrine System, 2445.

TOUCH AND PRESSURE

Type of psychology: Sensation and perception
Field of study: Auditory, chemical, cutaneous, and body senses

Receptors of touch and pressure are mechanoreceptors that convert mechanical energy into the electrical energy of nerve impulses. Touch receptors detect objects coming into light contact with the body surface and allow a person to reconstruct the size, shape, and texture of objects even if they are unseen; pressure receptors detect heavier contacts, weights, or forces and provide a sense of the position of body parts.

Principal terms
 ADAPTATION: a reduction over time of the nerve impulses sent by a
  sensory receptor under a constant stimulus
 EXPANDED-TIP TACTILE RECEPTOR: a touch receptor located in both hairy
  and nonhairy regions of the skin
 FREE NERVE ENDING: a mechanoreceptor located primarily in the skin
  and acting as a touch receptor
 HAIR END ORGAN: a touch receptor formed by sensory nerve branches
  surrounding a hair root in the skin; detects displacement of the hair
  shaft
 MECHANORECEPTOR: a sensory receptor that detects mechanical energy
  and converts it into the electrical energy of nerve impulses
 MEISSNER'S CORPUSCLE: a highly sensitive touch receptor located in
  nonhairy regions of the skin
 PACINIAN CORPUSCLE: a pressure receptor located just under the skin and
  in deeper body regions
 PROPRIORECEPTION: the sense of the position of the body parts
 RUFFINI'S END ORGAN: a pressure receptor located in deeper body
  regions and in the connective tissue capsules surrounding the joints
 SOMATIC SENSORY CORTEX: the region of the cerebrum receiving and
  integrating signals from sensory receptors

Overview

 The human body is supplied with an abundance of sensory receptors that detect touch and pressure. These receptors are members of a larger group of what are called mechanoreceptors; they are able to detect energy in mechanical form and convert it to the energy of nerve impulses. Mechanoreceptors occur both on body surfaces and in the interior, and they detect mechanical stimuli throughout the body. Touch receptors are located over the entire body surface; pressure receptors are located only under the skin and in the body interior. The two sensations are closely related. A very light pressure on the body surface is sensed by receptors in the skin and is felt as touch. As the pressure increases, mechanoreceptors in and immediately below the skin and at deeper levels are stimulated, and the sensation is felt as pressure.

Several different types of mechanoreceptors are located in the skin and primarily detect touch. One type, known as free nerve endings, consists simply of branched nerve endings without associated structures. Although located primarily in the skin, some mechanoreceptors of this type are also found to a limited extent in deeper tissues, where they detect pressure. A second mechanoreceptor type, termed Meissner's corpuscles, consists of a ball of nerve endings enclosed within a capsulelike layer of cells. These mechanoreceptors, which are exquisitely sensitive to the lightest pressure, occur in nonhairy regions of the skin, such as the lips and fingertips. A third mechanoreceptor type, the expanded-tip tactile receptor, occurs in the same nonhairy regions as Meissner's corpuscles and, in smaller numbers, in parts of the skin that are covered with hair. These mechanoreceptors often occur in clusters that are served by branches of the same sensory nerve cell. Meissner's corpuscles and the expanded-tip tactile receptors, working together in regions such as the fingertips, are primarily responsible for a person's ability to determine the size, surface texture, and other tactile features of objects touched. A fourth type of mechanoreceptor consists of a network of nerve endings surrounding the root of a hair. The combined nerve-hair root structure, called a hair end organ, is stimulated when body hairs are displaced. These mechanoreceptors, because hairs extend from the body surface, give an early warning that the skin of a haired region of the body is about to make contact with an object.

The remaining mechanoreceptors of this group are located in deeper regions of the body; because of their location, they detect pressure rather than touch. Pacinian corpuscles, which occur just under the skin and in deeper regions of the body, consist of a single sensory nerve ending buried inside a fluid-filled capsule. The capsule is formed by many layers of connective tissue cells, which surround the nerve ending in concentric layers, much like the successive layers of an onion. Pressure displaces the capsule and deforms its shape; the deforming pressure is transmitted through the capsule fluid to the surface of the sensory nerve ending. In response, the sensory nerve generates nerve impulses. The remaining type of pressure receptor, Ruffini's end organ, consists of a highly branched group of nerve endings enclosed in a capsule. These mechanoreceptors occur below the skin, in deeper tissues, and in the connective tissue capsules surrounding the joints. They detect heavy pressures on the body that are transmitted to deeper layers, and, through their locations in the joints, contribute to proprioception—the sense of the position of the body's limbs.

The various types of mechanoreceptors are believed to convert mechanical energy into the electrical energy of nerve impulses by essentially the same mechanism. In some manner, as yet incompletely understood, the mechanical forces deforming the cell membranes of sensory nerve endings open channels in the membranes to the flow of ions. The ions, which are electrically charged particles, produce the electrical effects responsible for generating nerve impulses.

The different mechanoreceptor types exhibit the phenomenon of adaptation to varying degrees. In adaptation, the number of nerve impulses generated by a sensory receptor drops off with time if the stimulus remains constant. In the pacinian corpuscle, for example, which is highly adaptive, adaptation results from flow of the capsule fluid. If pressure against the corpuscle is held at steady levels, deforming the capsule in one direction, the fluids inside the capsule flow in response to relieve the pressure. The new fluid distribution compensates for the applied pressure, and the nerve impulses generated by the pacinian corpuscle drop in frequency. Any change in the pressure, however, is transmitted through the fluid to the sensory nerve ending before the fluid has a chance to shift in response. As a result, a new volley of nerve impulses is fired by the sensory neuron on a change of pressure until the fluid in the corpuscle shifts again to compensate for the new pressure. In pacinian corpuscles, compensating movements of the fluid take place within hundredths or even thousandths of a second. Meissner's corpuscles and the hair end organs also adapt quickly.

The expanded-tip tactile receptors and Ruffini's end organs adapt significantly more slowly than the other mechanoreceptors. Expanded-tip tactile receptors adapt initially to a steady touch or pressure, but reach a base level at which they continue to generate nerve impulses under steady pressure. The Ruffini's end organs adapt only to a limited extent. The continuing nerve impulses arriving from these mechanoreceptors provide continuous monitoring of a constant stimulus. Thus, some of the mechanoreceptors are specialized to detect changes in touch or pressure, and some to keep track of constant stimuli.

Applications

The combined effects of touch and pressure receptors, along with the varying degrees of adaptation of different receptor types, allow the detection of a range of stimuli, varying from the lightest, most delicate, glancing touch, through moderate pressures, to heavy pressures that stimulate both the body surfaces and interior. People can explore the surface, texture, and shape of objects and can interpret the various levels of touch and pressure so well that they can reconstruct a mental image of objects touched by the fingers with their eyes closed.

Much of this mechanosensory ability depends on the degree to which the different receptor types adapt. The rapid adaptation of Meissner's corpuscles and the hair end organs explains why, if a steady, light to moderate pressure (not heavy enough to cause pain) is maintained on the body surface, the sensation of pressure quickly diminishes. If the pressure is heavy enough to cause pain, a person continues to be aware of the painful sensation, because pain receptors are very slow to adapt. If the degree or location of the pressure is altered, a person again becomes acutely aware of the pressure.

Awareness of continued touch depends primarily on the expanded-tip tactile receptors, which initially adapt but then continue to send nerve impulses when a light surface pressure is held constant. This allows a person to continue to be aware, for example, that some part of the body surface is touching an object. The limited adaptation of Ruffini's corpuscles keeps a person aware of stronger pressures that are felt deeply in the body. Through their locations in joints, these slow-adapting mechanoreceptors also help keep a person continually aware of the positions of the limbs.

The sensory effects of the fast- and slow-adapting mechanoreceptors can be demonstrated by a simple exercise such as pinching the skin on the back of the hand with a steady pressure only strong enough to cause slight pain. The feeling of pressure dissipates rapidly; however, one remains aware of the touch and pain. The rapid dissipation of the sensation of pressure is caused by the fast adaptation of Meissner's corpuscles and any pacinian corpuscles that may have been stimulated. Some degree of touch sensation is maintained, however, by residual levels of nerve impulses sent by the expanded-tip tactile receptors. The sensation of pain continues at almost steady levels because, in contrast to most of the mechanoreceptors, pain receptors adapt very little. If the pressure is released, the pain stops, and another intense sensation of pressure is felt as all the receptor types fire off a burst of nerve impulses in response to the change.

Mechanoreceptors located at deeper levels keep a person constantly aware of the positions of body parts and the degree of extension of the limbs with respect to the trunk. Ruffini's and pacinian corpuscles located within the connective tissue layers covering the bones, and within the capsules surrounding the joints, keep track of the angles made by the bones as they are pulled to different positions by the muscles. Ruffini's and pacinian corpuscles are among the most important mechanoreceptors keeping track of these movements.

Context

Touch and pressure receptors represent only a part of the body's array of mechanoreceptors. Other mechanoreceptors located more deeply in the body help monitor the position of body parts and detect the degree of stretch of body cavities.

In addition to the Ruffini's and pacinian corpuscles detecting the positions of the bones and joints, two further types of mechanoreceptors constantly track the tension developed by the muscles moving the limbs. One is buried within the muscle itself, and one in the tendons connecting the muscles to the bones. The mechanoreceptors buried within muscles, called muscle spindles, consist of a specialized bundle of five to twelve small muscle cells enclosed within a capsule of connective tissue. Sensory nerve endings surround the muscle cells in a spiral at the midpoint of the capsule, and also form branched endings among the muscle cells of the capsule. Because of their position within the muscle spindle, the nerve endings are stretched, and generate nerve impulses, when the surrounding muscle tissue contracts.

The mechanoreceptors of tendons, called Golgi tendon organs, are formed by nerve endings that branch within the fibrous connective tissue cells forming a tendon. The nerve endings of Golgi tendon organs detect both stretch and compression of the tendon as the muscles connected to them move and place tension on the limbs. The combined activities of the deeply located mechanoreceptors keep a person aware of posture, stance, and positions of the limbs. They also allow a person to perform feats such as bringing the thumbs or fingers together behind the back, or touching the tip of the nose with the forefinger with the eyes closed.

Mechanoreceptors are one of five different types of sensory receptors that also include thermoreceptors, which detect changes in the flow of heat to or from the body; nocioreceptors, which detect tissue damage and whose nerve impulses are integrated and perceived in the brain as pain; chemoreceptors, which detect chemicals in locations such as the tongue, where they are responsible for the sense of taste, and in the nasal cavity, where they contribute to the sense of smell; and photoreceptors, which detect light. The mechanoreceptors, thermoreceptors, and nocioreceptors together form what are known as the somatic or body senses.

Sensory nerve tracts originating from mechanoreceptors, particularly those arising from the body surfaces, and their connecting neurons within the spinal cord and the brain, are held in highly organized register with one another. Sensory fibers and their connecting nerves originating from the hand, for example, are located in a position near those originating from the wrist. In the cerebral cortex, the organization is retained, so that there is a projection of the body parts over a part of the cerebrum called the somatic sensory cortex. In this region, which occupies a band running from the top to the lower sides of the brain along anterior segments of the parietal lobes, segments corresponding to major body parts trace out a distorted image of the body from the top of the brain to the sides, with the genitalia, feet, and legs at the top, the arms and hands at the middle region, and the head, lips, tongue, and teeth at the bottom. Sensory information from the right side of the body is received and integrated in the somatic sensory cortex on the left side of the brain, and information from the left side of the body is received and integrated on the right side of the brain. The area of the somatic sensory cortex integrating signals from various body regions depends on the numbers of touch and other sensory receptors in the body regions. The lips and fingers, for example, which are generously supplied with sensory receptors, are represented by much larger areas in the somatic sensory cortex than the arms and legs. Reception and integration of signals in the somatic sensory cortex is partly under conscious control; a person can direct attention to one body part or another, and concentrate on the signals arriving from the selected region. The activities of touch, pressure, and other sensory receptors, integrated and interpreted in the somatic sensory cortex, supply people's link to the world around them and supply the information people require to survive and interact with the environment.

Bibliography

Berne, Robert M., and Matthew N. Levy, eds. *Physiology.* 2d ed. St. Louis: C. V. Mosby, 1988. Chapter 9 in this standard college physiology text, "The Somatosensory System," outlines the anatomy and physiology of the systems integrated in the detection of touch and pressure, with emphasis on the somatic sensory cortex of the brain, and the nerve tracts of the spinal cord connecting sensory receptors with the brain. Intended for students at the college level, but clearly enough written to be accessible to readers at the high school level.

Coren, Stanley. *Sensation and Perception.* New York: Academic Press, 1979. A simply written text providing an easily understood discussion of the senses, sensory cells, and routes traveled by sensory information through the spinal cord to the brain. Includes a clear and interesting description of the basics of perception in the cerebral cortex.

Guyton, Arthur C. *Textbook of Medical Physiology.* 7th ed. Philadelphia: W. B. Saunders, 1986. Chapter 48 in this readable and clearly written text, "Somatic Sensory Receptors and Their Basic Mechanisms of Action," outlines the fundamental activities of sensory receptors. Chapter 49, "Somatic Sensations: I. The Mechanoreceptive Sensations," presents more detailed information on the types of touch and pressure receptors and the nerve tracts connecting them to the somatic sensory cortex of the brain. Intended for college and medical students, but comprehensible to readers at the high school level.

Milne, Lorus Johnson, and Margery Milne. *The Senses of Animals and Men.* New York: Atheneum, 1962. A simple and entertaining survey of the senses and their importance in humans and other animals. Provides interesting and thought-provoking comparisons between the sensory systems of humans and other animals. Written for a popular audience.

Schmidt-Nielsen, Knut. *Animal Physiology, Adaptation, and Environment.* 4th ed. New York: Cambridge University Press, 1990. This standard college text, by one of the greatest animal physiologists, provides a deeply perceptive comparison of sensory systems in humans and other animals. Chapter 8 describes information and the senses. The text is remarkable for its lucid and entertaining description of animal physiology.

Stephen L. Wolfe

Cross-References

Neurons, 1661; Sensation and Perception Defined, 2207; Sensory Modalities and Stimuli, 2214; Signal Detection Theory, 2271; Temperature, 2533.

TRANSACTIONAL ANALYSIS

Type of psychology: Psychotherapy
Fields of study: Cognitive therapies; humanistic therapies; interpersonal relations

Transactional analysis (TA) is a school of psychotherapy and personality theory. Many of TA's key concepts, such as therapeutic contracts, games, and life scripts, have been accepted in the general psychotherapy community.

Principal terms

ADULT: the part of the personality that is objective, solves problems, and processes data

CHILD: the feeling, spontaneous, and impulsive part of the personality; the child ego state is subdivided into three subphases: free, adapted, and intuitive

DECISION: an early childhood choice in which the individual defines his or her life stance

DISCOUNTING: a response to the self or to another person that undermines self-esteem

EGO STATE: the building block of TA; the mental attitude of an individual at a given moment, such as parent, adult, or child

GAMES: a series of transactions in which one or both players end up feeling hurt or "not OK"

LIFE SCRIPT: a "script" that resembles a drama or mythological role that an individual reenacts as a result of family conditioning

PARENT: the part of personality that is incorporated from one's real parents; the parent ego state is either nurturing or critical

RACKET: an unhappy feeling that results from a game; chronic feelings that are maintained in order to justify an "I am not OK" life position

STROKE: a form of personal recognition that may include a touch, a kind word, or public praise; strokes may be positive or negative

Overview

Transactional analysis (TA) is a theory of personality and social interaction originated by Eric Berne in the mid-1950's. TA's popularity has been primarily as a form of psychotherapy and a method for improving social interactions between people in almost any setting—from the group therapy room to business and industry. Berne rejected psychoanalytic therapy, which he considered a type of game called "archaeology," in favor of his own short-term, action-oriented, commonsense approach to psychotherapy. Before entering a group psychotherapy session, Berne would ask himself, "How can I cure everyone in this room today?" In 1964, Berne's book *Games People Play* created a popular interest in a theory of personality and psychotherapy unequaled in the history of psychology; the book sold more than a million copies.

The basic concepts of transactional analysis describe an individual personality and the individual's repetitive patterns of interacting with others. Three distinct ego states compose the individual personality: "parent," "adult," and "child." Berne observed these as distinct phases in his patients' self-presentations. The child ego state within each individual is defined by the feeling, creative, and intuitive part within the person. The child ego state may be approval-seeking or defiant. The fun-loving or "free" side of the child state is curious, spontaneous, and impulsive. Parental discipline, when too harsh or inconsistent, often damages this spontaneous and free child; the adapted child is what then results. The adapted child can have a broken or rebellious spirit and may develop depression or addictions. In either case, the individual, authentic self becomes distorted because of an excessively compliant or defiant adaptation.

The adult ego state is objective and, in a sense, resembles a computer. The adult retrieves, stores, and processes data about physical and social reality. Problem solving and task-oriented behavior are the domain of the adult. If one were trying to build a bridge or do homework, the adult ego state would serve best; however, many problems require the assistance of the intuitive and creative child to be solved most effectively.

The parent ego state is an internalization of one's biological parents or other substitute authority figures in early childhood. The parent state judges, criticizes, and blames. This harsh side of the parent state is the critical parent. In contrast, Berne also recognized the nurturing parent that soothes, encourages, and gently supports the individual. The nurturing parent calls forth the free child, while the critical parent conditions the adapted child. The parent ego state is like a tape recording of the "dos and don'ts" of one's family of origin and culture; it may contain obsolete information. When in the parent state, one may point or shame with an extended index finger or disapproving scowl.

Transactions are basic units of analysis for the TA therapist. A transaction occurs when one individual responds to the behavior of another. Transactions are called complementary when both persons interact from compatible ego states. For example, a feverish child asks her parent for a glass of water, and the parent complies. A crossed transaction occurs when individuals in incompatible ego states interact. For example, a whining and hungry child asks a parent for an ice cream cone, and the parent (speaking from her adult ego state) reminds the child that it would not be nutritious. The child cannot incorporate the adult data. Another important type of transaction is the ulterior one. An ulterior transaction occurs when the spoken message is undercut by a hidden agenda. To exemplify this, Berne cited a cowboy who asks a woman to leave the dance and go look at the barn with him. The face value of his adult-to-adult question is subtly undercut by a child-to-child sexual innuendo.

Ulterior transactions, when not clearly understood by both parties, lead to "games." A game by definition is a social transaction in which either both or one member of the duo ends up feeling "bad." This bad feeling is experienced as a payoff by the game perpetrator; the game pays off by confirming the player's existential life position. For example, the game that Berne called "blemish" involves an existential life position of "I am not OK, you are not OK." In this game, the player exhaustively searches his or her partner for some defect, such as a personality quirk or physical imperfection. Once this defect or blemish is found, the player can hold it up as proof that others are not OK. One thus avoids examining one's own blemish while providing that "others are no good." An example of this can be seen in the chronic bachelor who cannot find a woman who measures up to his perfectionistic standards for marriage.

"Rackets" are the negative feelings that one experiences after a game. Racket feelings are chronic and originate in the early stroking patterns within one's family of origin. In the game of "blemish," the player will ultimately feel lonely and sad, while the victim may feel hurt and rejected. Berne compared rackets to stamp collecting: When one collects ten books of brown stamps from playing blemish, they can be cashed in for a divorce or suicide.

Life scripts emerge through repetitive interactions with one's early environment. Messages about what to expect from others, the world, and self become ingrained. A script resembles an actor's role in a drama. An important outcome of one's early scripting is the basic decision one makes about one's existential position. Specifically, the basic identity becomes constellated around feelings of being either OK (free child) or not OK (adapted child). Coping strategies are learned that reinforce the basic decision. Life scripts can often be discovered by asking individuals about their favorite games, heroes, or stories from their childhood. Once individuals become aware of their life scripts, they can be presented with the option of changing them. If a script does not support a person's capacity to be an authentic winner in life, the TA therapist will confront it. TA holds that people are all born to win.

Applications

Transactional analysis has been applied to the areas of individual and group psychotherapy, couples and family relationship problems, and communication problems within business organizations. This widespread application of TA should not be surprising, since TA's domain is wherever two human beings meet. Berne believed that the playing of games occurs everywhere, from the sandbox to the international negotiation table. Consequently, wherever destructive patterns of behavior occur, TA can be employed to reduce dysfunctional transactions.

TA's most common application is in psychotherapy. The TA therapist begins by establishing a contract for change with his client. This denotes mutual responsibilities for both therapist and client and avoids allowing the client to assume a passive spectator role. The therapist also avoids playing the "rescuer" role. For example, Ms. Murgatroyd (Berne's favorite hypothetical patient name), an attractive thirty-two-year-old female, enters therapy because her boyfriend refuses to make the commitment to marry her. Her contract with the therapist and group might be that she will either receive a marriage commitment from her boyfriend or will end the relationship. As her specific games and life script are analyzed, this contract might undergo a revision in which greater autonomy or capacity for intimacy becomes her goal.

During the first session, the therapist observes the client's style of interacting. The therapist will be especially watchful of voice tone, gestures, and mannerisms and will listen to her talk about her current difficulties. Since games are chronic and stereotypical ways of responding, they will appear in the initial interview. For example, her dominant ego state might be that of a helpless, whining child looking for a strong parent to protect her. Ms. Murgatroyd may describe her boyfriend in such bitter and negative terms that it is entirely unclear why a healthy adult would want to marry such a man. Discrepancies of this sort will suggest that a tragic script may be operating.

During the first few interviews, the transactional analysis includes game and script analysis. This might require some information about Ms. Murgatroyd's early childhood fantasies and relationships with parents, but would eventually return to her present behavior and relationship. This early history would be used primarily to help the therapist and client gain insight into how these childhood patterns of interacting are currently manifesting. Once the games and script have been clearly identified, the client is in a much better position to change.

After several interviews, in which Ms. Murgatroyd's past and recent history of relationships is reviewed, a pattern of her being rejected is evident. She acknowledges that her existential position is "I am not OK, you are not OK." Her repeated selection of men who are emotionally unavailable maintains her racket feelings of loneliness and frustration. She begins to see how she puts herself in the role of victim. Armed with this new awareness, she is now in a position to change her script. Through the support of the therapist and group, Ms. Murgatroyd can learn to catch herself and stop playing the victim.

Berne believed that the original script could best be changed in an atmosphere of openness and trust between the client and therapist. Hence the TA therapist will at all times display respect and concern for his or her client. At the appropriate time in therapy, the therapist delivers a powerful message to the client which serves to counteract the early childhood messages that originally instated the script. Ms. Murgatroyd's therapist, at the proper time, would decisively and powerfully counterscript her by telling her, "You have the right to intimacy!" or "You have the right to take care of yourself, even if it means leaving a relationship." Since the existential life position is supported by lifelong games and scripts, which resist change, TA therapists often employ emotionally charged ways of assisting a client's script redecision.

To catalyze script redecision, a client is guided back in time to the original scene where the destructive message that started the losing life script was received. Simply being told differently by a therapist is not always strong enough to create an emotionally corrective experience that will reverse a life script. Once in the early childhood scene, the client will spontaneously enter the child ego state, which is where the real power to change lies. This time, during the therapeutic regression, the choice will be different and will be for the authentic self.

Ms. Murgatroyd, who is struggling to change an early message, "Don't be intimate," needs to reexperience the feeling she had at the time she first received this message and accepted it from her adapted child ego state. In the presence of the therapist and group, she would role-play this early scene and would tell herself and the significant parent that she *does* have the right to be intimate. These words would probably be spoken amid tears and considerable emotional expression. The parent(s) would be symbolically addressed by her speaking to an empty chair in which she imagines her significant parent sitting: "Whether you like it or not, I'll be intimate!" She would tell herself that it is OK to be intimate. This time she will make a new decision about her script based on her authentic wants and needs, rather than on faulty messages from early childhood. Ms. Murgatroyd's further TA work might involve new contracts with the therapist and group as she integrates her new script into her daily life.

Context

Transactional analysis evolved as a form of short-term psychotherapy beginning in the mid-1950's. Eric Berne's early work in groups as a major in the Army during World War II helped him identify the need for both group and short-term therapy. The human growth and potential movement of the 1960's added further momentum to the transactional analysis approach. TA's recognition of the innate goodness of the free child prior to the damage of early parental injunctions and self-defeating scripts was consistent with the then-emerging humanistic schools of psychology. Berne began using TA as an adjunct to psychoanalysis, but he eventually rejected the psychoanalytic idea of the dynamic unconscious. Berne's move away from the unconscious and Freudian system paralleled developments in other schools of psychology. Both behavioral psychologists and the cognitive school wished to move away from what they saw as "depth psychology" fictions.

The general thesis of TA that current behavior is premised on responses to emotional trauma of early childhood is generally agreed upon by most psychologists. Early life experience teaches people a script or behavioral pattern, which they then repetitively act out in adulthood. Behavioral and humanistic schools alike recognize the formative role that early experiences play in adult behavior patterns; these ideas are not original to TA. TA's contribution is to have created a vocabulary that demystifies many of these ideas and provides a readily learned method of psychotherapy.

Most of the TA jargon and concepts can be readily seen to correspond to equivalent ones used by other psychologists. Sigmund Freud's constructs of the superego, ego, and id bear a noteworthy similarity to Berne's parent, adult, and child. The superego as the internalized voice of parental and societal values to regulate behavior nearly coincides with Berne's parent ego state. Freud's ego and the adult ego state similarly share the responsibility of solving the individual's problems with a minimum of emotional bias. Freud's id as the instinctual, spontaneous part of the personality shares many characteristics with Berne's child ego state.

Berne's concept of a game's "payoff" is clearly what the behaviorist call a reinforcer. The idea of scripts corresponds to the notion of family role or personality types in other personality theories. For example, an individual with a dominant child ego state would be labeled an orally fixated dependent type in Freudian circles.

The psychological role of dysfunctional families has become a topic of conversation for many nonspecialists. The explosion of twelve-step self-help groups has evidenced growing concern about America's mental health; the prominent role of shame and abandonment experiences in early childhood is receiving widespread interest. This surge of interest in making mental health services available to all society is a continuation of what TA practitioners pioneered several decades earlier. It is likely that future developments in the mental health field will draw upon the rich legacy of TA.

Finally, pure transactional analysis as practiced by Berne in the 1960's right before his death has been modified by TA therapists who combine it with emotive and experiential techniques. Many TA therapists found that life scripts failed to change when their clients merely executed new adult decisions. Powerful therapeutic experiences in which the individual regresses and relives painful experiences were necessary. These enable the client to make script redecisions from the child ego state, which proved to be an effective source of change. Future TA therapists are likely to continue enhancing their methods of rescripting by eclectically drawing upon new methods of behavior change that go beyond traditional TA techniques. The intuitive child ego state, upon which TA therapists freely draw, promises creative developments in this school of psychotherapy.

Bibliography

Berne, Eric. *Games People Play*. New York: Grove Press, 1964. A national bestseller that provides a highly readable introduction to the basic ideas of TA and games. Provides an interesting catalog of the most common games played in groups of many kinds. The reader will find that he or she can immediately apply the ideas contained here.

_____. *What Do You Say After You Say Hello?* New York: Grove Press, 1972. This is another excellent primary source for the reader who wants to apply TA to everyday life. Focuses on games and on Berne's final development of his script theory shortly before his death.

Corey, Gerald. *Theory and Practice of Counseling and Psychotherapy*. 4th ed. Pacific Grove, Calif.: Brooks/Cole, 1991. TA is covered in a brief twenty-five pages but is treated with excellent scholarship. Ideal for the reader who would like a sound overview of TA before moving on to the particular works of Berne. A two-page bibliography is included. TA is critically appraised and compared to other approaches.

Dusay, J., and K. Dusay. "Transactional Analysis." In *Current Psychotherapies*, edited by Raymond J. Corsini and Danny Wedding. 4th ed. Itasca, Ill.: Peacock, 1989. This forty-two-page article contains five pages of bibliography and is cowritten by a leading TA therapist and writer. Thorough and scholarly. The Dusays go into considerable depth in explaining Berne's ideas. A detailed discussion of ego-grams, the drama triangle, and many more key TA concepts are excellently covered. Recommended for the reader who wants a serious introduction to TA.

Goulding, Mary McClure, and Robert L. Goulding. *Redecision Therapy.* New York: Brunner/Mazel, 1979. This three hundred-page book is written by the two therapists who pioneered the integration of TA with Gestalt therapy. Both Gouldings studied directly with Berne and Fritz Perls. An overview of TA, contracts, and stroking is covered. The clinical use of TA with depression, grieving, and establishing "no suicide contracts" is handled with many case examples and some transcripts of actual sessions. Recommended for the advanced student of TA.

James, Muriel, and Dorothy Jongeward. *Born to Win.* Reading, Mass.: Addison-Wesley, 1971. Another TA work that became a best-seller. An optimistic and humanistic version of TA mixed with Gestalt experiments gives the reader a rich firsthand experience of TA. Contains many experiential and written exercises that enable readers to diagnose their own scripts and rackets. A practical program in how to apply the ideas of TA immediately to improve one's life is provided.

Paul August Rentz

Cross-References

Abnormality: Cognitive Models, 46; Abnormality: Humanistic-Existential Models, 60; Affiliation and Friendship, 142; Cognitive Therapy, 586; Group Therapy, 1120; Rational-Emotive Therapy, 2052; Self-Concept Origins, 2175.

TRUST, AUTONOMY, INITIATIVE, AND INDUSTRY: ERIKSON

Type of psychology: Developmental psychology
Field of study: Infancy and childhood

Children's self-perception, according to Erik Erikson, is formulated at a very early age. Should the early developmental needs of a child be denied, there is a likelihood that later psychological and behavioral problems will occur.

Principal terms
AUTONOMY: a child's self-assertion toward a parent without in any way harming the parent-child relationship
EGO: a unifying principle which makes sense of the many diverse experiences facing the growing child
IDENTITY: a reciprocal acceptance on the part of children to act and think like those on whom they depend
INDUSTRY: the recognition that building, creating, or making is a satisfactory and self-imaging activity
INITIATIVE: a child's instigation of a new game or decision on the next activity
PSYCHE: the soul or essential being of humankind
SELF-IMAGE: an accepted view of how one appears to the world
TRUST: the first stage of Erikson's model, in which the helpless infant knows that all basic needs will be met

Overview

Psychoanalyst Erik Erikson was one of the first to undertake intensive study of human development as it occurs over the course of the entire lifetime. He divided human development into eight "psychosocial" stages. The first four of these stages occur between birth and puberty, and they involve trust (versus mistrust), autonomy (versus shame and doubt), initiative (versus guilt), and industry (versus inferiority).

From the day they are born, infants will show whether they are contented or discontented—whether they sense that their needs are being fully met by a parent or other caregiver. A sense that their most basic needs are not being met will be reflected in unsettled sleep or continual crying. Continual reinforcement by the mother demonstrating that the infant's needs will be met provides the infant with a rudimentary sense of personal identity. Erikson postulates that infants look for and require a certain degree of uniformity in their handling and that this consistency on the part of the handler, in most cases the mother, creates and reinforces a sense of trust. Trust would seem a natural occurrence from a caring and nurturing mother, yet within this mother-child paradigm the possibility of mistrust exists.

The trust versus mistrust stage deals with the oral-sensory experiences of the small child. Eating and sleeping are the only major concerns. During this stage, the basis of trust or mistrust will develop. While feeding and caring for the infant are important, what seems more important during this period is the quality of the mother's attentiveness to the child. From the basic premise and understanding of trust, the growing infant will necessarily move into the next stage, which Erikson describes as the muscular-anal stage, during which the child begins to experience autonomy—a greater awareness of being an individual. This is not the first stage of being an individual, in the true sense, but is the early prototype model of how children will later perceive themselves. This is a point at which young infants realize that they can be autonomous from their principal provider yet feel relatively safe in what is still perceived as a hostile environment.

Erikson defines a sharp and concise relationship between the growth of the child and the ability to perform more advanced physical functions. During the period that is characterized by basic trust, bodily functions are enacted satisfactorily but without control. The child is not hindered by this lack of physical control, because the mothering figure takes care of all basic needs. Along with muscular development, mobility increases, and the growing child discovers more ways of becoming physically independent, although in a limited way. A definite sense of autonomy is experienced by the child between the ages of one and three. Assuming that the child has received nurturing, this newfound physical freedom will set up a dynamic within the child's psychic awareness that will most likely contradict those earlier childhood experiences. Wanting to be more autonomous is natural, but the fear of shame and doubt follow quickly behind this yearning to experience a more independent role in life.

At this stage, the infant must not feel compromised as more interesting experiences are presented to him or her. Since all the child's basic needs have been met, the appearance of wanting to be independent will not cause a loss of caregiving. The underpinning of trust must still be present and reinforced so that the exploring infant can take a more active and independent role in the world. Transition from the oral to the muscular stage need not be traumatic, as long as the caregiver is supportive and continues to reinforce the already present acceptance of trust. The consequence of moving into the muscular-anal stage is that the child gains more autonomy and thus a greater sense of identity, which will eventually lead to an understanding of himself or herself as a fully realized individual.

Shame and doubt develop in a child who feels unable to venture beyond the confines of the caregiver. Able to experiment with the social modalities of holding on and letting go, children learn how to regulate their infantile impulses. Allowing the child to experience and experiment in a caring environment will allow autonomous living to begin. Conversely, if the child continues to be forced into feeling a sense of shame during this period, the child's understanding of being a separate person will be severely restricted.

The third stage, that of initiative versus guilt, is reached in the growth and development of the child around the time of entering kindergarten (sometimes earlier), and it continues to about the child's seventh birthday. New ideas are presented that allow the possibility of further exploration of both the social and the phenomenal world. A major characteristic of this stage is the willingness on the part of the child to forget failure quickly and move on to the next endeavor. There is probably no other period in a young child's life that is more important than this stage, which is characterized by a yearning to learn and become a more integrated member of the child's immediate family and circle of friends. There is a strong sense that the child wants to share new ideas and become a part of the larger world, especially in terms of emulating the ideas of the schoolteacher.

Between the ages of six or seven and eleven years, the child enters an intense period of industry and activity; this is the fourth stage. What has been learned from earlier childhood experiences, both in the home and at school, will form the base for further exploration. Whereas play was an activity in and of itself, now the child wishes to produce and create something tangible from what was originally a play situation. At this stage, the child begins using prototypal tools, implements, and utensils, which may in some way reflect the type of work the child will experience in adulthood.

Applications

The first four stages of Erikson's eight-stage model of development deal with the child from birth to about eleven years of age. The other four stages deal with identity during the adolescent years, intimacy as a young adult, growth as an adult, and ego integrity as an older adult. For a child to develop a healthy and well-adjusted view of life, Erikson believes, the growing child must pass through each of these early stages. Each stage builds on the one immediately before.

When the basic tenets of trust, autonomy, initiative, and industry are fully integrated into the life of the child, there is unlikely to be a serious problem in later life. When one or all of these particular aspects of a child's growth meets its counterpart or negative side of these tenets (basic mistrust, shame and doubt, guilt, and inferiority), however, certain psychological imbalances become apparent in adulthood.

Studies of infantile schizophrenia probably best illustrate the denial of trust in the first two years of the infant's life. Should there be a lifelong denial of trust, the person will exhibit a definite schizoid or schizotypal personality disorder. Often this personality disorder will be accompanied by various states of depression. Depression can, in severe cases, lead to suicide or repeated suicide attempts. Such is the need and effect of trust on young children that their whole identities, in some psychic way, are tied up with the personal love and care given to them by their mother during this time. Basic mistrust and a later sense of insecurity will characterize the child who has not fully experienced basic trust in his or her parents.

In stage 2, shame and doubt act as the shadow side to autonomy and the ability to act in an individual, responsible way in society. Erikson maintains that the child who does not experience a well-regulated sense of autonomy will soon develop manipulative characteristics. At a time when the child should be exploring the environment and discovering new facets of that environment, there is a tendency to overmanipulate. The object or plaything no longer is interesting in terms of any intrinsic value but becomes something over which the child can project some authority and power. This is the basis for later neurotic disorders such as certain compulsive behavior patterns.

A child who is not given the room within a normal caring and monitored environment to express feelings of frustration and anger will tend to stifle these natural responses. Later in life, when similar stressful situations occur, the person may not have the coping skills to be able to deal properly with these same feelings. These inhibitors to normal expression and natural well-being are formulated when the child is growing up. Parents who cannot tolerate any form of aggressive behavior will create a problem for their child. When the child becomes an adult, he or she will need to be assertive in given situations; there is a high likelihood that this will not happen, because of the childhood inhibitions about confronting stressful situations. Instead, in order to inhibit the natural adaptive response to outside aggression, the person will appear overly agreeable and accommodating.

Again, the suppression of those earlier fears is evident. The normal coping skills are nonfunctional because their natural expression was inhibited during the early formative years. A person who adopts a neurotic style will rarely be able to conceal the underlying stress. Doubt and shame take on a broader and more potent meaning in adulthood. When initiative is called upon, the inhibitory devices first learned as a child become dominant. Instead of taking responsibility and acting in an independent manner, the individual will exhibit a childlike incompetence. An adult may even be unable and unsuited to take up a worthwhile position in society; industry, rather than being a part of the life experience, becomes something to be shunned. What develops is a feeling of inferiority and an inability to enter into the workplace fully as a productive and useful individual.

Context

Erik Erikson's *Childhood and Society* (1963) quickly became the seminal study on child growth and development. Erikson studied and practiced psychoanalysis; he was himself psychoanalyzed by Anna Freud while at the Vienna Psychoanalytic Institute. Erikson's work is comparable in significance to that undertaken by Jean Piaget, a Swiss psychologist who postulated that children learn through a series of cognitive stages. While Piaget was almost entirely concerned with how a child perceives the world in a cognitive sense, Erikson viewed the growth of the child in terms of an emotional and sensory perception of the world.

What Erikson's pioneering models and theories attempted to do was to lessen the many disparities between the accepted understanding of psychoanalysis, which mostly concentrated on the disturbed psyche of a person, and the broader influences of society. In an attempt to synthesize the two, Erikson added to the understanding of personality theories, which continue to be refined.

Erikson's works receive perhaps their broadest acknowledgment within the field of educational psychology; he is certainly one of the most widely read of American psychiatrists. Educators find Erikson's work relevant to the training of teachers, and it is very often coupled with the work of Piaget. Unfortunately, the two schools of thought tend to become intermingled, with the boundaries between Piaget's cognitive theories and Erikson's behavioral models becoming less than distinct. Erikson did not confine his work or his theories to the early years. Another important area of inquiry for Erikson was the issues and concerns facing the adolescent, especially as they relate to peer groups and school influences.

Overall, Erikson's views on childhood and his theory of identity crisis affected the main schools of psychotherapy only peripherally. While the behaviorist will acknowledge that a suppressed childhood can and often does lead to a maladjusted life in adulthood, Erikson is not considered any kind of final authority on the matter. What did become important in the study of the personality was Erikson's view of the ego and ego identity. Erikson was the first to see the inherent dangers of child psychoanalysis. A merely clinical approach to children's problems did not go far enough, in Erikson's view, and thus he became an early advocate of psychohistory. In his reaction to Freudian analysis, Erikson created a more humane approach to psychoanalysis. The eight stages of psychosocial development devised by Erikson continue to receive wide acknowledgment within the field of educational psychology and will continue to be used by educators and counseling psychologists alike.

Bibliography

Coles, Robert. *Erik H. Erikson: The Growth of His Work.* Boston: Little, Brown, 1970. This complete and scholarly work attempts to unify and examine the writings and teachings of Erikson. While the style is somewhat polemic at times, the book is quite valuable as a biography and source.

Erikson, Erik H. *Childhood and Society.* New York: W. W. Norton, 1963. In this classic study, Erikson presents his views and theories on identity and identity crisis—a phrase which he coined—as well as the psychosexual development of the child. The main view is that children grow through a series of progressive crises which should establish a sense of trust, autonomy, initiative, and competence.

_____. *Identity: Youth and Crisis.* New York: W. W. Norton, 1968. Using his own theory of identity crises developed in *Childhood and Society*, Erikson applies his understanding to those who are experiencing the uncertainty and confusion of adolescence. This work concentrates on such issues as peer culture, the school environment, and the inner feelings of adolescents.

_____. *Insight and Responsibility.* New York: W. W. Norton, 1964. This work acts in many ways as a source for Erikson's ideas. It consists of lectures that were given before 1964 and contains his essential ideas concerning psychotherapy, identity crises, the ego, and the beginnings of what later came to be known as psychohistory. Allows the reader a concise yet detailed introduction to Eriksonian therapy.

Roazen, Paul. *Erik H. Erikson: The Power and Limits of a Vision.* New York: Free Press, 1976. While Erikson tried to distance himself from the psychoanalytic approaches of Freud, Roazen shows that Erikson's views still have a basis in that movement. Contains further discussion on the life cycle, normality, and identity.

Richard G. Cormack

Cross-References

Attachment and Bonding in Infancy and Childhood, 307; Birth Order and Personality, 436; Ego Psychology: Erik Erikson, 867; Identity Crises: Erikson, 1255; Parenting Styles, 1740; Psychotherapy with Children, 2009; Separation, Divorce, and Family Life: Children's Issues, 2227.

THE TYPE A BEHAVIOR PATTERN

Type of psychology: Stress
Field of study: Stress and illness

The Type A behavior pattern has been related to coronary artery disease; individuals who have the Type A behavior pattern have been shown to be at a greater risk of coronary artery disease in some studies.

Principal terms
CATECHOLAMINES: hormones released from the adrenal glands in response to stressful situations
HARD-DRIVING BEHAVIOR: a Type A trait that comes from a perception of being more responsible, conscientious, competitive, and serious than other people
HURRY SICKNESS: the perception that more needs to be done or should be done in a given period of time
JOB INVOLVEMENT: a Type A trait that comes from the perception of having a challenging, high-pressure job
SPEED and IMPATIENCE: two traits of the Type A behavior pattern caused by a perception of time urgency

Overview

The Type A behavior pattern, often simply called the Type A personality, identifies behaviors which have been associated with coronary artery disease. Although these behaviors appear to be stress related, they are not necessarily involved with stressful situations or with the traditional stress response. Instead, the behaviors are based on an individual's thoughts, values, and approaches to interpersonal relationships. In general, Type A individuals are characterized as ambitious, impatient, aggressive, and competitive. Individuals who are not Type A are considered Type B. Type B individuals are characterized as relaxed, easygoing, satisfied, and noncompetitive.

Cardiologists Meyer Friedman and Ray H. Rosenman began work on the Type A behavior pattern in the mid-1950's. It was not until the completion of some retrospective studies in the 1970's, however, that the concept gained credibility. During the 1950's, it was noticed that younger and middle-aged people with coronary artery disease had several characteristics in common. These included a hard-driving attitude toward poorly defined goals; a continuous need for recognition and advancement; aggressive and at times hostile feelings; a desire for competition; an ongoing tendency to try to accomplish more in less time; a tendency to think and act faster and faster; and a high level of physical and mental alertness. These people were classified as "Pattern A" or "Type A."

Following their work on identifying the characteristics of the Type A personality or behavior pattern, Friedman and Rosenman began conducting studies to determine if it might actually cause coronary artery disease. First they conducted several correlational studies to determine if there was a relationship between the Type A behavior pattern and metabolic function in humans. They found that healthy persons with the Type A behavior pattern had elevated levels of fat in the blood (serum cholesterol and triglycerides), decreased blood-clotting time, increased catecholamine secretion (which increases heart rate, blood pressure, and heart contractility) during normal work hours, and decreased blood flow to some tissues. These studies indicated that the Type A behavior pattern may precede coronary artery disease.

Following these studies, Friedman, Rosenman, and their research team initiated the Western Collaborative Group Study in 1960. This large study, which went on for more than eight years, attempted to determine if the presence of the Type A behavior pattern increased the risk of coronary artery disease. The results of Rosenman and Friedman's study in 1974 indicated that the subjects with the Type A pattern had more than twice the incidence of the disease than subjects with the Type B pattern. More specifically, Type A individuals (when compared to Type B individuals) were twice as likely to have a fatal heart attack, five times more likely to have a second heart attack, and likely to have more severe coronary artery disease (of those who died). These results were found when other known risk factors, such as high blood pressure, smoking, and diet, were held constant. This study was followed by numerous other studies which linked coronary artery disease to the Type A behavior pattern. In 1978, the National Heart, Lung and Blood Institute sponsored a conference on the Type A behavior pattern. As a result of the Review Panel on Coronary-Prone Behavior and Coronary Heart Disease, a document was released in 1981 which stated that the Type A behavior pattern is related to increased risk of coronary artery disease.

Another product of the Western Collaborative Group Study was a method for assessing the Type A behavior pattern, developed by Rosenman in 1978. This method was based on a structured interview. A predetermined set of questions were asked of all participants. The scoring was based on the content of the participants' verbal responses as well as their nonverbal mannerisms, speech style, and behaviors during the interview process. The interview can be administered in fifteen minutes. Since the interview was not a traditional type of assessment, however, many interviewers had a difficult time using it.

In an effort to simplify the process for determining Type A behavior, many self-report questionnaires were developed. The first developed and probably the most-used questionnaire is the Jenkins Activity Survey, which was developed by C. David Jenkins, Stephen Zyzanski, and Rosenman in 1979. This survey is based on the structured interview. It gives a Type A score and three related subscores. The subscores include speed and impatience, hard driving, and job involvement. The Jenkins Activity Survey is a preferred method, because the questionnaire responses can be tallied to provide a quantitative score. Although this instrument is easy to use and provides consistent results, it is not considered as good as the structured interview because many believe the Type A characteristics can best be identified by observation.

The Type A behavior pattern continues to be studied, but research appears to have reached a peak in the late 1970's and early 1980's. Researchers are challenging the whole concept of coronary-prone behavior, because many clinical studies have not shown high correlations between the Type A behavior pattern and the progression of coronary artery disease. Other risk factors for coronary artery disease, such as smoking, high blood pressure, and high blood cholesterol, have received increasing attention.

Applications

The Type A behavior pattern, or personality, has been used to explain in part the risk of coronary artery disease; however, many risk factors for the disease have been identified. Since the various risk factors interact with one another, it is difficult to understand any one risk factor clearly.

Efforts have been made to explain the mechanism by which the Type A behavior pattern affects coronary artery disease. It has been theorized that specific biochemical and physiological events take place as a result of the emotions associated with Type A behavior. The neocortex and limbic system of the brain deliver emotional information to the hypothalamus. In a situation that arouses the Type A characteristics, the hypothalamus will cause the pituitary gland to stimulate the release of the catecholamines epinephrine and norepinephrine (also known as adrenaline and noradrenaline) from the adrenal glands, as well as other hormones from the pituitary itself. These chemicals will enter the blood and travel throughout the body, causing blood cholesterol and fat to increase, the ability to get rid of cholesterol to decrease, the ability to regulate blood sugar levels to decrease (as with diabetics), and the time for the blood to clot to increase. This response by the body to emotions is normal. The problem with Type A individuals arises because they tend to maintain this heightened emotional level almost continually, and the constant release of pituitary hormones results in these negative effects on the body being continuous as well.

The connection between Type A behavior and coronary artery disease actually results from the continuous release of hormones controlled by the pituitary gland. Through complex mechanisms, the constant exposure to these hormones causes several problems. First, cholesterol is deposited on the coronary artery walls as a result of the increase in blood cholesterol and the reduced ability to rid the blood of the cholesterol. Second, the increased ability of the blood to clot results in more clotting elements being deposited on the arterial walls. Third, clotting elements can decrease blood flow through the small capillaries which feed the coronary arteries, resulting in further complications with the cholesterol deposits. Fourth, increased insulin in the blood further destroys the coronary arteries. Therefore, the reaction of the pituitary gland to the Type A behavior pattern is believed to be responsible for the connection with coronary artery disease.

Fortunately, it is believed that people with the Type A behavior patttern can modify their behavior to reduce risk of coronary artery disease. As with many health problems, however, denial is prevalent. Therefore, it is important that Type A individuals become aware of their problem. In general, Type A individuals need to focus on several areas. These include hurry sickness, speed and impatience, and hostility.

Type A individuals try to accomplish more and more in less and less time (hurry sickness). Unfortunately, more is too often at the expense of quality, efficiency, and, most important, health. Type A individuals need to make fewer appointments related to work, and they need to schedule more relaxation time. This includes not starting the day in a rush by getting out of bed barely in time to get hurriedly to work. Finally, Type A individuals need to avoid telephone and other interruptions when they are working, because this aggravates hurry sickness. Therefore, it is recommended that individuals who suffer from hurry sickness avoid scheduling too much work; take more breaks from work (relaxation), including a lunch hour during which work is not done; and have calls screened in order to get blocks of working time.

Type A individuals typically do things rapidly and are impatient. For example, they tend to talk rapidly, repetitiously, and narrowly. They also have a hard time with individuals who talk slowly, and Type A individuals often hurry these people along by finishing their sentences. Additionally, Type A individuals try to dominate conversations, frequently focusing the discussion on themselves or their interests. In an effort to moderate speed and impatience, Type A individuals need to slow down, focus their speech in discussions to the specific problem, and cut short visits with individuals who waste their time. They should spend more time with individuals who enhance their opportunities.

The other area is hostility, or harboring destructive emotions. This is highly related to aggressiveness. Aggressive Type A individuals must learn to use their sense of humor and not look at situations only as challenges set up to bother or upset them. One way to accomplish this is for them consciously to attempt to socialize with Type B individuals. Obviously, this is not always possible, since the Type A individuals have certain other individuals with whom they must associate, such as colleagues at work and certain family members. Nevertheless, Type A individuals must understand their hostilities and learn to regulate them. In general, Type A individuals must learn to control their feelings and relationships. They must focus more attention on being well-rounded individuals rather than spending most of their time on work-related successes. Type A individuals can learn the Type B behavior pattern, resulting in a lower risk for coronary artery disease.

Context

The Type A behavior pattern was defined by two cardiologists, Meyer Friedman and Ray H. Rosenman, in the 1950's at the Harold Brunn Institute for Cardiovascular Research, Mt. Zion Hospital and Medical Center, in San Francisco. Since that time, many researchers have studied the Type A behavior pattern. Initially, most of the researchers were cardiologists. Gradually, more and more psychologists have become involved with Type A research.

Since the concept of relating coronary heart disease with human behavior was developed by cardiologists instead of psychologists, it was initially called the Type A behavior pattern rather than the Type A personality. "Personality" relates to an individual's inner traits, attitudes, or habits and is very complex and generally studied by psychologists. As Type A was defined, however, it only related specific behaviors with disease and was observed openly. Therefore, it seemed appropriate to label Type A a behavior pattern. Over the years, Type A has been assumed to be a personality; technically, this is not accurate, although many people now refer to it as the Type A personality.

Another reason Type A is most accurately considered a behavior pattern rather than a personality relates to the way it is assessed. Whether the structured interview or the written questionnaire is utilized, a predetermined set of questions and sequence are used. While this approach can assess a behavior pattern adequately, different skills which allow the interviewer to respond appropriately to an individual's answers and probe specific responses further are needed to assess personality.

The Type A behavior pattern evolved as a risk factor for coronary artery disease. The original need for this idea was not psychologically based. Instead, it was based on a need to understand further the factors that are involved with the development of coronary artery disease, a major cause of death. Therefore, the role of the Type A behavior pattern in psychology has been limited. Nevertheless, Type A studies have benefited humankind's understanding of an important disease and, to a certain extent, the understanding of psychology.

The future study of the Type A behavior pattern is in question. Research continually shows conflicting results about its role in coronary artery disease. As more research is conducted by both medical clinicians and psychologists, the true value of the Type A behavior pattern will become evident. Until then, health care professionals will continually have to evaluate the appropriateness of using the Type A behavior pattern as an identifier of the risk of artery or heart disease.

Bibliography

Chesney, Margaret A., and Ray H. Rosenman, eds. *Anger and Hostility in Cardiovascular and Behavior Disorders.* Washington, D.C.: Hemisphere, 1985. Integrating psychology and the Type A behavior pattern, this book provides in-depth information on the technical aspects of behavior. Although some portions of the book are technical, the introductions to each chapter provide historical and nontechnical information related to the broader topic of behavior.

Friedman, Meyer, and Ray H. Rosenman. *Type A Behavior and Your Heart.* New York: Alfred A. Knopf, 1974. Summarizes the history of Type A behavior and presents information as it relates to individuals. Very basic, it is meant to provide an understanding of Type A behavior for the general public. The basics of changing Type A behavior are also presented.

Friedman, Meyer, and D. Ulmer. *Treating Type A Behavior—and Your Heart.* New

York: Alfred A. Knopf, 1984. Friedman's second book written for the general public focuses on what an individual can do to change Type A behavior. It is nontechnical and provides basic information in an easy-to-read form.

Houston, B. Kent, and C. R. Snyder, eds. *Type A Behavior Pattern: Research, Theory, and Intervention.* New York: John Wiley & Sons, 1988. Contains thirteen chapters by various authors. The first three chapters nicely introduce the topic in relatively simple terms. Subsequent chapters tend to be more technical and require a better background for understanding. A wealth of references are listed throughout.

Jenkins, C. D., S. J. Zyzanski, and R. H. Rosenman. *The Jenkins Activity Survey.* New York: Psychological Corporation, 1979. Contains the survey used for assessing Type A behavior. Includes the scoring procedure, which is easy to understand and administer.

Price, Virginia Ann. *Type A Behavior Pattern.* New York: Academic Press, 1982. A good technical resource for Type A behavior. Very comprehensive. The introductory chapters provide the nontechnical reader with valuable, understandable information. More than three hundred references are listed at the end of the book.

Bradley R. A. Wilson

Cross References

Biofeedback and Relaxation, 416; Coping: Social Support, 700; Environmental Psychology, 978; Health Psychology, 1139; Stress: Cognitive Appraisals, 2404; The Concept of Stress, 2411; Effects of Stress, 2417; Theories of Stress, 2432; Stress and the Endocrine System, 2445; Stress and the Nervous System, 2452; Stress-Related Diseases, 2464.

VIOLENCE AND SEXUALITY IN THE MASS MEDIA

Type of psychology: Social psychology
Field of study: Aggression

The American mass media, especially films and television, contain high levels of violence. In some pornography, violence is presented in a sexual context. The consensus among social scientists, based on both laboratory experiments and field studies, is that nonsexual and sexual violence causes aggressive behavior in the audience but that nonviolent pornography does not.

Principal terms
AGGRESSION MACHINE: an apparatus used to measure physical aggression in which subjects think they are delivering electrical shocks to an experimental confederate
AGGRESSIVE CUES: stimuli that, because of their previous association with observed violence, can increase aggressive behavior
AROUSAL: an increase in physiological activity (heart rate, respiration rate, and so forth) in response to a stimulus
CATHARSIS HYPOTHESIS: the belief that exposure to media violence causes an emotional release that reduces the likelihood of subsequent aggressive behavior
DESENSITIZATION: a gradual reduction in arousal because of repeated exposure to a stimulus
DISINHIBITION: a reduction in restraints, such as anxiety or guilt, that ordinarily discourage aggression
EXCITATION TRANSFER: the theory that arousal from one source can intensify an emotional reaction to a different source (for example, that sexual arousal can increase the response to an aggressive cue)
IMITATION: the performance of behaviors that were learned by observing the actions of others
MEAN WORLD SYNDROME: the belief that society is more violent than it actually is
PRIMING: an increase in the availability of certain types of information in memory in response to a stimulus
RAPE MYTHS: false beliefs about the causes or consequences of rape (for example, "women who dress provocatively are responsible for their own victimization")
SCRIPT: the mental representation of a familiar sequence of behaviors, such as fixing dinner or robbing a bank

Overview
The world of the American mass media is much more violent than the real world.

Communication researcher George Gerbner has found that approximately 80 percent of television programs contain some violence, for an average of almost ten violent acts per hour. Some prime-time television programs and R-rated action films contain as many as fifty to 150 violent acts per hour. Cartoons average twenty-five violent acts per hour. It has been estimated that by the age of eighteen, the average American has witnessed 100,000 acts of violence, including 25,000 killings, on television alone. There are many cases of direct copying of media violence. For example, at least twenty-eight people have killed themselves in apparent imitation of the Russian roulette scene in the film *The Deer Hunter* (1978). Reactions to such anecdotal evidence, however, must be tempered by the knowledge that many millions of people have seen these programs and films.

In the early 1960's, psychologist Leonard Berkowitz devised a laboratory procedure to study the effects of filmed violence on aggressive behavior. In a typical experiment, subjects are made angry by a confederate or accomplice of the experimenter. They then watch a ten-minute film clip containing a high level of violence (a boxing match) or an equally exciting control film (a foot race). Finally, subjects are permitted to evaluate the confederate's work using an "aggression machine," an apparatus that they think delivers electric shocks to the confederate. Results of these studies consistently show that subjects who have seen a violent film deliver longer and more intense shocks than control subjects do. This experiment has been repeated at least 150 times, making it one of the more reliable findings in social psychology. Similar effects have been found with other measures of verbal and physical aggression.

Four variables have been shown to influence the amount of imitation of media violence. First, the more realistic the portrayal of violence, the greater the imitation. The same violence is more effective when presented as a real event than as fiction. "Aggression cues," or points of similarity between the filmed violence and the subject's real-life experience, such as a weapon or a character's name, can increase aggression. Second, more imitation occurs when violence is presented as justified. Violence committed by the hero in revenge for previous harm produces greater imitation than violence that is unfair to the victim. Third, imitation increases when violence is effective—that is, when aggressors are rewarded with wealth, happiness, and social approval. Fourth, imitation is more likely when the viewer is in a psychological state of readiness to aggress—for example, when he or she is emotionally aroused or angry. Anger, however, is not a necessary condition for imitation of violence.

Critics have argued that laboratory studies of aggression are so different from everyday experience that the results are not generalizable to the real world. This skepticism produced a second generation of studies using field research methodologies. These included correlational studies in which subjects' exposure to violent programs was related to ratings of their aggressiveness by parents, teachers, or peers; field studies in which the exposure of institutionalized boys to media violence was controlled and physical and verbal aggression was observed; "natural experiments" in which communities or nations that were slow to receive television were compared with others that received it sooner; and archival studies of the effects of highly publicized suicides or homicides on the suicide or homicide rate. Although the results of these studies are not as clear as those of laboratory experiments, they have generally supported the hypothesis.

In summary, there is substantial evidence from studies using a variety of research methods converging on the conclusion that filmed and televised violence increases aggression. Although any single study can be criticized on methodological grounds, there are no convincing alternative explanations for all of them.

Media violence can affect attitudes as well as behavior. The prevalence of crime and violence on television appears to cultivate a "mean world syndrome." For example, heavy viewers are more likely than infrequent viewers to overestimate the frequency of crime. It is not clear, however, whether television causes these attitudes or whether pessimistic and fearful people are more attracted to television.

Laboratory research on the effects of pornography has used procedures similar to those of aggression research. In several studies, male subjects were angered by a female confederate. They watched either violent pornography (a sexually explicit rape scene) or a control film. The men who saw the rape film showed more violence against women than did control subjects. Violent pornography, however, contains two distinct variables that might plausibly be related to aggression—violence and sexual explicitness. To determine whether either or both contribute to aggression, it is necessary to compare four conditions: sex plus violence (a sexually explicit rape scene), violence only (a nonexplicit rape scene), sex only (sexually explicit but with willing participants), and a control film. Researchers who have made this comparison find that the sex plus violence and violence only conditions increase aggression toward women (in about the same amount), but nonviolent pornography does not usually produce any more aggression than a control film. This suggests that the effect of violent pornography is a special case of the well-established effect of filmed violence. Nonviolent pornography does not increase aggression. This is important, because only a small percentage of pornography—for example, about 15 percent of pornography videotapes—contains violence.

Studies show that men exposed to violent (and, in some cases, nonviolent) pornography in laboratory experiments show undesirable changes in attitude. They are more likely to endorse rape myths, such as the belief that women secretly enjoy being raped. They recommend less severe punishment for the defendant in a hypothetical rape trial, suggesting that they regard rape as a less serious crime. There is no evidence, however, that these attitudes are directly related to the likelihood of raping someone. It should be noted that these attitude changes are small and temporary and that similar effects have been obtained with nonpornographic violence, such as R-rated "mad slasher" films.

Field research on the effects of pornography falls into two categories. Some researchers have examined the relationship between the availability of pornography and the incidence of reported rape in various locales. Others have interviewed convicted sex offenders to see whether they differ from nonoffenders in their history of exposure to pornography. Both approaches have produced mixed results, suggesting that, at most, pornography plays a minor role in sexual assault once alternative explanations have been removed.

Applications

The effects of media violence have been vigorously debated for several decades. Televised violence is of special concern because of its vivid and realistic nature and its easy accessibility to children. The most extensive government investigation of the effects of television on childen was the 1972 Surgeon General's Scientific Advisory Committee on Television and Social Behavior, which conducted forty scientific studies. They concluded that television can cause aggression, but their report contained so many qualifications that it was widely perceived as indicating that television is not really an important cause of aggressive behavior. This ambiguity may have resulted from the fact that the television networks were allowed to appoint five of the twelve commissioners and to blackball several proposed members. A 1982 update by the National Institute of Mental Health stated more directly that television violence is indeed a cause of aggression. In spite of these investigations and the lobbying of pressure groups such as Action for Children's Television, the amount of violence on television has changed little since the late 1960's. The television networks believe (with some justification) that violent programs are more popular, and they have considerable power to resist governmental regulation.

Pornography has also been an issue of great concern to the American public. The country's ambivalence about media sexuality is illustrated by the contrasting recommendations of two government commissions. The 1970 Commission on Obscenity and Pornography consisted primarily of social scientists. It funded nineteen original studies (all of nonviolent pornography) and concluded that pornography had no proven harmful effects. Political reaction to the report was primarily negative. In 1986, President Ronald Reagan appointed the Attorney General's Commission on Pornography (the Meese Commission), consisting primarily of antipornography activists with little social scientific background. The Meese Commission came to the following conclusions: Violent pornography causes aggression toward women and harmful attitude change; nonviolent pornography that is degrading to women (although the report was not very clear about what "degrading" means) does not cause aggressive behavior but produces harmful attitude change; and nonviolent and nondegrading pornography has no specific negative effects, although certain moral and aesthetic harms were claimed. In spite of the different effects attributed to each type, the commission concluded that all pornography should be banned and proposed ninety-two recommendations for doing so. Social scientists criticized the Meese Commission for failing to define categories of pornography clearly, for biased selection and presentation of research, for not distinguishing between low- and high-quality evidence, and for obscuring differences between the effects of violent and nonviolent pornography.

Attempts to regulate media violence and pornography would appear to be in conflict with the First Amendment to the United States Constitution, which states that "Congress shall make no law . . . abridging the freedom of speech, or of the press." The courts have historically permitted many exceptions to the First Amendment, however, and there is a long history of legal censorship of news and entertainment media. Social scientists disagree on whether there is enough evidence of antisocial effects of violence or pornography to justify censorship. Many social scientists would insist, however, that the Constitution places a strong burden of proof on the censor, that a much stronger case could be made for censorship of violence (including violent pornography) than of nonviolent pornography, and that attempts to censor media content because it is alleged to produce "bad attitudes" are in conflict with the free marketplace of ideas model assumed by the Constitution.

While social scientists see media violence as more harmful than pornography, the American public favors censorship of nonviolent pornography more than of violence. This suggests that people underestimate the effects of media violence, overestimate the effects of nonviolent pornography, or object to pornography for reasons other than its alleged harmful effects.

Context

Two early psychological approaches to the study of aggression made different predictions about the effects of media violence. Instinct and drive theories of aggression suggested that watching media violence would provide a "catharsis," or release of aggressive energy, which would reduce the likelihood of subsequent aggression. Social learning theory proposed that much of one's knowledge of how to behave comes from observing and sometimes imitating the behavior of others. Exposure to media violence would be expected to increase aggression. The majority of research has supported the social learning theory position.

There are several contemporary explanations for the effects of media violence. The imitation approach emphasizes the direct transmission of information about when, why, and how to commit aggressive behaviors. This theory accounts for copycat aggression but has difficulty explaining more general effects. The disinhibition approach points out that adults already know how to aggress, and that media violence reduces restraints that would normally cause people to inhibit their aggressive impulses by suggesting that aggression is socially acceptable. The arousal and desensitization approaches suggest that watching violence will have different short- and long-term effects. In the short run, violence is exciting and increases physiological arousal, which can spill over and energize real aggressive behavior. This effect would appear to be temporary. In the long run, each exposure produces progressively less arousal, called desensitization. This implies that a steady diet of media violence can make people indifferent to the pain and suffering of victims and increase their tolerance of real violence.

In the 1970's and 1980's, cognitive theories became more popular in psychology. The cognitive priming approach proposes that media violence increases the availability of aggressive thoughts in the viewer for as long as several days, and these thoughts increase the probability of aggressive behavior. A related approach suggests that media portrayals contribute to the formation and maintenance of aggressive behavioral scripts, which are later activated by real situations similar to those observed in the media.

The effects of violent pornography can be explained by the same theories that explain the effects of general film violence. Those who claim that nonviolent pornography causes aggression are faced with the problem of explaining how nonaggressive content (sexuality) can activate aggressive behavior. A variation on arousal theory, the excitation transfer theory, suggests that the physiological arousal caused by pornography can subsequently be confused with anger and can energize aggression. Any source of arousal, such as music or exercise, can have this effect if the timing is right. This theory predicts very subtle, temporary effects of exposure to pornography, and as noted, research does not consistently support it.

Effects of aggression and pornography on attitudes can be explained on the basis of theories of attitude change, which show that, not surprisingly, almost any media presentation produces small, temporary changes of attitude in the direction advocated by its author. Resistance to attitude change occurs when the audience has the information and the motivation to argue with the media effectively.

Bibliography

Donnerstein, Edward I., Daniel Linz, and Steven Penrod. *The Question of Pornography*. New York: Free Press, 1987. Review of laboratory research on effects of pornography. Distinguishes between the proven antisocial effects of violent pornography and the more speculative claims against nonviolent pornography. Accessible to the general reader.

Huesmann, L. Rowell, and Neil M. Malamuth. "Media Violence and Antisocial Behavior." *Journal of Social Issues* 42, no. 3 (1986): 125-139. This article is in a special issue of a psychological journal containing eleven articles that summarize the effects of media violence and pornography.

Joy, Leslie A., Meredith M. Kimball, and Merle L. Zabrack. "Television and Children's Aggressive Behavior." In *The Impact of Television*, edited by Tannis Mac-Beth Williams. Orlando, Fla.: Academic Press, 1986. Presents a study of the effects of the introduction of cable television in an isolated community in western Canada on the aggressive behavior of its children.

Liebert, Robert M., and Joyce Sprafkin. *The Early Window: Effects of Television on Children and Youth*. 3d ed. Elmsford, N.Y.: Pergamon Press, 1988. Excellent overview of the socializing effects of television. Discusses the effects of televised violence and the politics of governmental regulation of television content.

Signorelli, Nancy, and George Gerbner, comps. *Violence and Terror in the Mass Media: An Annotated Bibliography*. New York: Greenwood Press, 1988. Citations and paragraph-length summaries of 784 studies of violent media content and its effects. Very helpful when doing a literature survey.

Zillmann, Dolf, and Jennings Bryant, eds. *Pornography: Research Advances and Policy Considerations.* Hillsdale, N.J.: Lawrence Erlbaum, 1989. Fifteen papers dealing with the content and effects of pornography and the legal debate over pornography regulation. Papers are sometimes difficult but are generally rewarding.

Lloyd K. Stires

Cross-References

Aggression: Definitions and Theoretical Explanations, 162; Aggression: Reduction and Control, 169; Attitude-Behavior Consistency, 320; Attitude Formation and Change, 326; Sexism, 2240; Social Learning: Albert Bandura, 2304; Social Schemata, 2329.

VISION: BRIGHTNESS AND CONTRAST

Type of psychology: Sensation and perception
Fields of study: Cognitive processes; vision

Brightness refers to one's perception of the intensity of light reflected from a surface; contrast refers to one's perception of differences in light reflected from two surfaces. Contrast enhances perception of intensity differences, thereby accentuating lines, colors, and borders; it makes a dark area appear darker and a bright area appear brighter when they are juxtaposed.

Principal terms
ASSIMILATION: a diminishing of contrast between relatively similar hues bordering each other
COMPLEMENTARY COLOR: light that complements another light in that their addition produces white light and their juxtaposition produces high contrast
CONTRAST SENSITIVITY FUNCTION: a plot of sensitivity to difference in light intensity in adjacent regions versus the spatial frequency of a stimulus
HUE: the chromatic or color sensation produced by the wavelength of light
RETINA: the light-receptive surface of the eye where light is absorbed by pigment and transduced into neural impulses
SIMULTANEOUS CONTRAST: the tendency for the color of one area to affect perception of the color of an adjacent area
SUCCESSIVE CONTRAST: the tendency for an adapting stimulus to produce an afterimage, either in its complementary color or in its opposite degree of brightness

Overview

Brightness is the perception of intensity of light. Roughly, the more intense a light is, the brighter it seems to be. Intensity refers to the physical energy of light, as measured by a photometer. Brightness, however, is a perceptual phenomenon: It cannot be measured by physical instruments. It is a basic perception, difficult if not impossible to describe; it must be experienced. Measurements of brightness are generally observers' reports of their experience viewing lights of different intensities. Only in living systems—only in the eye of the perceiver—is the term "brightness" relevant.

The brightness of a spot of light, although related to the intensity of light reflected from that spot, is also influenced by other factors. It varies with the intensity of light reflected from the immediately surrounding area at any given time and at immediately preceding times. In general, a spot appears brighter if the surrounding areas are dark or are stimulated with light perceived as complementary in color; it also appears brighter if the eye has become accustomed to the dark ("dark-adapted"). These factors contribute contrast, the perception of differences in light intensity, which enhances brightness. Brightness and contrast are perceptually linked.

A light of a given physical intensity may appear quite bright when viewed with an eye that has been dark-adapted, perhaps by being covered for ten to fifteen minutes. That same light may seem dim in comparison to an eye exposed to bright light for the same time period. This is largely attributable to the fact that a dark-adapted eye has more photopigment available to respond to incoming light; when this pigment has been exposed, it becomes bleached and needs time to regenerate. The enhancement of differences in brightness by an adapting light or other stimulus preceding the test light is called successive contrast and is primarily attributable to the state of adaptation of the retina.

Simultaneous contrast can also affect brightness perception. In this case, a spot of light at one place on the retina can be made to appear brighter or dimmer depending only on changes in the lighting of adjacent retinal locations. A small gray paper square placed on a sheet of black paper appears brighter than an identical square on a sheet of white paper. This is mostly a result of lateral inhibition, or photoreceptors stimulated by the white background inhibiting the receptors stimulated by the square so it appears less dazzling on white than on black. In general, differences are enhanced when the stimuli are side by side.

Sensitivity to contrast also varies with the detail of the object being viewed. Reading a book involves attending to high spatial frequencies, closely spaced lines, and minute detail. Recognizing a friend across the room or finding one's car in a parking lot involves attention to much broader spatial frequencies; that is, the lines important for recognition are much farther apart. The visual system handles low, moderate, and high spatial frequencies, although not equally well. A contrast sensitivity function may be plotted to show which spatial frequencies are most easily detected—that is, to which frequencies the eye-brain system is most sensitive.

The peak of this function, the highest sensitivity to spatial frequency, is within the midrange of detectable frequencies. At this peak, it takes less physical contrast (a smaller intensity difference) for an observer to report seeing the border between areas of different frequency. At higher and lower spatial frequencies, sensitivity drops off, so greater intensity differences must be made for perception in those ranges.

While perceptual systems exaggerate physical contrast, they fail to notice lack of contrast, change, or movement. Changes in brightness, for example, can be made so gradually that no notice of them is taken at all. In fact, the visual system, while signaling changes well, does not respond to seemingly constant stimulation. When an image, a bright pattern of light projected on the retina, is stabilized so it does not move at all, the observer reports first seeing the image and then, in a few seconds, its fading from view. The field does not turn gray or black or become empty; it simply ceases to exist. A border circumscribing a pattern within another pattern, perhaps a red-filled circle within a green-filled one, may be stabilized on the retina. In this case, the inner border disappears completely: The observer continues to see an unstabilized green-filled circle with no pattern in it. The area that formerly appeared red—and which indeed does reflect long-wavelength light—is perceived only as a part of the homogeneous green circle. Thus, while borders and movement creating physical contrast are exaggerated in perception, a stimulus signaling no change at all is simply not perceived.

Applications

Brightness and contrast are especially well illustrated in color perception. In the retina, three different cone pigments mediate color perception. Each pigment maximally absorbs light of certain wavelengths: One maximally absorbs the short lengths that are perceived as blue, one the medium wavelengths perceived as green, and one the red or long-wavelength region of the spectrum. The outputs of the cones interact with one another in the visual system in such a way that reds and greens stand in opposite or complementary roles, as do blues and yellows, and black and white. A gray square reflects light of all wavelengths equally. It has no hue, or color. Yet when it is placed on a red background, it appears greenish; if placed on a blue background, that same gray square appears yellowish. In each case, the neutral square moves toward the complement of its background color. The background has induced the perception of hue, tinting the gray with the color of its complement. Brightness of the background can also affect hue. A royal-blue square against a moderately white background can appear deep navy when the background intensity is increased, or seem to be a powder blue when it is decreased. The same color in two different settings or under two different brightness conditions is not the same color.

The appearance of color is not a simple property of the color pigment itself but is defined in its relationship to others. Simultaneous color contrast can be quite startling, depending on the color relationships chosen. For example, if two squares of different hues but the same brightness are juxtaposed, colors appear very strong and exaggerated. One's attention goes immediately to the contrast. If they are complementary colors such as red and green, the contrast is heightened. If they are close to the complements of each other, they are perceived in the direction of complementarity.

Yet not all colors are contrasting. A color configuration that does not move toward contrast moves toward assimilation—toward being united with the major color present. For example, a painting's central blue feature may bring out subtly blue features elsewhere in the painting. Whenever colors show enough similarity to one another, they approach one another, emphasizing similarity rather than contrast. Both color contrast and assimilation are beautifully illustrated in Josef Albers' book *Interaction of Color* (1963).

Another visual demonstration of brightness effects is the Pulfrich pendulum effect, or the Pulfrich phenomenon. To observe this, tie a pendulum bob to a two-foot length of string. Swing this in a plane normal to the line of sight, moving it back and forth as a pendulum. Then observe this continuing motion while wearing glasses, one lens of which is darkened or covered with a sunglass cover. Suddenly the pendulum appears to move in an ellipse instead of an arc. This illusion is a brightness effect. The shaded or sunglass-covered eye does not receive as much light as the other eye at any given time. It takes this eye longer to integrate the light information it does receive and so, by the time it sends location information to the brain, the other eye is sending its information of another location. The brain interprets disparity, this difference in the locations, as depth. Therefore the pendulum appears to move closer and farther away from the observer in elliptical depth and not constantly in a single plane. Intriguingly, switching the covered eye changes the elliptical path from clockwise rotation to counterclockwise or vice versa.

The Pulfrich phenomenon is a demonstration of changes in perception with changes in brightness; such changes have very practical effects. Driving at dusk, for example, can be dangerous, because light levels are suddenly lower than expected. Although the eye gathers the available light for form, distance, and depth perception, it takes a longer period of time. Unaware of this, a driver may find reaction time to be longer than in the middle of the day and not allow enough braking distance. Similarly, an umpire may halt an evening soccer game earlier than the spectators think is necessary because of low light levels. The spectators can see well enough, as they gather the light needed to perceive what is happening. The players, on the other hand, notice that their reaction times are extended and that they are having trouble localizing the ball.

For a third application, the fact that contrast sensitivity shows peaks in particular spatial frequencies bears explanatory if not practical value. Robert Sekule, Lucinda Hutman, and Cynthia Owsley showed, in a 1980 study, that as one grows older, sensitivity to low spatial frequencies decreases. This may partly explain why older people may show greater difficulty recognizing faces or locating an automobile than the young even though the two groups may be equally able to discriminate fine structural details. Making an older person aware of this change in sensitivity may be of assistance in defining the difficulty and in providing assurance that this is not a memory problem or a sign of decreasing cognitive ability.

Context

In the late nineteenth century, much of the early development of psychology as a science came about through work in sensation and perception. As empirical evidence grew, theories of contrast perception took shape. Two of the most notable are those of Hermann von Helmholtz and Ewald Hering.

Helmholtz had a psychological theory—a cognitive theory that explained color and brightness changes with contrast as errors in judgment. Errors were attributed to lack of practice in making brightness judgments, not in any physiological change in the neural input. Something suddenly looked brighter simply because it was misinterpreted, probably because one was focusing on some other aspect.

At the same time, Hering insisted and provided convincing demonstrations that contrast involves no error in judgment but has a physiological base. The neural response of any region of the retina, he argued, is a function not only of that region but also of neighboring regions. These neighboring sensations were postulated as having an effect opposite in brightness, or in the complementary color, of the region being viewed. Hering showed with successive contrast and simultaneous contrast studies that the outputs of different places on the retina could be modified by one another.

In 1890, William James described this controversy and gave, in *The Principles of Psychology*, his support to Hering's physiological position. With some modifications, it may be supported today. Yet the Helmholtz theory has some supportive evidence as well. For example, John Delk and Samuel Fillenbaum showed in 1956 that an object's characteristic color influences an observer's perception of that object's color. In this way, for example, an apple cut out of red paper is identified as redder than it actually is. This line of evidence would support Helmholtz in his theory of errors in judgment.

Almost any modern consideration of contrast includes a discussion of brightness changes at borders, commonly called Mach bands. This dates to 1865, when Ernst Mach, an Austrian physicist, described borders as places where differences in brightness are shown side by side. One way to observe these is to create a shadow by holding a book or other object with a sharp edge between a light source and the surface it illuminates. The border of the shadow is not crisp; in fact, it seems to be made of several lines. On the inside there is a dark stripe, darker than the central shaded object that separates it from the unshaded region. Adjacent to this, on the bright side of the shadow, is another stripe that appears brighter than the rest of the illuminated surface. These additional bands are an example of brightness contrast at a border where the physical contrast between shadow and light is exaggerated in perception. As true brightness phenomena, Mach bands do not exist in the physics of the situation (that is, in the distribution of light intensity). They are purely a perceptual phenomenon, their brightness depending not only on the intensity of an area but also on the intensity of surrounding areas.

Bibliography

Albers, Josef. *Interaction of Color*. New Haven, Conn.: Yale University Press, 1963. Albers, an artist and teacher, presents commentary on form and color in addition to his paintings. Many of his works illustrate simultaneous contrast, successive contrast, assimilation, and other brightness effects. They are especially intriguing in that they were not designed to support psychological theories but to be viewed as art.

Barlow, H. B., and J. D. Mollon, eds. *The Senses*. Cambridge, England: Cambridge University Press, 1982. Clearly written yet somewhat technical, this text was designed for medical, psychology, education, and art students and may effectively be read in sections. Chapter 8 gives a good description of spatial frequency resolution in vision. Suggested reading even if only to glimpse the figures and graphs in this section.

Bloomer, Carolyn M. *Principles of Visual Perception.* New York: Van Nostrand Reinhold, 1976. Bloomer interweaves visual perception and art theory in an easily comprehensible explanation of perceptual principles complete with illustrations from the fine arts. She includes a full chapter on color, including illustrations of contrast, and suggestions for making one's own demonstrations. Annotated bibliography.

Gregory, Richard L. *Eye and Brain: The Psychology of Seeing.* 4th ed. Princeton, N.J.: Princeton University Press, 1990. An introduction to the basic phenomena of visual perception that was clearly written to be read and enjoyed by general readers as well as serious students. Gregory gives a full chapter on seeing brightness, including an excellent discussion of the eye's sensitivity to light. Clearly illustrated.

Rock, Irvin. *Perception.* New York: Scientific American Library, 1984. A carefully written and beautifully illustrated book. Rock describes characteristics of object perception, subjective contours, movement, and illusions. His treatment of contrast is in relation to illusions, color, and the intelligence of perception. For the general reader.

Bonnie S. Sherman

Cross-References

Color Vision, 611; Depth Perception, 796; Pattern Recognition as a Cognitive Process, 1747; Pattern Vision, 1752; Visual Illusions, 2622; Visual Neural Processing, 2629.

VISUAL DEVELOPMENT

Type of psychology: Sensation and perception
Field of study: Vision

Visual development involves the changes in the functioning of the human visual system that occur with age. Research has shown that even newborns can see well enough to start to learn about the world; by eight months of age, infants' visual functioning is comparable to that of adults.

Principal terms
 ACUITY: the ability to detect very small details in a pattern
 DEPTH CUE: a source of information in the two-dimensional retinal image that makes depth perception possible by specifying the three-dimensional characteristics of the scene being viewed
 DEPTH PERCEPTION: the ability to see three-dimensional features, such as the distance of an object from oneself and the shape of an object
 DETECTION: the ability to see that a surface is patterned
 DISCRIMINATION: the ability to see that two patterns differ in some way
 PATTERN: any two-dimensional picture consisting of an arrangement of black-and-white lines
 RECOGNITION: the ability to know that a pattern being viewed has been seen before

Overview

Researchers studying visual development pursue two major goals. First, they try to describe the visual capacities of humans at different ages, beginning with the newborn infant. Second, they attempt to explain what causes the changes in visual functioning that occur with age. For centuries, young infants' inability to describe verbally how they see the world made it impossible to pursue these goals through direct scientific study. Philosophers and early psychologists based their assertions about visual development on logical arguments and indirect evidence from experiments with adults.

In the 1960's, Robert Fantz made it possible for scientists to investigate these claims directly by developing procedures that measure three basic visual capacities in infants: the "detection," "discrimination," and "recognition" of two-dimensional patterns. Detection refers to the ability to see that a surface is patterned rather than uniform. Discrimination refers to the somewhat more complex ability of distinguishing between two (or more) patterns. Finally, recognition refers to the still more complex ability to determine whether a pattern has been seen previously.

Infants' detection of visual patterns has been tested by measuring their visual acuity. Visual acuity refers to the ability to see very small objects such as closely spaced, thin black stripes on a white background. An infant's acuity can be determined by using the "preferential-looking procedure" developed by Fantz. This procedure is based on the observation that infants consistently prefer to look at black stripes rather than a plain gray field. An infant is shown a striped pattern next to a plain gray field. If the infant consistently prefers to look at the striped side, then he or she must detect the stripes; otherwise, the striped pattern would look the same to him or her as the gray field, and the infant would not show a preference for it.

Visual acuity is influenced by two factors: spatial frequency and contrast. Spatial frequency refers roughly to the fineness or coarseness of a pattern. For the striped patterns described above, the smaller the space between stripes, the higher the spatial frequency of the pattern. Contrast refers to the difference between the brightest part of the white space in a pattern and the darkest part of the black space.

There is a dramatic improvement in acuity between birth and eight months of age. In addition, there are age-related changes in the spatial frequencies that are most easily detected. Newborns are best at detecting very low spatial frequencies. This means that, at birth, infants can most easily see coarse outlines such as a person's hairline. With age, visual acuity becomes best at progressively higher spatial frequencies. As a result, older infants and adults can detect details such as the eyes, nose, and mouth of a person's face. By eight months of age, an infant's visual acuity is about as good as an adult who could see better if he or she wore glasses but does not usually bother to do so.

Infants' discrimination of visual patterns has also been assessed by using the preferential-looking procedure. An infant is shown two patterns that differ in some way. If the infant consistently looks more at one pattern than the other, he or she must be able to discriminate between them on the basis of this difference. Many studies have documented that infants can discriminate patterns from birth onward. Before three months of age, an infant will look more at the pattern that appears to have the greater total amount of contrast. After three months, infants' preferences are more often based on the complexity and familiarity of the patterns. Among the preferred stimuli at this age are human faces, especially one's own mother.

Infants' recognition of visual patterns has been assessed by using the "habituation procedure," which was also developed by Fantz. This method involves two phases: a familiarization phase and a test phase. In the familiarization phase, infants are shown a pattern repeatedly. When infants become so bored that they no longer look at this pattern much, the test phase occurs. In this phase, infants are shown both the old pattern and a new one. Infants who are only a few days old will often remain bored with the old pattern but exhibit interest in the new pattern. This indicates that they must be able to discriminate between the old pattern and the new pattern. They also must be able to recognize the old pattern; otherwise, they would never be bored with it.

No one knows whether infants' recognition of a repeatedly shown picture is conscious. It is, however, surprisingly robust. Even two weeks after they are repeatedly shown a particular pattern, two-month-olds continue to prefer a different pattern.

Applications

The development of methods to test infants' ability to detect, discriminate, and recognize patterns led investigators to apply these same methods in other ways. Researchers have investigated infants' ability to see features of the world other than patterns. The same methods have also proved useful for diagnosing infants suspected of having abnormal vision.

For example, researchers have discovered that "saccadic" and "smooth pursuit" eye movements develop very early. When one's eyes are stationary, the picture one sees, called the visual field, has very sharp detail only in its center. Saccadic eye movements quickly shift the eyes from one position to another in order to move an object of interest to the center of the visual field where it can be seen most clearly. If the object then moves, smooth-pursuit eye movements keep it in the center of the visual field by steadily following it.

Even newborns perform saccadic eye movements. With age, infants become able to move their eyes to objects increasingly far from the center of the visual field. Infants are also capable of smooth-pursuit eye movements by two months of age. Before that time, they look at the location where an object has been for a second or two after it moves away. Then they quickly shift their eyes forward to a position roughly in line with the object's new location.

Mark Bornstein used the habituation procedure to show that infants' color vision is similar to that of adults. Adults see particular ranges of wavelengths of light as a single unique category of color; for example, they see wavelengths of 450 to 480 nanometers as blue. During the familiarization phase, Bornstein repeatedly presented four-month-olds with a particular wavelength of light until they lost interest. Infants then viewed two new wavelengths in the test phase. These were equally far from the original in terms of their wavelengths. To adults, however, one of the new wavelengths looked like a different color from the original wavelength, whereas the other was the same color. Infants looked more at the wavelength that adults saw as the different color than at the one that adults saw as the same color. This indicates that infants could see the color of the original wavelength and saw that one of the new wavelengths was the same color. Like adults, infants saw the other new wavelength as a new color. As a result, it was more interesting to them and they looked longer at it.

Finally, researchers have found that depth perception, the ability to see the distance and three-dimensional shape of objects, develops early in infancy. When one looks at an object, light enters the eye and is displayed on the retina, a light-sensitive structure at the back of the eye. The display of light on the retina is two-dimensional, however, somewhat like a picture. In order to see in three dimensions, the adult visual system uses three types of information contained in the flat retinal image: kinetic, binocular, and pictorial depth cues. The ability to use these three types of depth cues appears to develop in the same sequence for all individuals: Kinetic cues are used soon after birth, binocular cues start to be used at four months of age, and pictorial cues start to be used at around seven months.

Kinetic cues are based on how the retinal image moves over time. For example, as an object approaches, it fills an increasing portion of the visual field. Infants can use this expansion of the retinal image to see the approach of an object in the first month of life. Binocular cues are based on the fact that, because eyes in humans are several centimeters apart, the display of light on the two retinas almost always differs. By four months of age, infants can use the difference in the two retinal images of an object being observed to form an impression of how far away the object is. Pictorial cues were originally described by Leonardo da Vinci as ways of conveying distance in paintings. By seven months of age, infants are able to use pictorial cues such as perspective and shading to see the distance and shape of objects.

The methods of visual-development research have also been used successfully to diagnose infants with suspected visual abnormalities. For example, the absence of saccadic or smooth-pursuit eye movements may signal a visual deficit. In addition, the preferential-looking procedure for testing visual acuity has been used to determine whether an infant's vision is sufficiently impaired to require corrective surgery. This procedure has been standardized and used to diagnose children with problems such as cataracts, muscular weakness in the eyelids, and crossed eyes.

In some cases, infants who are suspected of being blind are found to have vision within normal limits. This saves the children's parents months of unnecessary worrying and prevents these infants from being treated as blind. In other cases, testing confirms that a child has a visual impairment. This often allows surgery to be performed early enough to be maximally effective.

Context

Philosophers concerned with questions about human nature and the origins of knowledge speculated for centuries about the visual capacities of infants. A central problem for many was the "nature versus nurture" issue. This refers to the question of whether visual abilities are inborn as part of the human biological heritage (the nature account) or learned through experience (the nurture account).

In the eighteenth and nineteenth centuries, empiricist philosophers such as John Locke, David Hume, Bishop Berkeley, and John Stuart Mill suggested that mature vision was primarily a learned skill. They maintained that infants at first see the world as a flat mosaic of lines and color. Gradually, by reaching for and manipulating objects and by moving around in the world, infants learn which parts of this mosaic constitute objects and surfaces. Eventually, they learn to infer other properties of these objects, such as how far away they are. This concept of impoverished initial endowment led the great early psychologist William James to write in 1890 that infants experience the world as "one great blooming, buzzing, confusion."

Research on visual development has had a dramatic impact on the age-old nature/nurture debate. It has shown that, like adults, even young infants are able to extract important information about the world. Because this competence is present before infants actively reach for objects, the traditional empiricist account is no longer tenable.

The research is more consistent with the view of the nature side of the nature/nurture debate, sometimes referred to as the "nativist theory." This view holds that people are biologically prepared to see the world. Many important visual abilities are present at birth, and others emerge in the first several months of infancy. For example, J. J. Gibson and Eleanor Gibson note that humans, like all animals, evolved in a world of objects and events. To survive, younger as well as older animals need to see the world in terms of these basic units and not as a meaningless mosaic of lines and colors. The Gibsons believe that, because they are essential to survival, many visual abilities are "built into" the infant.

Visual-development researchers now recognize two important qualifications to the nativist theory. First, it is unlikely that experience cannot have an effect on visual development. For example, animals raised in extremely abnormal conditions such as complete darkness fail to develop many visual abilities. Second, while many basic capacities seem to be inborn, there are certainly measurable changes in visual abilities in the first year. Some of these are probably caused by changes in the parts of the brain that are concerned with vision. Others, such as early improvements in visual acuity, are caused by changes in the optics and anatomy of the eye.

Bibliography

Bornstein, M. H. "Chromatic Vision in Infancy." In *Advances in Child Development and Behavior*, edited by H. W. Reese and L. P. Lipsitt. New York: Academic Press, 1978. Bornstein argues against the view that the division of wavelengths into colors is determined by the culture in which one lives. Instead, he reviews research with infants indicating that biological makeup plays a critical role in the way people perceive colors.

Granrud, C. E., ed. *Visual Perception and Cognition in Infancy*. Hillsdale, N.J.: Lawrence Erlbaum, 1991. A collection of chapters by leading researchers in the field, this book covers a wide range of topics in visual development. The authors review their own research findings and consider the theoretical implications of their work. The writing is mostly nontechnical but challenging.

Haith, Marshall M. *Rules That Babies Look By*. Hillsdale, N.J.: Lawrence Erlbaum, 1980. This book presents an entertaining description of how infants choose where to look and how their eye movements change with age. Easily the most readable summary of eye-movement research.

Maurer, Daphne, and Charles Maurer. *The World of the Newborn*. New York: Basic Books, 1988. This book won the American Psychological Association book award for 1988. The award was well deserved, because the book is both readable and informative in describing how newborns see as well as hear, feel, and think.

Mehler, Jacques, and Robin Fox, eds. *Neonate Cognition: Beyond the Blooming, Buzzing, Confusion*. Hillsdale, N.J.: Lawrence Erlbaum, 1985. This collection of chapters by leading researchers in the field is the predecessor of the more recent volume edited by Granrud, listed above. Presents many intriguing examples of the capabilities possessed by infants in the first eight months after birth.

Yonas, A., and C. E. Granrud. "The Development of Sensitivity to Kinetic, Binocular, and Pictorial Depth Information in Human Infants." In *Brain Mechanisms and Spatial Vision*, edited by David J. Ingle, David N. Lee, and Marc Jeannerod. Boston: Nijhoff, 1985. Describes a program of research that shows that infants begin to use the three types of depth cues at different ages. Summarizes many experiments and includes useful illustrations that make it easy to understand how infants' depth perception is studied.

Lincoln G. Craton

Cross-References

Cognitive Development Theory: Piaget, 553; Color Vision, 611; Depth Perception, 796; Infant Perceptual Systems, 1290; Pattern Vision, 1752; Visual Neural Processing, 2629.

VISUAL ILLUSIONS

Type of psychology: Sensation and perception
Field of study: Vision

When a figure is consistently perceived incorrectly or in a distorted fashion, that figure is called an illusion. Examples include the appearance of straight lines as curved, seemingly magnified line length, and lines seeming to exist when in fact no lines are there. By studying why illusions occur, scientists may learn how the human visual system normally works to select and interpret incoming information.

Principal terms
COGNITION: thought processes; the organization of information that occurs between a stimulus and a response
HORIZONTAL-VERTICAL ILLUSION: the appearance of a vertical line as longer than a horizontal line of the same length
ILLUSORY TRIANGLE: a triangle that is perceived in the absence of actual lines or edges forming a figure
MUELLER-LYER ILLUSION: the perception of a line bounded by outward-pointing arrows as smaller than a line of the same length bounded by inward-pointing arrows
POGGENDORFF ILLUSION: the perception that the two segments of a diagonal formed when the diagonal intersects two vertical lines, passes behind them, and emerges on their other side are not continuous
WUNDT-HERING ILLUSION: the perception of a straight horizontal line that crosses several radiating lines as curved

Overview

When most people view the Mueller-Lyer illusion shown in figure 1, the line with the outward-pointing arrows looks shorter than the line with the inward-pointing arrows. Both lines are really the same size. This misperception does not occur because there is too little light to see correctly or because the viewer's eyes are weak. Rather, there is no obvious reason for the error. Determining the factors underlying the perception of illusions is the main focus of research on illusions.

Accounts of why people see visual illusions fall into two main categories. Biological explanations focus on how the anatomy of the eye or processing in the nervous system may cause incorrect perception. Cognitive theories, which focus on thinking, propose that some kind of interpretation or decision making is involved in seeing illusions.

Several different biological accounts have been proposed. Two of the illusions which biological theories have tried to explain are the Wundt-Hering illusion and the illusory triangle, both shown in figure 1. In the Wundt-Hering illusion, the straight

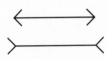 

Mueller-Lyer	Wundt-Hering	Illusory Triangle

Poggendorff   Horizontal-Vertical

Figure 1: EXAMPLES OF VISUAL ILLUSIONS

horizontal line looks curved. The illusory triangle is seen by most people even though in fact there is no outline around it. Biological theories try to account for these by describing how humans see edges. When a brighter surface abuts a darker surface, an edge is seen. According to one account, when cells in the human visual system are stimulated by a bright surface, they not only fire and send messages to the brain that a surface is present but also prevent other nearby cells from firing. This prevention of others cells from firing is called inhibition. When a person looks at a figure such as the Wundt-Hering illusion, the pattern of firing and inhibition may cause the horizontal line to look bowed. Other biological accounts propose that the human eyes and brain analyze the world by reducing all the patterns they see to dark and light bars. Because of the way the brain breaks down the dark and bright patterns, a person may "see" edges when no edges are there, as is the case with the illusory triangle.

Although it is clear that biology plays a role in why people see illusions, it is not the whole story. For example, biological theories are not concerned with how people interpret the illusions. Biological accounts also cannot explain why some illusions seem to go away as one continues to view them. It is therefore necessary to look at the cognitive theories that address thinking and learning.

One of the major cognitive accounts of illusions was presented by Richard Gregory. His account emphasized the roles of distance and size. Basically, an object that is close to a viewer looks larger than the same object if it is far away. Similarly, if two objects appear the same size, but one is close to the viewer while the other is far away, the viewer knows that the far one must be bigger. If one views a tree in a field,

Figure 2: THE MUELLER-LYER ILLUSION
CORRESPONDING TO AN INSIDE CORNER
AND AN OUTSIDE CORNER

one can close an eye, hold a thumb close to the open eye, and make one's thumb as big as the tree. One does not think the tree is the size of the thumb, and realizes the thumb is much closer than the tree to one's eye.

Gregory said that perception of the Mueller-Lyer illusion is based on misinterpreting cues for distance. Figure 2 shows an inside corner, corresponding to the inward-pointing arrows of the illusion, and an outside corner, corresponding to the outward-pointing arrows. Because the line with the inward-pointing arrows is seen as an inside corner, it is intepreted as being farther away than the other line. Because the two lines are the same size but one is interpreted as being farther away, that line appears longer—just as one knows the tree is bigger than one's thumb.

Gregory's theory is convincing; however, it does not explain why illusory distortion seems to go away as one gets more practice looking at some illusions. When one first looks at the Poggendorff illusion in figure 1, the right diagonal line seems too high to be a continuation of the left diagonal. If one repeatedly looks at the figure, however, the two diagonals appear to be one interrupted line. Stanley Coren and his associates proposed that as people have more practice looking at some illusions, they learn to scan the figures more accurately and so see the illusions less.

Neither the biological theories nor the cognitive theories fully explain why people see illusions. Biological theories do not account for the effects of learning on seeing illusions. Cognitive theories cannot explain why figures with bright edges result in stronger illusions than figures with dim edges. Both perspectives, however, contribute to a better understanding of how people see the world.

Applications

Although people may not realize it, they probably see illusions regularly. When they see a familiar tree cut down, people are surprised at how much shorter it looks than it did when it was upright. This demonstrates the horizontal-vertical illusion in figure 1, in which a vertical line looks longer than a horizontal line of the same length. People who play video games may have seen a figure move diagonally across the screen and behind a surface. They may then have expected the object to emerge from behind the surface lower than it actually did, just as would be expected for the Poggendorff illusion. These illusions can have significant implications. For example, an architect who wishes to design a structure that looks as tall as it is wide would actually have to make the length smaller than the width. A pilot who needs to estimate where another plane will emerge from behind a cloud bank it entered diagonally would have to take into account the distortion produced by the Poggendorff illusion.

Although illusions can affect important decisions, perception is reasonably accurate most of the time: People do not walk off cliffs because they see illusory surfaces or drive off straight roads because they appear curved. Yet the study of illusions has implications for most people. By studying how different groups of people see illusions, researchers can learn more about both how the visual system works and how differences between people cause them to see the world differently.

Differences in perception of illusions have been found among people of different ages. Children tended to see illusions such as the Mueller-Lyer and Wundt-Hering more than did young adults, who tended to see them more than did elderly people. Robert Pollack proposed that these differences occur because as people get older they become less sensitive to brightness and to the edges produced by differences in brightness. These age differences have implications for designing environments used by elderly people. For example, the edges of stairs should be bright so that elderly people can see them and avoid losing their footing.

Cross-cultural differences in perception of illusions have also been found. Researchers studied how traditional Zulu people of Africa saw the Mueller-Lyer illusion. The researchers assumed that since there were few right angles in the Zulus' environment, they would be less likely to interpret the illusion as corners and so would see the illusion less. As expected, traditional Zulus saw the figure more accurately than did Western people. Subsequent research was not entirely consistent with this. Pollack found that African-American children were less influenced by the illusion than were Euro-American children even though both groups came from similar environments. Pollack concluded that differences in the coloring of structures of the eye may cause these differences. What may be concluded from this research is that both culture and biology play a role in how people see the world. To understand other people, one needs to realize that their view of the world may differ from one's own for many reasons.

Context

People were aware of the existence of illusions long before there was a field called psychology. When the ancient Greeks built the Parthenon about two thousand years ago, they designed it to look perfect. Because the structure had a number of tall vertical columns, a horizontal roof would have looked bowed, like the horizontal line in the Wundt-Hering illusion. The Greeks purposely curved the roof in the opposite direction of the illusion so that it would look straight.

The scientific study of illusions began more recently, though still before psychology as a formal discipline existed. In the early and middle 1800's, scientists who considered themselves physicists and biologists started designing illusions and measuring how people saw them. These scientists believed that illusions could be used to study how the eyes and nervous system responded to the physical world. When the first psychological laboratory was founded by Wilhelm Wundt in 1879, illusions were included among the topics he investigated. Wundt was attempting to study thought. He believed that the study of illusions would help him break down thought into its building blocks. Then, in the early twentieth century, the study of illusions more or less ended.

The major psychological focus in the United States from about 1920 to 1950 was behaviorism. The behaviorists were interested only in measuring behavioral responses to objects in the environment. They were not interested in either cognition or biology and thus were not interested in illusions. In the 1950's, however, another change in psychology occurred. Psychologists became convinced that behaviorism alone could not explain human experience. Cognitive and biological processes were recognized as significant, and illusions were rediscovered as a means of studying these.

There is increasing interest in the field of psychology in thought processes, biological processes, and the interrelationships between the two. The study of illusions and the differences between groups in the perception of illusions will continue to shed light on these relationships. In addition, because society is increasingly technological, psychologists are concerned with people's use of this technology. Information, whether in computer graphics, video displays, or on the dashboards of cars, must be presented in such a way that it is seen accurately and not distorted by any illusion. The more that is known about how humans see, the more effectively machines can be designed to present information.

Although the study of illusions will continue to be significant for both theoretical and practical reasons, there is another reason to continue their study: They are fascinating. A person with otherwise accurate vision interprets two simple lines wrong simply because they have arrows on their ends, and sometimes sees a triangle when there is no triangle. People have been interested in illusions for at least two thousand years, and probably will continue to be for many more.

Bibliography

Block, J. Richard, and Harold Yuker. *Can You Believe Your Eyes?* Klamath Falls, Ore.: Gardner Press, 1989. A popular book for the layperson, this enjoyable work presents and describes excellent examples of hundreds of different illusions. Does not focus on the theories describing why illusions are seen; however, it does give the reader much to think about.

Coren, Stanley, and Joan Stern Girgus. *Seeing Is Deceiving: The Psychology of Visual Illusions.* Hillsdale, N.J.: Lawrence Erlbaum, 1978. Presents the history of people's interest in illusions, including the early research in the area, and provides a very complete summary of the theories and research on illusions through the late 1970's. Written for psychologists but can be appreciated by the layperson.

Gregory, Richard Langton. *Eye and Brain: The Psychology of Seeing.* New York: McGraw-Hill, 1978. An excellent introduction to the study of vision. An older book, but one that provides the reader with the background to understand more recent and more technical information. Includes a chapter specifically on illusions and one on perception and art in which illusions are also discussed.

Petry, Susan, and Glenn E. Meyer. *The Perception of Illusory Contours.* New York: Springer-Verlag, 1987. A collection of reports that was not written for the layperson; however, its examples of different illusory contour figures, such as the illusory triangle, can be very valuable to the nonexpert reader. Written by leading researchers; highly technical.

Rock, Irvin, ed. *The Perceptual World.* New York: W. H. Freeman, 1990. A collection of articles that originally appeared in *Scientific American.* Two deal specifically with theories of why people see illusions or illusory contour figures such as the illusory triangle. The remaining articles, while not specifically on illusions, provide a context for the study of illusions.

Eileen Astor-Stetson

Cross-References

Depth Perception, 796; Gestalt Laws of Organization, 1082; Pattern Vision, 1752; Perceptual Constancies, 1771; Vision: Brightness and Contrast, 2610; Visual Development, 2616; Visual Neural Processing, 2629.

VISUAL NEURAL PROCESSING

Type of psychology: Sensation and perception
Fields of study: Nervous system; vision

All the visual information that humans receive is sent to the brain on the fibers of nerve cells. Each cell is sensitive to particular features of the world at particular locations. The features that are detected are indicative of what kinds of things humans see best, and they explain why they sometimes see illusions.

Principal terms
CORTEX: a sheetlike layer of nerve cells covering the brain; the site where perception takes place
NEURON: a nerve cell with a long fiber that sends signals to other neurons or to muscles
RECEPTIVE FIELD: the region and pattern in space to which a single neuron responds
RETINA: the light-sensitive area at the back of the eye, containing the receptors that detect light
VISUAL RECEPTOR: a cell in the retina that converts light energy of a particular range of wavelengths into an electrical signal

Overview

The visual system has the job of taking an image of the light coming into the eye and extracting useful information from it. The visual system is organized into several levels, each with millions of neurons that share the same locations for their inputs and outputs.

The first stage of information processing takes place in the retina. There, light is changed into electrical signals in cells called receptors. Each receptor is sensitive only to a small area of the visual world: The receptor responds only when light strikes it. The part of the world to which the cell responds can be thought of as a receptive field, a location from which information is received. So the receptive field of the receptor is a small, roughly circular patch about as big as the cell itself.

There are four basic types of receptors, each specialized for picking up a different kind of light. The rod-shaped cells are the most numerous. They are sensitive to very low light levels and are the only cells active in night vision. The cones, the other kind of cells, come in three kinds, each most sensitive to a different color or wavelength of light. Cones can be most sensitive to either red, green, or blue light. The cones are the only kinds of cells in the fixation point, the part of the retina used to look directly at something. They become less common with increasing distance from the fixation point.

The fibers that leave the retina have a different kind of receptive field. Each is excited when a small light probe hits its center, and inhibited when light hits a surrounding patch. Half the cells have the reverse organization, with inhibition in the center and excitation in the surround (Stephen Kuffler, 1953). This organization has several advantages. First, the cells are not as sensitive to the absolute level of light, for the inhibitory and excitatory regions tend to cancel each other. Second, the cells become more sensitive to edges and discontinuities in the light distribution on the retina.

In addition to having a center-surround organization, these cells are sensitive to large, moving patterns, even if they are distant from the centers of the receptive fields. Once a cell is activated by a stimulus on the receptive field center or surround, a large moving contour as much as 90 degrees from the center can change the amount of activation. This is a weak effect, but the area over which it works is enormous: A receptive field center and surround might be 1 degree in diameter, more than a thousand times smaller than the area over which the periphery effect works. This means that in the real world, where texture and motion are everywhere, a cell might be more strongly affected by effects outside the center-surround receptive field than by events inside it (Bruce Bridgeman, 1988).

After further processing in another visual center, where more inhibition is added, visual signals reach the cortex. Here the receptive fields are no longer round; they appear elongated, like bars and edges with inhibitory surrounds (David Hubel and Torsten Wiesel, 1962). Some seem to respond best to bars and edges (simple cells), while others respond best to a bar or edge anywhere within the receptive field (complex cells), and still others prefer bars that end within the receptive field (hypercomplex cells). This information about receptive fields leads to the idea of feature detectors, nerve cells that code a psychologically meaningful aspect of the visual world. Extending this idea, one should expect to see neurons that detect more and more complex features, until finally there would be cells that would detect perceptual units—such as one's grandmother. It is easy to see why this idea does not work: How would the brain know that one cell means "grandmother" while another means something else? How would the cells become connected to detect new objects?

A closer look at the receptive fields in the cortex has resulted in a different theory of how perception works in the brain. Examined more precisely, a simple cell detects not a bar but a small patch of a grating with fuzzy bars. The cell is most sensitive at one location (the "bar" of the old bar-detector idea), and its sensitivity trails off on both sides. The spacing between bars is the spatial frequency of the grating; it expresses how frequently one encounters bars as one moves across the receptive field. The visual world is coded in a large number of cells sensitive to a range of orientations and spatial frequencies (Russell DeValois and Karen DeValois, 1988). Any pattern can be duplicated with enough gratings, and even the simplest visual scenes would be coded by many neurons operating together.

Beyond the stage at which it enters the cortex, visual information spreads out to more than a dozen separate maps of the retina, laid out over the cortex. Each appears to be specialized for a different function, such as movement or visual-motor coordination. The feeling that vision is a single sense is contradicted in the brain, where different functions are handled in different ways by different structures.

Applications

Since everything that one sees passes through the receptive fields at each stage of vision, the coding at these stages can affect perception. One does not see the outside world, but only the world as reported by one's nerve cells. Several illusions and properties of vision are explained by the coding in those cells. At the earliest level of visual processing, one sees things far more sharply at the fixation point than elsewhere because the receptive fields are smallest at the center of the retina. This pattern of smaller receptive fields at the center of vision is maintained throughout the many levels of visual processing in the brain.

Another illusion of vision, so compelling that one is normally quite unaware of it, is that high-quality color information is available only in a small region near the fixation point. Beyond 20 to 30 degrees from fixation, color resolution becomes quite poor because there are few color-sensitive receptive fields in those regions. Yet the feeling that everything is in full color is maintained by one's memory and imagery abilities.

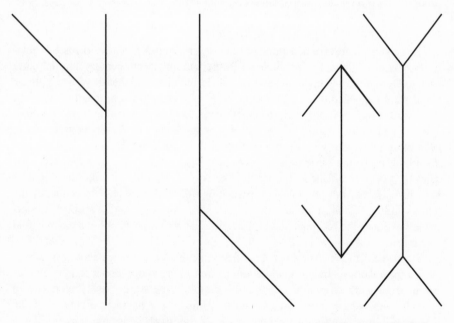

Poggendorff Illusion   Mueller-Lyer Illusion

Some illusions are caused by shortcuts that the visual system takes in processing sensory information. The Mueller-Lyer illusion (see figure) is an example. The difference in the apparent lengths of the parallel lines is probably caused by a combination of inhibitory interactions between the neurons that code for different line orientations and the lowest spatial frequencies that code the overall length of the figure. Perspective illusions may be caused by similar mechanisms. The Poggendorff illusion is another example of the codes in receptive fields resulting in an incorrect perception. The oblique lines are actually continuations of the same line but appear not to meet because of shortcuts that the visual system takes in coding the areas near the intersections of the obliques and the parallel lines.

Another area of application is in the growing field of high-definition television (HDTV). The problem is to compress more information into an existing television channel without degrading the quality of the picture. In conventional television, each point in the picture is recorded independently of all the others, in much the same way that the eye's retinal receptors pick up light. If the image is processed instead into patches of gratings, much as images are in the cortex, a picture that appears completely natural can be transmitted with only one-tenth as much information capacity. The reason for this is that people are very sensitive to "snow," pointlike errors in transmission. If an error is distributed over a fuzzy grating component, however, people tend not to notice it because their own visual systems code information in the same way. Using schemes such as this, engineers can squeeze ten times more information into a normal television channel.

Context

The search for feature detectors and the description of receptive fields is a relatively new development in psychology. In the late nineteenth century, physiologists such as Hermann von Helmholtz and Ewald Hering lamented that they knew nothing about what happened to visual information after it entered the retina. The development of electronics in the early twentieth century made it possible to record brain activity, and by the middle of the century, physiologists could record from single cells using electrodes with tips so small that they could record from a cell without disturbing it. At the same time, psychologists had developed a description of how sensory processes affected experience. The two streams of scientific development have not merged in a physiological psychology that takes as its subject matter the understanding of behavior and experience in terms of physiology. Part of that effort is the linking of the receptive fields of single cells with aspects of human perceptual experience.

One of the difficulties of this field is that most of what is known about experience comes from work on humans, while almost everything known about receptive fields comes from work on animals. It is also possible to measure sensory processes in animals with behavioral measures, and to compare the physical structures of the brains of humans and animals. One result of this work is an appreciation of the astonishing similarity of human and animal vision. As far as can be told, the visual systems of the Old World monkeys are nearly identical to those of humans. There are some minor differences at the margins, partly because human systems are simply larger than those of monkeys, but all the major features that can be identified are the same. The visual world of a macaque monkey is very much like a human's. Both have similar visual acuity and retinal structure, the same kinds of visual receptors with the same pigments, similar binocular vision, and so on. The study of animal vision, in a way, has brought humans and animals closer together; their common evolution is more clearly recognized. Study of the physiology of human experience gives scientists an appreciation of the human's place in nature.

The benefits of basic research are often unexpected, and the physiology of vision is no exception. The use of physiology-like coding schemes in television is an example. Other roles for visual physiology now include the design of human-machine interactions that are natural and easy to learn on the human side, and storage of visual information in electronic forms that are accessible and efficient. Many of the benefits are unpredictable, however, and the satisfaction of people's curiosity about how they are constructed and how they perceive their world cannot be measured.

Bibliography

Bridgeman, Bruce. *The Biology of Behavior and Mind.* New York: John Wiley & Sons, 1988. The first chapter describes the history and approach of physiological psychology, and the following two chapters give an overview of how the brain functions. Chapters 4 to 6 explain the physiology of the sensory systems, emphasizing vision. These chapters provide a good background for reading the remaining references given here.

DeValois, Russell L., and Karen K. DeValois. *Spatial Vision.* New York: Oxford University Press, 1988. Receptive fields are reviewed at all levels as they relate to pattern recognition, using a modern spatial-frequency approach. The first few chapters provide an excellent introduction to the subject.

Hubel, David. "Exploration of the Primary Visual Cortex." *Nature* 299 (October 7, 1982): 515-524. This article in a nonspecialized journal reviews Hubel and Wiesel's Nobel Prize-winning research on feature detectors in the cat. Though the text becomes technical in spots, the figures give an impression of what cortical receptive fields look like and how they are measured.

Kaufman, Lloyd. *Sight and Mind: An Introduction to Visual Perception.* New York: Oxford University Press, 1974. This beautifully written volume reviews the methods that the brain uses to make sense of visual input patterns. Includes work on thresholds, illusions, and color.

Kuffler, Stephen W. "Discharge Patterns and Functional Organization of Mammalian Retina." *Journal of Neurophysiology* (January 16, 1953): 37-68. Another seminal article, this was the first to describe the receptive fields of the cells whose fibers exit the eye. Using 1950's technology, the article's methods are more accessible than those of more recent computer-controlled studies. The antagonistic center-surround organization of retinal neurons is described here for the first time.

Bruce Bridgeman

Cross-References

The Central and Peripheral Nervous Systems, 494; The Cerebral Cortex, 500; Neurons, 1661; Pattern Recognition as a Cognitive Process, 1747; Pattern Vision, 1752; Visual Illusions, 2622; Visual System Anatomy, 2640.

THE VISUAL SPECTRUM

Type of psychology: Sensation and perception
Field of study: Vision

The visual spectrum (light) is a narrow band of electromagnetic radiation. Humans are able to detect electromagnetic wavelengths from about 370 to 700 nanometers with their unaided eyes; different wavelengths are interpreted by the brain as differences in color. Light provides humans with information which allows them to function more effectively in their physical environment.

Principal terms

COLOR: the brain's interpretation of electromagnetic radiation of different wavelengths within the range of visible light
ELECTROMAGNETIC RADIATION: energy which radiates from a source such as the sun and is created when atoms are exposed to sufficient heat
LIGHT: electromagnetic radiation with wavelengths between 370 and 700 nanometers (the range detectable by most human eyes)
NANOMETER: a billionth of a meter
WAVELENGTH: the measured distance from crest to crest of a wave

Overview

The visual spectrum is the rainbow of light, which is a very small portion of the spectrum of electromagnetic radiation. Electromagnetic radiation also includes everything from cosmic rays to radio waves. Someone looking at an apple and describing it as "red" is responding to the effects of light reflected from the surface of the apple to the eye and interpreted by the brain as color.

Electromagnetic radiation reaches the earth's environment from the sun. It is commonly described in terms of wavelength, although there are also particle theories which offer other explanations. Assuming that electromagnetic radiation is wavelike, scientists can measure the distance from the crest of one wave to the next. Visible light is roughly in the middle of the electromagnetic spectrum and ranges from about 370 to 700 nanometers. This relatively narrow range of wavelengths defines the visual spectrum and includes all the colors human beings are able to see. Within the visual spectrum, short wavelengths are seen as violet or blue, moderate wavelengths as green and yellow, and long wavelengths as orange and red.

If the wavelength of the electromagnetic radiation is relatively long, a person cannot see it. Wavelengths from the 700 nanometers of red light to wavelengths of about a centimeter (10 million nanometers) are described as heat or microwaves, and are used to cook food and transmit information. Television and radio use electromagnetic wavelengths in the range of 1 to 1,000 meters. Although the human eye cannot see these wavelengths, human technology has developed many instruments to detect and use them. Very short wavelengths, 400 nanometers and smaller, describe ultraviolet light, X rays, gamma rays, and cosmic rays.

Most living organisms are able to detect some form of electromagnetic radiation. There is considerable variety throughout the animal kingdom in the range of wavelengths detected. Some insects, such as bees, can detect shorter wavelengths. Bees make many of their decisions about where to land on a flower based on colors in the ultraviolet range that humans cannot even see. Human beings have an advantage when it comes to slightly longer wavelengths. Bees cannot detect red light; most human beings can. Snakes use the wavelengths longer than those detected by human vision to detect their prey. A snake can see heat.

The ability to discriminate different wavelengths of electromagnetic radiation has evolved as a means of gathering information about the environment. The ability to translate this information into the psychological experience of color allows humans to make discriminations that increase their potential for survival. The ability to see the difference between red and green light helps people to locate ripe red cherries in a tree or a brown deer in the green of the forest.

In a literal sense, objects do not have different colors. The grass in the lawn has chemicals known as pigments which either absorb the electromagnetic radiation to which they are exposed or reflect it back into the environment. If absorbed, the radiation is transformed into heat, a phenomenon one may observe while walking barefoot on a summer day across a paved road. Surfaces which are described as black absorb a high percentage of the radiation to which they are exposed.

White surfaces, on the other hand, have pigments that reflect a large percentage of the radiation to which the pigment is exposed. When many wavelengths of light enter the eye, the brain interprets the resulting combination of sensations as white light. Smooth surfaces, such as a still lake or a mirror, also reflect a large percentage of the light which strikes them, making them appear as white or a very pale color.

A person sees the grass as green because it absorbs most of the nongreen wavelengths of light and reflects the green wavelengths to the eye. What is referred to as color is the brain's interpretation of the pattern of wavelengths of light entering the eye and affecting the visual receptors. Waves in the visual spectrum have no more color than the waves that are used to X-ray a broken leg or transmit a television program. For color to be experienced, the right kind of nervous system is necessary. Just as different animals have nervous systems developed to make use of different wavelengths of radiation, human beings do not all see color in exactly the same way. Missing receptors or other abnormalities of the nervous system can make color meaningless or make a person confuse colors. This is referred to as color weakness or color blindness.

Applications

The light entering the eye can be controlled and modified for many different purposes. Colored glasses serve as filters, absorbing some of the light to which they are exposed and allowing other wavelengths to be transmitted to the eye. Dark-gray sunglasses reduce the amount of light reaching the eye by absorbing light in most wavelengths.

Yellow or red lenses reduce the amount of light from the shorter wavelengths that can reach the eye. These lenses are often called blue blockers, or ultraviolet (UV) blocking lenses. These lenses, which reduce the amount of UV light reaching the eye, are recommended for people who spend much of their time outdoors, even if the light is not bright enough to require dark lenses. UV light has been found to increase the possibility of the development of cataracts.

Yellow lenses have also traditionally been used by pilots and hunters. Their ability to block the blue end of the spectrum can increase the ability to detect objects in fog or hazy weather. They increase the contrast between objects of different colors. Some people find yellow lenses irritating; yellow lenses make everything look both brighter and more yellow, and they cause problems with color identification.

Sir Isaac Newton observed that if as few as three basic colors of light were present at the same time, the resulting combination would be white light. If the colors are combined selectively, all other colors can be created. This theory is the basis of many contemporary applications, such as color television. A television screen has thousands of small areas which can be turned off or illuminated by red, green, or blue light. As one steps away from the screen, the dots of colored light blend to create the impression of a colored image with thousands of different colors.

A normal human eye detects color in much the same way that a television creates it. The human eye has four types of cells. One type (the rods) responds to very dim light and is responsible for a person's ability to see with low levels of illumination, such as at twilight or in a darkened theater. The other three receptors are different types of cones. One responds best to wavelengths of 450 nanometers, one to wavelengths of 525 nanometers, and one to wavelengths of 555 nanometers. These wavelengths can be roughly described as blue, green, and red. Stimulating these cells individually would most likely produce the sensations of violet, blue-green, and a yellow-red. Responses of these cells to differing locations and intensities of light are combined by the brain to produce the sensation of color vision.

Context

When Sir Isaac Newton directed sunlight through a prism and projected the resulting band of colors on the wall, he described a series of colors that are now used to describe the spectrum. He reported seeing red, orange, yellow, green, blue, and violet light in the resulting spectral rainbow. He determined the separate identities of the colors by a series of experiments with prisms and filters. A red filter between the sunlight and the prism allowed only the red light from the spectrum to come through the prism, suggesting to Newton that red light is a separate entity not made of other combinations of wavelengths of light.

Newton's spectrum was observed using sunlight. When other sources of light are used (heated metals or gases), the light may be missing some wavelengths, or it may be more intense at some points of the spectrum. Since the source of light determines the wavelength of the light reflected to the eye, objects can appear to be different colors when the source of light is changed. A white vase looks pink under red light, and appears pale blue when the light is blue. The pants and shirt that match in the store under fluorescent light may not look the same color outside, in the light of the sun.

Even people's ability to perceive differences in wavelengths does not mean that all humans understand color in the same way. The visual spectrum has social and psychological as well as physiological characteristics. One can study the way people understand color by looking at how languages describe color differences. Some languages have very few labels for color and do not appear to make fine distinctions. Some languages only discriminate between black and white, or light and dark. Most languages have about a dozen major color names which correspond to the basic colors most people can identify. Even languages with a wide variety of color words do not have enough terms to differentiate the more than one thousand different colors the average person can distinguish.

Colors can also be described in terms of the effect that they have on people. Blues and greens are described as cool, while yellow, orange, and red are thought of as warm. (This contradicts physical law. When an object is heated, it glows red when it is relatively cool and gives off blue light when very hot.) Painters understand that blues and greens appear to recede from the plane of the surface to which they are applied, while oranges and reds appear to be closer to the viewer. Colors can be described as calming or as stimulating. Color preferences are thought to describe psychological states, and color therapy recommends the use of particular colors to control behavior.

The visual spectrum provides people with information about their world, and humans have developed sensitive structures to detect it. Human beings can live without color or light; however, its presence makes life easier and increases the variety of their experiences.

Bibliography

Ackerman, Diane. *A Natural History of the Senses.* New York: Random House, 1990. Provides a subjective look at the senses. The elegant descriptions of the experience of vision include interesting facts and comparisons which heighten an understanding of what it really means to see.

Hubel, David H. *Eye, Brain, and Vision.* New York: W. H. Freeman, 1988. A detailed but not overly difficult book by a well-known vision researcher. Includes many interesting facts about vision, and beautiful photographs and illustrations. The chapter on color vision has interesting information about the visual spectrum and how the eye and brain interpret it.

Mueller, Conrad George, and Mae Rudolph. *Light and Vision.* New York: Time, 1966. A commonly available book which uses striking photography and illustrations to present basic information about light and vision.

Smith, Jillyn. *Senses and Sensibilities.* New York: John Wiley & Sons, 1989. This interesting and readable book on the senses includes a good description of the spectrum as well as a number of interesting historical facts about early explorers in the vision field.

Watson, Philip. *Light Fantastic.* New York: Lothrop, Lee & Shepard, 1982. Written for children, but useful for anyone attempting to understand the visual spectrum. Provides simple instructions for the creation of demonstrations of the effects of light and color. The visual spectrum must be experienced to be appreciated.

Susan J. Shapiro

Cross-References

Color Blindness, 606; Color Vision, 611; Vision: Brightness and Contrast, 2610; Visual Neural Processing, 2629; Visual System Anatomy, 2640.

VISUAL SYSTEM ANATOMY

Type of psychology: Sensation and perception
Field of study: Vision

The anatomy of the visual system uniquely enables humans to perceive an astounding array of complex information over varying distances in a brief moment of time. An understanding of this system provides insights into visual impairments and how to overcome them, as well as the development of artificial vision in humans and machines.

Principal terms
ACCESSORY EYE STRUCTURES: those parts of the eye that contribute to focusing light onto the retina; principal ones are the cornea, iris, pupil, and lens
ACCOMMODATION: the ability of the lens to focus light on the retina by changing its shape
FOVEA: the central part of the retina that is densest in cone cells and is therefore the area of sharpest visual acuity
PHOTORECEPTOR: a specialized nerve cell that can transform light into a neural message; rods are specialized for black-and-white vision, cones for color vision
RETINA: the thin membrane on the back of the eye that contains photoreceptors
TRANSDUCTION: the process of changing physical energy, such as light, into neural messages
VISUAL CORTEX: the top six cell layers in the back of the brain that are specialized for organizing and interpreting visual information

Overview

Humans have three senses capable of detecting information at a distance: audition, smell, and vision. While smell depends on simple stimuli (odors), and hearing depends on time (sounds must change over time for meaningful audition to occur), the visual system is capable of analyzing complex stimuli, such as three dimensions, and may capture a multitude of diverse information in a brief moment of time (one picture may indeed be worth more than a thousand words). It is little wonder that most people consider vision their most prized sense. Indeed, the importance of the eye to the body is demonstrated by how well it is protected: It is encased in a bony socket, able to be covered reflexively or voluntarily by eyelids, and bordered by eyebrows and eyelashes to keep foreign matter from entering the open eye. What the visual system does that is so important is to transform a form of energy known as electromagnetic radiation (light) into a neurological experience that people call sight. How light becomes sight can be broken down into three phases: focusing, transduction, and neurological processing.

Focusing light is the primary responsibility of the accessory structures of the eye, depicted in section A of the figure. Light first enters the eye through a thin, transparent membrane called the cornea, which bends light waves to a narrower focus on the retina. The remainder of the eye is covered by the sclera, a protective tough white membrane. Light next passes through a chamber containing the aqueous humor, a transparent watery fluid that nourishes the cornea and the front of the eye.

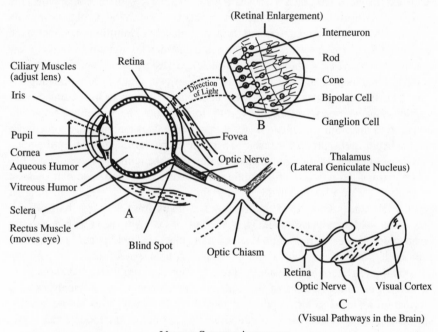

VISUAL SYSTEM ANATOMY

Light then enters a second, larger chamber through a small opening called the pupil. The size of the pupil is controlled by two pigmented muscles called the iris. These muscles, which provide one's eye color, regulate the amount of light entering the second chamber. When illumination is low, the iris dilates (widens) the pupil to allow more light in, and it constricts (narrows) the pupil as light brightens. Once light passes through the pupil, it enters a flexible structure called the lens, the shape of which can be changed by ciliary muscles. The lens flattens in order to focus light from distant objects on the retina and becomes rounder in order to focus closer objects on the retina. The focusing process resulting from the ability of the lens to change its shape is called accommodation.

After light rays are refracted (bent) by the lens, they are projected onto the retina, a thin membrane on the back of the eye that contains cells that record the light images. The light rays must pass through another nourishing fluid, the vitreous humor, that keeps the main chamber from collapsing. In the center of the retina is an area called the fovea, which contains the greatest number of light-sensitive cells. Vision is usually best when light falls directly on the fovea; consequently, people are constantly moving their eyes with rectus muscles to ensure that the image from what they are viewing falls directly on the retina.

Transforming electromagnetic radiation into neural activity is accomplished in the retina by photoreceptor cells (section B of the figure). Light passes through several cell layers in the retina until it strikes the two main types of photoreceptors: the approximately 6 million cones, which are specialized for day and color vision and are primarily located in the fovea, and the approximately 125 million rods, which are specialized for black-and-white and night vision and increase in number farther away from the fovea. When a photon (light particle) strikes a photoreceptor, it causes a chemical contained in the rod or cone to split in two, creating a neural impulse (message). Photoreceptors connect with bipolar cells, which in turn connect with ganglion cells, whose axons (output "wires") form the optic nerve sending retinal information to the brain. Interneurons form interconnections among these three types of retinal cells and sharpen the image. There are no photoreceptors where the optic nerve leaves the eye, resulting in a small blind spot in the retina.

After exiting the retina, half the optic nerve fibers, from the inside half (nearest the nose) of each eye's visual field, cross to the opposite hemisphere of the brain at the optic chiasm (section C of the figure). The fibers from the outer half of each eye's visual field do not cross over. Thus, if one looks straight ahead with one's right eye and puts a finger in front of that eye, dividing the visual field in half, information from the left half of the field would go to the left hemisphere; that from the right half would go to the right hemisphere. From the optic chiasm, nerve messages go to the lateral geniculate nucleus of the thalamus, which combines and analyzes such information as form, color, depth, and movement from both eyes before sending information to the visual cortex. In the visual cortex (the occipital lobe), many cells (called feature detectors) appear to respond only to specific visual stimuli, such as dots, lines, or movement. This "feature-detection" model assumes that the brain "sees" by putting together the simple features of light. An alternative, the "spatial frequency-filter" model, suggests that thousands of brain cells are simultaneously engaged in analyzing broad patterns of light and dark rather than synthesizing simple stimuli. However the brain deals with retinal information, one thing is certain: People interpret what their eyes detect in their brains.

Applications

Given the complex anatomical route that transpires before light becomes sight, it is remarkable that humans see as well as they do. Malfunctions anywhere in the visual system can cause distortions in visual perception. Retracing the pathway of the visual system, one can identify some common visual problems associated with anatomical defects and the corrective steps that can alleviate some of these problems.

Light first enters the cornea, which must remain transparent for visual clarity. If the aqueous humor chemical balance is upset, it can result in the cornea becoming cloudy. This can be corrected by a number of procedures, the most severe of which is a corneal transplant. The aqueous humor must recycle approximately every four hours to remain clear. If too much aqueous humor is produced or it is blocked from exiting, pressure builds up inside the eye, resulting in glaucoma. This disease can lead to blindness if not treated early.

The pupil allows light passing through the aqueous humor to enter the lens. As people age, it is common that the pupil does not open as wide, letting less light in, thus causing "night blindness," or difficulty in seeing under low illumination, a major problem. Another consequence of aging is the hardening of the lens, making it more difficult to accommodate to close objects. This is the reason why many adults, usually beginning in their forties, need reading glasses. Two other widespread problems associated with the lens are astigmatism, caused by surface and shape defects of the lens, and cataracts, a clouding of the lens that is present at birth in some but is most common in the elderly, affecting in varying degrees 75 percent of people over sixty-five years of age. Astigmatism can be corrected by lenses; cataracts by surgery.

The eye's shape is also important to proper vision. The vitreous humor, in conjunction with the sclera, helps to maintain the round shape of the eye. Sometimes impurities circulating through this fluid result in seeing spots before one's eyes. If the eyeball elongates between the lens and retina, nearsightedness (difficulty with distance vision) results; if the eyeball narrows between the lens and retina, farsightedness (difficulty with close vision) results. These two common problems are usually corrected with glasses or contact lenses. Continued eyestrain, such as from long periods of reading without resting one's eyes, may result in an elongation of the eyeball, leading to or worsening nearsightedness.

Retinal factors account for differences between day and night vision and problems with color vision. People see better at night by looking slightly to the side of an object, directing light slightly away from the fovea, thus using more rods than cones (which do not work well under dim illumination). Rods are connected to many ganglion cells; a small amount of light striking many rods can therefore effectively stimulate the ganglion cell which is connected to those rods. During daylight illumination, one sees best by looking straight at something, focusing light on the fovea. Acuity (visual sharpness) is best at the fovea, because cones are more densely packed there. Furthermore, because most cones are connected to only one ganglion cell, this ensures great acuity, since little information about which cone is being stimulated is lost. Cones are also responsible for color vision; animals such as dogs, which do not have cones, do not perceive color. In humans, many of the different defects in color vision are caused by having the wrong photopigments or by an absence of photopigments in the cones.

Defects in the optic nerve that prevent messages from the retina from reaching the visual cortex result in blindness. Researchers have wondered whether vision could be restored if a way could be found to bypass the damaged area and stimulate the visual cortex. William Dobelle and his associates reported in a 1977 study that such a possibility is more than science fiction. They found that if many electrodes (terminals that conduct electrical current into an area) were implanted in the visual cortices of blind volunteers' brains, stimulation of these electrodes would result in the volunteers reporting glowing patterns of light "before" their eyes. Advances in artificial vision techniques of this nature could have obvious benefits for the blind.

Research in the early 1960's by David Hubel and Torsten Wiesel demonstrated that cell development in the visual cortex is greatly affected by early experience. Studies with kittens and monkeys demonstrated that deprivation of early visual experience led to incomplete cell development in the visual cortex, thus leading to deficits in visual perception. If visual defects such as astigmatism or being cross-eyed in young children are not corrected early in life, the usual result is some type of permanent visual deficiency.

Context

It is interesting that those scientists who spent long nights observing light in the heavens, astronomers, produced the first valid insights into the function of the human eye. Johannes Kepler (1571-1630) is credited with being the first to suggest that the photoreceptive tissue of the eye is located in the retina. Christoph Scheiner, in 1625, demonstrated that the lens is the primary focusing device of the eye.

Scientific knowledge about the functioning of retinal cells began in 1876, when Franz Boll discovered in his research with fish eyes that the retina was a different color where light had shined on it. This discovery implicated a photochemical process as being crucial for visual transduction. Selig Hecht, in 1929, was among the first to describe how this process worked. In the meantime, Johannes von Kries had presented his duplicity theory of photoreceptors. Von Kries's theory, in 1895, distinguished between the functions of rods and cones. Haldan Keffer Hartline discovered the important function of the retinal interneurons in 1932; Hartline demonstrated how inhibitory messages coming from these cells help to sharpen visual perception.

While it had been known for many years that retinal cells send their messages to the visual areas of the brain's cortex, little was known about the organization and functioning of these cells until the work of David Hubel and Torsten Wiesel was first published in the early 1960's. Hubel and Wiesel, who won a Nobel Prize for their work, found that different areas in the visual field have corresponding receptive areas in the visual cortex. In other words, a kind of map of what one sees in one's field of vision is represented in the visual cortex. They also found that different layers of cortical cells are responsible for different types of visual stimulation.

As knowledge of the anatomy of the visual system increases, there are important benefits to humans and machines. The more they know about how the eye works, the more researchers and physicians can help the visually impaired. For example, advancements based on Dobelle's work with artificial vision may enable the totally blind to have increasingly more sophisticated visual experiences. Similarly, gains in knowledge about the visual system enable people to build machines that can respond more "intelligently" to their visual environments. Such developments are particularly useful in the field of robotics. Whether it exists in humans or machines, the vision of the future is one of fascinating possibilities.

Bibliography

Goldstein, E. Bruce. *Sensation and Perception.* 3d ed. Belmont, Calif.: Wadsworth, 1989. Goldstein's book is an advanced introduction to the field of sensation and perception, with more than half the chapters concerned with vision. An interesting chapter entitled "What Can Go Wrong with Your Eyes" contains information not commonly found in sensation and perception books. May be somewhat difficult reading for the layperson or high school student.

Gregory, Richard Langton. *Eye and Brain.* 4th ed. Princeton, N.J.: Princeton University Press, 1990. This inexpensive paperback is considered a classic in the field of visual perception. The book is written in a style that is easily accessible to the lay reader. Gregory's book contains many excellent illustrations. If one were to read one book on vision, this would be the book.

Keller, Helen. *The Story of My Life.* New York: Airmont, 1965. For anyone who has wondered what life would be like without a functioning visual system, this is a fascinating book to read. Presents the intriguing and courageous story of Keller's own triumph over adversity. The psychological consequences of visual disability are particularly notable.

MacKay, Donald MacCrimmon. *Behind the Eye.* Cambridge, Mass.: Basil Blackwell, 1991. Based on the Gifford lectures, given at the University of Glasgow by an expert in the field of visual processing in the brain. MacKay's book uniquely combines an understanding of neurophysiology and philosophy to approach not only the question of how the mind perceives but also the more fundamental question of what the mind is. Suitable for advanced undergraduates, but also accessible to the nonspecialist.

Matlin, Margaret W. *Perception.* 2d ed. Boston: Allyn & Bacon, 1988. Like Goldstein's book, this presents a general introduction to the field of perception. The chapters concerning vision are written in a scholarly style, but with more wit and style than most texts in the field. Matlin's book is probably easier fare for the layperson or high school student than Goldstein's.

Wolfe, Jeremy M., ed. *The Mind's Eye: Readings from Scientific American.* New York: W. H. Freeman, 1986. Twelve articles from *Scientific American* concerned with vision are featured in this book. The articles are divided into three sections: "Eyes," "Pathways to the Mind's Eye," and "In the Mind's Eye." The original writings of researchers in the field may sometimes be challenging reading for the nonspecialist, but the book is a valuable resource.

Paul J. Chara, Jr.

Cross-References

Color Blindness, 606; Color Vision, 611; Depth Perception, 796; Motion Perception, 1600; Nearsightedness and Farsightedness, 1634; Pattern Vision, 1752; Vision: Brightness and Contrast, 2610; Visual Development, 2616; Visual Neural Processing, 2629; The Visual Spectrum, 2635.

WITHIN-SUBJECT EXPERIMENTAL DESIGNS

Type of psychology: Psychological methodologies
Field of study: Experimental methodologies

Within-subject designs are experimental plans in which each participant in the experiment receives every level of the independent variable. Such designs are powerful, because individual differences cannot confound the effects of the independent variable.

Principal terms
> BALANCED LATIN SQUARE: a counterbalancing scheme in which each condition is preceded and followed equally often by every other condition
> BETWEEN-SUBJECT DESIGNS: experimental plans in which different participants receive each level of the independent variable
> CARRYOVER EFFECTS: confounding effects in within-subject designs caused by the order in which the levels of the independent variable are administered
> CONFOUNDING: the variation of other variables with the independent variable of interest, as a result of which any effects cannot be attributed with certainty to the independent variable
> COUNTERBALANCING: varying the order of conditions in order to distribute the effects of time of testing so that they are not confounded with conditions
> DEPENDENT VARIABLE: the behavior of subjects in an experiment that is measured and recorded by the experimenter
> INDEPENDENT VARIABLE: the factor of interest in an experiment, the comparison levels of which are manipulated by the experimenter
> REVERSAL DESIGN: a design in which an experimental condition intervenes between two periods in which behavior is measured but no treatment is given
> SMALL-n DESIGNS: experiments that use small numbers (n) of participants
> WITHIN-SUBJECT DESIGNS: experimental plans in which each subject receives each level of the independent variable

Overview

In an experiment, a particular comparison is produced while other factors are held constant. For example, in order to investigate the effects of music on reading comprehension, an experimenter might compare the effects of music versus no music on the comprehension of a chapter from a history textbook. The comparison that is produced—music versus no music—is called the independent variable. An independent variable must have at least two levels or values so that a comparison can be made. The behavior that is observed or measured is called the dependent variable, which would be some measure of reading comprehension in the example.

Presumably, any changes in reading comprehension during the experiment depend on changes in the levels of the independent variable. The intent of an experiment is to hold everything constant except the changes in the levels of the independent variable. If this is done, the experimenter can assume that changes in the dependent variable were caused by changes in the levels of the independent variable.

Experimental design concerns the way in which the levels of the independent variable are assigned to experimental subjects. This is a crucial concern, because the experimenter wants to make sure that the independent variable and not something else causes changes in behavior. Between-subject designs are plans in which different participants receive the levels of the independent variable. So, in terms of the example already mentioned, some people would read with music playing and other people would read without music. Within-subject designs are plans in which each participant receives each level of the manipulated variable. In a within-subject design, each person would read a history chapter both while music is playing and in silence. Each of these designs has unwanted features that make it difficult to decide whether the independent variable caused changes in the dependent variable.

Because different subjects receive each level of the independent variable in a between-subject design, the levels of the independent variable vary with the subjects in each condition. Any effect observed in the experiment could result from either the independent variable or the characteristics of the subjects in a particular condition. For example, the people who read while music is playing might simply be better readers than those who read in silence. This difference between the people in the two groups would make it difficult to determine whether music or reading ability caused changes in comprehension. When something other than the independent variable could cause the results of an experiment, the results are confounded. In between-subject designs, the potential effects of the independent variable are confounded with the different subjects in each condition. Instead of the independent variable, individual differences, such as intelligence or reading ability, could account for differences between groups. This confounding may be minimized by assigning participants to conditions randomly or by matching the different subjects in some way, but these tactics do not eliminate the potential confounding. For this and other reasons, many experimenters prefer to use within-subject designs.

Because each subject receives each level of the independent variable in within-subject designs, subjects are not confounded with the independent variable. In the example experiment, this means that both good and bad readers would read with and without music. Yet the order in which a subject receives the levels of the independent variable is confounded with the levels of the independent variable. Therefore, determining whether a change in the dependent variable occurred because of the independent variable or as a result of the timing of the administration of the treatment might be difficult. This kind of confounding is called a carryover effect.

The effects of one value of the independent variable might carry over to the period when the next level is being tested. Just as likely, an unwanted carryover effect could result because the subject's behavior changes as the experiment progresses. The subject might become better at the task because of practicing it or worse because of boredom or fatigue. Whatever the source of the carryover effects, they represent serious potential confounding.

Carryover effects can be minimized by counterbalancing. Counterbalancing means that the order of administering the conditions of an experiment is systematically varied. Consider the reading experiment: One condition is reading with music (M), and the comparison level is reading in silence (S). If all subjects received S before M, order would be confounded with condition. If half the subjects had M before S and the remaining subjects had S before M, the order of treatments would not be confounded with the nature of the treatments. This is so because both treatment conditions occur first and second equally often.

Complete counterbalancing is done when all possible orders of the independent variable are administered. Complete counterbalancing is easy when there are two or three levels of the independent variable. With four or more levels, however, complete counterbalancing becomes cumbersome because of the number of different orders of conditions that can be generated. With more than three levels, experimenters usually use a balanced Latin square to decide the order of administering conditions. In a balanced Latin square, each condition occurs at the same time period on average and each treatment precedes and follows each other treatment equally often. Imagine an experiment with four levels of the independent variable, called A, B, C, and D. One might think of these as four different types of music that are being tested in the reading-comprehension example. Suppose there are four subjects, numbered 1, 2, 3, and 4. In a balanced Latin square, the following would be the orders for the four subjects: subject 1—A, B, D, C; subject 2—B, C, A, D; subject 3—C, D, B, A; subject 4—D, A, C, B. Notice that across subjects each treatment occurs first, second, third, and fourth. Notice also that each treatment precedes and follows each other treatment. Although these four orders do not exhaust the possibilities for four treatments (there are a total of twenty-four), they do minimize the confounding from carryover effects.

Another feature favoring within-subject designs concerns inferential statistics. Because each participant serves in all conditions in within-subject designs, variability associated with individual differences among subjects has little influence on the statistical significance of the results. This means that within-subject designs are more likely than between-subject designs to yield a statistically significant result. Experimenters are more likely to find an effect attributable to the independent variable when its levels vary within subjects rather than between them.

A final reason within-subject designs are preferred to between-subject ones is that they require fewer subjects for testing. To try to minimize the confounding effects of individual differences in between-subject designs, experimenters typically assign many subjects randomly to each condition of the experiment. Since individual differences are not a hindrance in within-subject designs, fewer subjects can be tested, and there is a corresponding savings in time and effort.

Applications

Experimenters in all areas of psychology use within-subject designs. These designs are used whenever the independent variable is unlikely to have permanent carryover effects. Thus, if the characteristics of the subjects themselves are the variable of interest (such as place of birth or reading ability), those variables must be varied between subjects. If permanent carryover effects are of interest (such as learning to type as a function of practice), however, experimenters use within-subject plans.

Many experiments undertaken to solve practical problems use within-subject designs. These experiments are often small-n designs, which means that the number of subjects (n) is small—sometimes only one. Consider an experiment conducted by Betty M. Hart and her associates. They wanted to decrease the amount of crying exhibited by a four-year-old boy in nursery school. They observed his behavior for several days to find the baseline rate of crying episodes. During a ten-day period, the boy had between five and ten crying episodes each day that lasted at least five seconds. Hart and her associates noted that the teacher often tried to soothe the boy when he began crying. The researchers believed that this attention rewarded the crying behavior. Therefore, in the second phase of the experiment, the teacher ignored the boy's crying unless it resulted from an injury. Within five days, the crying episodes had decreased and remained at no more than one per day for a week. To gain better evidence that it was the teacher's attention that influenced the rate of crying, a third phase of the experiment reinstated the conditions of the baseline phase. The teacher paid attention to the boy when he whined and cried, and in a few days the level of crying was back to six or seven episodes per day.

The small-n design used by Hart and her associates is an example of a reversal design. In a reversal design, there is first a baseline phase, then a treatment phase, and finally a return to the baseline phase to make sure that it was the treatment that changed the behavior. Hart's experiment had a fourth phase in which the teacher again ignored the boy's crying, because the purpose of the treatment was to reduce the crying. In the fourth phase, the level of crying dropped to a negligible level.

When there is only one subject in an experiment, counterbalancing cannot be used to minimize carryover effects. Thus, the experience in the treatment phase of a reversal design might carry over into the second baseline phase. Experimenters seek an approximate return to the original behavior during the second baseline phase, but the behavior is seldom exactly as it was before the treatment period. Therefore, deciding about the effectiveness of the treatment introduced in the second phase may be difficult. This means that the reversal design is not a perfect experimental design. It has important applications in psychology, however, especially in clinical psychology, where practical results rather than strict experimental control are often very important.

Lise Saari conducted an experiment that used a more conventional within-subject design. Saari wanted to assess the effect of payment schedule on the performance and attitudes of beaver trappers. The trappers received an hourly wage from a forest-products company while they participated in the following experiment.

Initially, trapping performance was measured under the ordinary hourly payment plan. Later, the trappers worked under two incentive plans manipulated in a within-subject design. In the continuous-reward condition, trappers received an additional dollar for each animal that was trapped. In the second condition, trappers received a reward of four dollars when they brought in a beaver. They obtained the four dollars only if they correctly predicted twice whether the roll of a die would yield an even or an odd number. In this variable-ratio condition, the trapper could guess the correct roll one out of four times by chance alone. In summary, the trappers always received a one-dollar reward in the continuous-reward condition. In the variable-ratio condition, however, the payment of four dollars occurred once every four times on average. Therefore, the trappers averaged an extra dollar for each beaver in each condition.

To minimize carryover effects, counterbalancing the order of treatments occurred as follows. The trappers were split into two groups, which alternated between the two schedules, spending a week at a time on each. This weekly alternation of experimental payment continued for the entire trapping season.

Compared to the amount of trapping that occurred under the hourly wage, the results showed that beaver trapping increased under both the continuous and the variable-payment scheme. The increase was, however, much larger under the variable payment plan than under the continuous one. In addition, Saari found that the trappers preferred to work under the variable-ratio scheme. Since both plans yielded the same amount of extra money on average, the mode of giving the payment (continuous or variable) seems crucial.

The experiment by Saari has obvious important practical implications concerning methods of payment. Still, it is equally important that the design of the experiment was free of confounding. The counterbalancing scheme minimized the possibility of confounding the payment scheme with order. Thus, Saari could conclude that the change in attitudes and the increased trapping performance resulted from the variable payment plan, not from some confounding carryover effect.

Context

Within-subject designs have a long history of use in psychology. The psychophysics experiments conducted by Ernst Weber and Gustav Fechner in the nineteenth century were among the first within-subject experiments in psychology. The tradition of obtaining many observations on a few subjects started by Weber and Fechner continues in modern psychophysical scaling and signal-detection experiments.

One of the most famous small-n experiments in psychology is that reported by Hermann Ebbinghaus in his book *Über das Gedächtnis* (1885; *Memory*, 1913). Ebbinghaus tested himself in a series of memory experiments. In his work on remembering nonsense syllables and poetry, he discovered many laws of retaining and forgetting. These laws are now firmly established. Numerous modern experiments with larger numbers of experimental participants and various verbal materials have yielded results confirming Ebbinghaus' work. Among the most important findings are the shape of the curve of forgetting over time, the important role of practice in improving retention, and the benefits of distributing practice as opposed to cramming it.

B. F. Skinner pioneered the use of small-n designs for laboratory experiments on rats and pigeons in the 1930's. Skinner's work on schedules of reinforcement is among the most frequently cited in psychology. In his work, Skinner insisted on making numerous observations of few subjects under tightly controlled conditions. His ability to control the behavior of experimental subjects and obtain reliable results in within-subject plans such as the reversal design has led to the wide acceptance of within-subject plans in laboratory and applied experimental work.

Developmental psychologists regularly use a variant of the within-subject design. This is the longitudinal design, in which repeated observations are made as the subject develops and grows older. In a typical longitudinal experiment, a child first might receive a test of problem solving when he or she is three years old. Then the test would be repeated at ages five and seven.

The longitudinal design inherently confounds age or development with period of testing, since age cannot be counterbalanced for an individual. An alternative developmental design is the cross-sectional plan. In this design, subjects of different ages are tested at the same time. Since participants of different ages have grown up in different time periods with different people, age is confounded with generation of birth in the cross-sectional design. Thus, the cross-sectional plan is between subjects and cannot control for individual differences. Although the longitudinal design confounds age with time of testing, individual differences do not confound the results. Therefore, the longitudinal design is a valuable research tool for the developmental psychologist.

Because of their control, efficiency, and statistical power, within-subject designs are popular and important in psychology. All areas of applied and basic scientific psychology rely heavily on within-subject designs, and such designs are likely to remain important in the field.

Bibliography

Elmes, David G., Barry H. Kantowitz, and Henry L. Roediger III. *Research Methods in Psychology*. 4th ed. St. Paul, Minn.: West, 1992. A standard textbook on all aspects of research in psychology. Chapters 6 and 7 focus on experimental design and detail methods of counterbalancing. Chapter 8 discusses several small-n designs besides the reversal design. Can be understood by college students and sophisticated high school students.

Gescheider, George A. *Psychophysics: Method and Theory*. Hillsdale, N.J.: Lawrence Erlbaum, 1976. This is a standard work on psychophysical methods. Gescheider describes the many experimental plans used to examine the sensory judgments that people make. The student will find the discussion of method more valuable than the sections that deal with the theories of psychophysics.

Gravetter, Frederick J., and Larry B. Wallnau. *Essentials of Statistics for the Behavioral Sciences.* St. Paul, Minn.: West, 1991. This accessible statistics text shows the strength of within-subject designs. The authors do not assume that the reader has a sophisticated mathematical background, but understanding the statistical analysis of within-subject designs may require some effort.

Martin, David W. *Doing Psychology Experiments.* 2d ed. Monterey, Calif.: Brooks/Cole, 1985. This book is less rigorous than the one by Elmes et al. and may be more accessible to the high school student. Chapters 5 and 6 of this book examine many issues considered in this article. Martin presents many humorous examples that may help the reader comprehend the important principles of experimental design.

Sidman, Murray. *Tactics of Scientific Research.* New York: Basic Books, 1960. This sophisticated book is the standard reference for the logic and methods of small-n research. Sidman presents a strong case for developing a high degree of experimental control so that small numbers of subjects can be used in within-subject designs.

David G. Elmes

Cross-References

Complex Experimental Designs: Interactions, 625; Developmental Methodologies, 817; Psychological Experimentation: Independent, Dependent, and Control Variables, 1932; Psychophysical Scaling, 1963; Sampling, 2122; The Scientific Method in Psychology, 2148; Signal Detection Theory, 2271; Statistical Significance Tests, 2375.

WORK MOTIVATION

Type of psychology: Motivation
Fields of study: Motivation theory; social motives

Work motivation theories describe the psychological processes that affect people's choices regarding their work-related behaviors; the theories provide managerial guidelines for increasing worker productivity.

Principal terms

EXPECTANCY THEORY: a cognitive motivation model which proposes that people choose to perform behaviors they believe to be the most likely to lead to positive outcomes

EXTRINSIC MOTIVATION: motivation to perform an activity only because the activity leads to a valued outcome external to the activity itself

GOAL SETTING: a motivational technique used to increase productivity in which employees are given specific performance objectives and time deadlines

HIERARCHY OF NEEDS THEORY: a motivation theory which proposes that there are five categories of needs that influence values

INTRINSIC MOTIVATION: motivation to perform an activity because the activity itself is enjoyable

JOB ENRICHMENT: a motivational technique in which jobs are changed such that employees are given greater opportunities for learning and responsibility

SCIENTIFIC MANAGEMENT: an early managerial approach that emphasized work measurement, efficiency, and wage incentives

Overview

Motivation is the psychological process that directs people's choices regarding the type and intensity of their behavior. A common misconception among managers is that motivation is merely the desire to work hard. Consequently, managers often think that only productive workers possess motivation. In contrast, psychologists define motivation as a general process that influences virtually all behavior. Thus, psychologists believe that all workers are motivated. Some workers are motivated to work hard; other workers are motivated to stay home.

A basic principle that underlies most modern theories of motivation is that motivated behavior is performed to obtain pleasurable outcomes. Based on this principle, motivational theorists have defined two types of motivation: intrinsic motivation and extrinsic motivation. A behavior is intrinsically motivated if the valued or pleasurable outcome associated with the behavior is in the behavior itself. The intrinsically motivated employee works because the work itself is enjoyable. A behavior is extrinsically motivated if the valued outcome associated with the behavior is performed only as a means to obtain the outcome. The extrinsically motivated worker works not because the work is pleasurable but because working leads to a pleasurable outcome external to the job, such as money, status, security, or friendship.

The most popular and widely accepted theory of work motivation is the expectancy theory. Originally proposed by Victor Vroom, this model has been elaborated on by a large number of researchers. The expectancy theory describes the decision-making process that people experience when they choose which behavior to perform. It suggests that a person's motivation to perform some behavior is a function of three components: expectancy, instrumentality, and valence.

"Expectancy" refers to a person's beliefs about his or her ability to perform a behavior. "Instrumentality" refers to a person's beliefs about the likelihood that a number of outcomes will occur if the behavior is performed. "Valence" refers to how positively or negatively a person values these outcomes. The expectancy theory suggests that when people are deciding which of a number of behaviors they will perform, they consider the three components associated with each behavior and choose the behavior that is most likely to lead to positive outcomes. For example, a worker is given an opportunity to receive a bonus for completing a project early. The employee's motivation to work on the project is a function of the worker's beliefs about her ability to get the project done early (expectancy), her beliefs about the likelihood that she will actually receive a bonus for completing the project early (instrumentality), and the degree to which she values the bonus (valence). To the extent that the worker values the bonus, is certain that the bonus will be awarded if the project is completed early, and is certain that she is capable of completing the project, the worker will be motivated to complete the project early. Whether the worker attempts to complete the project, however, is influenced by her competing motivation to perform other behaviors. While the worker may be motivated to complete the project, she may also feel that other activities, such as going on vacation or calling in sick, are more likely to lead to equally or more pleasurable outcomes than the bonus.

The expectancy theory is considered a cognitive model. As such, the theory proposes that behavior is guided by choices based on beliefs and values. The theory describes the process of decision making. "Needs models" are another type of motivation model. Needs models complement the process-oriented cognitive models by suggesting the categories of outcomes that people typically value. Needs models also provide insight into how the values of outcomes change.

The most widely known needs model is the hierarchy of needs theory, proposed by Abraham Maslow. Maslow suggested that all people have five categories of needs, which are arranged in a hierarchy. From lowest level to highest level, these needs include physiological needs, safety needs, social needs, esteem needs, and self-actualization needs. Maslow argued that a person's first concern is to fulfill the lowest level of unsatisfied need. When a need is not satisfied, opportunities to fill the need gain value. As the need is met, opportunities to fill the satisfied need lose value, and opportunities to satisfy the next higher level of need gain value. For example, once a worker has enough air, water, and food, thus satisfying his or her physiological needs, the worker will become less concerned about these needs and will value opportunities to fill safety needs. The process of unsatisfied needs gaining value and satisfied needs losing value continues up the hierarchy through safety, social, and esteem needs. When all the lower-level needs are reasonably well satisfied, people will most highly value opportunities for self-actualization. Self-actualization can be thought of as the process of developing one's physical and mental skills to the limit of one's potential.

Maslow's theory helps define the distinction between extrinsic and intrinsic motivation. Extrinsic motivation usually involves performing a job as a way to meet physiological, safety, and social needs. Intrinsic motivation typically occurs when a job offers opportunities to meet higher-level needs. That is, the work itself becomes enjoyable when performance of the job leads to greater self-esteem and self-actualization.

Applications

The supervisor's job is to increase a subordinate's motivation to be productive. The supervisor does this by defining productivity and establishing a contingency between productive behavior and the attainment of an outcome the worker values. As mentioned above, that valued outcome can be either in the job itself, involving intrinsic motivation, or external to the job, involving extrinsic motivation. The expectancy theory offers a number of guidelines for helping supervisors establish productivity-outcome contingencies.

First, a supervisor must make certain that the employee believes she or he can be productive. That is, the supervisor must heighten the employee's expectancy beliefs. For example, the supervisor must clearly explain to the employee what behaviors or levels of performance constitute productivity. The supervisor may then need to provide training, giving the employee the skills necessary to meet the performance criteria. Additionally, the supervisor may need to coach the employee, convincing the employee that he or she has the potential to be productive.

Next, a supervisor must make certain that the employee believes that productive performance will lead to positive outcomes. (The supervisor must strengthen the employee's instrumentality beliefs.) In doing this, the supervisor must clearly explain the potential benefits of productive behavior, including any organizational policies regarding compensation and promotion. Finally, a supervisor must make certain that the employee values the outcome associated with productive behavior—that is, the supervisor must heighten the valence of productive performance. If the supervisor wants to increase intrinsic motivation, the supervisor must make certain that the employee can find the job itself enjoyable. If the supervisor wants to increase extrinsic motivation, he or she must offer a performance reward that the employee enjoys.

The expectancy theory provides useful theoretical guidelines for shaping employee motivation. Over the years, researchers have developed a number of specific techniques for increasing employee motivation to be productive. Two of the most useful techniques involve goal setting and job enrichment.

Goal setting involves assigning specific objectives for employee performance. For example, goal setting might be applied to the job of a computer disk-drive assembler in the following way. The assembler would meet with his or her supervisor. Using information about the worker's past performance, the supervisor and assembler would set a challenging goal regarding the number of disk drives to be assembled per week. The supervisor and assembler would then negotiate rewards for completing the goal on time. Each day, the supervisor would give the worker feedback by posting a running total of the number of disk drives assembled. At the end of the week, the worker's production would be reviewed and appropriate rewards would be given.

Edwin Locke and Gary Latham have studied goal setting extensively. They found that goals will lead to greater productivity if the goals are specific, difficult, and set with time deadlines. Further, goal setting programs will be more effective if the employee receives frequent feedback, allowing the employee to monitor his or her progress toward goal attainment. Additionally, goal setting will increase productivity if the employee is highly committed to the goal; giving employees the opportunity to participate in setting goals is one way to increase goal commitment. Finally, the effects of goal setting may be improved by establishing rewards for meeting goals on time. Other popular motivational techniques that involve goal setting include management by objectives (MBO) and organizational behavior modification (often called OBMod).

Job enrichment, a technique designed specifically to increase intrinsic motivation, was introduced by Frederick Herzberg. Herzberg argued that people will find a job enjoyable if the job provides opportunities to learn, to be responsible, and to experience a sense of achievement. For example, job enrichment might also be applied to the assembler's job. To enrich the job of the disk-drive assembler, the job might be changed so that the assembler assembled a whole computer rather than only the disk drives. This would require greater knowledge and skills. The assembler could be given greater responsibility and be made accountable for the quality of each of the computers he or she assembles. Additional responsibility could be given to the assembler by providing the assembler a budget and requiring the assembler to order all the parts needed for assembly. Finally, the assembler might be given the opportunity to schedule his or her own hours.

Herzberg, like Maslow, argued that people have an innate need to grow psychologically and develop their skills. Herzberg enriched the jobs of mechanics, secretaries, janitors, managers, and assembly-line workers. He found that giving workers challenging and interesting work, personal accountability for success and failures, control over organizational resources, and opportunities to self schedule increased production quantity, improved production quality, and heightened job satisfaction.

Context

Modern work motivation theories span three eras. The first period was the scientific management era, which began around the beginning of the twentieth century, when Frederick Winslow Taylor applied scientific methodology to the study of worker efficiency. Taylor assumed that workers were basically lazy and incapable of self-direction. He proposed that the best way to motivate workers was to simplify the worker's job as much as possible, to determine empirically the most efficient movements the worker needed to perform the job, and to make pay contingent on job performance. Taylor applied the principles of scientific management to steelworkers and was able to increase productivity dramatically. The result of scientific management was that managers treated employees as if they were simply part of the production machinery. By making jobs specialized and repetitive, the manager could structure and fine-tune a worker's performance. Job routinization, coupled with the assumption that employees were naturally uninterested in work, led managers to use extrinsic motivation techniques.

The next period of work motivation theory was the human relations era. This period began in the 1930's, with a classic study by Elton Mayo, Fritz Roethlisberger, and William Dickson at the Hawthorne Western Electric Plant. These researchers conducted numerous experiments and interviews that led them to question the fundamental assumptions of scientific management. The researchers found that workers were strongly influenced by social norms and that peers could have as much influence on productivity as rules and incentives. They also found that workers expressed a strong desire to have their opinions heard and to make decisions regarding their jobs. The outcome of the human relations era was that managers began to show greater concern for employees' opinions and social needs. Managers assumed that the best way to motivate employees was to alleviate employee morale problems and to improve social relations on the job.

It was not until the human potential movement that managers and psychologists began to emphasize intrinsic motivation. This period began in the 1960's, with a growing concern over job satisfaction. Attracted to the work of Maslow and Herzberg, managers began to recognize employees' needs for psychological growth. Managers thus assumed that the best way to motivate workers was to give workers more opportunities to learn and experience responsibility.

Beginning in the 1970's, motivational theorists and researchers became less concerned about finding the one best way to motivate employees. Instead, they took a more eclectic approach, elaborating on and integrating established motivation theories. For example, researchers have become interested in the degree to which extrinsic motivational strategies, such as performance bonuses, interfere with or supplement intrinsic motivation. As work roles become more central to people's identity, and as world economic competition increases, work motivation should remain a popular area of research; managers will continue to find motivation theories useful in improving job satisfaction and increasing worker productivity.

Bibliography

Campbell, J. P., and R. D. Pritchard. "Motivation Theory in Industrial and Organizational Psychology." In *Handbook of Industrial and Organizational Psychology*, edited by Marvin D. Dunnette. Chicago: Rand McNally, 1976. This chapter presents an overview of work motivation theories and research. Dunnette's handbook is a very useful reference for individuals interested in a wide variety of topics related to human behavior in the workplace.

Herzberg, Frederick. "One More Time: How Do You Motivate Employees?" *Harvard Business Review* 46, no. 1 (1968): 53-62. One of the most frequently cited articles on work motivation. Herzberg presents his controversial motivation-hygiene theory and describes the basics of job enrichment. Herzberg provides a compelling argument in a readable form.

Locke, Edwin A., and Gary P. Latham. *Goal Setting: A Motivational Technique That Works.* Englewood Cliffs, N.J.: Prentice-Hall, 1984. Locke and Latham present a no-nonsense technique for increasing motivation and improving worker performance. The authors' research suggests that a manager can improve an employee's performance through goal setting.

Maslow, Abraham H. *Toward a Psychology of Being.* 2d ed. New York: Van Nostrand Reinhold, 1968. Maslow describes his needs hierarchy model of motivation and presents an interesting discussion of self-actualization.

Pinder, Craig C. *Work Motivation: Theory, Issues, and Applications.* Glenview, Ill.: Scott, Foresman, 1984. A well-written, college-level textbook on motivation in the workplace. Detailed discussions of theories and research are included.

Porter, Lyman W., and Edward E. Lawler. *Managerial Attitudes and Performance.* Homewood, Ill.: Richard D. Irwin, 1968. This book presents an overview of the history of expectancy theory research and development. The authors present a useful version of the theory that incorporates both intrinsic and extrinsic motivation and integrates a number of popular models of motivation.

Taylor, Frederick Winslow. *The Principles of Scientific Management.* New York: W. W. Norton, 1967. This management classic, originally published in 1911, describes Taylor's studies at the Midvale Steel Mill. Taylor was one of the first authors to discuss such concepts as wage incentives, time and motion studies, employee selection, and planning.

Daniel Sachau

Cross-References

Human Resource Training and Development, 1197; Incentive Motivation, 1269; Industrial and Organizational Psychology, 1283; Motivation: Cognitive Theories, 1606; Motivational Constructs, 1616; Self-Actualization, 2168.

GLOSSARY

Absolute threshold: The smallest amount of stimulus that elicits a sensation 50 percent of the time.

Accommodation: In Piaget's theory of development, adjusting the interpretation (schema) of an object or event to include a new instance; in vision, the ability of the lens to focus light on the retina by changing its shape.

Acetylcholine (ACh): A cholinergic neurotransmitter important in producing muscular contraction and in some autonomic nerve transmissions.

Achievement motivation: The tendency for people to strive for moderately difficult goals because of the relative attractiveness of success and repulsiveness of failure.

Acquisition: In learning, the process by which an association is formed in classical or operant conditioning; in memory, the stage at which information is stored in memory.

Action potential: A rapid change in electrical charges across a neuron's cell membrane, with depolarization followed by repolarization, leading to a nerve impulse moving down an axon; associated with nerve and muscle activity.

Actor-observer bias: The tendency to infer that other people's behavior is caused by dispositional factors but that one's own behavior is the product of situational causes.

Actualizing tendency: The force toward maintaining and enhancing the organism, achieving congruence between experience and awareness, and realizing potentials.

Adaptation: Any heritable characteristic that presumably has developed as a result of natural selection and thus increases an animal's ability to survive and reproduce.

Addiction: Physical dependence on a substance; components include tolerance, psychological dependence, and physical withdrawal symptoms.

Adolescence: The period extending from the onset of puberty to early adulthood.

Adrenal glands: The suprarenal glands, small, caplike structures sitting each on top of one kidney; in general, they function in response to stress, but they are also important in regulating metabolic and sexual functions.

Affect: A class name given to feelings, emotions, or dispositions as a mode of mental functioning.

Affective disorders: Functional mental disorders associated with emotions or feelings (also called mood disorders); examples include depression and bipolar disorders.

Afferent: A sensory neuron or a dendrite carrying information toward a structure; for example, carrying sensory stimuli coming into the reticular formation.

Affiliation motive: The motive to seek the company of others and to be with one's own kind, based on such things as cooperation, similarity, friendship, sex, and protection.

Aggression: Behavior intended to harm or injure another person or thing.

Agoraphobia: An intense fear of being in places or situations in which help may not be available or escape could be difficult.

Allele: One of the many forms of a gene; it may be dominant (needing only one copy for the trait to appear) or recessive (needing two copies).

Altruism: A phenomenon in human and animal behaviors in which individuals unselfishly sacrifice their own genetic fitness in order to help other individuals in a group.

Alzheimer's disease: A form of presenile dementia, characterized by disorientation, loss of memory, speech disturbances, and personality disorders.

Amplitude: The peak deviation from the rest state of the movement of a vibrating object, or the ambient state of the medium through which vibration is conducted.

Anal stage: According to Freud, the second psychosexual stage of personality development, approximately from ages two to four; sexual energy is focused on the anus and on pleasures and conflicts associated with retaining and eliminating feces.

Analgesia: The reduction or elimination of pain.

Analytic psychology: A school of psychology founded by Carl Jung that views the human mind as the result of prior experiences and the preparation of future goals; it deemphasizes the role of sexuality in psychological disorders.

Androgens: Male sex hormones secreted by the testes; testosterone, the primary mammalian male androgen, is responsible for the development and maturation of male sexual structures and sexual behaviors.

Androgyny: The expression of both traditionally feminine and traditionally masculine attributes.

Anorexia nervosa: An eating disorder characterized by an obsessive-compulsive concern for thinness achieved by dieting; often combined with extreme exercising and sometimes part of a binge-purge cycle.

Anterograde amnesia: An inability to form new memories after the onset of amnesia.

Antidepressants: Drugs that are used in the treatment of depression, many of which affect or mimic neurotransmitters; classes of antidepressants include the tricyclics and MAO inhibitors.

Antisocial personality disorder: A personality disorder characterized by a history of impulsive, risk-taking, and perhaps chronic criminal behavior, and by opportunistic interpersonal relations.

Anxiety: A chronic fearlike state that is accompanied by feelings of impending doom and that cannot be explained by an actual threatening object or event.

Aphasia: Partial or total loss of the use of language as a result of brain damage, characterized by an inability to use and/or comprehend language.

Applied research: Research intended to solve existing problems, as opposed to "basic research," which seeks knowledge for its own sake.

Aptitude: The potential to develop an ability with training and/or experience.

Archetypes: In Jung's theory, universal, inherited themes—such as the motifs of the self, hero, and shadow—that exercise an influence on virtually all human beings.

Archival data: Information collected at an earlier time by someone other than the present researcher, often for purposes very different from those of the present research.

Artificial intelligence: The use of computers to simulate aspects of human thinking and, in some cases, behavior.

Assimilation: The interpretation of a new instance of an object or event in terms of one's preexisting schema or understanding; the fit, never perfect, is close enough.

Attachment: An emotional bond between infant and caregiver based on reciprocal interaction patterns.

Attention: The ability to focus mentally.

Attitude: A relatively stable evaluation of a person or thing; it can be either positive or negative, can vary in level of intensity, and has an affective, cognitive, and behavioral component.

Attribution: The process by which one gathers information about the self and others and interprets it to determine the cause of an event or behavior.

Attributional biases: Typical motivational and cognitive errors in the attribution process; tendencies that are shared among people in using information in illogical or unwarranted ways.

Autonomic nervous system: The division of the peripheral nervous system that regulates basic, automatically controlled life processes such as cardiovascular function, digestive function, and genital function.

Availability heuristic: A decision-making heuristic whereby a person estimates the probability of some occurrence or event depending on how easily examples of that event can be remembered.

Aversion therapy: A therapy that involves pairing something negative (such as electric shock) with an undesired behavior (such as drinking alcohol or smoking cigarettes).

Axon: The single fiberlike extension of a neuron that carries information away from the cell body toward the next cell in a pathway.

Beck Depression Inventory (BDI): A brief questionnaire used to measure the severity of depression; developed by Aaron Beck.

Behavior therapy: A branch of psychotherapy narrowly conceived as the application of classical and operant conditioning to the alteration of clinical problems, but more broadly conceived as applied experimental psychology in a clinical context.

Behaviorism: A theoretical approach which states that the environment is the primary cause of behavior and that only external, observable stimuli and responses are available to objective study.

Between-subject designs: Experimental plans in which different participants receive each level of the independent variable.

Bilingual: A person who has enough control of two languages to function well with both languages in a number of different contexts.

Binocular cues: Visual cues that require the use of both eyes working together.

Biofeedback: A psychophysiological technique in which an individual monitors a specific, supposedly involuntary, bodily function such as blood pressure or heart rate and consciously attempts to control this function through the use of learning principles.

Bipolar disorder: A disorder characterized by the occurrence of one or more manic episodes, usually interspersed with one or more major depressive episodes.

Bottom-up processing: Information processing guided by simple stimulus features of units rather than by a person's general knowledge, beliefs, or expectations.

Brain stem: The lower part of the brain, between the brain and spinal cord, which activates the cortex and makes perception and consciousness possible; it includes the midbrain, pons, medulla, and cerebellum.

Bystander effect: The tendency for an individual to be less likely to help as the number of other people present increases.

Cardinal trait: According to Allport's theory of personality, a single outstanding characteristic that dominates a person's life; few individuals are characterized by a cardinal disposition.

Case study: An in-depth method of data collection in which all available background data on an individual or group are reviewed; typically used in psychotherapy.

Catecholamines: A neurotransmitter group derived from the amino acid tyrosine that includes dopamine, epinephrine, and norepinephrine; they are activated in stressful situations.

Catharsis: A reduction of psychological tension and/or physiological arousal by expressing (either directly or vicariously) repressed aggressive or sexual anxieties.

Cell body: The principal portion of a cell such as a neuron, which contains genetic material and most of the cell cytoplasm.

Central nervous system: The nerve cells, fibers, and other tissues associated with the brain and spinal cord.

Central traits: According to Allport's theory, the relatively few (five to ten) distinctive and descriptive characteristics that provide direction and focus to a person's life.

Cephalocaudal development: A pattern of early physical growth consisting of motor development that proceeds from head to foot.

Cerebellum: The portion of the brain that controls voluntary muscle activity, including posture and body movement; located behind the brain stem.

Cerebral commissures: Fiber tracts, such as the corpus callosum and anterior commissure, that connect and allow neural communication between the cerebral hemispheres.

Cerebral cortex: The outer layer of the cerebrum; controls higher-level brain functions such as thinking, reasoning, motor coordination, memory, and language.

Cerebral hemispheres: Two anatomically similar hemispheres that make up the outer surface of the brain (the cerebral cortex); separated by the cerebral longitudinal fissure.

Cerebrospinal fluid: A fluid, derived from blood, that circulates in and around the ventricles of the brain and the spinal cord.

Cerebrum: The largest and uppermost portion of the brain; the cerebrum performs sensory and motor functions and affects memory, speech, and emotional functions.

Chaining: The process by which several neutral stimuli are presented in a series; they eventually assume reinforcing qualities by being ultimately paired with an innate reinforcer.

Children's Depression Inventory (CDI): A modified version of the Beck Depression Inventory (BDI) that was developed to measure the severity of depression in children; developed by Maria Kovacs.

Chromosomes: Microscopic threadlike bodies in the nuclei of cells; they carry the genes, which convey hereditary characteristics.

Circadian rhythm: A cyclical variation in a biological process or behavior that has a duration of about a day; in humans under constant environmental conditions, the rhythm usually reveals its true length as being slightly more than twenty-four hours.

Classical conditioning: A form of associative learning in which a neutral stimulus, called the conditioned stimulus (CS), is repeatedly paired with a biologically significant unconditioned stimulus (UCS) so that the CS acquires the same power to elicit response as the UCS; also called Pavlovian conditioning.

Clinical psychologist: A person with a Ph.D. in psychology, specially trained to assess and treat mental disorders and behavior problems.

Cochlea: The snail-shell-shaped portion of the inner ear, which contains the nerve connections to the auditory nerve.

Code-switching: A speech style used by many bilinguals that is characterized by rapid shifts back and forth between two languages within a single conversation or sentence.

Cognition: Mental processes involved in the acquisition and use of knowledge, such as attention, thinking, problem solving, and perception; cognitive learning emphasizes these processes in the acquisition of new behaviors.

Cognitive appraisal: An assessment of the meaningfulness of an event to an individual; events that are appraised as harmful or potentially harmful elicit stress.

Cognitive behavior therapy: Therapy that integrates principles of learning theory with cognitive strategies to treat disorders such as depression, anxiety, and other behavioral problems (such as smoking or obesity).

Cognitive dissonance theory: Leon Festinger's theory that inconsistencies among one's cognitions cause tension and that individuals are motivated to reduce this tension by changing discrepant attitudes.

Cognitive map: A mental representation of an external area that is used to guide one's behavior.

Cognitive processes: The processes of thought, which include attending to an event, storing information in memory, recalling information, and making sense of information; they enable people to perceive events.

Cognitive psychology: An area of study that investigates mental processes; areas within cognitive psychology include attention, perception, language, learning, memory, problem solving, and logic.

Cognitive science: A multidisciplinary approach to the study of cognition from the perspectives of psychology, computer science, neuroscience, philosophy, and linguistics.

Cohort: An identifiable group of people; in developmental research, group members are commonly associated by their birth dates and shared historical experiences.

Collective unconscious: In Jung's theory, memory traces of repeated experiences that have been passed down to all humankind as a function of evolutionary development; includes inherited tendencies to behave in certain ways and contains the archetypes.

Color: The brain's interpretation of electromagnetic radiation of different wavelengths within the range of visible light.

Color blindness: An inability to perceive certain colors; the most common type is green-minus color blindness, involving a defect in the eyes' green cones.

Compensation: In Adler's theory, a defense mechanism for overcoming feelings of inferiority by trying harder to excel; in Freud's theory, the process of learning alternative ways to accomplish a task while making up for an inferiority—a process that could involve dreams that adjust psychologically for waking imbalances.

Complementary color: Light that complements another light in that their addition produces white light and their juxtaposition produces high contrast.

Compulsions: Ritualistic patterns of behavior that commonly follow obsessive thinking and that reduce the intensity of the anxiety-evoking thoughts.

Concrete operations stage: The third stage of Piaget's theory, during which children acquire basic logical rules and concrete concepts; occurs between the ages of seven and eleven.

Conditioned response (CR): In Pavlovian conditioning, the behavior and emotional quality that occurs when a conditioned stimulus is presented; related to but not the same as the unconditioned response.

Conditioned stimulus (CS): A previously neutral stimulus (a sight, sound, touch, or smell) that, after Pavlovian conditioning, will elicit the conditioned response (CR).

Conditioned taste aversion: An avoidance of a food or drink that has been followed by illness when consumed in the past.

Conditioning: A type of learning in which an animal learns a concept by associating it with some object or by the administration of rewards and/or punishments.

Conditions of worth: In Rogers' theory, externally based conditions for love and praise; the expectation that the child must behave in accordance with parental standards in order to receive love.

Cone: One type of visual receptor found in the retina of the eye; primarily for color vision and acute daytime vision.

Confounding of variables: The variation of other variables along with the independent variable of interest, as a result of which any effects cannot be attributed with certainty to the independent variable.

Consciousness: A level of awareness that includes those things of which an individual is aware at any given moment, such as current ideas, thoughts, accessed memories, and feelings.

Consensual validation: The verification of subjective beliefs by obtaining a consensus among other people.

Consensus information: Information concerning other people's responses to an object; in attribution theory, high consensus generally leads people to attribute situational rather than personal causes to a behavior.

Conservation: In Piaget's theory, understanding that the physical properties (number, length, mass, volume) remain constant even though appearances may change; a concrete-operational skill.

Consistency information: Information concerning a person's response to an object over time. In attribution theory, high consistency implies that behavior is dispositional or typical of a person.

Consolidation: A neural process by which short-term memories become stored in long-term memory.

Construct: A formal concept representing the relationships between variables or processes such as motivation and behavior; may be empirical (observable) or hypothetical (inferred).

Construct validity: A type of validity that assesses the extent to which a test score (variable) correlates with other tests (variables) already established as valid measures of the item.

Consumer psychology: The subfield of psychology that studies selling, advertising, and buying; the goal of its practitioners is generally to communicate clearly and to persuade consumers to buy products.

Context dependence: The phenomenon in which memory functions more effectively when material is recalled in the same environment in which it was originally learned, compared with recall in a different environment.

Contingency: A relationship between a response and its consequence or between two stimuli; sometimes considered a dependency.

Contingency management: A method of behavior modification that involves providing or removing positive rewards in accordance with whether the individual being treated engages in the expected behavior.

Continuous reinforcement: A schedule in which each response is followed by a reinforcer.

Control group: A group of subjects that are like the experimental groups in all ways except that they do not experience the independent variable; used as a comparison measure.

Control variable: An extraneous factor that might influence the dependent variable, making it difficult to evaluate the effect of the independent variable; in an experiment, attempts are made to isolate or control such effects systematically.

Convergence: In perception, the turning of the eyes inward from parallel lines of sight to look at a nearby object; a depth cue.

Convergent thinking: Creative thinking in which possible solutions to a problem are systematically eliminated in search for the best solution; the type of ordinary thinking in which most people generally engage.

Conversion disorder: A psychological disorder in which a person experiences physical symptoms, such as the loss or impairment of some motor or sensory function (paralysis or blindness, for example), in the absence of an organic cause.

Coping: Responses directed at dealing with demands (in particular, threatening or stressful ones) upon an organism; these responses may either improve or reduce long-term functioning.

Correlation: The degree of relatedness or correspondence between two variables, expressed by a coefficient that can range from $+1.00$ to -1.00; 0.00 signifies no correspondence.

Cortex: The surface (or outer layer) of the brain, which receives sensory input, interprets it, and relates behavior to external stimuli; responsible for perception and conscious thought.

Cortical brain centers: The portions of the brain making up the cerebral cortex and controlling voluntary behavior, higher reasoning, and language skills; they develop rapidly during the first two years of life.

Countertransference: The phenomenon in which an analyst either shifts feelings from his or her past onto a patient or is affected by the client's emotional problems; caused by a patient's perceived similarity to individuals or experiences in the analyst's life.

Creativity: Cognitive abilities in areas such as fluency, flexibility, originality, elaboration, visualization, metaphorical thinking, and problem definition; the ability to originate something that is both new and appropriate.

Criterion group: A group used to validate a measurement instrument; in the case of interest inventories, it refers to persons in a particular occupational group.

Critical period: A time during which the developing organism is particularly sensitive to the influence of certain inputs or experiences necessary to foster normal development; in nonhuman animals, a specific time period during which a certain type of learning such as imprinting must occur.

Cross-sectional design: A design in which subgroups of a population are randomly sampled; the members of the sample are then tested or observed.

Cue-producing response: A response that serves as a cue for other responses; words (speech) can cue behaviors, and thoughts can cue other thoughts.

Cutaneous sense: Relating to the skin sense, as in responses to touch or temperature.

Cyclothymia: A milder version of a cyclical mood disorder in which mood swings can occur but are not as intense as in bipolar disorder.

Daily hassles: Seemingly minor everyday events that are a constant source of stress.

Dark adaptation: An increase in the sensitivity of rods and cones to light through an increase in the concentration of light-absorbing pigments.

Data: A collection of observations from an experiment or survey.

Death instinct: The unconscious desire for death and destruction in order to escape the tensions of living.

Debriefing: Discussing an experiment and its purpose with subjects after its completion; required if the experiment involved deception.

Decay: The disappearance of a memory trace.

Deduction: A type of logic by which one draws a specific conclusion from one or more known truths or premises; often formed as an "if/then" statement.

Defense mechanism: According to Freud, a psychological strategy by which an unacceptable sexual or aggressive impulse may be kept from conscious thought or expressed in a disguised fashion.

Deindividuation: The loss of self-awareness and evaluation apprehension that accompanies situations that foster personal and physical anonymity.

Delusion: A symptom of psychosis that consists of a strong irrational belief held despite considerable evidence against it; types include delusions of grandeur, reference, and persecution.

Dementia: Globally impaired intellectual functioning (memory reasoning) in adults as a function of brain impairment; it does not mean "craziness," but a loss or impairment of mental power.

Dendrite: A branching extension of a neuron through which information enters the cell; there may be one or many dendrites on a neuron.

Dependent variable: The outcome measure in a study; the effect of the independent variable is measured by changes in the dependent variable.

Depolarization: A shift in ions and electrical charges across a cell membrane, causing loss of resting membrane potential and bringing the cell closer to the action potential.

Depression: A psychological disorder characterized by extreme feelings of sadness, hopelessness, or personal unworthiness, as well as loss of energy, withdrawal, and either lack of sleep or excessive sleep.

Depth perception: The ability to see three-dimensional features, such as the distance of an object from oneself and the shape of an object.

Descriptive statistics: Procedures that summarize and organize data sets; they include mean, median, range, correlation, and variability.

Desensitization: A behavioral technique of gradually removing anxiety associated with certain situations by associating a relaxed state with these situations.

Determinism: The theory or doctrine that acts of the will, occurrences in nature, or social or psychological phenomena are causally determined by preceding events or natural laws.

Development: The continuous and cumulative process of age-related changes in physical growth, thought, perception, and behavior of people and animals; a result of both biological and environmental influences.

Developmental psychology: The subfield of psychology that studies biological, social, and intellectual changes as they occur throughout the human life cycle.

Deviancy: The quality of having a condition or engaging in behavior that is atypical in a social group and is considered undesirable.

Diagnosis: The classification or labeling of a patient's problem within one of a set of recognized categories of abnormal behavior, determined with the aid of interviews and psychological tests.

Diagnostic and Statistical Manual of Mental Disorders (DSM-III-R): A system created by the American Psychiatric Association for diagnosing and classifying mental disorders; used by mental health professionals and insurance companies.

Dichotic listening: A technique in which two different messages are simultaneously played through earphones, with a different message to each ear.

Diffusion of responsibility: The reduction of personal responsibility that is commonly experienced in group situations; diffusion of responsibility increases as the size of the crowd increases.

Discounting: Reducing the role of a particular cause in producing a behavior because of the presence of other plausible causes.

Discrimination: In perception, the ability to see that two patterns differ in some way; in intergroup relations, behavior (usually unfavorable) toward persons that is based on their group membership rather than on their individual personalities.

Discriminative stimulus: A stimulus that signals the availability of a consequence, given that a response occurs.

Dispersion: A statistical measure of variability; a measure (range, semi-interquartile range, standard deviation, or variance) that provides information about the difference among the scores.

Displacement: According to Freud, a defense mechanism by which a person redirects his or her aggressive impulse onto a target that may substitute for the target that originally aroused the person's aggression.

Display: A visual dance or series of movements or gestures by an individual or animal to communicate such things as dominance, aggression, and courtship to other individuals.

Display rules: Culturally determined rules regarding the appropriate expression of emotions.

Dispositional: Relating to disposition or personality rather than to situation.

Dissociative disorder: A disorder that occurs when some psychological function, such as memory, is split off from the rest of the conscious mind; not caused by brain dysfunction.

Dissonance: An unpleasant psychological and physiological state caused by an inconsistency between cognitions.

Distal stimulus: An object or other sensory element in the environment.

Distinctiveness information: Information concerning a person's response to an object under given conditions; in attribution theory, high distinctiveness suggests that individuals are behaving uniquely toward a given target/object.

Diurnal enuresis: The presence of enuretic episodes when the individual is awake.

Divergent thinking: Thinking that results in new and different responses that most people cannot, or do not, offer; the type of thinking most clearly involved in creativity.

Domestic violence: Physical, emotional, psychological, or sexual abuse perpetrated by a family member toward another family member; typically the abuse follows a repetitive, predictable pattern.

Dominance hierarchy: An ordered arrangement of dominant to subordinate individuals in an animal population that serves numerous social functions, including protection; a pecking order.

Dopamine: One type of neurotransmitter, a chemical that is released from one nerve cell and stimulates receptors on another, thus transferring a message between them; associated with movement and with treatment of depression.

Double bind: A form of communication that often occurs when a family member sends two messages, requests, or commands that are logically inconsistent, contradictory, or impossible, resulting in a "damned if one does, damned if one doesn't" situation; a hypothesis about the development of schizophrenia.

Double-blind method: A procedure in which neither the experimenter nor the subjects know who is receiving treatment and who is not; this controls for subject and experimenter biases and expectations.

Down syndrome: A chromosomal abnormality that causes mental retardation as well as certain physical defects, such as extra eyelid folds and a thick tongue; caused by an extra (third) chromosome on chromosome pair 21.

Drive: The tendency of a person or animal to engage in behaviors brought about by some change or condition inside that organism; often generated by deprivation (hunger or thirst) or exposure to painful or other noxious stimuli.

Drive reduction hypothesis: The idea that a physiological need state triggers a series of behaviors aimed at reducing the unpleasant state; drive reduction is reinforcing.

Dysfunctional family: A family grouping that is characterized by the presence of disturbed interactions and communications; particularly an abusive, incestuous, or alcoholic family.

Dyslexia: Difficulties in reading, usually after damage to the left cerebral hemisphere.

Dysphoria: A symptom of clinical depression; extreme sadness.

Dysthymic disorder: A form of depression in which mild to moderate levels of depressive symptoms persist chronically.

Early recollections: A projective technique in which the patient attempts to remember things that happened in the distant past; these provide clues to the patient's current use of private logic.

Eating disorders: Afflictions resulting from dysfunctional relationships to hunger, food, and eating.

Echoic memory: Sensory memory for sound.

Echolalia: An involuntary and parrotlike repetition of words or phrases spoken by others.

Eclectic therapy: Therapy in which a combination of models and techniques is employed, rather than a single approach.

Educational psychology: The subfield of psychology that studies the effectiveness of education, usually formal education; educational psychologists seek to develop new educational techniques and to improve the learning process.

Efferent nerve: A motor neuron or an axon carrying information away from a structure; for example, in the transmission of stimuli from the reticular formation to the cerebral cortex.

Ego: In psychoanalytic theory, the part of the personality responsible for perceiving reality and thinking; mediates between the demands of the pleasure-seeking id, the superego, and reality.

Egocentric thought: A cognitive tendency in childhood in which the child assumes that everyone shares his or her own perspective; the cognitive inability to understand the different perspective of another.

Elaborative rehearsal: Giving meaning to information to enable encoding it in memory.

Electroconvulsive therapy (ECT): A treatment for severe depression in which an electric current is passed through the brain of the patient.

Electroencephalogram (EEG): The graphic recording of the electrical activity of the brain (brain waves).

Electroencephalography: Measurement of the electrical output of the brain, which may then sometimes be brought under voluntary control by biofeedback and relaxation.

Embryonic phase: The period of rapid prenatal change that follows the zygote period; extends from the second to the eighth week after conception.

Emotion: A psychological response that includes a set of physiological changes, expressive behaviors, and a subjective experience.

Empathy: In therapy, the therapist's ability to focus attention on the needs and experience of the client; also refers to the therapist's ability to communicate an understanding of the client's emotional state.

Empirical evidence: Data or information derived objectively from the physical senses, without reliance on personal faith, intuition, or introspection.

Empiricism: A philosophy holding that knowledge is learned through experience and that infants begin life like blank slates, learning about their environment through experience.

Encoding: The transformation of incoming sensory information into a form of code that the memory system can accept and use.

Endocrine gland: A gland that produces one or more hormones and secretes them into the blood so that they can serve as intercellular messengers.

Endocrine system: A system of ductless glands in the bodies of vertebrate animals that secretes hormones which travel through the bloodstream to target tissues, whose functioning is altered by the hormones.

Endogenous behavior: An innate, or inborn, behavior that is established by the animal's inherited genetic code (DNA) and that is not influenced by the animal's experiences or environment.

Endorphins: A group of endogenous, opiatelike neuropeptides of the central nervous system that simulate analgesia and interfere with transmission of pain impulses; the brain's own morphine.

Enkephalins: Peptides containing five amino acids, within the endorphin group, that may act as neurotransmitters; the first of the endorphins to be discovered.

Enmeshment: An excessively close relationship between parent and child in which adult concerns and needs are communicated and in which overdependence on the child is apparent.

Entitlement: The expectation of special or unusually favorable treatment by others; commonly seen among narcissistic personalities.

Entropy: In Jung's analytic theory, a concept maintaining that aspects of a person's psychic energy which are not in balance will tend to seek a state of equilibrium.

Enuresis: The inability to control the discharging of urine; nocturnal enuresis is also called bed-wetting.

Environmental psychology: The subfield of psychology that studies the relationship between the environment and behavior, particularly the effects of the physical and social environments (such as noise or crowding) on behavior.

Environmental stressor: A condition in the environment, such as crowding, noise, toxic chemicals, or extreme temperatures, that produces stress (bodily or mental tension).

Epilepsy: A disorder of the nervous system in which the cortex produces electrical firing that causes convulsions and other forms of seizures; thought by some to be linked to the reticular formation.

Epinephrine: The neurotransmitter released from the adrenal gland as a result of innervation of the autonomic nervous system; formerly called adrenaline.

Episodic memory: A form of long-term memory involving temporal and spatial information, including personal experiences.

Equipotentiality: In Pavlovian conditioning, the idea that any stimulus paired with an effective unconditioned stimulus will come to elicit a conditioned response with equal facility.

Equity theory: A theory in attraction and work motivation that contends that individuals are motivated to remain in relationships they perceive to be fair, just, and equitable—that is, where one's outcomes are proportional to one's inputs, particularly when contrasted with others in the relationship.

Equivalence: A principle stating that an increase in energy or value in one aspect of the psyche is accompanied by a decrease in another area.

Estradiol: The primary sex hormone of mammalian females, which is responsible for the menstrual cycle and for development of secondary sex characteristics; a primary estrogen, secreted by the corpus luteum.

Ethnocentrism: An attitude of uncritically assuming the superiority of the in-group culture.

Ethology: A branch of zoology that studies animals in their natural environments; often concerned with investigating the adaptive significance and innate basis of behaviors.

Etiology: The factors that are thought to cause or contribute to the development of a particular disorder.

Eustress: Positive arousal or stress, appraised as a challenge rather than as a threat.

Evoked potential: A brain response triggered by electroencephalography using discrete sensory stimuli.

Excitation transfer: The theory that arousal from one source can intensify an emotional reaction to a different source (for example, that sexual arousal can increase the response to an aggressive cue).

Existentialism: A philosophical viewpoint emphasizing human existence and the human situation in the world that gives meaning to life through the free choice of mature values and commitment to responsible goals; the critical goal involves finding one's true self and living according to this potential.

Exogenous substances: Substances not normally occurring in the body, present only when administered; exogenous substances include substances such as drugs or synthetic test compounds mimicking endogenous substances.

Expectancy confirmation bias: Interpreting ambiguous information as being supportive of expectations; mistakenly "seeing" what is expected.

Expectancy theory: A cognitive motivation model which proposes that people choose to perform behaviors they believe to be the most likely to lead to positive outcomes; in work theory, workers are more motivated when they perceive congruence between their efforts, products, and rewards.

Experiment: One of several data collection methods; requires systematically manipulating the levels of an independent variable under controlled conditions in order to measure its impact on a dependent variable.

Experimenter bias: Biases introduced into a research study as a result of the expectations of the experimenter.

Expressive aphasia: Difficulties in expressing language, usually after damage to Broca's area in the left frontal lobe of the cerebral cortex.

External validity: The extent to which the results of a research study can be generalized to different populations, settings, or conditions.

Externalization: A defense mechanism in which one experiences unresolved, repressed inner turmoil as occurring outside oneself; holding external factors responsible for one's problems.

Extinction: A process by which the probability of a response is decreased; in classical or Pavlovian conditioning, a process in which the temporal contiguity of the conditioned stimulus and the unconditioned stimulus is disrupted and the learned association is lost; in operant or instrumental conditioning, a process in which undesirable behavior is not followed by reinforcement.

Extraneous variable: A variable that has a detrimental affect on a research study, making it difficult to determine if the result is attributable to the variable under study or to some unknown variable not controlled for; for example, in jury decision making, the effect of defendant attractiveness.

Extrinsic motivation: Motivation to perform an activity only because the activity leads to a valued outcome external to the activity itself.

Extrinsic religion: An immature religious orientation that uses religion for self-serving purposes such as security or a sense of social or economic well-being.

Factor analysis: A statistical technique wherein a set of correlated variables can be regrouped in terms of the degree of commonality they share.

Family therapy: A type of psychotherapy that focuses on correcting the faulty interactions among family members that maintain children's psychological problems.

Farsightedness: An inability to focus clearly on nearby objects that is caused by the point of focus of the lens falling behind the retina.

Feminist analysis: The examination of the ways in which inequality, injustice, or oppression devalues women and/or limits their potential, both individually and collectively.

Fetal phase: The third period of prenatal development, extending from the ninth week of pregnancy until birth.

Fetishism: A sexual behavior in which a person becomes aroused by focusing on an inanimate object or a part of the human body.

Field research: An approach in which evidence is gathered in a "natural" setting, such as the workplace; by contrast, laboratory research involves an artificial, contrived setting.

Fight-or-flight syndrome: A sequence of physiological changes, described by Walter B. Cannon, that occurs in response to threat and prepares the organism to flee from or fight the threat; includes increases in heart rate, blood pressure, and respiration.

Fixation: In psychoanalytic theory, an inability to progress to the next level of psychosexual development because of overgratification or undergratification of desires at a particular stage.

Flashback: A type of traumatic reexperiencing in which a person becomes detached from reality and thinks, feels, and acts as if a previous traumatic experience were happening again.

Flocking: A defensive maneuver in many mammalian and bird species in which a scattered group of individuals implodes into a compact cluster at the approach of a predator.

Flooding: A type of therapy in which a phobic person imagines his or her most-feared situation until fear decreases.

Fluid intelligence: The form of intelligence that reflects speed of information processing, reasoning, and memory capacity rather than factual knowledge (crystallized intelligence); associated with Raymond Cattell.

Forebrain: A developmentally defined division of the brain that contains structures such as the cerebral hemispheres, the thalamus, and the hypothalamus.

Forensic psychology: The application of psychological skills in the legal profession—for example, in jury selection, sanity determination, and assessing competency to stand trial.

Forgetting: The loss of information from memory.

Formal operations: According to Piaget, the fourth stage of cognitive development, reached at adolescence; characterized by the ability to engage in abstract thinking, hypothetical constructs, and unobserved logical possibilities.

Fovea: The central part of the retina, which is densest in cone cells and is therefore the area of sharpest visual acuity.

Free association: The psychoanalytic method in which a patient talks spontaneously without restriction; thought to reveal repressed conflicts of the unconscious.

Frequency: The number of complete back-and-forth movements or pressure changes (cycles) from the rest or ambient state that occur each second; measured in units called hertz.

Frequency distribution: The pairing of a measurement or score with the number of people or subjects obtaining that measurement.

Frontal lobe: The anterior portion of each cerebral hemisphere, containing control of motor areas and most of the higher intellectual functions of the brain, including speech.

Frustration: A psychological state of arousal that results when a person is prevented from attaining a goal.

Frustration-aggression hypothesis: A concept pioneered by John Dollard stating that aggressive behavior is born of frustration in attempting to reach a goal.

Fugue state: A flight from reality in which the individual develops amnesia, leaves his or her present situation, travels to a new location, and establishes a new identity.

Function word: A word that has little meaning in itself yet signals grammatical relationships between other words in a sentence, such as an article ("the" or "a") or a preposition (for example, "in," "on," "of").

Functional autonomy: A concept, pioneered by Gordon W. Allport, that many adult motives are independent in purpose from their childhood origins.

Functional disorders: Signs and symptoms for which no organic or physiological basis can be found.

Functional fixedness: An inability to think of novel uses for objects because of a fixation on their usual functions.

Functionalism: An early school of American psychology that argued for the study of the human mind from the standpoint of understanding consciousness in terms of its purpose rather than its elements.

Fundamental attribution error: Underestimating the influence of situations and overestimating the influence of personality traits in causing behavior.

Fundamental frequency: The lowest frequency in a harmonic series of complex overtones; the overtones are integer multiples of the fundamental.

Gamete: A reproductive sex cell; the female cell is known as the ovum, and the male cell is known as the sperm.

Gamma-Aminobutyric acid (GABA): The most common neurotransmitter in the brain, derived from the amino acid glutamic acid; an inhibitor that seems to affect mood and emotion.

Gender: Social maleness or femaleness, reflected in the behaviors and characteristics that society expects from people of one biological sex.

Gender identity: A child's accurate labeling of himself or herself by gender; also, a person's inner sense of femaleness or maleness.

Gender schema: A general knowledge framework that organizes information and guides perceptions related to males and females.

Gene: The basic unit of heredity; a segment of a DNA molecule that contains hereditary instructions for an individual's physical traits and abilities and for the cell's production of proteins.

General adaptation syndrome: The three-stage physiological response pattern of the body to stress that was proposed by Hans Selye; the three stages are the alarm reaction, resistance stage, and exhaustion stage.

Generalization: The process by which behavior learned in one situation transfers to new situations.

Generativity: In Erikson's theory of personality, the seventh stage, associated with the desire to leave a legacy; the need to take care of future generations through the experiences of caring, nurturing, and educating.

Genetics: The biochemical basis of inherited characteristics.

Genital stage: In Freud's theory, the fifth psychosexual stage, beginning at adolescence and extending throughout adulthood; the individual learns to experience sexual gratification with a partner.

Genotype: The genetic makeup of an individual.

Gestalt: A German word, for which there is no precise translation, that is generally used to refer to a form, a whole, or a configuration.

Gestalt school of psychology: A school of psychology which maintains that the overall configuration of a stimulus array, rather than its individual elements, forms the basis of perception.

Gestalt therapy: A form of psychotherapy, initiated by Fritz Perls, that emphasizes awareness of the present and employs an active therapist-client relationship.

Giftedness: A marked ability to learn more rapidly, perform more intricate problems, and solve problems more rapidly than is normally expected for a given age; operationally defined as an IQ score above 130 on an individually administered test.

Goal setting: A motivational technique used to increase productivity in which employees are given specific performance objectives and time deadlines.

Gray matter: Unmyelinated neurons that make up the cerebral cortex, so called because they lack the fatty covering (myelin) found on neurons of the white matter.

Group dynamics: The study of how groups influence individual functioning.

Gustation: The sense of taste.

Gyrus: A convolution on the surface of the brain that results from the infolding of the cortex (surface).

Habit: An association or connection between a cue and a response, such as stopping (the response) at a red light (the cue).

Habituation: A decrease in response to repeated presentations of a stimulus that is not simply caused by fatigued sensory receptors.

Hallucinogen: A drug that can alter perception (vision and audition, in particular); examples include LSD, PCP, peyote, psilocybin, and possibly marijuana.

Hardiness: A constellation of behaviors and perceptions, characterized by perceptions of control, commitment, and challenge, that are thought to buffer the effects of stress; introduced by Suzanne Kobasa.

Hawthorne effect: A phenomenon that occurs when a subject's behavior changes after the subject discovers that he or she is being studied.

Hedonic: Associated with the seeking of pleasure and the avoidance of pain.

Helplessness: The belief that one has little or no control over the events in one's life; viewed by Martin Seligman as an important cause of depression.

Heredity: The transmission of characteristics from parent to offspring through genes in the chromosomes.

Heuristic: A shortcut or rule of thumb used for decision making or problem solving that often leads to, but does not guarantee, a correct response.

Higher-order conditioning: The linking of successive conditioned stimuli, the last of which elicits the conditioned response; higher-order associations are easily broken.

Hindbrain: A developmentally defined division of the brain that contains the pons, medulla, and cerebellum.

Hippocampus: A structure located in the temporal lobe (lateral cortical area) of the brain that has important memory functions.

Homeostasis: A term referring to the idea that the body tries to maintain steady states—that is, to maintain physiological characteristics within relatively narrow and optimum levels.

Homophobia: A fear, prejudice, or hatred toward homosexuals, usually based upon irrational stereotyping.

Hormone: A chemical "messenger," usually composed of protein or steroids, that is produced and secreted by endocrine gland and released into the bloodstream; it targets specific genes in certain body tissue cells.

Hostile aggression: Aggressive behavior that is associated with anger and is intended to harm another.

Hue: The chromatic or color sensation produced by a certain wavelength of light.

Humanistic psychology: A branch of psychology that emphasizes the human tendencies toward growth and fulfillment, autonomy, choice, responsibility, and ultimate values such as truth, love, and justice; exemplified by the theories of Carl Rogers and Abraham Maslow.

Hypermetropia: Hereditary farsightedness caused by the length of the eyeball in the anterior-posterior direction being too short.

Hypnagogic hallucination: A vivid auditory or visual hallucination that occurs at the transition from wakefulness to sleep or from sleep to wakefulness; associated with narcolepsy.

Hypnosis: An altered state of consciousness brought on by special induction techniques (usually progressive relaxation instructions) and characterized by varying degrees of responsiveness to suggestions.

Hypnotic susceptibility: A subject's measured level of responsiveness to hypnotic suggestions on standardized scales.

Hypochondriasis: A psychological disorder in which the person is unrealistically preoccupied with the fear of disease and worries excessively about his or her health.

Hypothalamus: A small region near the base of the brain that controls the pituitary gland, autonomic nervous system, and behaviors important for survival, including eating, drinking, and temperature regulation.

Hypothesis: An educated guess about the relationship between two or more variables, derived from inductive reasoning; often tested by an experiment.

Iconic memory: Brief sensory memory for vision.

Id: The part of the psyche that contains the instincts and is directed solely by pleasure seeking; it is the most primitive part of the psyche and was thought by Freud to fuel the ego and superego.

Idealized self: Alienation from the real self that is characterized by grandiose, unrealistic conceptions of the self and unattainable standards; part of Karen Horney's psychology.

Identification: The internalization of parental or societal values, behaviors, and attitudes; in Freudian theory, a defense and resolution of incestuous feelings toward the opposite-sex parent that is important in the development of the superego.

Identity: A personal configuration of occupational, sexual, and ideological commitments; according to Erikson, the positive pole of the fifth stage of psychosocial development.

Identity crisis: According to Erikson, the central developmental issue in adolescence; encompasses a struggle between an integrated core identity and role confusion.

Idiographic study: The study of the unique patterns of the individual through methods such as case studies, autobiographies, and tests that examine patterns of behavior within a single person.

Illusions: Beliefs that are unsupported by evidence or that require facts to be perceived in a particular manner.

Imagery: The use of visualization to imagine the physical movements involved in executing a skill.

Imitation: The performance of behaviors that were learned by observing the actions of others.

Immune response: The body's response to invasion by disease-producing organisms; proteins (antibodies) are produced that mark the unwanted cells for destruction.

Immutable characteristics: Physical attributes (such as gender) that are present at birth and that other people assume gives them information as to the kind of person they are seeing.

Implosion therapy: A therapy in which the patient imagines his or her feared situation, plus elements from psychodynamic theory that the therapist thinks are related to the fear, until fear decreases.

Impression management: The attempt to control the impressions of oneself that others form; synonymous with "self-presentation."

Imprinting: The innate behavioral attachment that a young animal forms with another individual (for example, its mother), with food, or with an object during a brief critical period shortly after birth; especially seen in ducks and chicks.

In-group: A social group to which a person belongs or with which a person is identified, thereby forming part of the self-concept.

In-group bias: The tendency to discriminate in favor of one's own group.

Incentive: A motivating force or system of rewards that is presented to an individual if he or she behaves or successfully performs specified tasks according to the norms of society; a goal object.

Incompetency: The legally established lack of sufficient knowledge and judgment to maintain a given right or responsibility.

Incongruence: In Rogers' theory, inconsistency or distortion between one's real and ideal self; a lack of genuineness.

Independent variable: The factor that is manipulated by the experimenter in order to assess its causal impact on the dependent variable.

Individual psychology: Alfred Adler's school of personality theory and therapy; stresses the unity of the individual and his or her striving for superiority to compensate for feelings of inferiority.

Induction: A type of logic by which one arrives at a general premise or conclusion based on generalization from a large number of known specific cases.

Industrial and organizational (I/O) psychology: The subfield of psychology that studies behavior in business and industry; practitioners analyze placement, training, and supervision of personnel, study organizational and communication structures, and explore ways to maximize efficiency.

Inflection: An addition to the stem of a word which indicates subtle modulations in meaning, such as plurality (more than one) or tense (present time or past time); in English, inflections are all suffixes.

Information processing model: The approach of most modern cognitive psychologists; it interprets cognition as the flow of information through interrelated stages (input, processing, storage, and retrieval) in much the same way that information is processed by a computer.

Innate: A term describing any inborn characteristic or behavior that is determined and controlled largely by the genes.

Insanity: A legal term for having a mental disease or defect so great that criminal intent or responsibility and punishability are not possible; it renders one incompetent.

Insight: A sudden mental inspiration or comprehension of a problem that was previously unsolved.

Insomnia: Difficulty in falling asleep or in remaining asleep for sufficient periods.

Instinct: An innate or inherited tendency that motivates a person or animal to act in often complex sequences without reasoning, instruction, or experience; in Freudian theory, a biological source of excitation that directs the development of personality into adulthood, such as the life instinct (Eros) and death instinct (Thanatos).

Institutional racism: The behavior patterns followed in organizations and in society at large that produce discrimination against members of racial minorities regardless of the prejudice or lack thereof of individuals.

Instrumental aggression: Aggressive behavior that is a by-product of another activity; instrumental aggression occurs only incidentally, as a means to another end.

Instrumental conditioning: The learning of the relationship between a voluntary action and the reinforcements or punishments that follow that action; also known as operant conditioning.

Integration: The function of most of the neurons of the cerebral cortex; summarizing incoming sensory information and producing a consensus as to what the nervous system will do next.

Intelligence: The ability to perform various mental tasks, including reasoning, knowledge, comprehension, memory, applying concepts, and manipulating figures; thought to reflect one's learning potential.

Intelligence quotient (IQ): A measure of a person's mental ability (as reflected by intelligence test scores) in comparison with the rest of the population at a comparable age.

Intensity: A measure of a physical aspect of a stimulus, such as the frequency of a sound or the brightness of a color.

Interest inventory: A type of test designed to determine areas of interest and enjoyment, often for the purpose of matching a person with a career.

Interference: The loss or displacement of a memory trace because of competing information that is presented.

Intermittent reinforcement: Any reinforcement schedule in which some but not all responses are rewarded; particularly difficult to extinguish.

Internal validity: The extent to which the dependent variable is caused by the independent variable; if relevant plausible rival alternative hypotheses can be ruled out, the study has strong internal validity.

Interneuron: A neuron that receives information from a sensory neuron and transmits a message to a motor neuron; very common in the brain and important in integration.

Interrater reliability: The obtained level of agreement between two observers when scoring the same observations with the same behavioral taxonomy.

Interval schedule: A schedule in which reinforcer delivery is contingent upon performance of a response after a specified amount of time has elapsed.

Intrinsic motivation: Motivation based on the desire to achieve or perform a task for its own sake, because it produces satisfaction or enjoyment, rather than for external rewards.

Introspection: The self-report of one's own sensations, perceptions, experiences, and thoughts; analyses of and reports on the content of one's own conscious experiences.

Irradiation: Nervous excitement generated in a specific brain center by an unconditioned stimulus that spreads to surrounding areas of the cerebral cortex.

Kinesthetic: Related to the sensation of body position, presence, or movement, resulting mostly from the stimulation of sensory nerves in muscles, tendons, and joints.

Korsakoff syndrome: Alcohol-induced brain damage that causes disorientation, impaired long-term memory, and production of false memories to fill memory gaps.

Latency: In Freud's theory, the period between approximately age six and adolescence, when sexual instincts are not strongly manifested; strictly speaking, not a psychosexual stage.

Latent content: According to psychoanalytic theory, the hidden content of a dream, camouflaged by the manifest content.

Lateral geniculate nucleus: A subdivision of the thalamus in the brain, which receives the nerve impulse from the retina; it assembles visual information.

Laterality: Specialization by sides of almost symmetrical structures; speech is lateralized in human brains, because it is mainly controlled by the left hemispheres of almost all right-handed people.

Law of effect: Thorndike's basic law of instrumental conditioning, which holds that responses followed by certain events will be either more or less likely to recur.

Leakage: Nonverbal behavior that reveals information that a person wishes to conceal; especially useful in deception detection.

Learned helplessness: The hypothesized result of experiences in which behavior performed seems to bear no relationship to the appearance or control of a stressor.

Learning: A modification in behavior as the result of experience that involves changes in the nervous system which are not caused by fatigue, maturation, or injury.

Lesion: Damage or injury to brain tissue that is caused by disease or trauma or produced experimentally using mechanical, electrical, or chemical methods.

Levels-of-processing model: The perspective that holds that how well something is remembered is based on how elaborately incoming information is mentally processed.

Libido: The energy used to direct behavior that is pleasurable either for the self or others; directed toward the self, it results in self-gratification, follows the pleasure principle, and is immature.

Limbic system: An integrated set of cerebral structures (including the amygdala, hypothalamus, hippocampus, and septal area) that play a vital role in the regulation of emotion and motivation.

Linguistic relativity hypothesis: The idea that the structure of particular languages that people speak affects the way they perceive the world.

Linguistics: A field of inquiry that focuses on the underlying structure of language; linguists study phonology (the sound system), syntax (sentence structure), and semantics (meaning), among other topics.

Lipids: Fats and oils.

Lithium carbonate: An alkaline compound that modulates the intensity of mood swings and is particularly effective in the dampening of symptoms of manic excitability.

Loci method: A serial-recall mnemonic consisting of visualizing items to be remembered along a known path of distinct locations.

Locus of control: Beliefs concerning the sources of power over one's life; persons who believe they can generally control the direction of their lives have an internal locus of control, whereas those who believe that their lives are influenced more by fate have an external locus of control.

Long-term memory: A memory system of unlimited capacity that consists of more or less permanent knowledge.

Longitudinal study: A research methodology that requires the testing of the same subjects repeatedly over a specified period of time.

Loudness: The strength of sound as heard; related to sound pressure level but also affected by frequency.

Magnitude estimation: A technique for measuring perceptual experience by having persons assign numbers to indicate the "magnitude" of an experience.

Main effect: A statistically significant difference in behavior related to different levels of a variable and not affected by any other variable.

Major depressive episode: A disorder of mood and functioning, meeting clearly specified criteria and present for at least two weeks, which is characterized by dysphoric mood or apathy.

Mania: A phase of bipolar disorder in which the mood is one of elation, euphoria, or irritability; a disorder in which manic symptoms occur, including hyperactivity, agitation, restlessness, and grandiosity, and then are followed by a return to a normal mood state.

Manifest content: In Freudian theory, the content of a dream just as it is experienced or recalled; masks the dream's latent content.

Masculine protest: The denying of inferiority feelings through rebelliousness, violence, or maintaining a tough exterior.

Maturation: Development attributable to one's genetic timetable rather than to experience.

Mean: The arithmetic average of all the data measuring one characteristic; it can be used as a descriptive or inferential statistic.

Mechanoreceptor: A sensory receptor that is sensitive to mechanical stimulation, such as touch, movement of a joint, or stretching of a muscle.

Medical model: A view in which abnormality consists of a number of diseases that originate in bodily functions, especially in the brain, and have defined symptoms, treatments, and outcomes.

Medulla oblongata: The bulbous portion of the brain stem that directly connects with the spinal cord; controls cardiac and respiratory activity.

Melatonin: A hormone produced by the pineal gland within the forebrain that is usually released into the blood during the night phase of the light-dark cycle.

Memory: The mental processes that are involved in storing and recalling previously experienced images, information, and events.

Mere exposure: A psychological phenomenon in which liking tends to increase as a person sees more of something or someone.

Meta-analysis: A set of quantitative (statistical) procedures used to evaluate a body of empirical literature.

Metastasis: The transfer of disease from one part of the body to an unrelated part, often through the bloodstream or lymphatic system.

Midbrain: The section of the brain just above the hindbrain; influences auditory and visual processes and arousal.

Middle temporal gyrus (MT): The region of the occipital lobe in which motion perception is integrated.

Midlife crisis: A sense of reevaluation, and sometimes panic, that strikes some individuals during middle age; impulsive behavior, reassessment of goals, and career changes can result.

Mind-body problem: A psychological question originating from philosophy and religion that concerns how to understand the relationship between a physical body or brain and a nonphysical mind or subjective experience.

Mineralocorticoids: The proinflammatory hormones aldosterone and desoxycorticosterone, secreted by the adrenal cortex and having a role in salt metabolism.

Misattribution: Attributing an event to any factor other than the true cause.

Mnemonics: Strategies for improving memory through placing information in an organized context.

Monoamine oxidase (MAO) inhibitors: A class of antidepressant drugs.

Monoamines: A group of neurotransmitters derived from a single amino acid; they include serotonin and the catecholamines.

Monocular cue: A visual cue available to each eye separately; often used by artists to portray depth.

Monosynaptic reflex: A reflex system that consists of only one synapse, the synapse between the sensory input and motor output.

Monotic: Referring to the stimulation of only one ear.

Morpheme: The smallest part of a word that has a discernible meaning.

Morphology: The rules in a given language that govern how morphemes can be combined to form words.

Motivation: A hypothetical construct used to explain behavior and its direction, intensity, and persistence.

Motor neurons: The cells of the central nervous system responsible for causing muscular activity.

Multiple personality disorder: A rare mental disorder characterized by the development and existence or two or more relatively unique and independent personalities in the same individual.

Myopia: Hereditary nearsightedness caused by the length of the eyeball in the anterior-posterior direction being too long.

Nanometer: A billionth of a meter.

Narcolepsy: A condition in which an individual is prone to fall suddenly into a deep sleep.

Nativism: A philosophy which holds that knowledge is innate and that the neonate enters the world prepared for certain kinds of environmental inputs.

Natural selection: The process by which those characteristics of a species that help it to survive or adapt to its environment tend to be passed along by members that live long enough to have offspring.

Need: A state of an organism attributable to deprivation of a biological or psychological requirement; it is related to a disturbance in the homeostatic state.

Negative reinforcement: The procedure whereby the probability of a response is increased by the contingent removal of an aversive stimulus.

Neo-Freudian: A term for psychoanalysts who place more emphasis on security and interpersonal relations as determining human behavior than on the exclusively biological theories of Freud; Neo-Freudians include Adler, Jung, Horney, Sullivan, and Erikson.

Nerve impulse: Electrical activity transmitted through a nerve fiber.

Nervous system: An array of billions of neurons (conducting nerve cells) that transmits electrical information throughout the body and thereby controls practically all bodily processes.

Neurologist: A physician who specializes in the diagnosis and treatment of disorders of the nervous system.

Neuron: An individual nerve cell, the basic unit of the nervous system; receives and transmits electrical information and consists of a cell body, dendrites, and an axon.

Neuropsychology: The study of brain-behavior relationships, usually by using behavioral tests and correlating results with brain areas.

Neuropsychopharmacology: The field of study of the relationship among behavior, neuronal functioning, and drugs.

Neurosis: Any functional disorder of the mind or the emotions, occurring without obvious brain damage and involving anxiety, phobic responses, or other abnormal behavior symptoms.

Neurotransmitter: A chemical substance released from one nerve cell that communicates activity by binding to and changing the activity of another nerve cell, muscle, or gland; some stimulate, others inhibit.

Nomothetic study: A research approach that compares groups of people in order to identify general principles; the dominant method of personality research.

Nonparticipant observation: A field technique in which the researcher passively observes the behavior of the subjects, trying not to get involved in the setting.

Nonverbal communication: Communication through any means other than words; includes facial expression, tone of voice, and posture.

Normal distribution: A bell-shaped curve that often provides an accurate description of the distribution of scores obtained in research; it forms the basis of many statistical tests.

Observational learning: Learning that results from observing other people's behavior and its consequences.

Observational study: A research technique in which a scientist systematically watches for and records occurrences of the phenomena under study without actively influencing them.

Obsessions: Intrusive, recurrent, anxiety-provoking thoughts, ideas, images, or impulses that interfere with an individual's daily functioning.

Obsessive-compulsive disorder: A chronic, debilitating anxiety disorder characterized by continuous obsessive thinking and frequent compulsive behaviors.

Occipital lobe: The posterior portion of each cerebral hemisphere, where visual stimuli are received and integrated.

Oedipal complex: In Freudian theory, sexual attraction to the parent of the opposite sex, and jealousy of and fear of retribution from the parent of the same sex; first manifested in the phallic stage (in girls, sometimes called the "Electra complex").

Olfaction: The sense of smell.

Operant: The basic response unit in instrumental conditioning; a response which, when emitted, operates upon its environment and is instrumental in providing some consequences.

Operant conditioning: Learning in which a behavior increases or decreases depending on whether the behavior is followed by reward or punishment; also known as instrumental conditioning.

Operational definition: A description of a measurement or manipulation in terms that are unambiguous, observable, and easily identified.

Opiates: A class of drugs that relieve pain; opiates include morphine, heroin, and several naturally occurring peptides.

Oral stage: In Freudian theory, the first stage of psychosexual development, from birth to approximately age two; sexual energy focuses on the mouth, and conflicts may arise over nursing, biting, or chewing.

Organic disorder: A symptomatology with a known physiological or neurological basis.

Organizational effects: The early and permanent effects of a hormone; for example, the sex hormones, which produce differentiation in the developing embryo of primordial gonads, internal reproductive structures, and external genitalia.

Ossicle: Any of the three bones of the middle ear (the hammer, anvil, and stirrup) that are involved in conduction of sound into the inner ear.

Out-group: Any social group to which an individual does not belong and which, as a consequence, may be viewed in a negative way.

Overextension: The application of a word to more objects than ordinary adult usage allows; for example, when children refer to all small four-legged animals as "dog."

Overjustification effect: The tendency of external factors that are perceived to be controlling an individual's behavior to undermine the individual's intrinsic motivation to engage in that behavior.

Overtone: One of several sine waves simultaneously generated by most sound sources; these pure tones are all integer multiples of the fundamental.

Papilla: A small bundle of taste receptor cells surrounded by supportive cells and communicating with the exterior through a small pore.

Paradoxical intervention: A therapeutic technique in which a therapist gives a patient or family a task that appears to contradict the goals of treatment.

Parallel distributed processing (PDP): A neurally inspired model in which information is processed in a massively parallel and interactive network; the course of processing is determined by the connection strengths between units of the network.

Paranoia: A psychosis characterized by delusions, particularly delusions of persecution, and pervasive suspiciousness; paranoia rarely involves hallucinations.

Parasympathetic nervous system: A branch of the autonomic nervous system; responsible for maintaining or reestablishing homeostasis.

Parietal lobe: The side and upper-middle part of each cerebral hemisphere and the site of sensory reception from the skin, muscles, and other areas; also contains part of the general interpretive area.

Pavlovian conditioning: Learning in which two stimuli are presented one after the other, and the response to the first changes because of the response automatically elicited by the second; also called classical conditioning.

Penis envy: In Freudian theory, the strong envy that females develop of the male organ because they subconsciously believe they have been castrated; Freud proposed that penis envy dominates the female personality.

Perception: The psychological process by which information that comes in through the sense organs is meaningfully interpreted by the brain.

Perceptual constancy: The tendency to perceive figures as constant and stable in terms of shape, color, size, or brightness.

Peripheral nervous system: All the nerves located outside the bones of the skull and spinal cord.

Persona: A major Jungian archetype representing one's public personality; the mask that one wears in order to be acceptable to society at large.

Personality: An individual's unique collection of behavioral responses (physical, emotional, and intellectual) that are consistent across time and situations.

Personality disorder: A disorder involving deep-rooted behavior patterns that are inflexible and maladaptive and that cause distress in an individual's relationships with others.

Personality trait: A stable disposition to behave in a given way over time and across situations.

Phallic stage: In Freudian theory, the third stage of psychosexual development, from approximately age four to age six; sexual energy focuses on the genitals.

Phenomenology: An approach that stresses openness to direct experience in introspective or unsophisticated ways, without using analysis, theory, expectations, or interpretation.

Pheromone: A hormone or other chemical that is produced and released from the tissues of one individual and targets tissues in another individual, usually with a consciously or unconsciously detectable scent.

Phobia: An anxiety disorder involving an intense irrational fear of a particular thing (such as horses) or situation (such as heights).

Phoneme: A minimal unit of sound that can signal a difference in meaning.

Phonology: The specification for a given language of which speech sounds may occur and how they may be combined, as well as the pitch and stress patterns that accompany words and sentences.

Photoreceptor: A specialized nerve cell that can transform light into a neural message; rods are specialized for black-and-white vision, cones for color vision.

Pineal gland: A light-sensitive endocrine gland that is located toward the back of the brain and that controls reproductive cycles in many mammalian species.

Pitch: The highness or lowness of a sound as heard; related to frequency but also affected by loudness.

Pituitary: An endocrine gland located in the brain that controls several other endocrine glands and that cooperates with the hypothalamus of the nervous system in controlling physiology.

Placebo: A substance or treatment (such as a pill or an injection) that has no intrinsic effect but is presented as having some effect.

Placebo effect: The relief of pain or the causing of a desired behavioral effect as a result of a patient's belief that a substance or treatment which has no known psychological or biological effect will in fact be effective; for example, a sugar pill may relieve a backache if given by a trusted doctor.

Plasticity: The ability of neurons and neural networks to grow into specific patterns based partially upon the organism's genetics and partially upon the organism's learned experience; in the brain, neurons can modify the structural organization in order to compensate for neural damage.

Play therapy: A system of individual psychotherapy in which children's play is utilized to explain and reduce symptoms of their psychological disorders.

Pons: A part of the brain stem that serves as the nerve connection between the cerebellum and the brain stem.

Population: All members of a specified group that a researcher is interested in studying.

Positive reinforcement: A procedure used to increase the frequency of a response by presenting a favorable consequence following the response.

Positron emission tomography (PET) scanning: A brain-imaging technique that allows blood flow, energy metabolism, and chemical activity to be visualized in the living human brain.

Post-traumatic stress disorder (PTSD): A pathological condition caused by severe stress such as an earthquake or a divorce; it has an acute stage and a chronic stage, and symptoms involve reexperiencing the traumatic event.

Postsynaptic potential: A chemical stimulus produced in a postsynaptic cell; may excite the cell to come nearer to electrical firing, or may inhibit firing.

Power law: A statement of the lawful relationship between two variables that expresses one of them as the other raised to some exponent.

Pragmatism: A philosophical position that provided the framework of functionalism by proposing that the value of something lies in its usefulness.

Prejudice: Liking or disliking of persons based on their category or group membership rather than on their individual personalities; predominantly refers to unfavorable reactions.

Preoperational stage: In Piaget's theory, a transitional stage of the preschool child (ages two to seven, approximately), after mental representations (symbols) are acquired but before they can be logically manipulated.

Preparedness: The idea that, through evolution, animals have been genetically prepared to learn certain things important to their survival.

Presbyopia: Farsightedness resulting from decreased flexibility of the lens of the eye and other age-related factors.

Primacy effect: The tendency for things that are seen or received first to be better recalled and more influential than things that come later.

Primary motive: A motive that arises from innate, biological needs and that must be met for survival.

Primary reinforcer: A stimulus that acts as a natural, unlearned reinforcer.

Primary sex characteristics: The physiological features of the sex organs.

Priming: An increase in the availability of certain types of information in memory in response to a stimulus.

Prisoner's dilemma: A laboratory game used by psychologists to study the comparative strategies of cooperation and competition.

Probability: The proportion of times a particular event will occur; also, the study of uncertainty that is the foundation of inferential statistics.

Progesterone: A female sex hormone secreted by the corpus luteum of the ovary; maintains the lining of the uterus during pregnancy and the second half of the menstrual cycle.

Programmed instruction: A self-paced training program characterized by many small, increasingly difficult lessons separated by frequent tests.

Progressive muscle relaxation: A relaxation technique that systematically works through all the major muscle groups of the body by first tensing, then relaxing each group and paying attention to the changes.

Projective task: Any task that provides an open-ended response that may reveal aspects of one's personality; tasks or tests commonly include standard stimuli that are ambiguous in nature.

Proposition: A mental representation based on the underlying structure of language; a proposition is the smallest unit of knowledge that can be stated.

Prosocial behavior: Behavior intended to benefit another; can be motivated by either egoistic or altruistic concern.

Prototype: A "best example" of a concept—one that contains the most typical features of that concept.

Proxemics: The use of space as a special elaboration of culture; it is usually divided into the subfields of territory and personal space.

Proximo-distal development: Motor development that proceeds from the center of the body to its periphery.

Psychoactive drugs: Chemical substances that act on the brain to create psychological effects; usually classified as depressants, stimulants, narcotics (opiates), hallucinogens, or antipsychotics.

Psychoanalytic theory: A set of theories conceived by Sigmund Freud that see the roots of human behavior and mental disorders in unconscious motivation and early adulthood conflict.

Psychobiology: The study of the interactions between biological and psychological processes.

Psychogenic disorder: An illness that is attributable primarily to a psychological conflict or to emotional stress.

Psychometrics: The theory or technique of psychological measurement; the measurement of psychological differences among people and the statistical analysis of those differences.

Psychophysics: The study of the relationship between physical units of a stimulus, such as amplitude, and its sensory, experienced qualities, such as loudness.

Psychophysiology: The study of the interaction between the psyche (mind and emotions) and the physiology (physical processes such as blood pressure and heart rate) of the organism.

Psychosis: A general term referring to a severe mental disorder, with or without organic damage, characterized by deterioration of normal intellectual and social function and by partial or complete withdrawal from reality; includes schizophrenia and mood disorders such as bipolar disorder.

Psychosocial crisis: In Erikson's theory, a turning point in the process of development precipitated by the individual having to face a new set of social demands and new social relationships.

Psychosomatic disorder: A physical disorder that results from, or is worsened by, psychological factors; synonymous with psychophysiological disorder and includes stress-related disorders.

Psychosurgery: Brain surgery conducted to alter an inappropriate or maladaptive behavior.

Psychotherapy: A general category of treatment techniques for mental disorders; most psychotherapy uses talking as a tool and centers on the client-psychotherapist relationship to develop awareness and provide support.

Punishment: The procedure of decreasing the probability of a behavior by the response-contingent delivery of an aversive stimulus.

Pure tone: A sound produced by a vibration of a single frequency, the amplitude of which changes over time as a sinusoidal function; a sine wave.

Quasi-experiment: An experiment that does not allow subjects to be assigned randomly to treatment conditions.

Random assignment: The most common technique for establishing equivalent groups by balancing subject characteristics through the assigning of subjects to groups through some random process.

Rapid eye movement (REM) sleep: A special stage of sleep that involves desynchronized electrical brain activity, muscle paralysis, rapid eye movements, and narrative dream recall.

Ratio schedule: A reinforcement schedule in which reinforcer delivery is contingent upon the performance of a specified number of responses.

Rational-emotive therapy: A cognitive-based psychotherapy, pioneered by Albert Ellis, that attempts to replace or modify a client's irrational, inappropriate, or problematic thought processes, outlooks, and self-concept.

Realistic conflict theory: A theory from social psychology that suggests that direct competition for scarce or valued resources can lead to prejudice.

Receptive aphasia: Difficulties in comprehending spoken and written material, usually after damage to Wernicke's area in the left temporal lobe of the cerebral cortex.

Receptive field: The region and pattern in space to which a single neuron responds.

Receptor: A specific protein structure on a target cell to which a neurotransmitter binds, producing a stimulatory or inhibitory response.

Recessive gene: A gene whose corresponding trait will not be expressed unless the gene is paired with another recessive gene for that trait.

Reciprocal determinism: An interactional model proposing that environment, personal factors, and behavior all operate as interacting determinants of one another.

Reductionism: An aspect of the scientific method which seeks to understand complex and often interactive processes by reducing them to more basic components and principles.

Reflex: An unlearned and automatic biologically programmed response to a particular stimulus.

Reflex arc: The simplest behavioral response, in which an impulse is carried by a sensory neuron to the spinal cord, crosses a synapse to a motor neuron, and stimulates a response.

Regression: An ego defense mechanism that a person uses to return to an earlier stage of development when experiencing stress or conflict.

Regulators: Facial gestures and expressions by listeners that are informative for speakers; they convey comprehension or acceptance, or indicate when the other person may speak.

Reinforcement: An operation or process that increases the probability that a learned behavior will be repeated.

Reinforcer: A stimulus or event that, when delivered contingently upon a response, will increase the probability of the recurrence of that response.

Relative deprivation: The proposition that people's attitudes, aspirations, and grievances largely depend on the frame of reference within which they are conceived.

Reliability: The consistency of a psychological measure, which can be assessed by means of stability over repeated administrations or agreement among different observers.

Representativeness: A heuristic in which an estimate of the probability of an event or sample is determined by the degree to which it resembles the originating process or population.

Repression: In psychoanalytic theory, a defense mechanism that keeps unacceptable thoughts and impulses from becoming conscious.

Response cost: Negative consequences that follow the commission of an undesired behavior, decreasing the rate at which the misbehavior will recur.

Response hierarchy: An arrangement of alternative responses to a cue, in a hierarchy from that most likely to occur to that least likely to occur.

Resting membrane potential: The maintenance of difference in electrical charges between the inside and outside of a neuron's cell membrane, keeping it polarized with closed ion channels.

Retardation: A condition wherein a person has mental abilities that are far below average; other skills and abilities, such as adaptive behavior, may also be marginal; measured by an IQ score of less than 70.

Reticular formation: A core of neurons extending through the medulla, pons, and midbrain that controls arousal and sleeping/waking, as well as motor functions such as muscle tone and posture.

Retina: The light-sensitive area at the back of the eye, containing the photoreceptors (rods and cones) that detect light.

Retrieval: The process of locating information stored in memory and bringing it into awareness.

Retrograde amnesia: The type of amnesia that involves an inability to remember things that occurred before the onset of the amnesia.

Rhodopsin: The visual pigment in the cells of the rods that responds to light.

Rod: A photoreceptor of the retina specialized for the detection of light without discrimination of color.

Role: A social position that is associated with a set of behavioral expectations.

Role Construct Repertory Test: George A. Kelly's test for determining the nature of a person's system of constructs and psychological problems, which are related to significant others in the life of the person.

Rule-governed behavior: Behavior that is under the discriminative control of formalized contingencies.

Sample: A subset of a population; a group of elements selected from a larger, well-defined pool of elements.

Sampling error: The extent to which population parameters deviate from a sample statistic.

Satiety: A feeling of fullness and satisfaction.

Schema: An active organization of prior knowledge, beliefs, and experience which is used in perceiving the environment, retrieving information from memory, and directing behavior (plural, schemata).

Schizophrenia: Any of a group of psychotic reactions characterized by withdrawal from reality with accompanying affective, behavioral, and intellectual disturbances, including illusions and hallucinations.

Schwann cell: A type of insulating nerve cell that wraps around neurons located peripherally throughout the organism.

Script: An event schema in which a customary sequence of actions, actors, and props is specified; for example, behavior at a restaurant.

Seasonal affective disorder (SAD): Bipolar disorder that undergoes a seasonal fluctuation resulting from various factors, including seasonal changes in the intensity and duration of sunlight.

Secondary reinforcement: A learned reinforcer that has acquired reinforcing qualities by being paired with other reinforcers.

Secondary sex characteristics: Physical features other than genitals that differentiate women and men; for example, facial hair.

Self: The unified and integrated center of one's experience and awareness, which one experiences both subjectively, as an actor, and objectively, as a recipient of actions.

Self-actualization: A biologically and culturally determined process involving a tendency toward growth and full realization of one's potential, characterized by acceptance, autonomy, accuracy, creativity, and community; pioneered by Abraham Maslow.

Self-concept: The sum total of the attributes, abilities, attitudes, and values that an individual believes defines who he or she is.

Self-efficacy: The perception or judgment of one's ability to perform a certain action successfully or to control one's circumstances.

Self-esteem: The evaluative part of the self-concept; one's feeling of self-worth.

Self-image: The self as the individual pictures or imagines it.

Self-perception: A psychological process whereby individuals infer the nature of their attitudes and beliefs by observing their own behavior.

Semantic memory: The long-term representation of a person's factual knowledge of the world.

Semicircular canals: The three structures in the inner ear that together signal acceleration of the head in any direction.

Sensation: The process by which the nervous system and sensory receptors receive and represent stimuli received from the environment.

Sensorimotor stage: The first of Piaget's developmental stages, lasting from birth to about two years of age, during which objects become familiar and are interpreted by appropriate habitual, motor, and sensory processes.

Sensory memory: The persistence of a sensory impression for less than a second; it allows the information to be processed further.

Serial processing: A theory concerning how people scan information in memory that suggests that as the number of items in memory increases, so does the amount of time taken to determine whether an item is present in memory.

Set point: An organism's personal homeostatic level for a particular body weight, which results from factors such as early feeding experiences and heredity.

Sex: Biological maleness or femaleness, determined by genetic endowment and hormones.

Sex typing: The process of acquiring traits, attitudes, and behaviors seen culturally as appropriate for members of one's gender; gender-role acquisition.

Sexual instinct: In Freud's theory, the innate tendency toward pleasure seeking, particularly through achieving sexual aims and objects.

Shaping: The acquiring of instrumental behavior in small steps or increments through the reinforcement of successively closer approximations to the desired final behavior.

Short-term memory: A memory system of limited capacity that uses rehearsal processes either to retain current memories or to pass them on to long-term memory.

Significance level: The degree of likelihood that research results are attributable to chance.

Skinner box: The most commonly used apparatus for studying instrumental conditioning; manipulation of a lever (for rats, monkeys, or humans) or an illuminated disk (for pigeons) produces consequences.

Social categorization: The classification of people and groups according to attributes that are personally meaningful.

Social cognition: The area of social psychology concerned with how people make sense of social events, including the actions of others.

Social comparison: Comparing attitudes, skills, and feelings with those of similar people in order to determine relative standing in a group or the acceptability of one's own positions.

Social facilitation: The enhancement of a person's most dominant response as a result of the presence of others; for some tasks, such as simple ones, performance is enhanced, while for others, such as novel tasks, performance is impaired.

Social identity theory: A theory maintaining that people are motivated to create and maintain a positive identity in terms of personal qualities and, especially, group memberships.

Social learning theory: The approach to personality that emphasizes the learning of behavior via observations and direct reward; exemplified by the theories of Albert Bandura, Walter Mischel, and Julian Rotter.

Social loafing: The tendency to expend less effort while in the presence of others; most likely to occur on additive tasks in which one's individual effort is obscured as a result of the collective efforts of the group.

Social phobia: A condition characterized by fear of the possible scrutiny or criticism of others.

Social psychology: A subfield of psychology that studies how individuals are affected by environmental factors and particularly by other people.

Social support: The relationships with other people that provide emotional, informational, or tangible resources that affect one's health and psychological comfort.

Socialization: The process of learning and internalizing social rules and standards.

Sociobiology: The application of the principles of evolutionary biology to the understanding of social behavior.

Somatization disorder: A mental syndrome in which a person chronically has a number of vague but dramatic medical complaints that apparently have no physical cause.

Somatoform disorders: A group of mental disorders in which a person has physical complaints or symptoms that appear to be caused by psychological rather than physical factors; for example, hypochondriasis.

Somnambulism: The scientific term for sleepwalking; formerly a term for hypnosis.

Spectrum analysis: The ability of a system, such as hearing, to decompose a complex wave into its sine-wave components and their respective amplitudes.

Spinal cord: The part of the central nervous system that is enclosed within the backbone; conducts nerve impulses to and from the brain.

Spontaneous recovery: The recovery of extinguished behaviors over time in the absence of any specific treatment or training.

Sports psychology: The subfield of psychology that applies psychological principles to physical activities such as competitive sports; frequently concerned with maximizing athletic performance.

Sprouting: A process that occurs when remaining nerve fibers branch and form new connections to replace those that have been lost.

Stage theory of development: The belief that development moves through a set sequence of stages; the quality of behavior at each stage is unique but is dependent upon movement through earlier stages.

Standard deviation: A measure of how variable or spread out a group of scores is from the mean.

Standardization: The administration, scoring, and interpretation of a test in a prescribed manner so that differences in test results can be attributed to the testee.

Statistical significance: Differences in behavior large enough that they are probably related to the subject variables or manipulated variables—differences too large to be caused by chance alone.

Stereogram: A two-dimensional image that appears three-dimensional when viewed binocularly, typically consisting of two images of the same scene as viewed from slightly disparate viewpoints; when special glasses are worn, the images are fused into one image with the full three-dimensional effect.

Stereotype: A set of beliefs, often rigidly held, about the characteristics of an entire group.

Stimulants: Drugs that cause behavioral and/or physiological stimulation, including amphetamines, cocaine, and their respective derivatives; caffeine; nicotine; and some antidepressants.

Stimulus: An environmental circumstance to which an organism may respond; it may be as specific as a physical event or as global as a social situation.

Stimulus generalization: The ability of stimuli that are similar to other stimuli to elicit a response that was previously elicited only by the first stimuli.

Storage: The stage of memory between encoding and retrieval; the period for which memories are held.

Strange situation: A particular experimental technique designed to measure the quality of the mother-infant attachment relationship.

Stress: The judgment that a problem exceeds one's available resources, resulting from a primary appraisal of the problem and a secondary appraisal of the coping resources.

Stressor: Anything that produces a demand on an organism.

Striate cortex: The region of the occipital lobe that reconstitutes visual images for recognition.

Stroke: A vascular accident resulting from either the rupture of a vessel or the blocking of blood flow in an artery.

Structuralism: An early school of psychology that sought to define the basic elements of mind and the laws governing their combination.

Sublimation: According to Freud, a defense mechanism by which a person may redirect aggressive impulses by engaging in a socially sanctioned activity.

Suffix: A morpheme that attaches to the end of a word.

Superego: In Freudian theory, the part of the psyche that contains parental and societal standards of morality and that acts to prohibit expression of instinctual drives; includes the conscience and the ego-ideal.

Syllogism: A logical argument constructed of a major premise, a minor premise, and a conclusion, the validity of which is determined by rules of inference.

Symbiotic relationship: An overprotective, often enmeshed relationship between a parent and child.

Sympathetic nervous system: A division of the autonomic nervous system that prepares the organism for energy expenditure.

Synapse: The junction between two neurons over which a nerve impulse is chemically transduced.

Synchronized electroencephalogram: A regular, repetitive brain-wave pattern that is caused by multitudes of neurons firing at the same time and the same rate in a given brain region.

Systematic desensitization: An exposure therapy in which the phobic person is gradually presented with a feared object or situation.

Systems theory: A concept in which the family grouping is viewed as a biosocial subsystem existing within the larger system of society; intrafamilial communications are the mechanisms of subsystem interchange.

Tachistoscope: An experimental apparatus for presenting visual information very briefly to the right or left visual field; sometimes called a T-scope.

Tardive dyskinesia: Slow, involuntary motor movements, especially of the mouth and tongue, which can become permanent and untreatable; can result from psychoactive drug treatment.

Temporal lobe: The lower portion on the side of each cerebral hemisphere, containing the sites of sensory interpretation, memory of visual and auditory patterns, and part of the general interpretive area.

Test-retest reliability: A common way of determining consistency, by administering the same test twice to the same persons.

Testosterone: The principal male sex hormone produced by the testes.

Thalamus: A portion of the diencephalon, located at the base of the forebrain, which receives sensory information from the body and relays these signals to the appropriate regions of the cerebrum.

Thematic Apperception Test (TAT): A personality test in which individuals demonstrate their needs by describing what is happening in a series of ambiguous pictures.

Theory: A model explaining the relationship between several phenomena; derived from several related hypotheses which have survived many tests.

Therapy: The systematic habilitation of a disorder.

Thermoreceptor: A sensory receptor specialized for the detection of changes in the flow of heat.

Threshold: The minimum stimulus intensity necessary for an individual to detect a stimulus; usually defined as that intensity detected 50 percent of the time it is presented.

Thyroxine: The major hormone produced and secreted by the thyroid gland; stimulates protein synthesis and the basal metabolic rate.

Timbre: The sound quality produced by the respective amplitude and frequency of the overtones, or underlying sine waves that make up a complex wave.

Top-down processing: A situation in which a person's perception of a stimulus is influenced by nonstimulus factors such as the person's general knowledge, beliefs, or expectations.

Trait theory: A way of conceptualizing personality in terms of relatively persistent and consistent behavior patterns that are manifested in a wide range of circumstances.

Transduction: The process of changing physical energy, such as light, into neural messages.

Transference: The phenomenon in which a person in psychoanalysis shifts thoughts or emotions concerning people in his or her past (most often parents) onto the analyst.

Transvestite: A person who, for fun or sexual arousal, often dresses and acts like a member of the opposite sex (going "in drag"); most are heterosexual males.

Tricyclics: A class of antidepressant drugs.

Turner's syndrome: A condition in which there is only one X sex chromosome, with no second female X or male Y; causes the development of female structures.

Two-factor theory: A behavioral theory of anxiety stating that fear is caused by Pavlovian conditioning and that avoidance of the feared object is maintained by operant conditioning.

Type A personality: A behavior pattern that describes individuals who are driven, competitive, high-strung, impatient, time-urgent, intense, and easily angered; some researchers have associated this pattern with increased risk of heart disease.

Unconditional positive regard: The attempt by a therapist to convey to a client that he or she genuinely cares for the client.

Unconditioned response (UR): An innate or unlearned behavior that occurs automatically following some stimulus; a reflex.

Unconditioned stimulus (US): A stimulus that elicits an unconditioned response; the relation between unconditioned stimuli and unconditioned responses is unlearned.

Unconscious: The deep-rooted aspects of the mind; Freud claimed that it includes negative instincts and urges that are too disturbing for people to be aware of consciously.

Unipolar depression: A disorder characterized by the occurrence of one or more major depressive episodes but no manic episodes.

Validity: A statistical value that tells the degree to which a test measures what it is intended to measure; the test is usually compared to external criteria.

Vicarious learning: Learning (for example, learning to fear something) without direct experience, either by observing or by receiving verbal information.

Visual cortex: The top six cell layers in the back of the brain, which are specialized for organizing and interpreting visual information.

Visual dyslexia: The lack of ability to translate observed written or printed language into meaningful terms.

Voyeurism: The derivation of sexual pleasure from looking at the naked bodies or sexual activities of others without their consent.

Wavelength: The distance traveled by a wave front in the time given by one cycle (the period of the wave); has an inverse relation to frequency.

White matter: The tissue within the central nervous system, consisting primarily of nerve fibers.

Within-subject design: An experimental plan in which each subject receives each level of the independent variable.

Working through: A psychoanalytical term that describes the process by which clients develop more adaptive behavior once they have gained insight into the causes of their psychological disorders.

Yerkes-Dodson law: The principle that moderate levels of arousal tend to yield optimal performance.

Zeitgeber: A German word meaning "time giver"; a factor that serves as a synchronizer or entraining agent, such as sunlight in the morning.

SURVEY
OF
SOCIAL
SCIENCE

ALPHABETICAL LIST

CATEGORY LIST

SURVEY
OF
SOCIAL
SCIENCE

INDEX

Page ranges appearing in boldface type indicate that an entire article devoted to the topic appears on those pages; a single page number in bold denotes definition of a term in the Glossary.

INDEX